Social Influence:

The Ontario Symposium, Volume 5

ONTARIO SYMPOSIUM ON PERSONALITY AND SOCIAL PSYCHOLOGY

SOCIAL INFLUENCE:

The Ontario Symposium, Volume 5

Edited by

MARK P. ZANNA
University of Waterloo
JAMES M. OLSON
University of Western Ontario
C. PETER HERMAN
University of Toronto

LAWRENCE ERLBAUM ASSOCIATES, PUBLISHERS
1987   Hillsdale, New Jersey   London

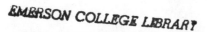

Lawrence Erlbaum Associates, Inc., Publishers
365 Broadway
Hillsdale, New Jersey 07642

Library of Congress Cataloging-in-Publication Data

Social influence.

   "Papers from the Fifth Ontario Symposium on Personality and Social Psychology, held at the
University of Waterloo, August 21–23, 1984"—Pref.
   Includes bibliographies and indexes.
   1. Attitudes—Congresses.   2. Attitude change—
Congresses.   3. Influence (Psychology)—Congresses.
4. Persuasion (Psychology)—Congresses.   I. Zanna,
Mark P., 1944–   II. Olson, James M., 1953–   .   III. Herman,
C. Peter, 1946–   .   IV. Ontario Symposium on
Personality and Social Psychology (5th : 1984 : University
of Waterloo)
HM291.S58838   1987   302'.13   86-24291

ISBN 0-89859-678-5

Printed in the United States of America
10   9   8   7   6   5   4   3   2   1

Contents

III. COMMENTARY

Preface

This volume presents papers from the Fifth Ontario Symposium on Personality and Social Psychology, held at the University of Waterloo, August 21–23, 1984. The contributors are active researchers in the area of social influence, whose chapters, we believe, document the continuing vitality of this topic. One of the purposes of this volume is to provide an accurate picture of our current knowledge about social influence processes. Thus, the chapters describe important recent developments in this area. A second and perhaps more important purpose of this volume is to bring together scholars with different perspectives on the social influence process in order to stimulate further research and theorizing in this area.

To date, five Ontario Symposia on Personality and Social Psychology have been held. The series is designed to bring together scholars from across North America who work in the same substantive area, with the goals of identifying common concerns and integrating research findings. The first Ontario Symposium, held at the University of Western Ontario in August 1978, dealt with social cognition (see Higgins, E. T., Herman, C. P., and Zanna, M. P. (Eds.) (1981). *Social cognition: The Ontario Symposium*. Vol. 1 Hillsdale, NJ: Lawrence Erlbaum Associates); the second, held at the University of Waterloo in October 1979, had the theme of variability and consistency in social behavior (see Zanna, M. P., Higgins, E. T. and Herman, C. P. (Eds.) (1982). *Consistency in social behavior: The Ontario Symposium*. Vol. 2. Hillsdale, NJ: Lawrence Erlbaum Associates); the third, held at the University of Toronto in May 1981, addressed the social psychology of physical appearance (see Herman, C. P., Zanna, M. P. and Higgins, E. T. (Eds.) (1985). *Physical appearance, stigma, and social behavior: The Ontario Symposium*. Vol. 3. Hillsdale, NJ: Lawrence

Erlbaum Associates); and the fourth, held at the University of Western Ontario in October 1983, was concerned with relative deprivation and social comparison processes (see Olson, J. M., Herman, C. P. and Zanna, M. P. (Eds.) (1986). *Relative deprivation and social comparison: The Ontario Symposium.* Vol. 4. Hillsdale, NJ: Lawrence Erlbaum Associates). Participation by Canadian faculty and graduate students in this series of conferences has been gratifying. We hope that the symposia have contributed to (and will continue to stimulate) the growth of personality and social psychology in Ontario and Canada.

Once again, we are deeply indebted to the Social Sciences and Humanities Research Council of Canada, to the Faculty of Arts of the University of Waterloo, and to the Department of Psychology of the University of Waterloo for their financial support. We are also grateful to David Reynolds for helping coordinate the conference, which was attended by more than 60 persons from over 15 universities, and the graduate students at the University of Waterloo for "housing" many of the out-of-town graduate students who attended the symposium. As editors, we would like to thank the contributors to this volume for providing comments on earlier drafts of other participants' chapters, and Larry Erlbaum and Jack Burton for their continuing support and editorial guidance. Finally, Betsy Zanna, Mary Olson and Janet Polivy provided support and encouragement throughout the project.

Mark P. Zanna
James M. Olson
C. Peter Herman

Social Influence:

The Ontario Symposium, Volume 5

COMMUNICATION AND PERSUASION

1 The Heuristic Model of Persuasion

Shelly Chaiken
New York University

Implicit in traditional information-processing models of persuasion such as McGuire's (1972) reception-yielding framework and the cognitive response approach (Greenwald, 1968; Petty, Ostrom, & Brock, 1981) is the view that recipients of persuasive messages engage in a considerable amount of information processing in deciding whether to accept a message's overall position; that is, people are often assumed to attend to, comprehend, and cognitively elaborate upon persuasive argumentation, and to think in some depth about the issue discussed in the persuasive message (see Eagly & Chaiken, 1984, for a fuller discussion of these approaches). In contrast to this *systematic* conceptualization of persuasion (see Chaiken, 1978, 1980), this chapter focuses in more detail on an alternative conceptualization called the "heuristic" model of persuasion (Chaiken, 1978, 1980, 1982; Chaiken & Eagly, 1983; Eagly & Chaiken, 1984). The thrust of the heuristic conceptualization is that opinion change in response to persuasive communications is often the outcome of only a minimal amount of information processing. According to the model, people exert little cognitive effort in judging the validity of a persuasive message and, instead, may base their agreement with a message on a rather superficial assessment of a variety of extrinsic persuasion cues such as surface or structural characteristics of the message itself (e.g., its length or number of arguments), communicator characteristics (e.g., expertise, likability, physical attractiveness), and audience characteristics (e.g., positive or negative audience reactions to the message). The idea that people often perform tasks and make decisions and other judgments after only minimal information processing has gained increasing attention in both cognitive psychology (e.g., Craik & Lockhart, 1972; Schneider & Shiffrin, 1977; Shiffrin & Schneider, 1977) and social psychology (e.g., Abelson, 1976;

Bargh, 1984; Cialdini, 1985; Langer, 1978). Moreover, within the social influence area per se, this idea has found expression in Petty and Cacioppo's (1981; Cacioppo & Petty, Chapter 2, this volume) "central versus peripheral" framework and in Cialdini's (1985; Chapter 7, this volume) attempt to understand compliance phenomena in terms of a set of "compliance principles" not unlike some of the simple decision rules featured in the heuristic model of persuasion. Nevertheless, aside from the heuristic model, the central versus peripheral framework, and a few informal observations by persuasion theorists (e.g., McGuire's (1969) discussion of the "lazy organism" message recipient), the view that people may often be minimalist information processors is largely absent in contemporary cognitive accounts of the persuasion process (see Eagly & Chaiken, 1984).

The heuristic model asserts that many distal persuasion cues are processed by means of simple schemas or decision rules (or cognitive heuristics) that people have presumably learned on the basis of past experiences and observations (Abelson, 1976; Nisbett & Ross, 1980; Stotland & Canon, 1972). For example, with respect to communicator expertise, people may have learned (or been taught) that statements by experts are usually more veridical than statements by persons who lack expertise and may then apply the expert credo, "statements by experts can be trusted," in response to a cue conveying high expertise. Given a cue conveying that a communicator is likable, people may call upon a liking-agreement heuristic such as "people agree with people they like" or "people I like usually have correct opinions on issues." Such a liking-agreement heuristic might derive from people's past direct experience with others or, alternatively, may stem from a lower-order rule suggesting a fairly consistent association between the concepts of liking and interpersonal similarity (Stotland & Canon, 1972). Contextual cues in persuasion settings may also affect opinion change by way of simple decision rules. For example, in response to a cue indicating that other recipients or an overheard audience approve(s) of a communication (e.g., Landy, 1972), people may call upon a consensus heuristic such as "if other people think the message is correct then it is probably valid." And, regarding the heuristic processing of message cues, people's past experiences may have taught them that strong, compelling persuasive messages typically contain more arguments, longer and more detailed arguments, arguments supported by statistics, or arguments derived from highly credible sources (e.g., "According to the Wall Street Journal, the inflation rate is decreasing"). If so, it is likely that people will have abstracted rules such as "length implies strength," "more arguments are better arguments," and "arguments based on expert opinions are valid." According to the heuristic model, people may apply such rules in judging the probable validity of persuasive communications without fully absorbing the semantic content of persuasive argumentation. Consequently, people may agree more with messages containing many (versus few) arguments, with messages that are longer (versus shorter), or with messages containing arguments that are embellished with statistics or ascribed to credible sources.[1]

The extent to which people in persuasion settings do base their judgments of message validity and subsequent agreement with these messages on the kinds of simple decision rules discussed above might be viewed more generally as examples of the way in which people's judgments are influenced by the representativeness heuristic discussed by Tversky and Kahneman (1974, 1981; Kahneman & Tversky, 1973). The representativeness heuristic implies that people base their judgments about whether a particular target observation belongs to a particular category on the degree to which salient features of the target case are representative of or similar to features that are presumed to be characteristic of the general category. In other words, the resemblance of the target case to a prototypical case serves as a powerful cue in affecting judgments about the target case. Thus, in persuasion settings, people who agree more with longer messages or messages containing more arguments or with expert or likable communicators' messages could be viewed as having determined message validity by assessing the degree to which these salient features of the persuasion setting are representative of features presumed to be characteristic of the prototypical "valid persuasive message."

In essence, whereas the more systematic information-processing approaches to understanding persuasion emphasize relatively detailed processing of message content and the role of message- and topic-relevant cognitions in determining opinion change, the heuristic model deemphasizes detailed processing and postulates that simple decision rules often mediate the persuasive impact of a variety of persuasion variables. To better understand the distinction between systematic and heuristic processing, it is useful to differentiate yielding to a message's overall conclusion (e.g., "supervised probation should be used as an alternative to imprisonment") from yielding to persuasive argumentation (e.g., "probation costs taxpayers less than imprisonment"). According to the systematic view of persuasion, distal persuasion variables (e.g., source factors such as communicator credibility, message factors such as number of arguments, contextual factors such as perceived audience evaluation of a message) indirectly affect

---

[1]As noted in the text, a number of Cialdini's (Chapter 7) compliance principles, or heuristics, parallel some of the simple decision rules postulated by the heuristic model. Specifically, the compliance principles of "Social Validation," "Authority," and "Friendship/Liking" are directly analogous to the consensus, expertise, and liking/agreement rules. Whether other compliance heuristics identified by Cialdini (e.g., the "reciprocity" principle) can be applied to understanding persuasion phenomena and, similarly, whether simple persuasion heuristics such as the length/strength rule can be applied to understanding compliance phenomena would seem fruitful questions for subsequent research. It should also be noted that the example persuasion heuristics discussed in this chapter represent an illustrative (and researched) list of decision rules that people may use in persuasion settings rather than an exhaustive list of such principles.

yielding to a message's conclusion and therefore persuasion via their more direct impact on either argument-reception processes (e.g., McGuire, 1972; Wyer, 1974) or argument-acceptance processes (e.g., Fishbein & Ajzen, 1975; Greenwald, 1968; McGuire, 1972; Wyer, 1974). According to the heuristic model, however, such independent variables may directly influence the recipient's global judgment that the message is valid and thus his or her willingness to yield to the message's conclusion without necessarily influencing his or her attention to, comprehension of, or acceptance of persuasive argumentation. Consistent with Shiffrin and Schneider's (1977; Schneider & Shiffrin, 1977) distinction between controlled and automatic processing, systematic processing of persuasive messages is probably most often a controlled process in the sense that it requires attention, is effortful, and is presumably capacity limited. In contrast, heuristic processing of persuasion cues may sometimes occur without much active control or attention by message recipients. Thus, it is possible that people may sometimes be unaware of the extent to which they apply simple decision rules in processing persuasion cues. Nevertheless, under many circumstances message recipients no doubt apply such decision rules quite self-consciously (Chaiken, 1982). For example, an investor may self-consciously decide to accept a stockbroker's recommendations about stock purchases because the broker is a recognized expert on such matters and the investor feels unable or unwilling to critically evaluate the evidential base underlying the broker's recommendations.

Other theoretical perspectives in persuasion such as Kelman's (1961) identification model of opinion change, Brehm's (1966) reactance theory, Heider's (1958) balance theory, Eagly's attributional analysis (Eagly, Chaiken, & Wood, 1981), and Staats' (e.g., Staats & Staats, 1958) classical conditioning approach share with the heuristic model the view that persuasion is not invariably the outcome of message recipients' reception (i.e., attention, comprehension) and/or acceptance of persuasive argumentation. Yet, the heuristic model is novel in its explicit cognitive focus on the mediational role of simple schemas or cognitive heuristics. Moreover, of the above *peripheral* (Petty & Cacioppo, 1981) approaches, only the heuristic model and the attributional perspective are in accord with the implicit motivational assumption of most contemporary (and more *systematic*) information-processing models of persuasion that a message recipient's primary goal in a persuasion setting is to assess the validity of a message's overall conclusion.

In this regard, it should be clear that the heuristic model is not synonymous with what Petty and Cacioppo (1981, 1983; Cacioppo & Petty, Chapter 2, this volume) refer to as the "peripheral route to persuasion." As most clearly articulated in their 1981 text (Petty & Cacioppo, pp. 255–256), the central versus peripheral framework represents a *typological* distinction between various attitude change processes in which theoretical approaches that specify factors or *motives* in persuasion settings that produce attitude change without any active message- or issue-relevant thinking are classified under the peripheral label. Although the heuristic model would, in this framework, be classified as a peripheral approach, the two formulations are not identical because the peripheral label is also used by these authors to refer to theoretical approaches that feature assumptions about the psychological mediation of persuasion and motivational goals of message recipients that are not shared by the heuristic model. For example, the peripheral label is used by Petty and Cacioppo (1981) to refer to classical and to operant conditioning models of attitude change as well as Kelman's identification model, Brehm's reactance theory, and Schlenker's (1980) impression-management theory that feature motivational orientations other than assessing the validity of persuasive messages (see Eagly & Chaiken, 1984, for an elaborated discussion of various motivational bases of persuasion). Finally, it should be noted that under the "central route" to persuasion, Petty and Cacioppo classify persuasion models that emphasize detailed processing of argumentation and the importance of issue-relevant thinking. Unlike the peripheral term, then, the central route does correspond to the "systematic" conceptualization of persuasion (Chaiken, 1978, 1980, 1982; Chaiken & Eagly, 1983). Yet, unlike the Petty and Cacioppo (e.g., 1986) framework, which posits two mutually exclusive routes to persuasion (cf. Stiff, 1986), systematic and heuristic processing are viewed as parallel modes of information processing (Chaiken, 1982; Eagly & Chaiken, 1984).

EMPIRICAL EVIDENCE SUPPORTING THE HEURISTIC MODEL

Consistent with the heuristic model, there are numerous studies suggesting that communicator attributes may exert a relatively direct impact on persuasion (see Chaiken, 1978, 1986, for a more detailed review). For example, Norman (1976) found that an attractive communicator was equally persuasive regardless of whether his message did or did not include supportive argumentation. If the attractiveness cue were mediated by message recipients' processing of message content, the attractive communicator should have been more persuasive with the message that included (versus excluded) argumentation. Similar findings were reported by Mills and Harvey (1972). Further, Miller, Maruyama, Beaber, and Valone (1976) found that fast-talking communicators were perceived as more credible and were more persuasive than slow-talking communicators. Finding no evidence that the persuasive impact of speech rate in their study was mediated either by comprehension effects or by counterargument disruption, Miller et al. concluded that their subjects may have predicated their opinion judgments simply on the basis of whether the communicator seemed credible.

Role of Motivation and Ability

Better evidence that persuasion cues may often be heuristically processed stems from experiments that have examined subjects' motivation or ability to engage in effortful cognitive processing. Unlike systematic processing, which is effortful and may generally be avoided in the interest of cognitive economy (Chaiken, 1978, 1980; Eagly & Chaiken, 1984; Taylor & Fiske, 1978), heuristic processing is relatively effortless and thus may predominate in many persuasion settings (particularly those outside of the experimental social psychology laboratory). However, when motivation to engage in message- and issue-relevant thinking is high, and at least a modicum of ability exists, people may be more likely to engage in the kind of systematic processing specified by the traditional information processing models of persuasion because such processing should, in the long run, be a more reliable means of judging message validity than relying on simple decision rules (Chaiken, 1980; Eagly & Chaiken, 1984). These economic and reliability considerations suggest that persuasion cues whose impact is mediated by simple decision rules should exert a *greater* persuasive impact when message recipients are unmotivated or unable to process systematically. In these situations, the likelihood is low that people will either notice or generate message- or issue-relevant information that might contradict a global judgment of message validity based on some available extrinsic cue like message length. Conversely, such extrinsic persuasion cues should exert a *lesser* persuasive impact when recipients are *highly motivated* and *able* to process systematically. In these latter situations, heuristic processing still might proceed in parallel with systematic processing. However, the greater systematic processing that occurs in such situations should reduce the impact of persuasion cues that are typically processed heuristically (Chaiken, 1982, 1983). For example, although long messages may often lead to greater persuasion than short messages because people apply the "length implies strength" heuristic, careful scrutiny of the semantic content of persuasive argumentation may provide information contradicting this simple heuristic (e.g., the message is long but consists of inferior arguments). Thus, in situations characterized by high motivation and/or high ability to process systematically, a variable such as message length may not exert a detectable impact on opinion change.

Motivation.   Experiments that have presumably varied subjects' motivation to systematically process information by manipulating issue involvement (personal importance or relevance of a message topic) or response involvement (consequentiality of recipients' opinion judgments) have yielded persuasion findings consistent with the predictions outlined above. In these studies, manipulations of source credibility (Johnson & Scileppi, 1969; Rhine & Severance, 1970) and attractiveness (Wilson & Donnerstein, 1977, Experiment I) have significantly affected subjects' opinion judgments under conditions of low, but not high, involvement.

In the first explicit test of the heuristic-systematic framework, Chaiken (1980) examined the persuasive impact of communicator likability in two experiments, one in which response involvement was manipulated (Experiment I) and one in which issue involvement was manipulated (Experiment II). In accord with predictions, both studies found that the persuasive impact of communicator likability was greater under low (versus high) involvement. Moreover, via regression analyses (Experiment I only) that attempted to predict opinion change from various measures designed to tap both systematic and heuristic processing (e.g., message-oriented versus communicator-oriented thoughts), this research was able to document that when involvement was high, subjects based their opinion judgments primarily on their responses to persuasive argumentation, a finding consistent with the systematic view of persuasion. In contrast, and in accord with the heuristic model, when involvement was low, subjects' opinion judgments were primarily determined by their perceptions of the communicator. In two conceptually similar studies, Petty and Cacioppo were able to replicate the basic persuasion findings of these experiments using a different manipulation of communicator attractiveness (Petty, Cacioppo, & Schumann, 1983) and a manipulation of communicator expertise (Petty, Cacioppo, & Goldman, 1981). Unfortunately, while both studies found that the manipulated communicator characteristic exerted a significantly greater impact on persuasion when involvement was low (versus high), neither provided any additional information regarding the cognitive mediation of these opinion change effects.

The above studies all examined the persuasive impact of communicator variables as a function of involvement. Other studies that have manipulated involvement in conjunction with extrinsic surface or structural characteristics of persuasive messages have yielded highly compatible findings. Langer, Blank, and Chanowitz (1978) found that compliance with a small, inconsequential request was equally high regardless of whether the request (to make 5 Xerox copies) was supported by a vacuous reason ("May I use the Xerox machine because I have to make copies") or a more valid reason ("May I use the Xerox machine because I'm in a rush"). In contrast, compliance with a larger, more consequential request (to make 20 Xerox copies) was substantially lower when the request was accompanied with a vacuous (versus valid) reason. These findings suggest that the mere inclusion of arguments in a message, regardless of their quality, can enhance persuasion under uninvolving conditions. However, under more involving conditions in which people are presumably attending to the semantic content of the message, the intrinsic quality of an argument, rather than its mere presence, is the more important determinant of persuasion. In a more definitive test of this hypothesis within a traditional persuasion setting, Petty and Cacioppo (1984) found that, under low involvement, message recipients indicated greater agreement with communications that contained nine rather than three arguments, regardless of the quality of these arguments. Under high involvement, however, recipients agreed more with messages containing nine (versus three) high quality arguments but less with messages containing nine (versus three) low quality arguments. Moreover, in accord with the Chaiken (1980, Experiment I) correlational findings, these authors found that subjects' opinion judgments were more highly related to message-relevant thinking under high (versus low) involvement, as would be expected if heightened involvement motivates people to engage in systematic processing. In contrast, subjects in the low involvement conditions of this study presumably used a simple decision rule such as "more arguments are better arguments" in making their opinion judgments.

In a recently completed study (Axsom, Yates, & Chaiken, 1985), we examined whether findings similar to those just described with respect to communicator and surface message characteristics could be obtained with a contextual persuasion cue such as an overheard audience's reaction to a persuasive message. Although past research suggests that recipients may be less persuaded when an overheard audience expresses disapproval (versus approval) of a message (Chaiken & Fowler, 1979; Hylton, 1971; Hocking, Margreiter, & Hylton, 1977; Landy, 1972; Silverthorne & Mazmanian, 1975), the psychological mechanism(s) underlying this cue's persuasive impact remain unclear. The purpose of the Axsom et al. study was to investigate whether heightened agreement with a message that other listeners approve of might reflect a simple consensus heuristic. To explore this idea, subjects (under the guise of listening to one side of a debate) were exposed to an audio-taped message that advocated probation as an alternative to imprisonment. A between-subjects design manipulated the focal extrinsic cue (audience response: positive vs. negative), an intrinsic message cue (argument quality: strong vs. weak), and involvement (high vs. low). Argument quality was varied by preparing two versions of the probation message, one containing six strong persuasive arguments and one containing six weak arguments. In the positive audience condition, subjects heard a tape of the message in which an (ostensibly present) audience interrupted the speaker several times with short but loud bursts of clapping and responded to his summary statement with long and enthusiastic applause. In contrast, in the negative audience condition, only one or two tentative clappers were heard responding to the speaker's points and his final summary was met with an indifferent, barely polite smattering of applause. Finally, in order to vary subjects' motivation to process systematically, in the low-involvement conditions of the study subjects were told that the experiment was "only preliminary" and that the probation issue was being considered for the distant future in a faraway location (Minnesota). In contrast, in the high-involvement conditions, subjects were told that the experiment was "quite important" (as were their responses) and that the probation issue was currently being considered for adoption in their own area (middle Tennessee).

In line with our hypothesis that the extrinsic audience cue would have a detectable impact on persuasion only when motivation to process systematically was low, subjects' postmessage agreement ratings revealed that only low-involvement subjects were significantly influenced by the audience manipulation, with those overhearing the positive (versus negative) audience manifesting greater persuasion. Moreover, consistent with the heuristic perspective, the audience manipulation had little impact on various measures designed to assess systematic processing (e.g., argument recall, message- and issue-oriented cognitions). Instead, subjects' perceptions of how much the audience approved of the message proved to be a significant predictor of persuasion for low-involvement (but not high-involvement) subjects. In contrast to these findings, high-involvement subjects were not differentially affected by the audience manipulation. As expected, however, these subjects manifested a greater tendency to engage in systematic processing and, consequently, were significantly influenced by the argument quality manipulation, with those exposed to strong (versus weak) arguments evidencing greater persuasion. Presumably, high (versus low) involvement subjects were unaffected by the audience manipulation because their more careful scrutiny of the message's intrinsic features (persuasive arguments) provided them with information that contradicted the simple consensus heuristic that "if other recipients approve of the message it's probably valid."

Ability. All of the previously discussed involvement studies have yielded findings consistent with the earlier proposition that cues that are typically processed heuristically will exert a greater impact on persuasion when people lack the motivation to engage in systematic processing of persuasive messages. In addition to motivation, however, ability to process systematically must be considered. Given the types of messages used in previous research (relatively easy-to-comprehend and easy-to-evaluate arguments) and the fact that intrinsic message cues such as amount (Chaiken, 1980) and quality of argumentation (Axsom et al., 1985; Petty et al., 1981; Petty & Cacioppo, 1984) affected persuasion under conditions of high involvement, it is likely that subjects possessed reasonably high ability to engage in message- and issue-relevant thinking. Regardless of motivation, however, there are at least two reasons to expect that heuristically processed persuasion cues will exert a greater impact on opinion change when ability to process systematically is low.

The first reason for this prediction rests on (1) the assumption that heuristic and systematic processing of persuasion cues represent parallel, rather than mutually exclusive, modes of information processing (Chaiken, 1982; Eagly & Chaiken, 1984), and (2) theory and research on controlled versus automatic processing which suggests that factors that render a task more difficult or otherwise reduce capacity to process information should primarily harm controlled, rather than automatic, processing (Schneider & Shiffrin, 1977; Shiffrin & Schneider, 1977). Thus, even in persuasion situations in which motivation to process systematically is relatively high, situational or individual difference factors (e.g., distractions or lack of knowledge) that adversely affect this mode of processing should not, at the same time, decrease the likelihood that heuristic processing will be activated by relevant extrinsic persuasion cues. As a consequence, when message recipients lack the ability to process systematically, intrinsic message cues such as quality of persuasive argumentation should exert a relatively minimal impact on opinion judgments. Moreover, recipients' decreased abilities to comprehend, evaluate, and elaborate on persuasive argumentation should reduce the likelihood that they will either notice or generate information that might contradict a judgment of message validity based upon some available extrinsic persuasion cue such as message length or communicator attractiveness.

A second reason underlying the prediction that the persuasive impact of heuristically processed extrinsic cues will increase as ability to engage in systematic processing decreases stems from (1) the assumption noted earlier that, regardless of processing mode employed, message recipients are primarily oriented toward assessing the validity of a message's overall conclusion, and (2) the idea that the extent to which recipients utilize one mode of processing information rather than another depends in part on the *sufficiency* of a particular mode for determining the validity of a message's overall recommendation (see Eagly & Chaiken, 1984). As Eagly and Chaiken (1984) have argued, although the sufficiency principle suggests that recipients often move from less effortful to more effortful modes of information processing in order to more confidently assess message validity (see Wood & Eagly, 1981, for an empirical demonstration), the reverse direction may also be observed under certain circumstances. Indeed, an inability or reduced ability to engage in systematic processing of persuasive communications may represent a circumstance in which message recipients may quite self-consciously decide to employ a simple decision rule in evaluating message validity. In line with this hypothesis, some research in the decision-making literature indicates that as a task becomes more complex, people tend to increase their reliance on simplifying choice heuristics (e.g., Payne, 1976; Newell & Simon, 1972). An extreme instance in which recipients might self-consciously decide to rely on a simple decision rule in evaluating message validity might occur when the persuasive message contains insufficient information on which to predicate an opinion judgment and the recipient lacks much prior knowledge regarding the topic discussed in the message. Consistent with this conjecture, a study by McCroskey (1970) that employed a relatively unfamiliar persuasion topic (federal control of education) found that communicator credibility significantly affected persuasion only when the persuasive message contained minimal evidence in support of its overall conclusion. When the message contained more (and stronger) evidence, subjects' opinion judgments were unaffected by the communicator's credibility (see also, Chaiken, 1980, Experiment 2). Presumably, subjects in the minimal evidence condition considered a message containing so little information a meager basis for assessing message validity and thus felt it necessary to rely also on information regarding the communicator's credibility in forming their opinion judgments.

In summary, when ability to engage in detailed systematic processing is impaired, the persuasive impact of extrinsic cues that affect opinion change via simple decision rules may be enhanced for two reasons. First, in a more passive manner, message recipients may not gain access to message- and issue-relevant information that might serve to contradict the validity of a simple heuristic (e.g., "length implies strength") and, thus, suppress the persuasive impact of the relevant extrinsic cue (e.g., message length). Second, in a more active manner, recipients who desire to maximize the validity of their opinions but whose ability to process systematically is impaired may, by default or by design, self-consciously decide to rely on a simple decision rule in judging the probable validity of a persuasive message.

A number of findings in the persuasion literature are consistent with the idea that manipulations that make a task more difficult or reduce information processing capacity primarily harm systematic, rather than, heuristic processing. For example, manipulations that distract recipients from processing counterattitudinal messages often enhance persuasion by interfering with their ability to critically evaluate persuasive argumentation (e.g., Osterhouse & Brock, 1970) and, when compelling but inherently complex messages are transmitted by a modality that impairs ability to process systematically (e.g., video- or audiotape), compared to one that enhances this ability (e.g., written presentation), recipients show less comprehension of the message's supportive argumentation and are less persuaded (Chaiken & Eagly, 1976). Nevertheless, neither high levels of distraction nor presenting messages in a difficult-to-process medium appear to dampen the persuasive impact of extrinsic cues. Indeed, consistent with the hypothesis that such cues will exert a greater persuasive impact when ability to process systematically is low, Kiesler and Mathog (1968) found that a manipulation of communicator credibility had a somewhat stronger impact on persuasion when subjects were distracted (vs. were not distracted) from paying attention to message content, and Chaiken and Eagly (1983) found that a manipulation of communicator likability had a significantly stronger persuasive impact when subjects received video- or audio-taped (vs. written) messages.

Findings compatible with these earlier results have been obtained in two recent experiments. For example, Yalch and Elmore-Yalch (1984) reasoned that the amount of quantitative information contained in a persuasive message would influence recipients' abilities (and, possibly their motivation as well) to process message content and, consequently, their reliance on extrinsic persuasion cues. In their experiment, subjects read a message advocating the use of automatic teller machines that was attributed to either an expert or inexpert source and contained either quantitative or qualitative information. Consistent with predictions, the findings of this study indicated that the communicator expertise manipulation significantly affected persuasion only when quantitative (vs. qualitative) messages were received. Moreover, subjects generated fewer message-oriented cognitions when they received the quantitative version of the persuasive message. Although these findings are compatible with the idea that extrinsic cues are more likely to affect persuasion when ability to process systmatically is low, it is possible (as authors note) that the message quantitativeness variable affected motivation to process systematically as much as it affected ability.

In a recent study (Ratneshwar & Chaiken, 1986), we attempted to address the ability issue more directly by utilizing what we considered to be a more clear-cut manipulation of ability (vs. motivation) to process systematically. In the study we varied subjects' ability to comprehend a short persuasive message using a manipulation modeled after those used by Bransford and his colleagues (e.g., Bransford & Johnson, 1972) in their research on the role of relevant contextual knowledge in comprehension. Specifically, we developed a 200-word written message describing a novel product—a replacement eraser for a pencil—that, in the absence of a picture that depicted the product's components (discussed in the message), was relatively incomprehensible to pilot subjects. In the study, subjects in the high-comprehensibility conditions were exposed to both the written message and a "full context" picture depicting the product's components, their appropriate spatial relations, and the significance of these relations in a meaningful functional context (i.e., atop a pencil). In a medium comprehensibility condition, subjects received the written message as well as a "partial context" picture that depicted the product's components but did not preserve their appropriate spatial relations and did not show the product in a meaningful functional context. Finally, subjects in the low-comprehensibility conditions received only the written message. Cross-cutting the comprehensibility manipulation was a manipulation of our focal extrinsic persuasion cue, communicator expertise: Some subjects were led to believe that the *inventor* who held the patent on the novel product described in the message was a Stanford University professor who specialized in "innovation and entrepreneurial development" and who had numerous other patents and a published book on creativity to his credit. In contrast, other subjects were told that the inventor was a local real-estate agent who had been trying, without success, to find a publisher for a book he was hoping to write on creativity and product design. Subjects, who participated in small group sessions, were told that the purpose of the study was to investigate consumers' reactions to novel products and that the product information they would receive conformed to official Patent Office specifications. After exposure to the persuasive message, subjects' attitudes toward the product and the inventor, their comprehension of the message, and other responses were assessed.

As expected, our contextual manipulation appropriately influenced subjects' abilities to comprehend the persuasive message: Subjects in the low (vs. medium or high) comprehensibility conditions manifested significantly less comprehension of the message. In addition, subjects considered the inventor to be significantly more expert when he had been described as a Stanford Professor (vs. local real-estate agent). On subjects' ratings of how useful they considered the replacement eraser to be, neither the comprehension nor expertise main effect proved significant. However, as we had predicted, an interaction between comprehensibility and source expertise ($p < .07$) indicated that subjects' product evaluations were significantly influenced by the source manipulation only when their abilities to comprehend the message were low: Low-comprehension subjects rated the product as much more useful when the inventor possessed high (vs. low) expertise (Ms = 1.50 vs. − .05 on a −4 to +4 scale where +4 signified very useful, $p < .01$). In contrast, in the medium- and high-comprehensibility conditions (combined), subjects rated the product's usefulness equivalently, regardless of whether the source was portrayed as expert or inexpert (Ms = .36 vs. .44, F < 1). Moreover, subjects' postmessage product evaluations proved to be more highly correlated with their perceptions of source expertise in the low (vs. medium and high) comprehensibility condition of the experiment (rs = .55 vs. .25, $p < .03$). Finally, in line with our assumption that our comprehensibility manipulation would primarily affect subjects' abilities to systematically process message content, rather than their motivation to do so, subjects' self-reports of the amount of effort that had put into trying to understand the persuasive message were not significantly affected by either the comprehensibility manipulation, the expertise manipulation, or their interaction.

Notwithstanding the Ratneshwar and Chaiken (1986) experiment, it seems reasonable to expect that many variables that adversely affect peoples' abilities to scrutinize and evaluate persuasive argumentation would also tend to undermine their motivation to engage in message- and issue-relevant thinking. In the achievement area, for example, research indicates that low expectancies regarding one's ability to succeed at some task often result in decreased performance, presumably because of a reduction in effort spent on that task (see Frieze, Parsons, Johnson, Ruble, & Zellman, 1978). Similarly, in persuasion settings it may often be the case that variables that tax recipients' abilities to successfully evaluate a persuasive communication (e.g., distractions, inherently complex argumentation) will also tend to decrease the amount of effort that recipients are willing to put into this task. Thus, in general, it may be infrequent that ability-impairing manipulations exert a unique impact on ability. Rather, such manipulations probably influence the persuasive impact of extrinsic cues by way of their influence on both ability and motivation to engage in message- and issue-relevant thinking.

Individual Differences in Motivation and/or Ability. The research summarized thus far has demonstrated how variations in manipulated situational factors (e.g., message comprehensibility, response-involvement, distraction) may influence the persuasive impact of extrinsic persuasion cues via their impact on either motivation or ability to process systematically. In addition, those studies that have manipulated subjects' levels of issue-involvement (e.g., Chaiken, 1980, Experiment 2; Petty et al., 1981) have provided some insights regarding how certain temporary and domain-specific recipient predispositions may influence mode of processing and, thus, the persuasive impact of extrinsic persuasion cues. In this section we consider recent research that has examined the impact of non-manipulated individual difference factors on information processing and the persuasive impact of extrinsic persuasion cues. As will be seen, due to the nature of these individual difference constructs, it is not clear at this time whether their influence on the persuasive impact of extrinsic cues is primarily due to their effect on motivation or ability alone, on *both* motivation and ability for systematic processing or, perhaps, on motivation for heuristic processing.

Wood, Kallgren, and Priesler (1985) examined the relative persuasive effectiveness of argument quality (an intrinsic message cue) and message length (an extrinsic message cue) among subjects who, prior to the experiment, differed in terms of their abilities to retrieve attitude-relevant information from memory. High retrieval (i.e., high knowledge) subjects were expected to be more influenced by the intrinsic message cue of argument quality whereas low-retrieval (i.e., low-knowledge) subjects were expected to be more influenced by the extrinsic cue of message length. Consistent with these predictions, Wood et al. found that subjects with little prior knowledge about the message topic (preserving the environment), but not highly knowledgeable subjects, showed significantly greater agreement with long, rather than short, messages, even though these messages contained an equivalent number of distinct persuasive arguments. In addition, low-knowledge subjects were unaffected by the argument quality manipulation whereas high-knowledge subjects exhibited greater opinion change when the message contained strong, rather than weak, persuasive arguments. Moreover, consistent with the authors' assumption that low-knowledge subjects would evidence less systematic processing of the persuasive message, fewer message-oriented cognitions were generated by low (vs. high) knowledge subjects on a thought-listing task. Because subjects were selected on the basis of their differential abilities to access attitudinally-relevant information from memory, Wood et al. argued that their findings were primarily due to the impact of the retrieval variable on subjects' abilities to engage in message- and issue-relevant thinking. Nevertheless, as the authors point out, because high (vs. low) retrieval subjects also considered the message topic more personally relevant, differential motivation for systematic processing may also have been a contributing factor.

Elaborating on Cohen's (1957; Cohen, Stotland, & Wolfe, 1955) early work, Cacioppo and Petty (1982) developed a 34-item Need for Cognition (NFC) scale that measures chronic individual differences in people's tendencies to "engage in and enjoy thinking." In addition to providing psychometric evidence regarding the NFC scale's reliability and validity (Cacioppo & Petty, 1982), these authors have recently demonstrated its applicability to persuasion settings. Reasoning that high- (vs. low-) NFC subjects would be more likely to engage in message- and issue-relevant thinking in response to a persuasive message, Cacioppo, Petty, and Morris (1983) predicted and found that a manipulation of an intrinsic persuasion cue, argument quality, had a significant impact on the postmessage opinions expressed by high, but not low, NFC subjects. Although Cacioppo et al. viewed their findings as reflecting high- and low-NFC subjects' differential motivation for systematic (or central) processing, because higher scores on the NFC scale have been shown to be positively and significantly correlated with academic achievement scores (Cacioppo & Petty, 1982), the impact of NFC on systematic processing may also be a product of peoples' differential abilities to engage in message- and issue-relevant thinking.

In contrast to the Cacioppo, Petty, and Morris (1983) experiment that focused on the greater responsiveness of high- (vs. low-) NFC subjects to an intrinsic persuasion cue, recent research in our laboratory (Axsom et al., 1985; Chaiken, Axsom, Hicks, Yates, and Wilson, 1985) has focused on investigating whether *low*- (vs. high-) NFC individuals may be more likely to use simple decision rules in evaluating the validity of persuasive messages. This prediction stems directly from the assumption (discussed earlier) that the persuasive impact of extrinsic cues should be enhanced when motivation and/or ability for systematic processing is low because, in such situations, people may not gain access to message- and issue-relevant information that might serve to contradict the validity of a simple heuristic (e.g., length implies strength) and thus suppress the persuasive impact of relevant extrinsic cues (e.g., message length). Another idea underlying this prediction, however, is that low-NFC individuals, in addition to their postulated tendency to dislike complex thinking, may actively *prefer* to employ simple decision rules when performing tasks and making judgments.

Evidence for the hypothesis that people lower in Need for Cognition may be more prone to employ simple decision rules has been obtained in two recent experiments in which high- and low-NFC subjects (identified on the basis of a pre-experimental questionnaire) were exposed to persuasive messages in contexts in which we manipulated two different types of extrinsic persuasion cues. In one study (Chaiken et al., 1985), subjects, under the guise of judging the physical characteristics of a speaker based only on his audiotaped voice, were exposed to a persuasive message advocating that their University (Vanderbilt) should adopt comprehensive examinations for graduating seniors (arguments for this message were adapted from Petty and Cacioppo, 1984). Although all subjects listened to a message that contained six distinct persuasive arguments, some subjects heard a version of the tape in which the speaker began by stating that he would discuss 10 reasons for his position whereas the remaining subjects heard a version in which the speaker stated that he would discuss 2 reasons. Attesting to the success of our argument number manipulation, subjects exposed to a message that purportedly contained 10 (vs. 2) arguments estimated that the message contained significantly more persuasive arguments. And, in support of our hypothesis, a significant interaction between the number of arguments manipulation and NFC status ($p < .05$) on subjects' postmessage agreement scores indicated that low, but not high, NFC subjects agreed much more with the speaker's message when he claimed to have 10 (vs. 2) arguments.

Findings compatible with these were also obtained in the audience cue study described earlier (Axsom et al., 1985) in which involvement, argument quality, and audience reaction to the persuasive message (positive versus negative) were manipulated. In that study, NFC scores were available for only a subset of participating subjects. Nevertheless, for this subsample, analyses of subjects' postmessage opinions revealed that that low- (vs. high-) NFC subjects were more responsive to the extrinsic audience cue, although this effect obtained only when involvement was low. Specifically, a three-way interaction between the audience manipulation, involvement, and NFC status ($p < .05$) showed that high-NFC subjects were unaffected by the audience manipulation, regardless of whether involvement was high or low and that low-NFC subjects were unaffected by the audience manipulation when involvement was high. However, when low-NFC subjects were not induced to process systematically (i.e., when involvement was low), they agreed significantly more with the message when the audience's response to the message was positive, rather than negative ($p < .02$).

The results of the number of arguments study and the audience cue study thus support our hypothesis that people who are lower (vs. higher) in Need for Cognition will be more responsive to extrinsic persuasion cues (particularly when situational-inducements to process systematically are absent). As noted above, this hypothesis flows directly from the assumption that the lesser amount of systematic processing engaged in by low- (vs. high-) NFC individuals (Cacioppo et al., 1983) fails to provide them with message- and issue-relevant information contradicting the validity of simple decision rules (e.g., the length strength rule, the consensus heuristic). However, it was also suggested that low- (vs. high-) NFC individuals may, in fact, prefer to rely on simplifying heuristics when they make decisions and other judgments. Some tentative evidence for the latter idea comes from three recent pilot studies in which three different samples of college-aged subjects (Ns = 341, 367, and 174) completed a questionnaire containing 20 Need for Cognition items (Cacioppo & Petty, 1982) and 8 additional items (randomly distributed throughout the NFC items) designed to tap subjects' self-reported tendencies to rely on simple decision rules (e.g., ''I generally agree with people I like and disagree with people I dislike,'' ''I trust statements made by experts,'' ''If most people think something is correct, then chances are it is'').[2] For all three samples, factor analyses revealed that only one major factor (by the scree test) characterized all 28 test items. Although the (non-NFC) heuristic items tended to have somewhat lower loadings on this factor than did many (though not all) of the original NFC items, in none of the three replications was there any evidence that the two sets of items tapped different constructs. These data should be considered tentative given the fact that our subjects responded to the heuristic items in the context of responding to a larger number of NFC items (a context that may overestimate the extent to which these

---

[2]This questionnaire was administered to subjects during class time in their introductory psychology courses. Because of time constraints, we could not administer a questionnaire that contained all of the original 34 Need for Cognition items. The 20 items that we did select for presentation were chosen because they had the highest item-total correlations (for original items and item-total correlations, see Cacioppo and Petty, 1982).

two item subsets cohere). Nevertheless, they are consistent with the idea that lower Need for Cognition scores reflect, not only a lesser tendency to enjoy and to engage in thinking, but also a greater preference for simple heuristics in decision making.

Before concluding this section, it is instructive to consider one last study because of its implications for understanding how a more affectively laden individual difference variable may impact on mode of information processing and persuasion. In this study (Jepson & Chaiken, 1986) we explored how individual differences in subjects' levels of anxiety about a specific health threat, cancer, might influence information processing and opinion change in response to a persuasive message that advocated regular cancer-related check-ups. In the study, subjects first completed a questionnaire that included a number of items designed to tap cancer-specific anxiety (e.g., "how scared are you of getting cancer?" "how upsetting do you find it when you read or hear something about cancer?") as well as items tapping other variables (e.g., perceived susceptibility to cancer). Next, in line with the experimenter's request that subjects help him to evaluate the quality of various health messages on different topics, subjects were instructed to read a two-page essay that advocated regular cancer-related check-ups for all young adults and, while performing this task, to list their thoughts, criticisms, and other comments about the message on a piece of paper that was provided. Thus, the 86 subjects in this study were given explicit instructions to critically evaluate the merit of the message and, moreover, were given an unlimited amount of time to read the message and to list their thoughts. After completing this task, subjects' opinion on the message topic, their recall of the message's arguments, and other responses were assessed.

The major purpose of the Jepson and Chaiken (1986) study was to investigate the relationship between subjects' levels of cancer-specific anxiety and the amount of systematic processing they evidenced. Several indices of systematic processing were obtained: The number of message-relevant thoughts generated on the thought-listing task, the number of these message-relevant thoughts that cited logical errors in the message (six inferential errors had been strategically placed throughout the message), and the number of arguments that subjects were able to recall. Despite the fact that our instructions demanded a critical set from all subjects, correlational analyses revealed significant or near significant linear relationships between all of our systematic processing indices and the anxiety index: Subjects who manifested higher (vs. lower) levels of cancer-specific anxiety found fewer inferential errors ($p < .001$), listed fewer message-relevant thoughts ($p < .03$), and tended to recall fewer persuasive arguments ($p < .07$). Interestingly, in contrast to these objective measures of systematic processing, high- (vs. low) anxiety subjects reported putting more time and effort into reading and evaluating the message ($p < .03$). Finally, consistent with our expectation that agreement with our experimental message would increase as subjects detected fewer logical errors, subjects who manifested higher (vs. lower) levels of cancer-specific anxiety exhibited greater opinion change ($p < .005$).[3]

These findings are consistent with observations that have been made in the health literature that people who are anxious about or vulnerable to a health threat, or otherwise experiencing stress may engage in less careful or less extensive processing of health-relevant information (e.g., Cohen & Lazarus, 1973; Janis & Mann, 1977; Klagsbrun, 1971; McIntosh, 1974). Moreover, at least some researchers in this area (e.g., Wortman & Dunkel-Schetter, 1979) have speculated that such affective reactions tend to reduce people's confidence in their abilities to make decisions and process relevant information in such a way that they may quite self-consciously desire to rely on other people's advice when it comes to decision making. One implication of this assertion (that we are currently investigating) for understanding people's responses to health appeals is that variables such as health-specific anxiety or perceived vulnerability to a health threat may lead, not only to less systematic processing of health messages, as shown by the Jepson and Chaiken study, but also to a greater reliance on the kinds of simple rules specified by the heuristic model.

Finally, it should be pointed out that our prediction in the Jepson and Chaiken (1986) study that a heightened level of cancer-specific anxiety would lead to *less* systematic processing of our experimental message is directly opposite to the prediction we might have made had we considered a variable such as perceived vulnerability (see footnote 3) or health-specific anxiety only in terms of its "colder" cognitive (vs. affective) aspects. By focusing exclusively on the cognitive aspects of variables such as these, we might have been tempted to predict that greater perceived vulnerability would have led to a *greater* amount of systematic processing because individuals with a heightened sense of vulnerability and/or anxiety regarding a particular health threat would, no doubt, perceive a message dealing with that threat to be much more personally relevant than would individuals who did not view themselves as vulnerable or who were not anxious. As reviewed earlier, studies that have manipulated the personal relevance or

---

[3]Although subjects' (preexperimental) ratings of their vulnerability, or susceptibility, to cancer proved to be only negligibly correlated with our cancer-specific anxiety index ($r = .09$), the observed relationship between perceived vulnerability and systematic processing paralleled, for the most part, the findings reported in the text for the cancer-specific anxiety index. Specifically, greater perceived vulnerability to cancer was associated with fewer message-relevant cognitions ($p < .05$), fewer logical errors detected ($p = .11$), and lesser argument recall ($p < .05$). Unlike the findings reported in the text, however, greater perceived vulnerability was associated with a nonsignificantly greater tendency to report less effort processing the cancer message ($p = .21$) and significantly less opinion change ($p < .01$). It should also be noted that the cancer-specific anxiety/systematic processing findings reported in the text were replicated in a second study which showed, in addition, that our cancer-specific anxiety index was only negligibly correlated with Spielberger's (1972) measure of trait anxiety ($r = .09$, ns) and that the observed effects of cancer-specific anxiety on systematic processing of our cancer message were not attributable to individual differences in trait anxiety.

importance of message topics (i.e., issue-involvement) have generally found that higher levels of personal relevance encourage greater systematic processing. Thus, the Jepson and Chaiken (1986) study represents an exception to the idea that higher levels of issue-involvement will uniformly lead to greater systematic processing of persuasive messages and, moreover, suggests than when investigating the impact of involvement-like variables on information processing and persuasion, both the affective and cognitive aspects of such variables need to be taken into account (see Chaiken & Stangor, in press for a more detailed discussion of the persuasive impact of involvement). More generally, our own findings as well as other research on the effect of arousal on information processing and task performance (e.g., Easterbrook, 1959; Yerkes & Dodson, 1908) suggest that very high levels of stress and/or arousal (however induced) may inhibit systematic processing and, perhaps, encourage heuristic processing (Nemeth, 1986). Indeed, within the area of minority group influence, Nemeth (this volume, Chapter 10) has hypothesized and shown that individuals exposed to majority (vs. minority) group points of view engage in less active and thoughtful information processing and, further, that this processing difference may reflect, at least in part, the fact that exposure to majority (vs. minority) positions leads individuals to experience greater stress (e.g., Nemeth & Wachtler, 1983).

Salience and Vividness

All of the aforementioned research suggests that when motivation or ability to process persuasive messages in a systematic manner is low, opinion change is more likely to reflect recipients' use of simple decision rules. In addition, recent research also suggests that increasing the salience and/or vividness of persuasion cues that are typically processed in heuristic fashion may also increase the likelihood that people will apply simple decision rules in judging the probable validity of persuasive messages.

In two experiments (utilizing a total of three different persuasion topics), Chaiken and Eagly (1983) presented subjects with either a videotaped, audiotaped, or written persuasive message that was attributed to either a likable or unlikable communicator. Based on the assumption that nonverbal communicator cues in the two broadcast modalities would draw recipients' attention to the communicator, we reasoned that the liking-agreement heuristic ("people generally agree with people they like") would be more likely to be activated when subjects were exposed to videotaped or audiotaped, rather than written, messages. Consistent with our reasoning, the communicator likability manipulation exerted a significantly greater impact on the postmessage opinions expressed by subjects in the video and audiotaped (vs. written) modalities; subjects in the two broadcast modalities agreed significantly more with the likable (vs. unlikable) communicator's message, whereas subjects who received written messages were unaffected by the likability manipulation. Moreover, additional findings from these experiments indicated that subjects thought more about the communicator in the two broadcast modalities (as indexed by subjects' responses to a thought-listing task) and, to a greater extent than subjects exposed to written messages, based their opinion judgments on their perceptions of the communicator.

The results of the Chaiken and Eagly (1983) experiments, which are consistent with prior research on salience effects (e.g., McArthur, 1981; Taylor & Fiske, 1978) as well as the hypothesis that vivid (vs. nonvivid) information is more impactful (Nisbett & Ross, 1980; Taylor & Thompson, 1982), suggest that manipulations that make other types of persuasion cues salient or inherently more vivid should also increase their persuasive impact. Of course, manipulations that make message content more salient (e.g., instructional sets that lead recipients to focus attention on persuasive argumentation) should enhance the likelihood that recipients engage in systematic processing and, consequently, the persuasive impact of intrinsic cues such as argument quality. However, increasing the salience or vividness of extrinsic cues such as communicator likability, communicator expertise, or message length should increase their persuasive impact. Moreover, according to the heuristic model, the enhanced persuasive impact of such cues would be ascribed to the activating effect of their increased salience or vividness on people's tendencies to utilize the simple decision rules that are associated with these cues.

Consistent with this reasoning about the effects of increasing attention to extrinsic cues, Pallak (1983) obtained findings suggesting that increasing the vividness of a communicator's physical attractiveness enhances the likelihood that people will retrieve and make use of the liking/agreement rule in making their opinion judgments (see Chaiken, 1986, for an elaborated discussion of how the liking/agreement heuristic may often underlie communicator attractiveness effects in persuasion). In the Pallak study, vividness was manipulated by presenting subjects with either a high-quality color photograph of the (male) communicator or a degraded xerox copy of the photo. In addition to this manipulation, for some subjects, the message that was attributed to the communicator contained strong persuasive arguments while, for others, the message contained weak arguments. The results of this study indicated that when the communicator's physical appearance was not vivid, subjects apparently processed the persuasive message systematically: They agreed more with high- (vs. low-) quality messages, and their postmessage opinions were highly correlated with their message-oriented cognitions (as indexed by a thought-listing task). In contrast, when the communicator's appearance was made vivid, subjects manifested greater heuristic (and also lesser systematic) processing: In this condition, postmessage opinions were unaffected by the argument quality manipulation and were more highly correlated with subjects' perceptions of the communicator than with their message-oriented cognitions.

As implied by both the Chaiken and Eagly (1983) and Pallak (1983) research, any factor in a persuasion setting that increases either the salience or vividness of extrinsic persuasion cues may enhance their persuasive impact, presumably because of the increased likelihood that the simple decision rules associated with such cues will be activated and, thus, utilized by recipients of persuasive messages. For example, Pallak, Murroni, and Koch (1983) have argued and provided some evidence for the notion that an emotionally toned (vs. rationally toned) message may draw attention to a communicator's attractiveness and, thus, facilitate the persuasive impact of this extrinsic cue. The range of variables in persuasion settings that may enhance the salience and/or vividness of extrinsic persuasion cues may prove to be fairly broad, particularly when novel variables such as Pallak's (1983) vividness-of-appearance manipulation are considered in addition to more traditional persuasion variables such as communication modality. Thus, further research investigating the impact of such variables on information processing and persuasion would seem fruitful.

More Direct Evidence for Heuristic Processing

Although the research summarized thus far in this chapter supports the utility of the heuristic model, it has provided only indirect empirical evidence for the cognitive mediation of opinion change specified by this persuasion framework. Under conditions of low motivation and/or low ability to process message content systematically, and also under conditions of high cue salience, extrinsic persuasion cues such as number of arguments, message length, audience reaction, and communicator expertise, likability, or physical attractiveness appear to have an enhanced impact on opinion change (relative to conditions of high motivation and ability and low cue salience). Moreover, those studies that have included measures designed to index more effortful, systematic processing of message content (e.g., measures of argument recall and message- and issue-relevant thinking) have indicated that the observed persuasive impact of these extrinsic persuasion cues has *not* been mediated by recipients' attention to, comprehension of, or elaboration of persuasive argumentation (Axsom, Yates, & Chaiken, 1985; Chaiken, 1980; Chaiken & Eagly, 1983; Pallak, 1983; Pallak, Murroni, & Koch, 1983; Petty & Cacioppo, 1984; Wood, Kallgren, & Priesler, 1985). Further, in many of these studies (Axsom et al., 1985; Chaiken, 1980; Chaiken et al., 1985; Chaiken & Eagly, 1983; Pallak, 1983; Wood et al., 1985), additional correlational findings have indicated that the persuasive impact of extrinsic persuasion cues *has* covaried with subjects' perceptions and/or judgments regarding these cues (e.g., the Chaiken [1980] finding that low-, but not high-, involvement subjects' opinions were best predicted by their perceptions of communicator attractiveness). At the same time, however, this research has provided little *direct* evidence that subjects in these studies have actually used the kinds of simple decision rules specified by the heuristic model (e.g., the liking-agreement rule, the length-strength rule).

As noted earlier in this chapter, because people may sometimes be unaware of the extent to which they use simple decision rules in processing extrinsic persuasion cues (or unwilling to acknowledge their use of such rules), self-report measures may not be very useful in documenting the role that such cognitive heuristics play in persuasion. Indeed, in the only previous study that included a measure designed to assess subjects' possible use of a simple heuristic (Chaiken, 1980, Experiment 2), only a partial corrrespondence was found between subjects' self-reported use of the liking-agreement rule and the extent to which they agreed more with a likable (vs. unlikable) communicator's message. To obtain more direct evidence for the cognitive mediation of opinion change specified by the heuristic model, recent research in our laboratory (Chaiken et al., 1985; Hicks & Chaiken, 1984; Wilson, Axsom, Lee, & Chaiken, 1985) has featured priming tasks that are designed to vary either the accessibility or both the accessibility and perceived reliability of various decision rules.[4] Consequently, we hypothesize that these priming tasks will affect the likelihood that subjects will utilize the decision rules whose accessibility and/or reliability has been manipulated in a subsequent persuasion setting. In all of these studies, subjects are first exposed to a priming manipulation that is typically presented to them as a self-contained judgment or memory study. Then, in the context of participating in a second, ostensibly unrelated, experiment, subjects are exposed to a persuasive message in a setting in which we manipulate the extrinsic persuasion cue that corresponds to whatever decision rule has been made more or less accessible or more or less reliable by the earlier priming task. In order to minimize subjects' motivation for systematic processing (and to increase their reliance on simple decision rules) during the persuasion phase of these studies, we typically lead them to believe that their task is something other than forming an opinion on the issue discussed in the message.[5] Our major prediction in these experiments has

---

[4]The following undergraduates aided us considerably in our priming studies by helping with subject-recruitment, serving as experimenters, and transferring raw data to the computer: Breck Collins, Mark Lee, David Livert, Kelly Madison, Martha Miller, and Erin O'Connor.

[5]One of our major problems in conducting these experiments has been how to undermine subjects' tendencies to pay rapt attention to the persuasive messages that they receive. Although we believe that heuristic processing of persuasive messages is a very common occurrence in natural settings (see Cialdini, Chapter 7 for a similar argument), systematic processing of messages in laboratory settings seems to be the norm given the implicit demands that are often placed on the subjects to pay careful attention to stimulus information. To the extent that our various strategies for undermining subjects' motivation for systematic processing during the persuasion phases of our priming experiments were not wholly successful, relatively weak priming effects would be expected. Indeed, as detailed in the text, these laboratory studies tended to yield statistically weak, albeit consistently predictable, priming effects. Moreover, measures of systematic processing (e.g., argument recall, message- and issue-relevant cognitions generated on thought-listing tasks) included in some of the experiments suggested that our attempts to keep systematic processing to a minimum were not entirely successful.

been that primed (vs. nonprimed) subjects will, in the subsequent persuasion setting, be more responsive to our manipulated extrinsic persuasion cue. Further, in all but the first of these studies, subjects' levels of Need for Cognition were assessed (typically during a pretest) in order to test the hypothesis that our priming manipulations would be more likely to influence the behavior of low- (vs. high-) NFC subjects. As noted earlier, people who score lower (vs. higher) on the NFC dimension may be especially prone to utilize simple decision rules in persuasion settings.

Our first study in this series (Hicks & Chaiken, 1984) examined the effects of manipulating subjects' perceptions that expert communicators could be trusted. In the priming phase of the study, subjects (who thought their task was to judge how problem-solving groups got along in group settings) read a summary of a "panel-discussion" in which various medical researchers presented their views on the value of annual physical examinations. In a "high association" version of this transcript, the various highly expert medical researchers manifested a great deal of consensus on the value of yearly physicals. In contrast, in the "low association" version, these expert researchers revealed a fair amount of disagreement about the value of exams and the frequency with which the public should have them. In the second phase of the study, subjects listened to a brief audiotaped message in which a speaker argued that people should sleep much less than 8 hours per night (subjects were led to believe that this was one of many speeches available for the study and that their task was to judge the speaker's mood). For half the subjects, the speaker's credentials conveyed high expertise on the sleep topic while for the other half, the speaker's credentials conveyed low expertise (a subsequent check on the expertise manipulation revealed that it was successful and, moreover, that the priming manipulation did not differentially influence subjects' ratings of the communicator's expertise).

Analyses of the opinion change data from this first experiment yielded only partial support for our priming hypothesis. Specifically, a marginal 3-way interaction involving the two manipulated factors and subject sex ($p < .07$) indicated that our prediction was upheld only among female subjects. Male subjects evidenced equivalent amounts of opinion change regardless of level of association or level of expertise (or their interaction). In contrast, in line with our original prediction, female subjects manifested greater opinion change in response to the expert (vs. inexpert) communicator's message in the high association condition of the experiment ($p < .07$) but negligibly less opinion change in response to the expert's message in the low association condition (ns). Although sex differences were not anticipated in this study, two possible explanations occurred to us. First, the failure to find any effects for male subjects may have been due to the relatively small proportion of males in the sample (male cell ns ran as low as 4 whereas female cell ns ran no lower than 9). Second, because of their greater expertise in judging nonverbal cues (Hall, 1984), perhaps females were more involved in the "mood detection" task (our pretext for exposing subjects to the persuasive message) and, thus, more likely than males to process the message heuristically.

In our second priming study (see Chaiken et al., 1985, and Wilson et al., 1985, for more extensive descriptions) we investigated the effects of manipulating subjects' perceptions of the reliability of the "length implies strength" rule on their subsequent tendencies to agree with a (purportedly) longer versus shorter persuasive message. In the first phase of this experiment, subjects were told that we were interested in "how good certain folk rules of thumb" really were. Subjects were asked to judge the goodness of the "more is better" rule by examining six sets of statements on six different topics that had (supposedly) been prepared by undergraduates in an earlier study. Each set of statements appeared on a separate sheet of paper that contained a position statement at the top (e.g., probation should be used more frequently as an alternative to imprisonment) and then numbered, handwritten arguments supporting that position. High-Association subjects received 6 sets of statements designed to increase their faith in the length-strength rule (i.e., each statement set contained either many high quality arguments or very few low quality arguments where argument quality had been determined by pilot testing). In contrast, subjects in the Low-Association condition read statements designed to convey a zero-order relationship between length and strength. For each statement set received, subjects jotted down the total number of arguments listed by the (hypothetical) undergraduate-writer, the quality of each argument, and the overall quality of the statement. Afterwards, subjects were asked (as their "final experimental task") to judge the overall reliability of the "more is better" folk heuristic. Subsequent analysis of this measure indicated that the association manipulation exerted a strong impact on subjects' reliability judgments.[6]

After completing this (priming) phase of the study, subjects were "debriefed" by the experimenter who then left the room after turning the "shared experimental time-slot" over to a different experimenter. This second experimenter introduced his study as an investigation of "people's abilities to judge the physical characteristics of a speaker just based on hearing his or her voice." Next, the experimenter played a short audiotaped message (purportedly selected at random from a pool of available "speeches") that advocated mandatory comprehensive exams for graduating seniors. Two versions of the tape were prepared in order to vary the apparent number of arguments contained in the message: In one version, the speaker claimed that he had "9" reasons for his

---

[6]It should be noted that this somewhat heavy-handed approach to manipulating the perceived reliability of the length-strength rule was adopted because earlier pilot efforts to affect these perceptions by passively exposing subjects to sets of arguments that systematically varied the relationship between argument number and argument quality had shown that subjects generally failed to detect the covariation between these two variables (see Chapman & Chapman, 1967; Nisbett & Ross, 1980). In addition, in this experiment as well as the others, subjects' responses to a detailed postexperimental questionnaire revealed little, if any, suspicion regarding the relationship between the various "mini studies" that they participated in or any awareness of our priming hypotheses.

position while in the other version, he claimed to have "3" reasons (a third control condition in which the speaker made no mention of the number of reasons in his message was also included in the study but is not discussed here because of its minimal relevance). In actuality, the message contained six distinct persuasive arguments. After listening to the message, subjects indicated their opinions on the exam topic, their physical descriptions of the speaker (to lend credibility to the cover story), and other responses.

Analyses of the opinion data from this experiment proved compatible with our priming hypotheses. On an overall basis, subjects agreed more with the message when it purportedly contained nine (vs. three) persuasive arguments ($p < .06$). However, as predicted, this main effect was qualified by the Association $\times$ Number of Arguments interaction ($p < .07$): The tendency for subjects to agree more with the message that supposedly contained nine (vs. three) arguments obtained *only* for high- (vs. low-) association subjects whose perceptions of the reliability of the length-strength rule had been heightened (vs. lowered) in the first phase of the study. In addition, when subjects' levels of Need for Cognition were taken into account (NFC was assessed in a classroom pretest and subjects were divided at the median into high- and low-NFC groups), a marginally significant 3-way interaction between the two manipulated variables and NFC ($p < .09$) indicated that the two-way interaction pattern just described was primarily due to low-NFC subjects: The Association $\times$ Arguments interaction was significant for low NFC ($p < .02$), but not high NFC, subjects. Thus, as we had anticipated, our priming manipulation exerted a greater impact on the opinions expressed by subjects who, on a chronic basis, were more predisposed to utilize a simple decision rule in forming their opinion judgments.

Subjects in our third priming study, which dealt with the liking/agreement heuristic, participated in what they believed were three different "mini" experiments. The first ("consumer-behavior") study was a brief survey included only to lend added credence to our cover story that our experimenter had been hired by the psychology department to run a "bunch of short experiments for various faculty members." The second ("memory") study represented our vehicle for manipulating the accessibility and perceived reliability of the liking/agreement rule, and the third ("impression formation") study was our vehicle for presenting subjects with a persuasive message from a likable or unlikable communicator. (In order to add further credibility to our 3-experiment cover story, subjects were "debriefed" after each "mini" experiment.) Three conditions of the "memory" study were run: In the high accessibility/high reliability condition, subjects memorized 8 sentences, all of which conveyed the general idea that people agree with people they like (e.g., "When people want good advice, they go to their friends"). In contrast, in the high accessibility/low reliability condition, subjects memorized 8 sentences that conveyed the idea that people don't always agree with people they like and, in fact, that disliked persons sometimes have good ideas (e.g., "Best friends do not necessarily make the best advisors"). Finally, in a low accessibility (control) condition, subjects memorized

8 sentences about sports and games (e.g., "In baseball, good hitting will usually beat good fielding").

After "debriefing" subjects as to the purpose of the "memory" study (supposedly an investigation of the facilitative role of organizing themes such as sports and interpersonal relations in memory), the experimenter introduced the "final experiment." Subjects were asked to read a "transcript of an interview with a student" and then "give their impressions of the student's personality." In the transcript, the student-communicator's likability was manipulated by having him either praise or insult fellow students at his (and the subjects') university (cf. Chaiken, 1980). Further, the transcript contained information indicating that the communicator felt strongly that people should sleep less than 8 hours per night. After reading the transcript, subjects indicated their opinions on the sleep issue, their perceptions of the communicator, and other responses.

Analyses of the opinion data from this third experiment proved statistically weak on an overall basis but, nevertheless, consistent with our priming hypotheses. The 3-way (Association × Likability × NFC status—again assessed in a classroom pretest) interaction implied by our hypothesis attained marginal significance in the overall analysis of variance ($p < .10$). To explore the data in a more refined manner, an a priori contrast was performed (separately for low and high NFC subjects) that tested the hypothesis that the persuasive advantage of the likable (vs. unlikable) communicator would be greatest for subjects in the high accessibility/high reliability condition, moderate in the (control) low accessibility condition, and slightly reversed in the high accessibility/low reliability condition (where some of the prime sentences had indicated a negation to the liking/agreement rule). This contrast attained marginal significance for low-NFC subjects ($p < .09$): Low-NFC subjects in the high accessibility/high reliability condition exhibited a somewhat greater tendency to agree with the likable (vs. unlikable) communicator (Ms = 8.38 vs. 6.81) in comparison to low NFC subjects in the low accessibility control condition (Ms = 8.00 vs. 7.46) and, unlike both of these subject groups, low-NFC subjects in the high accessibility/low reliability condition agreed somewhat *less* with the likable (vs. unlikable) communicator (Ms = 5.14 vs. 6.43). The same a priori contrast proved nonsignificant for high-NFC subjects (F < 1). Thus, in this study, only subjects who were presumed to be predisposed to utilize simple decision rules in persuasion settings were affected by our priming manipulation.

Despite our growing awareness that priming effects on social judgment were somewhat elusive, we designed a final experiment (briefly summarized earlier as "number of arguments" study). In the study we focused again on the length-strength rule but, unlike our second study which made this rule accessible for all subjects (while manipulating its perceived reliability), this fourth experiment used a more subtle priming task designed to vary only the accessibility of this decision rule. Using a three-experiment scenario virtually identical to the one used in the liking/agreement study, subjects first completed a (filler) consumer-behavior survey and then participated in a second "memory" study (priming phase) and a third "mental imagery" study (persuasion phase). In the "memory" study, subjects in the priming condition memorized 8 phrases relevant to the length-strength rule (e.g., "The more the merrier," "The bigger the boat, the farther it floats") whereas subjects in the control condition memorized 8 irrelevant phrases (e.g., "Absence makes the heart grow fonder"). After completing a recognition memory test and being "debriefed" (the memory study was described as an investigation of why proverbs are well-remembered), subjects participated in the "mental imagery" study which was described as an investigation of "how people form images of another person's physical appearance based only on hearing that person's voice." After this introduction, the experimenter played a short (and, purportedly, randomly selected) audiotaped message of a "Vanderbilt junior's talk for a speech class." In the message the speaker endorsed mandatory comprehensive exams for graduating seniors and, in the beginning of his speech stated that he had either "ten" or "two" reasons for his opinion (in fact, the message contained six arguments). As in the previous studies, after exposure to the message, subjects indicated their own opinions on the exam topic and responded to other ancillary measures.

Analyses of the opinion change data from this final experiment yielded findings that were statistically weak on an overall basis but, nevertheless, consistent with our previous studies and our priming hypotheses. Although neither the two-way (Priming × Arguments) nor three-way (Priming × Arguments × NFC) interactions attained conventional levels of significance in the overall ANOVA, primed (vs. control) subjects did tend to express greater agreement with the message that purportedly contained 10 (vs. 2) arguments and, more importantly, this effect proved to be most evident among subjects who scored lower (vs. higher) on the Need for Cognition scale. Indeed, the *only* group of subjects in this study who agreed significantly more with the message when it was said to contain 10 (vs. 2) arguments were low-NFC subjects for whom the length/strength rule had been made more accessible (Ms = .63 vs. − .24, $p <$ .03). Low-NFC subjects in the control condition expressed only negligibly greater agreement with the 10 (vs. 2) arguments message (Ms = .20 vs. .05, F < 1) and high NFC subjects evidenced a nonsignificant tendency to agree less with the message when it purportedly contained 10 (vs. 2) arguments, regardless of whether they had or had not been primed (p's < .23).

On a study-by-study basis, none of the four priming experiments just described yielded statistically robust effects favoring our priming hypotheses. Nevertheless, taken together, the four studies reveal a relatively strong and consistent pattern. As originally hypothesized, priming manipulations that vary either the accessibility or both the accessibility and perceived reliability of simple persuasion heuristics such as the liking/agreement or expertise or length/strength rules do influence the likelihood that recipients will use these decision rules to evaluate message validity in subsequent persuasion settings. When such rules are made more accessible to subjects or when the reliability attributed to these rules is increased, the extrinsic cues that are associated with these rules exert a stronger impact on people's reactions to subsequent persuasive messages. In addition, these priming effects have been shown by our studies to be more pronounced among subjects who, on a chronic basis, are most prone to utilize simple decision rules in evaluating the validity of persuasive messages. Thus, we consider these studies to have been fairly successful in terms of their goal of providing somewhat more direct evidence that people in persuasion settings actually do utilize the kinds of simple decision rules specified by the heuristic model of persuasion.

SUMMARY, IMPLICATIONS, AND CONCLUSIONS

As noted at the outset of this chapter, a major implication that the heuristic model has for understanding persuasion phenomena is the idea that opinion change in response to persuasive communications is often the outcome of only minimal information processing on the part of recipients. Research stimulated by the heuristic model and related formulations (e.g., Cialdini's "compliance principles," see Chapter 7; Petty and Cacioppo's notion of the "peripheral route" to persuasion, see Chapter 2) thus has the potential to help redress prior theoretical perspectives' possible overestimation of the extent to which people carefully scrutinize argumentation and engage in in-depth issue-relevant thinking when exposed to persuasive messages.

Among its more specific implications for persuasion phenomena, the heuristic model suggests an alternative mediational explanation for the impact of a number of distal variables that have traditionally been thought to influence persuasion via other psychological mechanisms. For example, Kelman (1961) distinguished between internalization-based and identification-based attitude change and postulated that source expertise and source attractiveness, respectively, may be antecedent conditions for these two qualitatively different modes of social influence. Following Kelman's distinction, researchers have traditionally assumed that the persuasive impact of communicator expertise can be attributed to the impact of this variable on recipients' processing of argumentation, whereas the heightened persuasive impact of attractive communicators is independent of people's processing of message content and instead reflects their desires to establish a self-defining relationship with the communicator. Although empirical evidence (e.g., Kelman, 1961; Mills & Harvey, 1972; Norman, 1976) suggests that there are some circumstances under which these two source variables *do* influence opinion change via these qualitatively different mechanisms, the heuristic model suggests that very often the persuasive impact of *both* source variables can be attributed to recipients' use of simple decision rules so that (1) credibility effects, like attractiveness effects, may often be independent of recipients' processing of persuasive argumentation, and (2) heightened agreement with liked communicators, like heightened agreement with credible communicators, may often be motivated by people's desires to hold correct opinions (see earlier discussion of assumptions underlying the heuristic model).

Research testing the heuristic model has also provided some insights regarding the *conditions* under which a variety of extrinsic persuasion cues (i.e., communicator variables such as expertise, likability, and physical attractiveness; message cues such as number of arguments and message length; contextual cues such as audience reactions to a message) are most likely to be important determinants of persuasion. As reviewed in this chapter, existing research indicates that these extrinsic cues tend to exert their maximal impact on persuasion when motivation for systematic processing is low (e.g., when issue- or response-involvement is low) or when, regardless of motivation, ability to process systematically is impaired (e.g., when distractions are present or when an incomprehensible message is received) or when these extrinsic cues are made highly salient or inherently vivid (e.g., when a vivid, rather than pallid, photograph of the communicator is presented). Moreover, in accord with the cognitive mediation assumed by the heuristic model, existing research has provided both indirect and direct evidence that the persuasive impact of these extrinsic cues is often mediated by simple decision rules such as the liking/agreement heuristic, the expertise credo, the length-strength rule, and the consensus heuristic.

As implied in the very beginning of this chapter (see discussion of types of decision rules and how they arise out of past experiences and observations) and as more explicitly noted by Eagly and Chaiken (1984), *prior learning* is an important determinant of whether message recipients utilize the simple rules and schemas specified by the heuristic model. To employ such rules in judging message validity, people must have learned and stored in memory the (procedural, Smith, 1984) knowledge structures that are relevant to available extrinsic persuasion cues. For example, in order for a cue such as communicator likability to be processed heuristically, recipients via their past experiences with liked and disliked persons (or, via direct instruction from socialization agents) must have learned and stored in memory the liking/agreement heuristic ("people generally agree with people they like"). Moreover, as suggested by the priming studies that were reviewed in this chapter, the persuasive impact of such cues should be a function of the *strength* of their associated decision rules or schemas: Recipients whose past experiences and observations with likable and unlikable persons, for example, have yielded few exceptions to the liking/agreement rule (i.e., the schema has "low" probabilism, Stotland & Canon, 1972) should perceive a relatively strong associative connection between the concepts of liking and interpersonal agreement and should thus be more likely to agree with likable communicators than recipients whose past experiences have yielded many exceptions to the liking-agreement rule (i.e., the liking-agreement schema has "high" probabilism).

The extent to which people engage in heuristic processing depends not only on whether they have learned and stored in memory relevant knowledge structures, but also on whether these knowledge structures are *activated* upon presentation of the extrinsic persuasion cues that are associated with them. Although more research is needed on this issue, the Chaiken and Eagly (1983) and Pallak (1983) experiments (reviewed in the section on salience and vividness) suggest that increasing attention to extrinsic persuasion cues (e.g., communicator likability or attractiveness) enhances the likelihood that recipients retrieve from memory and utilize relevant knowledge structures (e.g., the liking-agreement rule) in forming their opinion judgments. Another (and, to date, unresearched) factor that should influence whether relevant decision rules are activated in a particular setting is the recipient's motivational goals in that setting. If an individual is relatively uninterested in assessing the validity of a particular persuasive communication (and, instead has other goals that are unrelated to such an assessment; see Eagly and Chaiken, 1984, for a discussion of other motivational bases of persuasion), it is less likely that knowledge structures of potential relevance for judging message validity would be activated. Finally, an obvious factor that influences recipients' tendencies to utilize the simple decision rules specified by the heuristic model is whether the persuasion setting contains cues that *can* be processed heuristically. When no such cues are available for processing in persuasion settings, recipients, even when not highly motivated, may engage in at least some message- and issue-relevant thinking (see Eagly and Chaiken, 1984 for a discussion of the "sufficiency" principle in determining mode of processing in persuasion settings).

As noted earlier in this chapter, heuristic processing of persuasion cues represents a relatively effortless mode of information processing. Consequently, because people may prefer less effortful processing modes for reasons of cognitive economy (Chaiken, 1978, 1980; Taylor & Fiske, 1978), heuristic processing may predominate in many persuasion settings unless recipients are especially motivated to engage in the message- and issue-relevant thinking featured in more traditional information processing models (e.g., Fishbein & Ajzen, 1975; Greenwald, 1968; McGuire, 1972). Nevertheless, like the judgment heuristics identified by Tversky and Kahneman (1974, 1981; Kahneman & Tversky, 1973), the simple decision rules specified by the heuristic model, although often valid indicators of message validity, may sometimes lead to less than optimal decisions. Thus, in the long run, an overreliance on simple decision rules may inflate Type I and Type II errors: Using the heuristic mode, people may sometimes accept (or reject) message conclusions they might otherwise have [correctly] rejected (or accepted) had they invested the time and effort to attend to, comprehend, and elaborate on persuasive argumentation.

A further liability of heuristic processing concerns its implications for attitudinal persistence and attitude-behavior relations. On an initial basis, persuasive message-induced opinions may not differ in magnitude as a function of whether recipients have based these opinions primarily on their reactions to extrinsic persuasion cues or primarily on the basis of their understanding of message content and their own message- and issue-relevant cognitions (Chaiken,

1980; Chaiken & Eagly, 1983). Nevertheless, because heuristic processing will generally fail to provide the recipient with supportive cognitions for his/her newly adopted opinion, opinions formed via this mode of processing should be relatively temporary and unpredictive of subsequent attitudinally relevant behavior (but see Chaiken & Stangor, in press). In contrast, opinions adopted or changed after carefully scrutinizing persuasive argumentation should be supported by message- and issue-relevant cognitions and, thus, more enduring and more predictive of subsequent behavior. In accord with this reasoning, two studies that have explicitly examined opinion change over time (Chaiken, 1980; Chaiken & Eagly, 1983) have found that heuristic (vs. systematic) processing does tend to confer less opinion persistence. In addition, Pallak et al. (1983) found that attitudes formed on the basis of heuristic (vs. systematic) processing were less highly correlated with (contemporaneously measured) behavioral intentions. Although this finding is consistent with the idea that attitudes formed on the basis of heuristic processing should be less predictive of subsequent behavior than attitudes formed on the basis of systematic processing, this attitude-behavior hypothesis awaits empirical confirmation.

In considering the relationship between some of the findings reviewed in this chapter and the broader literature on heuristics and biases in decision making (e.g., Kahneman, Slovic, & Tversky, 1982; Sherman & Corty, 1984), an interesting discrepancy arises. Unlike the simple persuasion heuristics discussed here whose persuasive impact seems to decline as recipients become more motivated and/or able to process persuasive messages systematically, the judgment heuristics identified by Tversky and Kahneman (e.g., 1974)—for example, the availability and representativeness heuristics—seem to impact on subjects' judgments in decision-making settings regardless of task motivation and, for the more complicated problems, regardless of task ability (e.g., Kahneman & Tversky, 1972; Lichtenstein & Slovic, 1971, 1973; Tversky & Kahneman, 1973, 1974). This apparent contradiction between the findings in the two literatures may be due to two factors. First, there are probably differences in the ability levels required to arrive at judgments not bound by heuristics in the two literatures (i.e., persuasive communications versus statistically based decision problems). More specifically, the problems typically used to explore the biasing effects of heuristics in decision making studies may fall beyond the ability levels of most individuals; thus motivational factors would be largely irrelevant in influencing the likelihood that people would not fall prey to such cognitive heuristics. Supporting this view, some decision-making research indicates that carefully structured problems that highlight relevant statistical information can sometimes enable subjects to overcome their dependence on cognitive heuristics (e.g., Ajzen, 1977; Fischhoff, Slovic, & Lichtenstein, 1979). A second factor that may account for the fact that motivation and ability seem to affect the use of heuristics in the persuasion literature but not in the decision-making literature may be that there are differences in the *strength* with which the rules highlighted in the two literatures are generally held by individuals. In contrast to the judgment heuristics studied in decision-making situations, the decision rules featured in the heuristic model are closer to simple folk sayings, grounded more in casual observation and tied less to any formal tenets of logic and statistics. Thus, it may be easier for individuals to identify exceptions to the simple heuristics studied in persuasion research. If so, only a modicum of ability would be needed to overcome an inappropriate reliance on these more informal folk heuristics (see also Yates & Chaiken, 1983).

In conclusion, it should be pointed out that the heuristic model, like most other contemporary cognitive perspectives in persuasion, does not constitute a general theory of persuasion. First, although the range of extrinsic cues whose persuasive impact may sometimes be mediated by simple decision rules may eventually prove broader than those identified by existing research, this set will obviously not exhaust the variety of distal variables that have long interested persuasion researchers. In addition, although some of these other distal variables such as involvement, communication modality, and others that affect motivation, ability, or cue salience have been shown to influence the likelihood that heuristic (vs. systematic) processing of persuasion cues will predominate in a given persuasion setting, assumptions about *why* such variables influence processing mode are not inherent in the heuristic model. Rather, like many of the assumptions made by researchers testing other persuasion frameworks (e.g., the cognitive response model; Petty et al., 1981; Eagly & Chaiken, 1984), such assumptions require importing concepts from other theoretical perspectives in both social psychology (e.g., Taylor and Fiske's [1978] "cognitive miser" view of information processing) and cognitive psychology (e.g., Shiffrin and Schneider's [1977] automatic versus controlled processing framework). Despite these limitations, the research discussed in this chapter suggests that the heuristic model does hold some promise for enriching our understanding of certain persuasion phenomena. A more definitive judgment regarding the model's worth depends on further empirical evaluation and its "heuristic" value for subsequent persuasion research.

ACKNOWLEDGMENTS

Preparation of this chapter and the author's research was supported in part by NSF Grant No. BNS-8309159. The author is grateful to the following postdoctoral fellows and graduate students who collaborated on much of the research reported in this chapter and provided comments on an earlier draft of the manuscript: Danny Axsom, Andrew Hicks, Christopher Jepson, Ratti Ratneshwar, Dawn Wilson, and Suzanne Yates. In addition, the critical comments of Robert Cialdini, Beth Meyerowitz, Wendy Wood, and Mark Zanna on an earlier draft are greatly appreciated.

REFERENCES

Abelson, R. P. (1976). Script processing in attitude formation and decision-making. In J. S. Carroll & J. W. Payne (Eds.), *Cognition and social behavior.* Hillsdale, NJ: Lawrence Erlbaum Associates.

Axsom, D., Yates, S. M., & Chaiken, S. (1985). *Extending the heuristic model of persuasion: The effect of audience response, involvement, and need for cognition on opinion change.* Unpublished manuscript, Vanderbilt University, Nashville, TN.

Ajzen, I. (1977). Intuitive theories of events and the effects of baserate information on prediction. *Journal of Personality and Social Psychology, 35,* 303–314.

Bargh, J. A. (1984). Automatic and conscious processing of social information. In R. S. Wyer, Jr. & T. K. Srull (Eds.), *Handbook of social cognition* (Vol. 3, pp 1–43). Hillsdale, NJ: Lawrence Erlbaum Associates.

Bransford, J. D., & Johnson, M. K. (1972). Contextual prerequisites for understanding: Some investigations of comprehension and recall. *Journal of Verbal Larning and Verbal Behavior, 11,* 717–726.

Brehm, J. W. (1966). *A theory of psychological reactance.* New York: Academic Press.

Cacioppo, J. T., & Petty, R. E. (1982). The need for cognition. *Journal of Personality and Social Psychology, 42,* 116–131.

Cacioppo, J. T., Petty, R. E., & Morris, K. J. (1983). Effects of need for cognition on message evaluation, recall, and persuasion. *Journal of Personality and Social Psychology, 45,* 805–818.

Chaiken, S. (1978). *The use of source versus message cues in persuasion: An information processing analysis.* Unpublished doctoral dissertation, University of Massachusetts-Amherst.

Chaiken, S. (1980). Heuristic versus systematic information processing and the use of source versus message cues in persuasion. *Journal of Personality and Social Psychology, 39,* 752–766.

Chaiken, S. (1982/October). *The heuristic/systematic processing distinction in persuasion.* Paper presented at the Symposium on Automatic Processing, Society for Experimental Social Psychology, Nashville, IN.

Chaiken, S. (1983/May). *Heuristic processing of persuasion cues.* Invited paper presented at Midwestern Psychological Association Meetings, Chicago.

Chaiken, S. (1986). Physical appearance and social influence. In C. P. Herman, M. P. Zanna, & E. T. Higgins (Eds.), *Physical appearance, stigma and social behavior: The Ontario symposium* (Vol. 3). Hillsdale, NJ: Lawrence Erlbaum Associates.

Chaiken, S., Axsom, D., Hicks, A. P., Yates, S. M., & Wilson, D. K. (1985). *Priming simple decision rules in persuasion settings.* Unpublished manuscript, Vanderbilt University, Nashville, TN.

Chaiken, S., & Eagly, A. H. (1976). Communication modality as a determinant of message persuasiveness and message comprehensibility. *Journal of Personality and Social Psychology, 34,* 605–614.

Chaiken, S., & Eagly, A. H. (1983). Communication modality as a determinant of persuasion: The role of communicator salience. *Journal of Personality and Social Psychology, 45,* 241–256.

Chaiken, S., & Fowler, D. (1979) *The effect of perceived audience opinion on persuasion.* Unpublished manuscript, University of Toronto.

Chaiken, S. & Stangor, C. (in press). Attitudes and attitude change. *Annual Review of Psychology, 38.*

Cialdini, R. B. (1985). *Influence: Science and practice.* Glenview, IL: Scott, Foresman.

Chapman, L. J., & Chapman, J. P. (1967). Genesis of popular but erroneous observations. *Journal of Abnormal Psychology, 72,* 193–204.

Cohen, A. R. (1957). Need for cognition and order of communication as determinants of opinion change. In C. I. Hovland (Ed.), *The order of presentation in persuasion*. New Haven, CT.: Yale University Press.

Cohen, F., & Lazarus, R. S. (1973). Active coping processes, coping dispositions, and recovery from surgery. *Psychosomatic Medicine, 35,* 375–389.

Cohen, A. R., Stotland, E., & Wolfe, D. M. (1955). An experimental investigation of need for cognition. *Journal of Abnormal and Social Psychology, 51,* 291–294.

Craik, F. I. M., & Lockhart, R. S. (1972). Levels of processing: A framework for memory research. *Journal of Verbal Learning and Verbal Behavior, 11,* 671–684.

Eagly, A. H., & Chaiken, S. (1984). Cognitive theories of persuasion. In L. Berkowitz (Ed.), *Advances in experimental social psychology* (Vol. 17). New York: Academic Press.

Eagly, A. H., Chaiken, S., & Wood, W. (1981). An attribution analysis of persuasion. In J. H. Harvey, W. J. Ickes, & R. F. Kidd (Eds.), *New directions in attribution research* (Vol. 3). Hillsdale, NJ: Lawrence Erlbaum Associates.

Easterbrook, J. A. (1959). The effect of emotion on the utilization and the organization of behavior. *Psychological Review, 66,* 183–201.

Fishbein, M., & Ajzen, I. (1975).*Belief, attitude, intention, and behavior: An introduction to theory and research.* Reading, MA: Addison-Wesley.

Fishhoff, B., Slovic, P., & Lichtenstein, S. (1979). Subjective sensitivity analysis. *Organizational Behavior and Human Performance, 23,* 339–359.

Frieze, I. H., Parsons, J. E., Johnson, P. B., Ruble, D. N., & Zellman, G. L. (1978). *Women and sex roles: A social psychological perspective.* New York: W. W. Norton.

Greenwald, A. G. (1968). Cognitive learning, cognitive response to persuasion, and attitude change. In A. G. Greenwald, T. C. Brock, & T. M. Ostrom (Eds.), *Psychological foundations of attitudes.* New York: Academic Press.

Hall, J. A. (1984). *Nonverbal sex differences: Communication accuracy and expressive style.* Baltimore, MD: The Johns Hopkins University Press.

Heider, F. (1958). *The psychology of interpersonal relations.* New York: Wiley.

Hicks, A. P., & Chaiken, S. (1984).*Use of the expertise/agreement heuristic in assessing the validity of a persuasive message.* Unpublished manuscript, Vanderbilt University, Nashville, TN.

Hocking, J., Margreiter, D., & Hylton, C. (1977). Intra-audience effects: A field test. *Human Communication Research, 3,* 243–249.

Hylton, C. (1971). Intra-audience effects: Observable audience response. *Journal of Communication, 21,* 253–265.

Janis, I. L., & Mann, L. (1977).*Decision making: A psychological analysis of conflict, choice, and commitment.* New York: Free Press.

Jepson, C., & Chaiken, S. (1986, August). *The effect of anxiety on systematic processing of persuasive communications.* Paper presented at the Annual Meeting of the American Psychological Association, Washington, D.C.

Johnson, H. H., & Scileppi, J. A. (1969). Effects of ego-involvement conditions on attitude change to high and low credibility communicators. *Journal of Personality and Social Psychology, 13,* 31–36.

Kahneman, D., Slovic, P., & Tversky, A. (Eds.). (1982). *Judgment under uncertainty: Heuristics and biases.* New York: Cambridge University Press.

Kahneman, D., & Tversky, A. (1972). Subjective probability; A judgment of representativeness. *Cognitive Psychology, 3,* 430–454.

Kahneman, D., & Tversky, A. (1973). On the psychology of prediction. *Psychological Review, 80,* 237–251.

Kelman, H. C. (1961). Processes of opinion change. *Public Opinion Quarterly, 25,* 57–78.

Kiesler, S. A., & Mathog, R. (1968). The distraction hypothesis and attitude change: The effects of inference and credibility. *Psychological Reports, 23,* 1123–1133.

Klagsbrun, S. C. (1971). Communications in the treatment of cancer. *American Journal of Nursing, 71,* 944–948.

Landy, D. (1972). The effects of an overheard audience's reaction and attractiveness on opinion change. *Journal of Experimental Social Psychology, 8,* 276–288.

Langer, E. J. (1978). Rethinking the role of thought in social interaction. In J. H. Harvey, W. J. Ickes, & R. F. Kidd (Eds.), *New directions in attribution research* (Vol. 2). Hillsdale, NJ: Lawrence Erlbaum Associates.

Langer, E. J., Blank, A., & Chanowitz, B. (1978). The mindlessness of ostensibly thoughtful action: The role of "placebic" information in interpersonal interaction. *Journal of Personality and Social Psychology, 36,* 635–642.

Lichtenstein, S. C., & Slovic, P. (1971). Reversals of preferences between bids and choices in gambling decisions. *Journal of Experimental Psychology, 89,* 46–55.

Lichtenstein, S. C., & Slovic, P. (1973). Response-induced reversals of preference in gambling: An extended replication in Las Vegas. *Journal of Experimental Psychology, 101,* 16–20.

McArthur, L. Z. (1981). What grabs you? The role of attention in impression formation and causal attribution. In E. T. Higgins, C. P. Herman, & M. P. Zanna (Eds.), *Social cognition: The Ontario Symposium* (Vol. 1), Hillsdale, NJ: Lawrence Erlbaum Associates.

McCroskey, J. C. (1970). The effects of evidence as an inhibitor of counter persuasion. *Speech Monographs, 37,* 188–194.

McGuire, W. J. (1969). The nature of attitudes and attitude change. In G. Lindzey & E. Aronson (Eds.), *The handbook of social psychology* (Vol. 3, 2nd ed.). Reading, MA: Addison-Wesley.

McGuire, W. J. (1972). Attitude change: The information processing paradigm. In C. G. McClintock (Ed.), *Experimental Social Psychology.* New York: Holt, Rinehart, & Winston.

McIntosh, J. (1974). Processes of communication, information seeking, and control associated with cancer: A selective review of the literature. *Social Science and Medicine, 8,* 167–187.

Miller, N., Maruyama, G., Beaber, R. J., & Valone, K. (1976). Speed of speech and persuasion. *Journal of Personality and Social Psychology, 34,* 615–624.

Mills, J., & Harvey, J. (1972). Opinion change as a function of when information about the communicator is received and whether he is attractive or expert. *Journal of Personality and Social Psychology, 21,* 52–55.

Nemeth, C. (1986). The differential contributions of majority and minority influence. *Psychological Review, 93,* 1–10.

Nemeth, C., & Wachtler, J. (1983). Creative problem solving as a result of majority vs. minority influence. *European Journal of Social Psychology 13,* 45–55.

Newell, A., & Simon, H. A. (1972). *Human problem solving.* Englewood Cliffs, NJ: Prentice-Hall.

Nisbett, R., & Ross, L. (1980). *Human inference: Strategies and shortcomings of social judgment.* Englewood Cliffs, NJ: Prentice-Hall.

Norman, R. (1976). When what is said is important: A comparison of expert and attractive sources. *Journal of Experimental Social Psychology, 12,* 294–300.

Osterhouse, R. A., & Brock, T. C. (1970). Distraction increases yielding to propoganda by inhibiting counterarguing. *Journal of Personality and Social Psychology, 15,* 344–358.

Pallak, S. R. (1983). Salience of a communicator's physical attractiveness and persuasion: A heuristic versus systematic processing interpretation. *Social Cognition, 2,* 156–168.

Pallak, S. R., Murroni, E., & Koch, J. (1983). Communicator attractiveness and expertise, emotional versus rational appeals, and persuasion: A heuristic versus systematic processing interpretation. *Social Cognition, 2,* 120–139.

Payne, J. W. (1976). Task complexity and contingent processing in decision making: An information search and protocol analysis. *Organizational Behavior and Human Performance, 16,* 366–387.

Petty, R. E., & Cacioppo, J. T. (1981). *Attitudes and persuasion: Classic and contemporary approaches.* Dubuque, IA: W. C. Brown.

Petty, R. E., & Cacioppo, J. T. (1984). The effects of involvement on responses to argument quantity and quality: Central and peripheral routes to persuasion. *Journal of Personality and Social Psychology, 46,* 69–81.

Petty, R. E., Cacioppo, J. T., & Goldman, R. (1981). Personal involvement as a determinant of argument-based persuasion. *Journal of Personality and Social Psychology, 41,* 847–855.

Petty, R. E., Cacioppo, J. T., & Schumann, D. (1983). Central and peripheral routes to advertising effectiveness: The moderating role of involvement. *Journal of Consumer Research, 10,* 135–146.

Petty, R. E., Ostrom, T. M., & Brock, T. C. (1981). Historical foundations of the cognitive response approach to attitudes and persuasion. In R. E. Petty, T. M. Ostrom, & T. C. Brock (Eds.), *Cognitive responses in persuasion.* Hillsdale, NJ: Lawrence Erlbaum Associates.

Ratneshwar, S., & Chaiken, S. (1986). *When is the expert source more persuasive? A heuristic processing analysis.* Paper presented at American Marketing Association Summer Educators' Conference, Chicago, IL.

Rhine, R. J., & Severance, L. J. (1970). Ego-involvement, discrepancy, source credibility, and attitude change. *Journal of Personality and Social Psychology, 16,* 175–190.

Schlenker, B. R. (1980). *Impression management: The self-concept, social identity and interpersonal relations.* Monterey, CA: Brooks/Cole.

Schneider, W., & Shiffrin, R. M. (1977). Controlled and automatic human information processing: I. Detection, search, and attention. *Psychological Review, 84,* 1–86.

Sherman, S. J., & Corty, E. (1984). Cognitive heuristics. In R. S. Wyer, Jr., & T. K. Srull (Eds.), *Handbook of social condition* (Vol. 1). Hillsdale, NJ: Lawrence Erlbaum Associates.

Shiffrin, R. M., & Schneider, W. (1977). Controlled and automatic human information processing: II. Perceptual learning, automatic attending, and a general theory. *Psychological Review, 84,* 127–190.

Silverthorne, C. P., & Mazmanian, L. (1975). The effects of heckling and media of presentation on the impact of a persuasive communication. *Journal of Social Psychology, 96,* 229–236.

Smith, E. R. (1984). Model of social inference processes. *Psychological Review, 91,* 392–413.

Spielberger, C. D. (1972). *Anxiety: Current trends in theory and research* (Vol. 1). New York: Academic Press.

Staats, A. W., & Staats, C. K. (1958). Attitudes established by classical conditioning. *Journal of Abnormal and Social Psychology, 57,* 37–40.

Stiff, J. B. (1986). Cognitive processing of persuasive message cues: A meta-analytic review of the effects of supporting information on attitudes. *Communication Monographs, 53,* 75–89.

Stotland, E., & Canon, L. K. (1972). *Social psychology: A cognitive approach.* Philadelphia: Saunders.

Taylor, S. E., & Fiske, S. T. (1978). Salience, attention, and attribution: Top of the head phenomena. In L. Berkowitz (Ed.), *Advances in experimental social psychology* (Vol. 11). New York: Academic Press.

Taylor, S. E., & Thompson, S. C. (1982). Stalking the elusive "vividness" effect. *Psychological Review, 89,* 155–181.

Tversky, A., & Kahneman, D. (1973). Availability: A heuristic for judging frequency and probability. *Cognitive Psychology, 5,* 207–232.

Tversky, A., & Kahneman, D. (1974). Judgment under uncertainty: Heuristics and biases. *Science, 185,* 1124–1131.

Tversky, A., & Kahneman, D. (1981). The framing of decisions and the psychology of choice. *Science, 211,* 453–458.

Wilson, D. W., & Donnerstein, E. (1977). Guilty or not guilty? A look at the "simulated" jury paradigm. *Journal of Applied Social Psychology, 7,* 175–190.

Wilson, D. K., Axsom, D., Lee, M., & Chaiken, S. (1985/August). *Evidence for heuristic pro-*

cessing of persuasive messages. Paper presented at the meeting of the American Psychological Association, Los Angeles.

Wood, W., & Eagly, A. H. (1981). Stages in the analysis of persuasive messages: The role of causal attributions and message comprehension. *Journal of Personality and Social Psychology, 40*, 246–259.

Wood, W., Kallgren, C. A., & Priesler, R. M. (1985). Access to attitude-relevant information in memory as a determinant of persuasion: The role of message attributes. *Journal of Experimental Social Psychology, 21*, 73–85.

Wortman, C. B., & Dunkel-Schetter, C. (1979). Interpersonal relationships and cancer: A theoretical analysis. *Journal of Social Issues, 35*, 120–155.

Wyer, R. S. (1974). *Cognitive organization and change: An information-processing approach.* Hillsdale, NJ: Lawrence Erlbaum Associates.

Yalch, R. F., & Elmore-Yalch, R. (1984). The effect of numbers on the route to persuasion. *Journal of Consumer Research, 11*, 522–527.

Yates, S. M., & Chaiken, S. (1983/October). *Cognitive heuristics in persuasion and decision making.* Paper presented at the Association for Consumer Research Conference, Chicago.

Yerkes, R. M., & Dodson, J. D. (1908). The relation of strength of stimulus to rapidity of habit formation. *Journal of Comparative Neurology of Psychology, 18*, 459–482.

2

Stalking Rudimentary Processes of Social Influence: A Psychophysiological Approach

John T. Cacioppo
University of Iowa

Richard E. Petty
University of Missouri-Columbia

Social psychologists have been studying attitudes and persuasion ever since the discipline began (Allport, 1935), and over the past 70 years thousands of experiments have been conducted and scores of theories have promulgated. Unfortunately, for almost any variable studied—even a seemingly simple one like source credibility—the accumulated literature invariably shows that the variable can increase persuasion, decrease persuasion, or have no effect (see McGuire, 1985). Also, an embarrassment of riches holds when it comes to the number of theories that exists concerning the underlying *processes* of attitude formation and change (Insko, 1967; Petty & Cacioppo, 1981).

As a result of the many conflicting findings and different theories that had arisen by the late 1960s, interest in attitude change research began to decline. Reviewers of the attitudes literature in the 1970s were generally quite critical of either the attitude construct (e.g., Wicker, 1971) or the "reigning confusion" (Sherif, 1976) characterizing the accumulated literature (see also Fishbein & Ajzen, 1972). One of the major problems was that, as suggested above, persuasion variables seemed to have so many different effects and there were numerous theories that explained subsets of these effects. In a review of the attitudes literature (Petty & Cacioppo, 1981), we have suggested that the many existing theories of persuasion could be thought of as emphasizing one of two relatively distinct *routes* to persuasion. In some instances, persuasion occurred when change was based on a careful and thoughtful consideration of the issue-relevant arguments supporting an issue position. We called this the "central route" to persuasion. In other circumstances, however, persuasion occurred when attitude change was based on some simple cue in the persuasion context that induced change without necessitating scrutiny of the true merits of the arguments presented. When simple cues induced agreement with little issue-relevant thinking, we called this the "peripheral route" to persuasion. Attitude changes induced via the central route are postulated to be more enduring, resistant to counterpersuasion, and predictive of behavior (see Fig. 2.1).

The central and peripheral routes to persuasion are two key processes in a general theory of persuasion called the Elaboration Likelihood Model (ELM) (Petty & Cacioppo, 1980, 1981, 1985, in press). More specifically, we view the

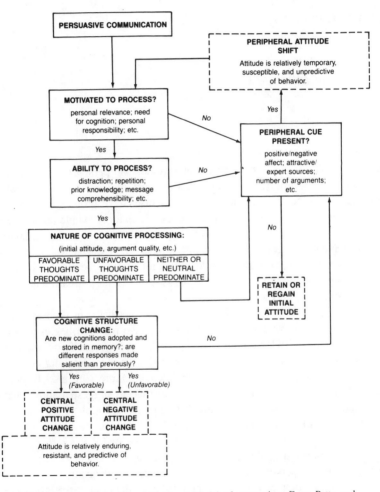

FIG. 2.1. The Elaboration Likelihood Model of persuasion. From Petty and Cacioppo (1985).

two routes to persuasion as anchoring a continuum of elaboration likelihood. By elaboration in a persuasion setting, we mean the extent to which a person carefully scrutinizes the issue-relevant information in a message by relating it to information stored previously in memory. In some persuasion situations, the likelihood of message elaboration and issue-relevant thinking is high. In these situations people are: (a) highly *motivated* to devote the cognitive work necessary to evaluate the message, perhaps because the message has direct personal relevance, personal responsibility is high, or they are the kind of people who typically enjoy thinking (Cacioppo, Petty, & Morris, 1983; Petty & Cacioppo, 1979; Petty, Cacioppo, & Harkins, 1983); and (b) highly *able* to evaluate the message, perhaps because the message is repeated several times, distractions are few, or they have considerable issue-relevant knowledge (Cacioppo & Petty, 1979c, 1980b; Petty, Wells, & Brock, 1976). In other situations, however, motivation and/or ability to process issue-relevant information is quite low. In these situations simple cues may induce agreement without argument scrutiny.

This continuum, which goes from persuasion situations in which the likelihood of message elaboration is very low to persuasion situations in which the likelihood of message elaboration is very high, is important because of the different consequences of elaboration (see Fig. 2.1), and because it appears that variables operate differently depending upon where along the continuum the variable is tested. For example, Fig. 2.2 depicts the effects that we have obtained for the variable "source credibility" when it is examined along the elaboration likelihood continuum. When people are generally unmotivated or unable to think about an issue, such as when personal relevance is very low, credibility serves as a simple acceptance or rejection cue affecting agreement with little or no argument processing (top panel). When elaboration likelihood is very high, such as when a message has certain relevance, credibility is unimportant as a simple cue. Instead, attitude change is determined mostly by the cogency of the issue-relevant arguments presented (bottom panel). When the elaboration likelihood is more moderate, such as when people are uncertain as to the personal relevance of a message, source credibility affects the extent of information processing (middle panel). That is, when elaboration likelihood is intermediate, source factors can help a person decide if a message merits or needs scrutiny (see recent review by Petty & Cacioppo, in press). The ELM, then, provides a framework for organizing the conflicting pattern of data characterizing variables such as source credibility.

Importantly, it is also possible to place theories of attitude change along the elaboration continuum. At the low end of the continuum are theories that require very little, if any, issue-relevant elaboration to produce influence. Theories of attitude change such as classical conditioning and operant conditioning (e.g., Lott & Lott, 1968; Staats & Staats, 1958) which emphasize associating an object, issue, or person, with some simple affective cue typify this influence. For

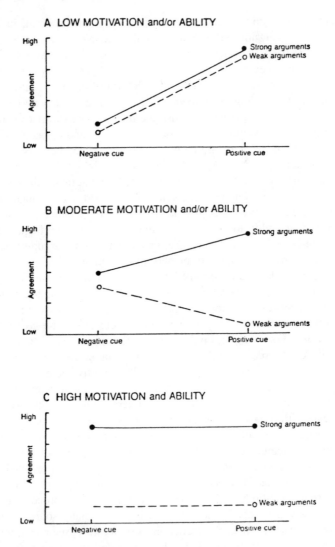

A LOW MOTIVATION and/or ABILITY

B MODERATE MOTIVATION and/or ABILITY

C HIGH MOTIVATION and ABILITY

FIG. 2.2.   The Elaboration Likelihood Model of Source Factors. From Petty and Cacioppo (1984).

instance, Gorn (1982) provided evidence that subjects developed a preference for an inexpensive product that was associated with liked rather than disliked background music.

Moving a little further up the continuum are theories in which again some simple cue provides the basis of the attitude change, but the cue may be used more deliberately. For example, it is possible for people to adopt the opinion of a similar other without carefully scrutinizing issue-relevant arguments if the person "identifies" with the source (Kelman, 1961), employs the "balance" principle (Heider, 1946), or makes use of a learned similarity "heuristic" (Chaiken, see Chapter 1). As with the process of affective association, these theories can be characterized as peripheral in that the resulting attitude is based primarily on a simple cue rather than scrutiny of the information central to the merits of the advocacy.

Finally, at the high end of the continuum are theories that emphasize issue-relevant thinking, and the integration of issue-relevant beliefs into a coherent position. The cognitive response approach (Greenwald, 1968; Petty, Ostrom, & Brock, 1981), the theory of reasoned action (Ajzen & Fishbein, 1980), and inoculation theory (McGuire, 1964), for example, emphasize processes characterized by the high end of the elaboration continuum. The ELM, then, provides a general framework for organizing the existing theories of persuasion and indicating when the different underlying processes of persuasion are likely to be invoked. Consistent with this model, the logic of experimental designs and postcommunication attitude assessments have suggested that simple affective associations (e.g., Gorn, 1982) and cognitive inferences (e.g., Chaiken, 1980; Taylor, 1975) are more powerful determinants of persuasion when the personal relevance or consequences of a message are low rather than high, whereas the quality of issue-relevant arguments are more important when personal relevance is high rather than low (e.g., Petty & Cacioppo, 1979; Petty, Cacioppo, & Goldman, 1981; for an extended discussion of the ELM, see Petty & Cacioppo, in press).

ASSESSING ATTITUDINAL PROCESSES

Although many different processes ranging from simple affective associations to extended elaboration of issue-relevant arguments have been posited to operate in persuasion contexts, our knowledge of these processes has traditionally relied on people's postcommunication attitude ratings and self-reports. In a prototypical persuasion experiment, for instance, self-reports are used to assess the efficacy of the experimental manipulations, the effects of these manipulations on verbal or overt behavior, and the operation of the assumed intervening sequence of events (cf. Gerard, 1964; McGuire, 1985). This is a great deal to ask of any single measurement strategy.[1]

A second feature of research on social influence is that multiple self-report measures and truly clever experimental designs have been employed to allow inferences to be drawn regarding the processes underlying these data (e.g.,

---

[1]These points, of course, apply not only to the study of attitudes but to the study of social processes generally (see recent review by Cacioppo & Petty, 1985).

Moreland & Zajonc, 1977; Zanna & Cooper, 1974). However, these inferences are themselves not infrequently followed by equally clever counterarguments (e.g., Birnbaum & Mellers, 1979; Greenwald, 1975) and occasionally by theoretical impasses (e.g., See Kiesler & Munson, 1975) or disinterest (Wicker, 1969). The inclusion of chronometric or behavioral measures to augment self-report indices has strengthened the grounds for theorizing about social influence, but common to these methods is that the measured responses (e.g., reaction time, recall, compliance behavior) trail and reflect upon an entire sequence of events since they are obtained following the posited social process. Inferences regarding the timing, nature, and intensity of the underlying attitudinal processes based solely on the study of these measures can be called into question, since these measures may: (1) occur at various points after the events constituting the posited social process(es); (2) be unrepresentative of all but the material in short term memory and material in long-term memory which is easily accessible at the time of measurement; and/or (3) be colored by the cognitive strategy by which responses are requested (e.g., coherent verbal reports or ratings, reaction time—see discussions by Cacioppo & Petty, 1985; Ericcson & Simon, 1980; Nisbett & Wilson, 1977).[2]

Affect—which is widely viewed as a fundamental antecedent if not the major component or essence of attitudes—is a case in point. Philosophers and theorists have spoken of affect and emotion as being characterized by actions and feelings beyond a person's control, as when an individual is described as being *insanely* jealous, in a *blind* rage, or *dumbfounded* with astonishment.

> One speaks of "being in the grip" of a strong emotion and that seems a particularly apt figure of speech . . . One experiences a loss of control, a sense of functioning on a more primitive and less reflective level (Winton, Putnam, & Krauss, 1984, p. 195).

Individuals may voice explanations for affective states, but these explanations can be influenced by rationalization, ego-defensive processes, and naive inference-making. Although the notion of an "affective reaction" assumes a precipitating circumstance or stimulus, the perception or registration of the eliciting stimulus need not be reportable or conscious (Kunst-Wilson & Zajonc, 1980), nor does the affect need have verbal or elaborate cognitive antecedents (Greenwald, 1982; cf. Lazarus, 1984; Zajonc, 1980, 1984). Tomkins (1981), for instance, has distinguished "primary affects" from more cognitively refined "affect complexes." Primary affects and emotions are generally viewed as limited

---

[2]A possible but infrequently found exception to this rule is experimental designs which accommodate the collection of either self-report measures or reaction-time measures to a secondary task at various points in time during the process of interest. This procedure has been criticized recently, however, for altering the nature of the normally occurring process.

in number; manifesting in some form at all evolutionary levels; having some relevance to basic adaptive processes; relying little upon learning, memory, and cognition; emerging early in infants; and possessing pancultural display characteristics. Affect complexes, on the other hand, account for the myriad of human emotions such as pride, shame, and embarrassment which involve cognitive if not conscious self-reflection.

Previous attempts to study the basic affective foundations of attitudes and the affective processes in attitude development and change have been characterized either by the use of *verbal* measures—a strategy which may misrepresent the role of affect by misgauging the nature, intensity, and timing of attitude-relevant affect; or *visceral* measures—a strategy which may misrepresent the role of affect by misgauging the valence of the reaction and the relative importance and timing of affect when the visceral measures are contrasted with verbal measures of cognition (e.g., see Breckler, 1984). The purpose of the present chapter is to survey our research on somatic markers of feeling and knowing, and to outline the inferential context in which these markers are viewed as valid. We then return to a brief discussion of the applicability of psychophysiological assessments in studies of the ELM.

BRIDGES BETWEEN SOCIAL INFLUENCE CONSTRUCTS AND SOMATIC DATA

Theoretical analyses of somatic activity during problem solving, imagery, and emotion have shared assumptions regarding the specificity and adaptive utility of somatic responses (Cacioppo & Petty, 1981a; Ekman & Friesen, 1975; Izard, 1971; McGuigan, 1978; Sokolov, 1972; Tomkins, 1962; Zajonc & Markus, 1982). Darwin (1872/1965), for instance, posited three general principles to account for the origin of distinctive facial expressions. In the first, termed the principle of serviceable associated habits, Darwin (1872/1965) posited that the distinctive facial expressions have an adaptive origin:

> Certain complex actions are of direct or indirect service under certain states of mind, in order to relieve or gratify certain sensations, desires, etc; and whenever the same state of mind is induced, however feebly, there is a tendency through the force of habit and association for the same movements to be performed, though they may not then be of the least use. (p. 28)

Thus, for instance, disgust is characterized by facial actions which serve to expel noxious materials from the mouth and the feeling of disgust—even in the absence of a noxious gustatory stimulus, is associated with the same pattern of facial actions.

In the principle of antithesis, Darwin posited that diametrical psychological states produce a strong involuntary tendency to perform movements of a directly opposite nature. Thus, the drawing of the corners of the mouth upwards and back in the form of a smile may have evolved to characterize positive feelings because these muscular actions contrast with the serviceable facial actions associated with negative emotions. Finally, Darwin posited the principle of direct action of the nervous system, which states that excitatory stimuli lead to discharges in the nervous system, causing effects such as trembling and tachycardia.

Tomkins (1962, 1963), whose theoretical work has contributed to our understanding of the antecedents and properties of emotion, has long resisted the belief in social psychology that physiological measures are incapable of distinguishing between positive and negative affective states and therefore are useful only in assessing general arousal:

> The low visibility of the affects and the difficulties to be encountered in attempting to identify the primary affects have already been described. Yet our task is not as difficult as it might otherwise have been, for the primary affects, before the transformations due to learning, seem to be innately related in a one-to-one fashion with an organ system which is extraordinarily visible. (Tomkins, 1962, p. 204)

Tomkins was, of course, referring to the facial efference system—an organ system we know from common experience is capable of more complex and variable actions than captured by the notion of general arousal. Indeed, consistent with much of Darwin's and Tomkin's thinking, Ekman and Friesen (Ekman, 1972; Ekman & Friesen, 1969) have found that people from various cultures distinguished the facial expressions for the emotions of happiness, sadness, surprise, anger, disgust, and fear; that the facial expressions accompanying pleasant and unpleasant emotional states could be distinguished, as to some extent could the intensity of these positive and negative reactions; and that a large portion of variance in people's observable facial displays could be attributed to socially learned prescriptions, termed display rules, for regulating expressions of emotion (see recent review by Fridlund, Ekman, & Oster, in press).

Recently we proposed that several additional principles were supported by studies of somatic patterning using electromyography (EMG): (1) there are foci of somatic activity in which changes mark particular psychological processes (e.g., linguistic vs. nonlinguistic information processing, positive vs negative affect); (2) inhibitory as well as excitatory changes in somatic activity can mark a psychological process; (3) changes in somatic activity are patterned temporally as well as spatially; (4) changes in somatic activity become less evident as the distance of measurement from a focal point increases; and (5) foci can be identified a priori by (i) analyzing the overt reactions that initially characterized the particular psychological process of interest but which appeared to drop out with practice, and (ii) observing the somatic sites that are involved during the "acting out" of the particular psychological process of interest. Together, these principles were termed the model of skeletomuscular patterning (Cacioppo & Petty, 1981a).

The first, second, and fifth principles are illustrated in research by Schwartz and his colleagues (Schwartz, Fair, Salt, Mandel, & Klerman, 1976a, 1976b). They found that, even in the absence of noticeable facial expressions, the level of EMG activity increased over the zygomatic major (whose action pulls the ends of the mouth upwards and back) and depressor anguli oris (whose action pulls the corner of the mouth downward) muscle regions and tended to decrease over the corrugator supercilii (whose action pulls the brows together and down) region following instructions to imagine a *happy* situation, whereas EMG activity increased primarily over the corrugator supercilii region following instructions to imagine a *sad* situation (see Fig. 2.3 for an atlas of selected facial muscles). In addition, Schwartz and his colleagues found that this patterning of facial muscle activity reliably distinguished positive and negative emotional imagery in nor-

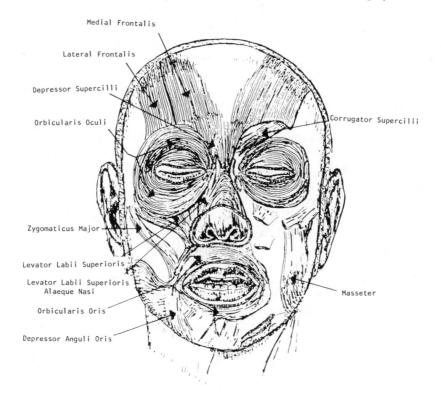

FIG. 2.3.   The facial musculature. The superficial muscles are depicted on the left and the deep muscles are revealed on the right. From Cacioppo, Losch, Tassinary, and Petty (in press).

mals and clinically depressed patients; and that the depressed patients showed an attenuated pattern of facial EMG activity during happy imagery and an exaggerated pattern of facial EMG actitivy to sad imagery.

Patterns of Efference Accompanying Simple Physical and Attitudinal Tasks

The interesting results in the clinical domain obtained by Schwartz and their colleagues led us to conduct a study to test more explicitly the model of skeletomuscular patterning (Cacioppo, Petty, & Marshall-Goodell, 1984). Ekman and Friesen (1975, 1978) have emphasized that specific, overt emotional expressions are evident in the lower (e.g., mouth), middle (e.g., eyes, nose), and upper (e.g., brows) regions of the face. Hence, EMG activity was monitored over muscles which control the movement of facial landmarks in the lower (e.g., zygomatic major), middle (e.g., levator labii superioris, which raises the lip and dilates the nostril in the primitive expression of disgust), and upper (e.g., corrugator supercilii) regions of the face to determine whether invisibly small muscle actions were evoked and varied as a function of the affective tone of attitudinal processing. Subjects were led to believe they were participating in a study on involuntary neural responses during "action and imagery." Subjects on any given trial either: (a) lifted a "light" (16 gram) or "heavy" (35 gram) weight (action); (b) imagined lifting a "light" (16 gram) or "heavy" (35 gram) weight (imagery); (c) silently read a neutral communication as if they agreed or disagreed with its thesis (action); or (d) imagined reading an editorial with which they agreed or disagreed (imagery). Based on the model of skeletomuscular patterning, we expected that the affective processes invoked by the positive and negative attitudinal tasks would lead to distinguishable patterns of EMG activity over the corrugator supercilii, zygomatic major, and possibly the levator labii superioris (which is involved in expressions of disgust) regions, whereas the simple physical tasks would lead to distinguishable EMG activity over the superficial forearm flexors (whose actions control flexion about the wrist).

Imagining performing rather than actually performing the tasks was, of course, associated with lower mean levels of EMG activity. More importantly, and consistent with the model of skeletomuscular patterning, multivariate analyses revealed that the site and overall form of the task-evoked EMG responses were generally similar across the levels of this factor. Analyses further revealed that EMG activity over the corrugator supercilii, zygomatic major, and levator labii superioris muscle regions in the face varied as a function of whether subjects thought about the topic in an agreeable or disagreeable manner, EMG activity over the superficial forearm flexors was higher during the physical than attitudinal tasks, and EMG activity over the forearm (but not over the facial muscles) varied across the simple physical tasks.

To probe whether subjects had suspicions regarding facial efference being the focus of the study, subjects were interviewed at the end of each session and were asked specifically what they believed to be the experimental hypothesis. Since subjects might reason that they should not disclose how much they "knew," we emphasized that it was important that they respond honestly and accurately. The postexperimental interviews failed to reveal any evidence for the operation of experimental demands. All subjects appeared convinced of the cover story (e.g., that the sensors were used to detect involuntary physiological reactions), and no subject articulated anything resembling the experimental hypothesis. Instead, the postexperimental interviews of subjects indicated that they tended to organize the experimental trials in terms of whether they imagined or performed some task (e.g., lifting a weight or silently reading a text) rather than in terms of whether the task was physical or attitudinal.

Finally, following the study two judges viewed videotapes of subjects during trials on which the subjects performed positive and negative attitudinal tasks. The judges' task was to guess the valence of the task performed each trial based on their observations of the subjects' facial displays during the trial. Judges performed at chance level. It seems to us to strain plausibility to argue that subjects chose to support the experimental hypothesis by making socially imperceptible facial responses to the attitudinal tasks. Indeed, Hefferline, Keenan, and Harford (1959) found they could operantly condition an invisibly small thumb-twitch even though subjects remained ignorant of their behavior and its effect; and they reported that subjects could not produce this covert behavior in the absence of EMG feedback when deliberately trying to do so. Together these data suggest both that experimental demands are not necessary for the selective facial EMG activation observed during affective processing and imagery and, more interestingly, that attitudinal processing can have discriminable effects on facial EMG patterning.

Patterns of Efference During Silent Language Processing

One final set of observations of interest from this study is that EMG activity over the region of the muscles of speech (i.e., perioral EMG activity) was higher during the attitudinal than physical tasks even though the tasks required no overt verbalization and perioral EMG activity did not vary as a function of the affective tone of people's attitudinal processing. These data are consistent with the notion that problem solving and silent language processing influence perioral EMG activity (see reviews by Garrity, 1977; McGuigan, 1970). However, these data, like the previous research, are not particularly informative regarding the specificity of the relationship between perioral EMG activity and information processing since the type of stimulus presented and/or the type of subject employed has been varied along with the extent of linguistic processing presumably manipulated. For instance, although poor readers show greater perioral EMG activity while reading than good readers (e.g., Edfeldt, 1960; Faaborg-Anderson & Edfeldt, 1958), it is unclear whether this effect is caused by differences in the cognitive work involved in comprehending or in encoding the material, the manner in which the material is being processed, attentional differences in the readers, differences in self-monitoring between the readers, and/or differences in apprehension. Since the literature on social influence is characterized both by theories based on the premise that people commonly engage in cognitive deliberations regarding the content of persuasive appeals (Fishbein & Ajzen, 1972; Greenwald, 1968; see, also, Sherman, Chapter 3, Wolfe, Chapter 9) and by theories based on the contrasting premise that social influence can be achieved much of the time mindlessly (Langer, Blank, & Chanowitz, 1978), automatically (Chaiken, 1983; Cialdini, 1984) and possibly without awareness (Kunst-Wilson & Zajonc, 1980), we have proposed the ELM as a general framework to organize the processes postulated by these various theories, and we have attempted in our psychophysiological research to extend the model of skeletomuscular patterning to determine precisely how facial efference generally and perioral EMG activity in particular serves as a marker for cognitive and affective processing.

In most of our initial investigations of perioral EMG activity, we employed the instructional manipulations used commonly to study encoding operations. The paradigm involves presenting target words (e.g., trait adjectives) to subjects while randomly varying the question pertaining to each trait word (Craik & Tulving, 1975). In this paradigm, somatic responses attributable to features of subjects and stimuli are assigned to the error term, and what generally remains is variance due to the instructional factor (the "cue-question"), which serves as the operationalization of the predominant type of informational analysis operating during the presentation of the target word (cf. Baddeley, 1978; Cermak & Craik, 1979). Results of research in this paradigm have generally shown that the more semantic (i.e., meaning-oriented) the cued analysis, the more likely subjects are to remember the stimulus word (see review by Craik, 1979), although these effects are especially evident when semantic processes are cued both at the time of encoding and at the time of retrieval (Morris, Bransford, & Franks, 1977; Tulving, 1978). These data have been interpreted as indicating the existence of qualitatively different processes by which incoming information is related to one or more existing domains of knowledge (Cermak & Craik, 1979; Craik, 1979).

Semantic and Nonsemantic Processing.   The purpose of our initial study was to determine whether perioral (orbicularis oris) EMG activity was higher when subjects performed tasks which required that they think about the meaning and self-descriptiveness of a word rather than about the orthographic appearance of the word (Cacioppo & Petty, 1979b). EMG activity over a nonoral muscle region (superficial forearm flexors of the nonpreferred arm) was also recorded to determine whether task-evoked changes in EMG activity were specific or general (e.g., part of an arousal response). The Subjects were shown cue-questions asking them whether or not the succeeding trait-adjective was printed in upper-case letters, or whether or not the word was self-descriptive. Half of the trait adjectives were printed in upper-case letters and half were printed in lower-case; and half of the trait adjectives were highly self-descriptive, while half were not at all self-descriptive. Subjects responded yes or no by pressing one of two micro-switches. Results revealed several interesting results. First, the self-referent task led to better recall than the orthographic task, replicating previous studies in social psychology (e.g., Rogers, Kuiper, & Kirker, 1977). Second, the self-referent task led to greater increases in perioral EMG activity than the orthographic task. Third, EMG activity over a nonoral muscle group did not vary as a function of the orienting task, making it unlikely that the association between self-referent processing and perioral EMG activity was due to subjects being generally more aroused or tense when performing the self-referent than orthographic task.

This orienting-task paradigm has also been used in social psychology to investigate possible differences in the existence of different processes by which incoming information is related to one or more existing domains of social knowledge. Studies have shown that trait words are better recalled when rated for their descriptiveness of oneself or one's best friend than of people about whom one has little or no direct knowledge (e.g., Bower & Gilligan, 1979; Keenan & Baillet, 1980). These data have been interpreted as indicating structural differences in domains of social knowledge in memory. As Ferguson, Rule, and Carlson (1983) note, the domains of knowledge (e.g., one's self) accessed by tasks (e.g., self-referent task) that produce relatively better recall of the incoming stimuli are thought to be characterized by greater elaboration (i.e., more associates), integration (i.e., stronger interassociative bonding), and/or differentiation (i.e., more chunking of associates into distinct, but related subsets). Ferguson et al. further reported data from this paradigm using a between-subjects design showing that self-referent and evaluative orienting tasks yielded similar response latencies and levels of recall. They argued that: (a) evaluation constitutes a central dimension along which incoming information such as trait words is categorized and stored, and (b) both evaluative and self-referent tasks facilitated the use of the evaluative dimension and minimized the use of other irrelevant dimensions in rating traits. This led them to conclude that, given the centrality of the evaluative dimension in the organization of memory, "no unique memorial status need be attributed to the self or familiar others" (Ferguson et al., 1983, p. 260).

Evaluative and Self-Referent Processing. In an experiment bearing upon both the effects of information processing on perioral EMG activity and on Ferguson et al.'s analysis, subjects were exposed to 60 trait adjectives spanning a range of likeability (Cacioppo & Petty, 1981b). Each trait adjective was preceded by one of five cue-questions, which defined the processing task. The cue questions were: (a) Does the following word rhyme with ---'' (Rhyme), (b) ''Is the following word spoken louder than this question?'' (Volume discrimination), (c) ''Is the following word similar in meaning to ---?'' (Association), (d) ''Is the following word good (bad)?'' (Evaluation), and (e) ''Is the following word self-descriptive?'' (Self-reference). Finally, as in all of our facial EMG research, subjects in this study knew bioelectrical activity was being recorded, but they did not realize that activity over which they had voluntary control was being monitored.

Results revealed that mean recognition confidence ratings were ordered as follows: self-reference, evaluation, association, rhyme, and volume discrimination. Importantly, all means except the last two differed significantly from one another. These data, which were obtained using a within-subjects rather than a between-subjects design, have been conceptually replicated by McCaul and Maki (1984) and argue against Ferguson et al.'s contention that evaluative and self-referent processing are fundamentally the same. In addition we found that: (a) the mean amplitude of perioral (orbicularis oris) EMG activity was lowest for the nonsemantic tasks of rhyme and volume discrimination, intermediate for the task of association, and equally high for the tasks of evaluation and self-reference (in a subsequent section of this chapter, we show that these tasks, too, can be differentiated using psychophysiological measures); (b) cardiac activity and the mean amplitude of EMG activity over a nonoral muscle region (i.e., nonpreferred superficial forearm flexors region) did not vary as a function of the type of task performed; and (c) the association between task and perioral EMG activity was temporally specific, with task-discriminating EMG activity observed only while subjects analyzed the aurally presented trait adjectives and formulated their response.

Affect-laden Information Processing in Persuasion Contexts.   Given evidence that perioral EMG activity varies as a function of semantic processing and that EMG activity over selected facial muscle regions (e.g., corrugator supercilii, zygomatic major) can discriminate between positive and negative affective states, we reasoned that facial EMG measures might prove informative regarding elementary processes evoked by the anticipation and presentation of personally involving persuasive communications. Brock (1967) and Greenwald (1968), for instance, posited that recipients of persuasive communications ''cognitively responded'' to message arguments, generating new associations, links, and counterarguments in the process. Miller and Baron (1973), on the other hand, argued that recipients did *not* engage in extensive cognitive activity when confronted by a persuasive communication (see also, Langer et al., 1978; Miller, Maruyama, Beaber, & Valone, 1976). Experimental results based on subjects' reported attitudes and the thoughts and ideas they listed in retrospective verbal protocols ("thought listings") provided support for the former position (Petty & Cacioppo, 1977; cf. Cialdini & Petty, 1981), but others have expressed concerns that these data reflect post hoc rationalizations produced in response to postexperimental questioning rather than processes evoked by the persuasive communication.

An initial study supported the applicability of psychophysiological principles and procedures to the particular social psychological paradigm of interest: Localized increases in perioral EMG activity were observed when individuals followed the experimental instruction to "collect their thoughts" about an impending counterattitudinal editorial (Cacioppo & Petty, 1979a, Experiment 1). More importantly, a follow-up study was conducted in which subjects anticipated and heard a proattitudinal, counterattitudinal, or neutral communication (Cacioppo & Petty, 1979a, Experiment 2). Students were recruited for what they believed was an experiment on "biosensory processes," and as in the previous research, they were unaware that somatic responses were being monitored. After subjects adapted to the laboratory, we obtained recordings of basal EMG activity, forewarned subjects that in 60 sec they would be hearing an editorial with which they agreed, an editorial with which they disagreed, or an unspecified message, obtained another 60 sec of physiological recording while subjects sat quietly, and obtained yet another 120 sec of data while subjects listened to a proattitudinal appeal, counterattitudinal appeal, a news story about an archeological expedition. Subjects were not told to collect their thoughts in this study, but rather somatovisceral activity was simply monitored while subjects awaited and listened to the message presentation. This allowed us to assess the extent to which spontaneous thinking accompanied the anticipation of a persuasive communication.

As expected, subjects evaluated more positively and reported having more favorable thoughts and fewer counterarguments to the proattitudinal than to the counterattitudinal advocacy. Although unexpected, we also found that subjects reported enjoying the "neutral" message (which concerned an obscure archeological expedition) as much as they did the proattitudinal editorial. Analyses of perioral EMG indicated that perioral activity increased following the forewarning of an impending and personally involving counterattitudinal advocacy, and it increased for all conditions during the presentation of the message. This selective activation of perioral EMG activity during the postwarning-premessage period provided convergent evidence for the view that people engage in anticipatory cognitive activity to buttress their beliefs when they anticipate hearing a personally involving, counterattitudinal appeal. Moreover, the pattern of subtle facial EMG activity was found to reflect the positive/negative nature of the persuasive appeal before and during the message. Presentation of the proattitudinal and *neutral* messages was accompanied by a pattern of facial EMG activity similar to that found to accompany pleasant emotional imagery, whereas both the anticipation and presentation of the counterattitudinal message was associated with a pattern of EMG activity similar to that found to accompany unpleasant emotional imagery.

Patterns of Facial Efference and Affect

Although this study indicates that facial EMG activity can find applications in studies of social influence, one can question whether electromyographic studies of visually imperceptible emotional expressions are useful only in distinguishing positive from negative states. Brown and Schwartz (1980), for instance, used standardized affective imagery instructions and observed that happy emotional imagery increased the mean amplitude of EMG activity over the zygomatic major region, whereas sad, anger, and fear imagery increased the EMG activity over the corrugator supercilii muscle region. Changes in EMG activity over the masseter and lateral frontalis (whose action raises the outer eyebrows and wrinkles the forehead) muscle regions failed to distinguish these imagery conditions even though these muscles can be involved when forming overt facial expressions of emotions.

The Valence and Intensity of Affective Reactions.   The inability of low-level facial EMG activity to discriminate among the negative affects would not seem to be a major limitation in studies of attitudes, however, if facial EMG activity, at least when recorded in controlled laboratory settings, could be used to gauge the intensity as well as the valence of affective reactions which were sufficiently mild to be unaccompanied by noticeable emotional expressions. Physiological measures have traditionally been viewed in social psychology as useful only in assessing general arousal and therefore incapable of distinguishing between positive and negative affective states. Evidence from several laboratories now indicate, however, that facial EMG responses differentiate positive and negative affective states (e.g., see recent review by Fridlund & Izard, 1983). If these subtle, transient, and distinctive patterns of facial EMG activity vary in magnitude with the intensity of the affective states, then they would potentially constitute an objective, continuous, and sensitive probe of affective processes underlying attitude formation and change. In a study designed to examine this question, subjects were exposed to slides of moderately unpleasant, mildly unpleasant, mildly pleasant, and moderately pleasant scenes (Cacioppo, Petty, Losch, & Kim, 1986). Subjects viewed each slide for 5 seconds and rated how much they liked the scene that was depicted, how familiar the scene appeared, and how aroused it made them feel. Judgments of the videorecordings of subjects' facial actions during the 5-second stimulus presentations indicated that the scenes were sufficiently mild to avoid evoking socially perceptible facial expressions. Nevertheless, analyses revealed that EMG activity over the corrugator supercilii and orbicularis oculi muscle regions differentiated the direction and intensity of people's affective reaction to the scenes: The more subjects liked the scene, the lower the level of EMG activity over the corrugator supercilii region; moreover, EMG activity was higher over the orbicularis oculi region when moderately pleasant than mildly pleasant or unpleasant stimuli were presented. EMG activity over the zygomatic major region also tended to be greater for liked than disliked scenes, with EMG activity being significantly higher when liked than disliked scenes were presented.[3] Importantly, neither EMG activity over the corrugator supercilii region nor EMG activity over the zygomatic major region covaried with reported arousal, nor did EMG activity over the perioral (orbicularis oris) region or a peripheral muscle region (sueprficial forearm flexors) vary as a function of stimulus likeability. These data, therefore, are more consistent with the view of response specificity in the facial actions accompanying cognition and affect than with the view that somatic activity increases generally as affective intensity increases (Cacioppo & Petty, 1981a; Winton et al., 1984).

The Topography of EMG Activity.   A second potential limitation of facial EMG measures involves the manner in which EMG activity has been conceptualized. For instance, when trying to articulate the theoretical connections between neurophysiological principles regarding efferent activity (cf. Henneman, 1980a, 1980b; Rinn, 1984; Willis & Grossman, 1977) and the form and function of somatic (e.g., facial EMG) responses in studies of social processes (e.g., regarding the spontaneous/deliberate nature of an emotional expression), we realized that unambiguous links could not be derived as long as EMG activity was equated with the mean amplitude of the response. Yet most psychophysiological research using the electromyogram, including most of that reviewed above, has employed the measure of the average amplitude recorded in a given period—such as during a task (see reviews by Fridlund & Izard, 1983; McGuigan, 1978; Schwartz, 1975). This is noteworthy because the extraction of mean amplitude, which itself is a relatively recent advance in the analysis of the aperiodic electromyogram (Lippold, 1967; McGuigan, 1979), ignores the form

---

[3]The pattern of EMG activity obtained over the orbicularis oculi muscle region was not expected but based on data from a pilot study is reliable even when a visual focal point was employed. An interesting account for these data can be derived from Ekman and Friesen's (1982) important work on "felt" smiles. Ekman and Friesen suggest that people display a smile—whether happy or not—when they wish to present a happy image, but that people display both a smile and crow's feet at the outer edges of their eyes when they feel happy. Ekman and Friesen hypothesize that the common elements in the facial expression of the person who actually experiences a positive emotion are the action of two muscles: "the zygomatic major pulling the lip corners upwards toward the cheekbone; and the orbicularis oculi which raises the cheek and gathers skin inwards from around the eye socket" (p. 242). Since there was no reason in this setting for subjects to feign positive affective reactions to the experimental stimuli, it is possible that the heightened EMG activity over the orbicularis oculi region may be related to the variations in the subjects' *feelings* of positive regard for the depicted scenes.

of the response as it unfolds over time. Thus, neither the temporal nor frequency domain of EMG activity is represented, and the amplitude domain is represented in a limited fashion. One implication of interest here is that an implicit but unintended assumption in (facial) EMG research has been that cognitive and affective processes are graded but static "events." This is, of course, a gross oversimplification which suffers from many of the same problems as does using photographs rather than videotapes to study overt facial actions (cf. Ekman, 1982b).

We found that a variety of statistical and mathematical procedures had been employed in studies using the electromyogram (e.g., gradients of mean amplitude within epochs, fast Fourier transform, cross correlations, coherency analysis, ratio of evoked amplitude to basal level), but perhaps surprisingly none has proven generally applicable or satisfactory (e.g., Grabiner & Robertson, in press; O'Donnell, Rapp, Berkhout, & Adey, 1973; Person, Gundarov, Kudina, Vojtenko, & Konjuxova, 1967; Lippold, 1967; Malmo, 1975; McGuigan, Dollins, Pierce, Lusebrink, & Corus, 1982; Robertson & Grabiner, in press; Sokolov, 1972). Consequently, an analytical procedure to quantify the time and amplitude dimensions of the EMG response was developed (Cacioppo, Marshall-Goodell, & Dorfman, 1983; Cacioppo & Dorfman, 1985).[4]

Perioral EMG Activity and the Utilization of Cognitive Resources.   The empirical and theoretical power gained by considering the form rather than simply the mean amplitude of EMG activity is illustrated in a recent study on the effects of simple cognitive tasks on perioral EMG activity. Recall that we had found perioral EMG activity, as indexed by mean amplitude, to be greater during semantic than nonsemantic processing, but that perioral EMG activity was equivalent across the semantic (e.g., evaluative and self-referent) tasks even though subjects expressed greater recognition confidence in having seen trait words used in the self-reference than evaluation tasks (Cacioppo & Petty, 1981b). In a follow-up study, subjects performed orthographic, grammatical, evaluative, and self-referent orienting tasks (Cacioppo, Petty, & Morris, 1985). EMG activity and response latency were assessed during each trial, either task difficulty (Replication 1) or reported cognitive effort (Replication 2) was assessed following each trial, and recall was assessed at the conclusion of the study.

Analyses of the cognitive measures revealed that recall was poorest when trait words were judged in terms of their orthographic appearance, moderately poor

---

[4]Although discussion of this analysis is beyond the scope of the present chapter, interested readers may wish to consult Cacioppo et al. (1983) for the theoretical rationale for using moment-based parameters to characterize the time and amplitude dimensions of the (integrated) EMG response, and for evidence that the topographical analysis is capable of differentiating unique waveforms, provides a reliable and valid index of EMG activity obtained under conditions of submaximal isometric muscle contraction, and represents a significant improvement over mean amplitude.

and moderately good when words were judged in terms of their grammatical and evaluative features, respectively, and best when words were judged in terms of their self-descriptiveness—all this despite the finding that subjects took longest to perform the grammatical task and rated this task as the most difficult and most cognitively effortful to perform. Clear evidence was again obtained, therefore, that the orienting tasks invoked distinctive analyses of the trait words. More interestingly here, multivariate analyses of the topography of facial EMG activity in general, and perioral (orbicularis oris) EMG activity in particular, revealed that the form rather than the mean amplitude of the task-evoked EMG responses differentiated these simple cognitive tasks, with significant differences emerging during semantic and nonsemantic processing and between evaluative and self-referent tasks. Subsequent regression analyses revealed that perioral EMG activity covaried more closely with reported cognitive effort than with recall. These results suggest that long-term memory for incoming information is affected both by short-term memory processes and by the accessibility and structure of existing knowledge domains, but that short-term memory processes have the more direct effect on perioral EMG activity. For example, one can invoke extensive short-term processing, and exhibit heightened perioral EMG activity, when there is so little in long-term memory that there are few cues to assist retrieval and when there is so much in long-term memory that there are conflicting retrieval cues. Consider two students in an introductory college chemistry class, one of whom had high school chemistry, the other of whom did not. Although the latter student may have to utilize more cognitive resources (and show greater elevations in perioral EMG activity) to simply comprehend the class lectures as they are presented, the former student nevertheless could well transfer more of the class material to long-term memory because of a more highly developed schema for chemistry.

Spontaneous and Deliberately Modified Expressions of Emotion.   It should be noted that the EMG patterning observed in our research has been subtle and is easily distorted, requiring optimal experimental conditions to obtain. As Ekman (1972) and Friesen (1972) have demonstrated, facial actions are clearly controllable and serve communicative and deceptive as well as emotionally expressive functions. In a recent study, we examined the patterns of facial EMG activity that characterized spontaneous facial expressions to mildly pleasant or unpleasant visual stimuli and those that characterized expressions that were deliberately modified in response to these stimuli (Cacioppo & Bush, 1985). Based on the work by Ekman and his colleagues, it was hypothesized that the timing of the spontaneously produced and deliberately constructed EMG responses would differ, with the latter developing more slowly and over a longer period of time (cf. Ekman, 1982a).

Facial EMG activity was recorded as subjects viewed slides of mildly pleasant or mildly unpleasant faces and scenes. Each slide was presented for 5 seconds, and during the first set of slides subjects were simply instructed to examine each when it was presented and to rate how much they liked it following its presentation. Following this initial series of slides, subjects were told to imagine two individuals were seated in front of them—one of whom was a close friend and another of whom was a stranger. Subjects were instructed that as they examined the photographs projected onto the screen, they should either try not to reveal through their facial displays whether the stimulus was pleasant or unpleasant (deliberately posed unexpressive facial displays) or through subtle facial displays, try to communicate to the friend, but not the stranger, whether the stimulus was pleasant or unpleasant (deliberately posed expressive facial displays). Subjects were given an opportunity to practice prior to the experimental trials, the order of these last two instructions was counterbalanced across replications of the study, and data from the few trials on which emotional facial expressions were noticeable were deleted prior to analysis.

Results revealed that the facial EMG activity associated with spontaneous affect versus the interpersonal communication of affect were distinguished in the predicted manner. EMG activity over the corrugator supercilii was again greater in response to unpleasant than pleasant visual stimuli; deliberately masked facial displays were characterized generally by a maintenance of EMG activity at prestimulus levels across the facial muscles; and deliberately posed expressive facial displays were characterized by affect-discriminating EMG responses which developed more intensely and were maintained over a longer period of time than spontaneous emotional expressions. Since the focus of this study was on socially imperceptible patterns of facial activity, one cannot be completely confident that these results would generalize to cases where subjects are simply told to exaggerate their emotional expression. Nevertheless, this preliminary study has broad implications for the study of attitude formation and change if, as these data suggest, the temporal parameters of facial efference can be used to distinguish between spontaneous and deliberately managed expressions of emotion.

INFERENTIAL CONTEXT AND IMPLICATIONS

Previous research on affect and emotion has identified two or three stable dimensions of experience: valence (pleasantness/unpleasantness), intensity (calm/excited), and control (spontaneous/voluntary) (e.g., Osgood, 1966). Our research thus far indicates that at least the first two of these dimensions of affect have reliable effects on facial EMG activity, and the preceding study suggests the third dimension may also have discriminable somatic effects. Studies of emotion have further revealed that emotions can be highly transient, occur in combinations ("blends"), and at times go undetected using verbal reports, visual observations, or response latencies (e.g., Ekman, 1982b; Haggard & Issacs, 1966; Kunst-Wilson & Zajonc, 1980; Schwartz, 1975; Tomkins, 1962). While the analyses of the dynamic aspects of overt expressive behaviors using videotapes (in contrast to drawings or photographs) to augment verbal reports has revealed a wealth of information regarding communication and emotion (Ekman & Friesen, 1978; Izard, 1971, 1977), there is room for yet other convergent, concomitant measures because not all social processes are accompanied by visually (Ekman, Schwartz, & Friesen—cited in Ekman, 1982b) or socially perceptible (Love, 1972; Rajecki, 1983) expressive behaviors. Love (1972), for instance, videotaped people's facial expressions while they were exposed to a proattitudinal or counterattitudinal appeal and reported detecting no differences in overt expressions. As noted above, we replicated this result while also demonstrating that the mean amplitude of the EMG activity recorded over facial muscle regions (e.g., corrugator, zygomatic) during the communication differentiated between subjects who were exposed to a proattitudinal appeal from those who were exposed to a counterattitudinal appeal (Cacioppo & Petty, 1979a). The social psychological research on overt facial actions illustrates the utility of convergent operations which allow measurement of social processes as they unfold over time (e.g., Ekman & Friesen, 1974, 1975; Ekman, Friesen, & Ancoli, 1980; Izard, 1977; Zuckerman, DePaulo, & Rosenthal, 1981), while the research on facial EMG suggests that psychological events (e.g., positive/negative affect) too subtle or fleeting to evoke an overt expression may nevertheless be tracked (Cacioppo et al., 1986).

Several caveats are in order, however. First, although the effects on which we have focused have been obtained repeatedly in our laboratory and by others (e.g., McGuigan, 1978; McHugo, Lanzetta, Sullivan, Masters, & Englis, 1985; Ohman & Dimberg, 1984), these effects are subtle, transient, and easily masked by noise (e.g., electrostatic interference from power lines, individual variability, muscular tension or muscular fatigue). Second, difficulties in extracting psychologically and behaviorally relevant information from ongoing somatovisceral processes are to be expected given the nonpsychological (e.g., homeostatic, reflexive) functions served by the human organism, the paucity of current knowledge about the neurophysiological mechanisms serving psychological processes, and the methodological limitations inherent in studying human subjects using noninvasive somatovisceral recording procedures (cf. Coles, Donchin, & Porges, 1985). Indeed, although somatovisceral measures have been used with some success to index psychological states such as the use of deception (cf. Fridlund, Ekman, & Oster, in press; Lykken, 1981; Podlesny & Raskin, 1977; Waid & Orne, 1981) and the intensity or direction of reported attitudes (cf. Cacioppo & Sandman, 1981; Tursky & Jamner, 1983; Petty & Cacioppo, 1983), physiological measures of enduring and accessible psychological states have oftentimes proven to be expensive, cumbersome, and less sensitive than traditional methods in social psychology such as verbal reports (e.g., Rogers, 1983; cf. Crider, 1983;

Shapiro & Schwartz, 1970) or simple variations on these assessments such as the bogus pipeline (Jones & Sigall, 1971; see review by Petty & Cacioppo, 1983).

Consider, for instance, the limits to the utility of facial EMG as a physiological measure of attitudes. Electrodermal activity (e.g., Rankin & Campbell, 1955), pupil size (e.g., Hess, 1965), and heart rate (e.g., Katz, Cadoret, Hughes, & Abbey, 1965) have all been used to study attitudes, but these physiological measures have at best proven sensitive to variations in the extent of strong emotion underlying an attitude (cf. Cacioppo & Sandman, 1981; Petty & Cacioppo, 1983; Zanna, Detweiler, & Olson, 1984). Although measures of facial efference may overcome this particular problem (Cacioppo et al., 1986), we do not envision facial EMG to be an effective physiological measure of attitudes in many contexts. At the simplest level, people are capable of suppressing, falsifying, and distorting their facial expressions, making it difficult to determine their true feelings toward a stimulus using measures of facial actions, at least in some contexts (Zuckerman, Larrance, Spiegel, & Klorman, 1981; cf. Cacioppo & Petty, 1985).

Second, attitudes are generally conceived as being global and enduring evaluations of a stimulus (e.g., Petty & Cacioppo, 1981; Zanna & Rempel, 1984). People's positive attitudes toward their children endure despite moments of displeasure and occasional thoughts of abandonment. Facial efference, on the other hand, can be extremely transient and specific, marking perhaps a positive thought and feeling one moment and the realization of an undesirable consequence the next. This is not to say that attitudes and facial EMG will never covary; when people are left to simply think about an unequivocally counterattitudinal vs proattitudinal issue, for instance, the predominant thought and feeling can be expected to vary so dramatically and consistently that facial EMG should differentiate the individuals in these conditions (Cacioppo & Petty, 1979a). But the same general factors mitigating attitude-behavior correspondence when comparing a general measure of attitude with a specific measure of behavior can also be expected to vitiate the correspondence between a person's general and enduring attitude toward a stimulus and the facial efference associated with transient, specific, and possibly issue-irrelevant (e.g., a speaker's facial expression—cf. McHugo et al., 1985) affective reactions.

Third, conditions can be anticipated in which even general expressions of attitudes and of affect diverge. Avid smokers, for instance, may generally hold that the consumption of cigarettes is foolish, harmful, and negative, but nevertheless have consistent and positive affective reactions toward the act of smoking cigarettes (Fishbein, 1980).

Finally, and relatedly, the accessing of one's attitude toward a stimulus can but need not be accompanied by an unequivocal affective reaction. For instance, mild affective reactions habituate with repeated presentations of a stimulus, yet people's evaluation of the stimulus need not become neutral (e.g., Hare, 1973). Similarly, individuals appear able to categorize a familiar stimulus as being good or bad with minimal if any affective involvement (e.g., Cacioppo & Petty, 1980a; Cacioppo et al., 1985; Gordon & Holyoak, 1983). This is not to suggest that affect cannot precede inferences, but simply to suggest that individuals, like well-programmed computers, can access a previously formulated attitude and can perhaps even apply a set of criteria to categorize a stimulus as being *good* or *bad, wise* or *foolish,* or *harmful* or *beneficial* without invoking emotion. To the extent that this analysis is accurate, at least in relative if not absolute terms, then interesting questions arise regarding the differences in the consequences of social judgments (e.g., attitudes, attributions, inferences) grounded primarily in cognition versus those based primarily in affect (cf. Zanna & Rempel, 1984).

Yet a major advantage of somatovisceral measures and manipulations— providing means for studying the *process* by which the social world impinges on individual action and experience, has remained largely unexploited; and it is in this respect that we have applied most of our psychophysiological research to the ELM. For instance, the somatic nervous system is the ultimate mechanism through which humans interact with and modify their environments. Moreover, the muscles of facial expression differ from most other skeletomuscles in that they are linked to connective tissue and fascia rather than to skeletal structures (cf. Rinn, 1984). Thus, neural activation of the facial muscles of expression is somewhat unique in function in that it generally does not operate directly on the physical environment, but rather its effect is often mediated by the construction of facial configurations which communicate information (e.g., ideas, inferences), misinformation (e.g., deception), and emotion (e.g., threat, approval). It is not unreasonable, therefore, to suggest that an understanding of people's actions and experiences, and perhaps particularly those pertaining to communication and social interaction, may be enriched if the operation of central events is analyzed in terms of its output. Specifically, the location, intensity, and timing of EMG activity recorded over facial muscle regions, although the consequence of a number of central and peripheral factors (Fridlund & Izard, 1983; Henneman, 1980b; Rinn, 1984; Willis & Grossman, 1977), can be particularly informative regarding social processes.

To study the processes outlined in the ELM, our psychophysiological research has departed from earlier traditions in a couple of respects. First, verbal, behavioral, and/or chronometric measures of processes presumably involved in attitude development and change ranging from affective arousal to cognitive processing have been supplemented using continuous, noninvasive video and psychophysiological recordings for the purpose of tracking the means by which the social world impinges on individual action and experience. Potentially important in this regard is the development of a mathematical procedure that allows representation of the temporal features of nonnegative bounded waveforms, since the topographical analysis of EMG responses provides a means for studying the changes across time in imperceptible as well as perceptible facial actions (e.g., Cacioppo et al., 1984).

Second, monitoring facial efference to track affect-laden information processing places particular importance on the interpretive context in which the measures are collected—just as is the case when reaction time is used to study cognitive processes (cf. Cacioppo & Petty, 1985). For instance, although more extensive cognitive analyses of a linguistic stimulus tend to result in longer reaction times and greater perioral EMG activity, knowing either of the latter does not indicate the presence of the former. Following work in cognitive psychophysiology (cf. Donchin, 1982), we have used psychophysiological measures as markers rather than as universal correlates of cognitive and affective processes (Cacioppo & Petty, 1985, in press-a). Physiological measures of psychological states and processes have possessed a particular attraction to attitude researchers, apparently because these measures have some of the attributes one would want in a "valid" index. A continuous record of physiological activity can be collected while individuals do nothing more than act naturally as they are exposed to various attitude stimuli (e.g., see Cooper, 1959; Hess, 1965; Rankin, 1955). Moreover, several physiological indices, such as cardiovascular, electrodermal, and electrocortical, are difficult for novices to control—though they are not difficult for novices to affect (cf. White & Tursky, 1982). And although there are individual differences in physiological responding, variations in environmental and social stimuli can also be shown to have clear and powerful effects across individuals (Cacioppo & Petty, 1983; Lacey & Lacey, 1958; Schwartz & Shapiro, 1973; Waid, 1984). Finally, high expectations regarding the validity of psychophysiological measures are raised by anecdotes regarding what can be learned about an individual's feelings and inclinations if only one scrutinizes another's bodily responses sufficiently closely (e.g., Darwin, 1872/1965; Galton, 1884). It is worth emphasizing, therefore, that verbal, nonverbal, and physiological measures have different attributes, distinctive utilities and disutilities, and only partially overlapping ranges of construct validity. All are potentially useful in limited contexts—for instance, as markers (i.e., temporally stable indicators of the presence of a particular psychological process or state)—and none is "purer" than any other (see recent review by Cacioppo & Petty, 1985).

As we noted above, the limits in self-report data correspond to potential strengths in psychophysiological assessments. For a physiological reaction (or syndrome) to serve as a marker for a psychological process, it should be shown that, *within a given experimental context,* the physiological reaction: (a) can be measured reliably and is stable across time; (b) occurs infrequently in the absence of the psychological process of interest; and (c) generally emerges at the onset and returns to basal levels at the offset of the psychological process of interest—although reliable time-lags between the two levels can be accommodated (Iacono, 1983). Thus, when the regions of construct validity between specific verbal and physiological measures diverge, each can potentially provide information about social influence and behavior not easily attainable from the other.

The fact that the ranges of validity for these measures are not identical makes each worthwhile.

The overlapping regions of construct validity for psychophysiological and self-report data are also informative, for they define the contexts and provide the means for assessing the construct validity of simple, inexpensive self-report measures. Given the results from a variety of measurement strategies identify a specific context in which people are willing and able to report accurately what are the processes underlying their attitudes, one could reasonably rely on simple verbal indices to draw inferences within measurement context. The initial research often must be conducted within a context in which verbal and physiological indices lead to the same theoretical inference. Once bridges between social psychological constructs and psychophysiological data have been established, the latter can fruitfully be extended to regions in which the validity of self-report measures is more suspect.

As a case in point, the research reviewed in this chapter suggests that facial EMG activity may be used to assess the extent and affectivity of information processing. Since the central, in contrast to peripheral, route to persuasion involves the expenditure of cognitive resources on processing issue-relevant information, facial EMG holds promise as an objective and continuous probe of the extent to which persuasion processes are central; but this relationship would be expected to hold only when peripheral processes involved only minimal (silent) language processing. Although such persuasion contexts theoretically exist (e.g., see Harkins & Petty, 1981), peripheral processes can also involve the effortful processing of information that has little or no relevance to the actual merits of the recommended position (see Petty & Cacioppo, in press, Ch. 2). Hence, facial EMG should be a useful measure of message elaboration only when the persuasion context is such that the focus of most of the silent language processing is message and issue-relevant information.

Interestingly, it may also be possible to index the extent to which information processing activity is relatively objective rather than biased by assessing the extent of differential hemispheric activation during message processing. For example, in two studies we found that individuals who produced a relatively polarized profile of thoughts (unfavorable–favorable thoughts) in response to a persuasive message also demonstrated relative right hemispheric EEG activation as assessed over the parietal lobes (Cacioppo, Petty, Quintanar, 1982). Although this relationship appears quite reliable, the boundary conditions for this effect (e.g., aural vs. visual presentations) have not yet been established.

Note that the ongoing somatovisceral reactions which serve as markers of psychological events (e.g., muscle action potentials across the face marking a positive or negative affective reaction) need not represent an instrumental component of the psychological event. Noninstrumental physiological reactions (e.g., associated movements) as well as instrumental physiological events can favor the involvement of a particular psychological process (e.g., semantic versus emotional reactions to an appeal) or of a given physiological mechanism (e.g., unitary arousal vs. a highly specific, behaviorally adaptive response system). Whether or not a given physiological reaction is necessary for a particular process, while interesting in its own right, is not critical for a measure to serve as an episodic marker.

Finally, although our research has not been designed to answer questions about the role of facial efference in affective experience, the observed correspondence between subtle patterns of facial efference and subject's transient and idiosyncratic affective reactions is certainly consistent with the view that facial efference is a significant determinant of emotion as well as with the view emphasized above that facial efference can serve as emotional readout. It is possible, for instance, that subjects in the present study rated their affective reactions as more intense *because* greater discriminably patterned feedback had been evoked. Research on the temporal specificity of striated muscular activity (e.g., Henneman, 1980b), facial actions (e.g., Ekman & Friesen, 1978), and facial EMG activity (e.g., Cacioppo et al., 1984) is clearly consistent with recent arguments that the temporal parameters of the afference resulting from spontaneous versus deliberate facial actions are distinguishable just as are the spatial parameters that differentiate the feedback resulting from expressions of, say, happiness and sadness (Tomkins, 1981).

As is well known, evidence has also been reported questioning the contributions of facial efference to affective experience (cf. Tourangeau & Ellsworth, 1979). However, several mechanisms of action linking spontaneous facial efference to affective experience can be suggested that do not cast the relationship between facial efference and affective experience as an invariant. In addition to innate afferent mechanisms (e.g., Izard, 1977; Tomkins, 1962, 1963), one might point to the processes of classical conditioning (wherein facial feedback from spontaneous expressions of emotion have been paired so frequently with particular emotional experiences that this feedback has come to serve as a conditioned stimulus), self-perception (e.g., why would one smile spontaneously at another unless liking was involved), and behavioral confirmations (e.g., facial expressions, like overt actions toward another, should influence the social feedback individuals receive). While deliberate facial expressions of emotion may invoke some of these mechanisms in a weakened form (e.g., even the effects attributable to social feedback should be weakened by leakage from other channels—cf. Zuckerman et al., 1981), the construction and maintenance of a deliberate expression of emotion and the monitoring of the communicative effectiveness of the expression can also subsume processing capacity. When an individual's processing resources are sufficiently limited in an emotionally evocative context that the capacity allocated to the construction, maintenance, and monitoring of an expressive display diminishes what can be allocated to the evocative stimulus, then one might expect deliberate expressions of emotion to actually attentuate the affective experience or to introduce feelings of negative affect such as anxiety or distress. For instance, expressing and maintaining an unfelt smile in the face of danger may prove to be an effective means of attenuating fear because of the disruption of the normal (i.e., spontaneous) pattern of efference and feedback found in this situation *and* because of the reduction in the processing capacity that can be allocated to the fear-evoking situation. Of course, the latter process would not hold for deliberately constructed facial expressions when the expression is so well practiced as to have achieved automaticity, the emotionally evocative stimulus requires little to no processing capacity, or the emotionally evocative stimulus persists sufficiently long that any diminution of processing resources which can be allocated to the stimulus becomes trivial.

In sum, previous research has demonstrated that overt facial expressions vary as a function of people's emotional reactions; that overt perioral activity is associated with language processing; and that the electromyogram is an effective technology for examining neuromuscular actions in the absence of overt muscle contractions. The results of our psychophysiological research point to a procedure for tracking various aspects of cognitive and affective information processing. For instance, results have indicated that facial EMG can mark the valence and intensity of transient and specific affective reactions even in the absence of emotional expressions that are noticeable, at least under normal viewing conditions. Although the pattern of facial efference is unlikely to yield a satisfactory physiological marker of attitudes per se, the present results do suggest that facial EMG may provide a useful technology for tracking silent language processing as well as the rudimentary positive or negative feelings a person has toward a stimulus and the more elementary processes underlying a variety of social judgments and behaviors such as attitude development and change. It is also possible that questons regarding whether episodes of "instrumental" and "hostile" aggression studied in social psychological laboratories differ in terms of their emotional underpinnings (cf. Rajecki, 1983), questions regarding whether cognitive dissonance is characterized phenomenologically by the perception of arousal or by an unpleasant affective reaction (see recent reviews by Cacioppo & Petty, 1985; Fazio & Cooper, 1983) and a number of other elusive questions of interest to social psychologists may be amenable to psychophysiological probes.

ACKNOWLEDGMENT

This research was supported by National Science Foundation Grant Nos. BNS-8414853, BNS-8444909, and BNS-8418038. Address correspondence to John T. Cacioppo, Department of Psychology, University of Iowa, Iowa City, Iowa 52242, or to Richard E. Petty, Department of Psychology, University of Missouri, Columbia, Missouri 65211.

REFERENCES

Ajzen, I., & Fishbein, M. (1980). *Understanding attitudes and predicting social behavior.* Englewood Cliffs, NJ: Prentice-Hall.

Allport, G. W. (1935). Attitudes. In C. Murchison (Ed.), *Handbook of social psychology* (Vol. 2). Worcester, MA: Clark University Press.

Baddeley, A. D. (1978). The trouble with levels: A reexamination of Craik and Lockhart's framework for memory research. *Psychological Review, 85,* 139–152.

Birnbaum, M. H., & Mellers, B. A. (1979). Stimulus recognition may mediate exposure effects. *Journal of Personality and Social Psychology, 37,* 391–394.

Bower, G. H., & Gilligan, S. G. (1979). Remembering information related to one's self. *Journal of Research in Personality, 13,* 420–432.

Breckler, S. J. (1984). Empirical validation of affect, behavior, and cognition as distinct attitude components. *Journal of Personality and Social Psychology, 47,* 1191–1204.

Brock, T. C. (1967). Communication discrepancy and intent to persuade as determinants of counterargument production. *Journal of Experimental Social Psychology, 3,* 269–309.

Brown, S. L., & Schwartz, G. E. (1980). Relationships between facial electromyography and subjective experience during affective imagery. *Biological Psychology, 11,* 49–62.

Cacioppo, J. T., & Bush, L. (1985). The effects of voluntary control over facial expressions on facial EMG responses. *Psychophysiology, 22,* 585–586.

Cacioppo, J. T., & Dorfman, D. D. (1985). Topographical analysis of non-negative bounded waveforms: Applications to psychophysiological data. *Psychophysiology, 22,* 577. (abstract)

Cacioppo, J. T., Losch, M. E., Tassinary, L. G., & Petty, R. E. (1986). Properties of affect and affect-laden information processing as viewed through the facial response system. In R. A. Peterson, W. D. Hoyer, & W. R. Wilson (Eds.), *The role of affect in consumer behavior: Emerging theories and applications.* Lexington, MA: D. C. Heath.

Cacioppo, J. T., Marshall-Goodell, B., & Dorfman, D. D. (1983). Skeletomuscular patterning: Topographical analysis of the integrated electromyogram. *Psychophysiology, 20,* 269–283.

Cacioppo, J. T., & Petty, R. E. (1979a). Attitudes and cognitive response: An electrophysiological approach. *Journal of Personality and Social Psychology, 37,* 2181–2199.

Cacioppo, J. T., & Petty, R. E. (1979b). Lip and nonpreferred forearm EMG activity as a function of orienting task. *Journal of Biological Psychology, 9,* 103–113.

Cacioppo, J. T., & Petty, R. E. (1979c). Effects of message repetition and position on cognitive response, recall, and persuasion. *Journal of Personality and Social Psychology, 37,* 97–109.

Cacioppo, J. T., & Petty, R. E. (1980a). The effects of orienting task on differential hemispheric EEG activation. *Neuropsychologia, 18,* 675–683.

Cacioppo, J. T., & Petty, R. E. (1981a). Electromyograms as measures of extent affectivity of information processing. *American Psychologist, 36,* 441–456.

Cacioppo, J. T., & Petty, R. E. (1981b). Electromyographic specificity during covert information processing. *Psychophysiology, 18,* 518–523.

Cacioppo, J. T., & Petty, R. E. (Eds.). (1983). *Social psychophysiology: A sourcebook.* New York: Guilford Press.

Cacioppo, J. T., & Petty, R. E. (1985a). Social processes. In M. G. H. Coles, E. Donchin, & S. Porges (Eds.), *Psychophysiology: Systems, processes, and applications.* New York: Guilford Press.

Cacioppo, J. T., & Petty, R. E. (1985b). Physiological responses and advertising effects: Is the cup half full or half empty? *Psychology and Marketing, 2,* 115–126.

Cacioppo, J. T., Petty, R. E., Losch, M. E., & Kim, H. S. (1986). Electromyographic activity over facial muscle regions can differentiate the valence and intensity of affective reactions. *Journal of Personality and Social Psychology, 50,* 260–268.

Cacioppo, J. T., Petty, R. E., & Marshall-Goodell, B. (1984). Electromyographic specificity during simple physical and attitudinal tasks: Location and topographical features of integrated EMG responses. *Biological Psychology, 18,* 85–121.

Cacioppo, J. T., Petty, R. E., & Morris, K. J. (1983). Effects of need for cognition on message evaluation, recall, and persuasion. *Journal of Personality and Social Psychology, 45,* 805–818.

Cacioppo, J. T., Petty, R. E., & Morris, K. J. (1985). Semantic, evaluative, and self-referent processing: Memory, cognitive effort, and somatovisceral activity. *Psychophysiology, 22,* 371–384.

Cacioppo, J. T., Petty, R. E., & Quintanar, L. R. (1982). Individual differences in relative hemispheric alpha abundance and cognitive responses to persuasive communications. *Journal of Personality and Social Psychology, 43,* 623–636.

Cacioppo, J. T., & Sandman, C. A. (1981). Psychophysiological functioning, cognitive responding, and attitudes. In R. E. Petty, T. M. Ostrom, & T. C. Brock (Eds.), *Cognitive responses in persuasion.* Hillsdale, NJ: Lawrence Erlbaum Associates.

Cermak, L. S., & Craik, F. I. M. (Eds.). (1979). *Levels of processing in human memory.* Hillsdale, NJ: Lawrence Erlbaum Associates.

Chaiken, S. (1980). Heuristic versus systematic information processing and the use of source versus message cues in persuasion. *Journal of Personality and Social Psychology, 39,* 752–766.

Chaiken, S. (1983, October). *The heuristic/systematic processing distinction in persuasion.* Paper presented at the symposium on automatic processing, Society for Experimental Social Psychology, Nashville, Indiana.

Cialdini, R. B. (1984). Principles of automatic influence. In J. Jacoby & C. S. Craig (Eds.), *Personal selling: Theory, research, and practice.* Lexington, MA: D.C. Heath.

Cialdini, R. B., & Petty, R. E. (1981). Anticipatory opinion effects. In R. E. Petty, T. M. Ostrom, & T. C. Brock (Eds.), *Cognitive responses in persuasion.* Hillsdale, NJ: Lawrence Erlbaum Associates.

Coles, M. G. H., Donchin, E., & Porges, S. (Eds.). (1985). *Psychophysiology: Systems, processes, and applications.* New York: Guilford Press.

Cooper, J. D. (1959). Emotion and prejudice. *Science, 130,* 314–318.

Craik, F. I. M. (1979). Human memory. *Annual Review of Psychology, 30,* 63–102.

Craik, F. I. M., & Tulving, E. (1975). Depth of processing and the retention of words in episodic memory. *Journal of Experimental Psychology: General, 104,* 268–294.

Crider, A. (1983). The promise of social psychophysiology. In J. T. Cacioppo & R. E. Petty (Eds.), *Social psychophysiology: A sourcebook.* New York: Guilford Press.

Darwin, C. (1965). *The expression of the emotions in man and animals.* Chicago: The University of Chicago Press. (Originally published, 1872).

Donchin, E. (1982). The relevance of dissociations and the irrelevance of dissociationism: A reply to Schwartz and Pritchard. *Psychophysiology, 19,* 457–463.

Edfeldt, A. W. (1960). *Silent speech and silent reading.* Chicago: University of Chicago Press.

Ekman, P. (1972). Universal and cultural differences in facial expressions of emotion. In J. Cole (Ed.), *Nebraska symposium on motivation, 1971* (Vol. 19). Lincoln: University of Nebraska Press.

Ekman, P. (1982a). *Emotion in the human face* (2nd ed.). Cambridge: Cambridge University Press.

Ekman, P. (1982b). Methods for measuring facial action. In K. R. Scherer & P. Ekman (Eds.), *Handbook of methods in nonverbal behavior research* (pp. 45–90). Cambridge: Cambridge University Press.

Ekman, P., & Friesen, W. V. (1969). The repertoire of nonverbal behavior. *Science, 1,* 49–98.

Ekman, P., & Friesen, W. V. (1974). Detecting deception from the body or face. *Journal of Personality and Social Psychology, 29,* 288–298.

Ekman, P., & Friesen, W. V. (1975). *Unmasking the face.* Englewood Cliffs, NJ: Prentice-Hall.

Ekman, P., & Friesen, W. V. (1978). *Facial coding action system (FACS): A technique for the measurement of facial actions.* Palo Alto, CA: Consulting Psychologists Press.

Ekman, P., & Friesen, W. V. (1982). Felt, false, and miserable smiles. *Journal of Nonverbal Behavior, 6,* 238–252.

Ekman, P., Friesen, W. V., & Ancoli, S. (1980). Facial signs of emotional experience. *Journal of Personality and Social Psychology, 39,* 1125–1134.

Ericcson, K. A., & Simon, H. A. (1980). Verbal reports as data. *Psychological Review, 87,* 215–251.

Faaborg-Anderson, K., & Edfeldt, A. W. (1958). Electromyography of intrinsic and extrinsic laryngeal muscles during silent speech: Correlation with reading activity. *Acta Otolaryngologica, 49,* 478–482.

Fazio, R. H., & Cooper, J. (1983). Arousal in the dissonance process. In J. T. Cacioppo & R. E. Petty (Eds.), *Social psychophysiology: A source book* (pp. 122–152). New York: Guilford Press.

Ferguson, T. J., Rule, B. G., & Carlson, D. (1983). Memory for personally relevant information. *Journal of Personality and Social Psychology, 44,* 251–261.

Fishbein, M. (1980). A theory of reasoned action: Some applications and implications. In H. Howe & M. Page (Eds.), *Nebraska Symposium on Motivation* (Vol. 27). Lincoln: University of Nebraska Press.

Fishbein, M., & Ajzen, I. (1972). Attitudes and opinions. In M. Rosenzweig & L. Porter (Eds.), *Annual review of psychology* (Vol. 23). Palo Alto, CA: Annual Reviews.

Fridlund, A. J., Ekman, P., & Oster, H. (in press). Facial expressions of emotion: Review of literature, 1970–1983. In A. Siegman (Ed.), *Nonverbal communication.* Hillsdale, NJ: Lawrence Erlbaum Associates.

Fridlund, A. J., & Izard, C. E. (1983). Electromyographic studies of facial expressions of emotions and patterns of emotion. In J. T. Cacioppo & R. E. Petty (Eds.), *Social psychophysiology: A sourcebook.* New York: Guilford Press.

Friesen, W. V. (1972). *Cultural differences in facial expression in a social situation: An experimental test of the concept of display rules.* Unpublished doctoral dissertation, University of California, San Francisco.

Galton, F. (1884). Measurement of character. *Fortnightly Review, 42,* 179–185.

Garrity, L. I. (1977). Electromyography: A review of the current status of subvocal speech research. *Memory & Cognition, 5,* 615–622.

Gerard, H. B. (1964). Physiological measurement in social psychological research. In P. H. Leiderman & D. Shapiro (Eds.), *Psychobiological approaches to social behavior.* Stanford: Stanford University Press.

Gorn, G. J. (1982). The effects of music in advertising on choice behavior: A classical conditioning approach. *Journal of Marketing, 46,* 94–101.

Gordon, P. C., & Holyoak, K. J. (1983). Implicit learning and generalization of the "mere exposure" effect. *Journal of Personality and Social Psychology, 45,* 492–500.

Grabiner, M. D., & Robertson, R. N. (1985). Utilization of digital discriminators for quantification of the surface electromyograms. *EMG & Clinical Neurophysiology, 25,* 489–498.

Greenwald, A. G. (1968). Cognitive learning, cognitive response to persuasion, and attitude change. In A. Greenwald, T. Brock, & T. Ostrom (Eds.), *Psychological foundations of attitudes.* New York: Academic Press.

Greenwald, A. G. (1975). On the inconclusiveness of "crucial" cognitive tests of dissonance versus self-perception theory. *Journal of Experimental Social Psychology, 11,* 490–499.

Greenwald, A. G. (1982). Is any*one* in charge? Personanalysis versus the principle of personal unity. In J. Suls (Ed.), *Psychological perspectives on the self* (Vol. 1). Hillsdale, NJ: Lawrence Erlbaum Associates.

Haggard, E. A., & Issacs, F. S. (1966). Micromomentary facial expressions as indicators of ego mechanisms in psychotherapy. In C. A. Gottschalk & A. Averback (Eds.), *Methods of research in psychotherapy.* New York: Appleton-Century-Crofts.

Hare, R. D. (1973). Orienting and defensive responses to visual stimuli. *Psychophysiology, 10,* 453–464.

Harkins, S. G., & Petty, R. E. (1981). Effects of source magnification of cognitive effort on attitudes: An information processing view. *Journal of Personality and Social Psychology, 40,* 401–413.

Hefferline, R. F., Keenan, B., & Harford, R. A. (1959). Escape and avoidance conditioning in human subjects without their observation of the response. *Science, 1,* 1338–1339.

Heider, F. (1946). Attitudes and cognitive organization. *Journal of Psychology, 21,* 107–112.

Henneman, E. (1980a). Organization of the motoneuron pool: The size principle. In V. B. Mountcastle (Ed.), *Medical physiology* (14th ed., Vol. 1). St. Louis: Mosby.

Henneman, E. (1980b). Skeletal muscle: The servant of the nervous system. In V. B. Mountcastle (Ed.), *Medical physiology* (14th ed., Vol. 1). St. Louis: Mosby.

Hess, E. H. (1965). Attitude and pupil size. *Scientific American, 212,* 46–54.

Iacono, W. G. (1983). Psychophysiology and genetics: A key to psychopathology research. *Psychophysiology, 20,* 371–383.

Insko, C. A. (1967). *Theories of attitude change.* New York: Appleton-Century-Crofts.

Izard, C. E. (1971). *The face of emotion.* New York: Appleton-Century-Crofts.

Izard, C. E. (1977). *Human emotions.* New York: Plenum.

Jones, E. E., & Sigall, H. (1971). The bogus pipeline: A new paradigm for measuring affect and attitude. *Psychological Bulletin, 76,* 349–364.

Katz, H., Cadoret, R., Hughes, K., & Abbey, D. (1965). Physiological correlates of acceptable and unacceptable statements. *Psychological Reports, 17,* 78.

Keenan, J. M., & Baillet, S. D. (1980). Memory for personality and socially significant events. In R. S. Nickerson (Ed.), *Attention and performance VIII.* Hillsdale, NJ: Lawrence Erlbaum Associates.

Kelman, H. C. (1961). Process of opinion change. *Public Opinion Quarterly, 25,* 57–78.

Kiesler, C. A., & Munson, P. A. (1975). Attitudes and opinions. In M. R. Rosenzweig & L. W. Porter (Eds.), *Annual review of psychology* (Vol. 26). Palo Alto, CA: Annual Reviews.

Kunst-Wilson, W. R., & Zajonc, R. B. (1980). Affective discrimination of stimuli that cannot be recognized. *Science, 207,* 557–558.

Lacey, J. I., & Lacey, B. C. (1958). Verification and extension of the principle of autonomic response stereotypy. *American Journal of Psychology, 71,* 50–73.

Langer, E., Blank, A., & Chanowitz, B. (1978). The mindlessness of ostensibly thoughtful action: The role of "placebic" information in interpersonal intraction. *Journal of Personality and Social Psychology, 36,* 635–642.

Lazarus, R. S. (1984). On the primacy of cognition. *American Psychologist, 39,* 124–129.

Lippold, O. C. J. (1967). Electromyography. In P. H. Venables & I. Martin (Eds.), *Manual of psychophysiological methods* (pp. 245–298). New York: Wiley.

Lott, A. J., & Lott, B. E. (1968). A learning theory approach to interpersonal attitudes. In A. G. Greenwald, T. C. Brock, & T. M. Ostrom (Eds.), *Psychological foundations of attitudes.* New York: Academic Press.

Love, R. E. (1972). *Unobtrusive measurement of cognitive reactions to persuasive communications.* Unpublished doctoral dissertation, Ohio State University.

Lykken, D. T. (1981). *A tremor in the blood: Uses and abuse of the lie detector.* New York: McGraw-Hill.

Malmo, R. B. (1975). *On emotions, needs, and our archaic brain.* New York: Holt, Rinehart, and Winston.

McCaul, K. D., & Maki, R. H. (1984). Self-reference versus desirability ratings and memory for traits. *Journal of Personality and Social Psychology, 47,* 953–955.

McGuigan, F. J. (1970). Covert oral behavior during the silent performance of language tasks. *Psychological Bulletin, 74,* 309–326.

McGuigan, F. J. (1978). *Cognitive psychophysiology: Principles of covert behavior.* Englewood Cliffs, NJ: Prentice-Hall.

McGuigan, F. J. (1979). *Psychophysiological measurement of covert behavior: A guide for the laboratory.* Hillsdale, NJ: Lawrence Erlbaum Associates.

McGuigan, F. J., Dollins, A., Pierce, W., Lusebrink, B., & Corus, C. (1982). Fourier analysis of covert speech behavior. *Pavlovian Journal of Biological Science, 17,* 49–52.

McGuire, W. J. (1964). Inducing resistance to persuasion: Some contemporary approaches. In L. Berkowitz (Ed.), *Advances in experimental social psychology* (Vol. 1). New York: Academic Press.

McGuire, W. J. (1985). Attitudes and attitude change. In G. Lindzey & E. Aronson (Eds.), *The handbook of social psychology* (3rd ed.). Reading, MA: Addison-Wesley.

McHugo, G. J., Lanzetta, J. T., Sullivan, D. G., Masters, R. D., & Englis, B. G. (1985). Emotional reactions to a political leader's expressive displays. *Journal of Personality and Social Psychology, 49,* 1513–1529.

Miller, N., Maruyama, G., Beaber, R., & Valone, K. (1976). Speed of speech and persuasion. *Journal of Personality and Social Psychology, 34,* 615–625.

Moreland, R. L., & Zajonc, R. B. (1977). Is stimulus recognition a necessary condition for the occurrence of exposure effects? *Journal of Personality and Social Psychology, 35,* 191–199.

Morris, C. D., Bransford, J. D., & Franks, J. J. (1977). Levels of processing versus transfer appropriate processing. *Journal of Verbal Learning and Verbal Behavior, 16,* 519–533.

Nisbett, R. E., & Wilson, T. D. (1977). Telling more than we can know: Verbal reports on mental processes. *Psychological Review, 84,* 231–259.

O'Donnell, R. D., Rapp, J., Berkhout, J., & Adey, W. R. (1973). Autospectral and coherence patterns from two locations in the contracting biceps. *Electromyography and Clinical Neurophysiology, 13,* 259–269.

Ohman, A., & Dimberg, U. (1984). An evolutionary perspective on human social behavior. In W. M. Waid (Ed.), *Sociophysiology.* New York: Springer-Verlag.

Osgood, C. E. (1966). Dimensionality of the semantic space for communicating via facial expressions. *Scandanavian Journal of Psychology, 7,* 1–30.

Person, R. S., Gundarov, V. P., Kudina, L. I., Vojtenko, G. A., & Konjuxova, G. P. (1967). Primeneie metoda korreljacionnogo analiza v elektromiografi. *Navosti Medicinskogo Priborostroenija, 1,* 16–20.

Petty, R. E., & Cacioppo, J. T. (1977). Forewarning, cognitive responding and resistance to persuasion. *Journal of Personality and Social Psychology, 35,* 645–655.

Petty, R. E., & Cacioppo, J. T. (1979). Issue-involvement can increase or decrease persuasion by enhancing message-relevant cognitive responses. *Journal of Personality and Social Psychology, 37,* 1915–1926.

Petty, R. E., & Cacioppo, J. T. (1980). Effects of issue involvement on attitudes in an advertising context. *Proceedings of the Division 23 Program, 88th Annual American Psychological Association Meeting,* 75–79.

Petty, R. E., & Cacioppo, J. T. (1981). *Attitudes and persuasion: Classic and contemporary approaches.* Dubuque, IA: W. C. Brown.

Petty, R. E., & Cacioppo, J. T. (1983). The role of bodily responses in attitude measurement and change. In J. T. Cacioppo & R. E. Petty (Eds.), *Social psychophysiology: A sourcebook* (pp. 51–101). New York: Guilford Press.

Petty, R. E., & Cacioppo, J. T. (1984). Source factors and the elaboration likelihood model of persuasion. *Advances in Consumer Research, 11,* 668–672.

Petty, R. E., & Cacioppo, J. T. (1986). The elaboration likelihood model of persuasion. *Advances in Experimental Social Psychology, 19,* 123–205.

Petty, R. E., & Cacioppo, J. T. (1986). *Communication and Persuasion: Central and Peripheral Routes to Attitude Change.* New York: Springer-Verlag.

Petty, R. E., Cacioppo, J. T., & Goldman, R. (1981). Personal involvement as a determinant of argument-based persuasion. *Journal of Personality and Social Psychology, 41,* 847–855.

Petty, R. E., Cacioppo, J. T., & Harkins, S. G. (1983). Group size effects on cognitive effort and attitude change. In H. H. Blumber, A. P. Hare, V. Kent, & M. Davies (Eds.), *Small groups and social interaction* (Vol. 1, pp. 165–181). London: Wiley.

Petty, R. E., Ostrom, T. M., & Brock, T. C. (Eds.). (1981). *Cognitive responses in persuasion.* Hillsdale, NJ: Lawrence Erlbaum Associates.

Petty, R. E., Wells, G. L., & Brock, T. L. (1976). Distraction can enhance or reduce yielding to propaganda: Thought disruption versus effort justification. *Journal of Personality and Social Psychology, 34,* 874–884.

Podlesny, J. A., & Raskin, D. C. (1977). Physiological measures and the detection of deception. *Psychological Bulletin, 84,* 782–799.

Rajecki, D. W. (1983). Animal aggression: Implications for human aggression. In R. G. Geen & E. J. Donnerstein (Eds.), *Aggression: Theoretical and empirical reviews* (Vol. 1, pp. 189– 211). New York: Academic Press.

Rankin, R. E., & Campbell, D. T. (1955). Galvanic skin response to negro and white experimenters. *Journal of Abnormal and Social Psychology, 51,* 30–33.

Rinn, W. E. (1984). The neuropsychology of facial expression: A review of the neurological and psychological mechanisms for producing facial expression. *Psychological Bulletin, 95,* 52–77.

Robertson, R. N., & Grabiner, M. D. (in press). Relationship of IEMG to two methods of counting surface spikes during different levels of isometric tension. *EMG & Clinical Neurophysiology.*

Rogers, R. W. (1983). Cognitive and physiological processes in fear appeals and attitude change: A revised theory of protection motivation. In J. T. Cacioppo & R. E. Petty (Eds.), *Social psychophysiology: A sourcebook.* New York: Guilford Press.

Rogers, T. B., Kuiper, N. A., & Kirker, W. S. (1977). Self-reference and the encoding of personal information. *Journal of Personality and Social Psychology, 35,* 677–688.

Schwartz, G. E. (1975). Biofeedback, self-regulation, and the patterning of physiological processes. *American Scientist, 63,* 314–324.

Schwartz, G. E., Fair, P. L., Salt, P., Mandel, M. R., & Klerman, G. L. (1976a). Facial expressions and imagery in depression: An electromyographic study. *Psychosomatic Medicine, 38,* 337–347.

Schwartz, G. E., & Shapiro, D. (1973). Social psychophysiology. In W. F. Prokasy & D. C. Raskin (Eds.), *Electrodermal activity in psychological research.* New York: Academic Press.

Shapiro, D., & Schwartz, G. E. (1970). Psychophysiological contributions to social psychology. *Annual Review of Psychology, 21,* 87–112.

Sherif, C. W. (1976). *Orientation in social psychology.* New York: Harper & Row.

Sokolov, A. N. (1972). *Inner speech and thought.* New York: Plenum.

Staats, A. W., & Staats, C. K. (1958). Attitudes established by classical conditioning. *Journal of Abnormal and Social Psychology, 57,* 37–40.

Taylor, S. E. (1975). On inferring one's attitudes from one's behavior: Some delimiting conditions. *Journal of Personality and Social Psychology, 31,* 126–131.

Tomkins, S. S. (1962). Affect, imagery, consciousness: The positive *affects* (Vol. 1). New York: Springer.

Tomkins, S. S. (1963). *Affect, imagery, consciousness: The negative affects* (Vol. 2). New York: Springer.

Tomkins, S. S. (1981). The role of facial response in the experience of emotion: A reply to Tourangeau and Ellsworth. *Journal of Personality and Social Psychology, 40,* 355–357.

Tourangeau, R., & Ellsworth, P. C. (1979). The role of facial response in the experience of emotion. *Journal of Personality and Social Psychology, 37,* 1519–1531.

Tulving, E. (1978). Relation between encoding specificity and levels of processing. In L. S. Cermak & F. I. M. Craik (Eds.), *Levels of processing in human memory* (pp. 19–92). Hillsdale, NJ: Lawrence Erlbaum Associates.

Tursky, B., & Jamner, L. (1983). Evaluation of social and political beliefs: A psychophysiological approach. In J. T. Cacioppo & R. E. Petty (Eds.), *Social psychophysiology: A sourcebook.* New York: Guilford Press.

Waid, W. (1984). *Sociophysiology.* New York: Springer-Verlag.

Waid, W. M., & Orne, M. T. (1981). Cognitive, social, and personality processes in the physiological detection of deception. In L. Berkowitz (Ed.), *Advances in experimental social psychology* (Vol. 14). New York: Academic Press.

White, L., & Tursky, B. (1982). *Clinical biofeedback: Efficacy and mechanisms.* New York: Guilford Press.

Wicker, A. W. (1969). Attitudes versus actions: The relationship of verbal and overt behavioral responses to attitude objects. *Journal of Social Issues, 25,* 41–78.

Wicker, A. W. (1971). An examination of the "other-variables" explanation of attitude-behavior inconsistency. *Journal of Personality and Social Psychology, 19,* 18–30.

Willis, W. D., Jr., & Grossman, R. G. (1977). *Medical neurobiology* (2nd ed.). St. Louis: Mosby.

Winton, W. M., Putnam, L. E., & Krauss, R. M. (1984). Facial and autonomic manifestations of the dimensional structure of emotion. *Journal of Experimental Social Psychology, 20,* 195–216.

Zajonc, R. B. (1980). Feeling and thinking: Preferences need no inferences. *American Psychologist, 35,* 151–175.

Zajonc, R. B. (1984). On primacy of affect. *American Psychologist, 39,* 117–123.

Zajonc, R. B., & Markus, H. (1982). Affective and cognitive factors in preferences. *Journal of Consumer Research, 9,* 123–131.

Zanna, M. P., & Cooper, J. (1974). Dissonance and the pill: An attribution approach to studying the arousal properties of dissonance. *Journal of Personality and Social Psychology, 29,* 703–709.

Zanna, M. P., Detweiler, R. A., & Olson, J. M. (1984). In W. Waid (Ed.), *Sociophysiology.* New York: Springer-Verlag.

Zanna, M. P., & Rempel, J. K. (in press). Attitudes: A new look at an old concept. In D. Bar-Tal & A. Kruglanski (Eds.), *The social psychology of knowledge.* New York: Cambridge University Press.

Zuckerman, M., DePaulo, B. M., & Rosenthal, R. (1981). Verbal and nonverbal communication of deception. *Advances in Experimental Social Research, 14,* 1–59.

Zuckerman, M., Larrance, D. T., Spiegel, N. H., & Klorman, R. (1981). Controlling nonverbal displays: Facial expressions and tone of voice. *Journal of Experimental Social Psychology, 17,* 506–524.

3

Cognitive Processes in the Formation, Change, and Expression of Attitudes

Steven J. Sherman
Indiana University

When I was first asked to be a participant in this Fifth Ontario Symposium, my initial suggestion to Mark Zanna was a rather simple and straightforward talk. I would discuss the effects of imagining and explaining hypothetical events and outcomes on attitudes and relate these effects to other work that has looked at cognitive processes in social influence. But this initial intention was not followed (so much for intentions, even those involving commitment, predicting subsequent behavior). Perhaps I had simply become bored with the imagination-explanation area; or perhaps stemming from a desire to focus on the bigger picture, I noticed that some general issues kept arising (e.g., attentional processes; automatism and control). I felt that it might make a more meaningful presentation if I focused on general issues of cognitive processes in social influence and used imagination-explanation research as well as other areas of research to exemplify these processes.

What happened after that decision can only be described as a delusion of grandeur. I have never been one for developing or drawing out process models. It has always seemed to me that such models were highly speculative and that the models as a whole, or even their component parts, were difficult to test or to verify over other equally plausible models. Yet I plunged ahead. I decided that if I was going to discuss general issues concerning attitudes I might as well consider the entire process beginning with attitude formation, going on to change or resistance to change, and ending in the expression of attitudes in subsequent behavior—all the relevant factors, processes, and stages. I do, however, limit discussion of this sequence to cases where it occurs primarily in response to a persuasive message.

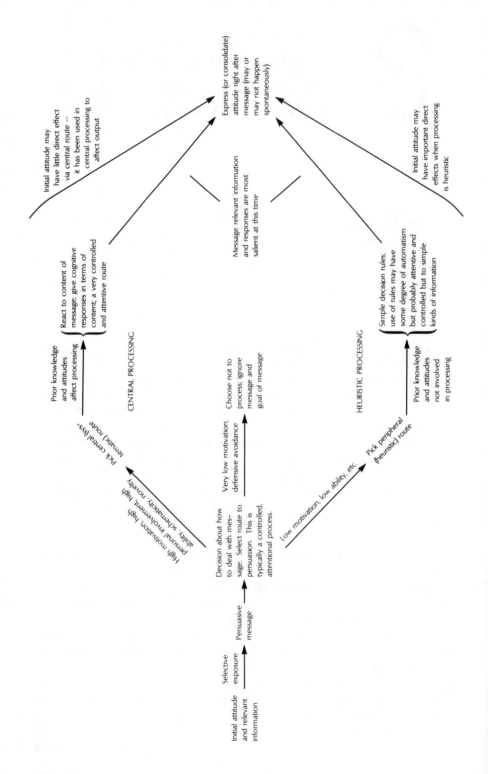

Express (or consolidate) attitude right after message (may or may not happen spontaneously)

Initial attitude may have little direct effect via central route – it has been used in central processing to affect output

React to content of message; give cognitive responses in terms of content; a very controlled and attentive route

Prior knowledge and attitudes affect processing

CENTRAL PROCESSING

Message relevant information and responses are most salient at this time

Simple decision rules; use of rules may have some degree of automatism but probably attentive and controlled but to simple kinds of information

Prior knowledge and attitudes not involved in processing

HEURISTIC PROCESSING

Initial attitude may have important direct effects when processing is heuristic

Pick central (sys-tematic) route

High motivation, high personal involvement, high ability; schematicity, novelty

Choose not to process; ignore message and goal of message

Very low motivation; defensive avoidance

Decision about how to deal with mes-sage. Select route to persuasion. This is typically a controlled, attentional process.

Low motivation, low ability, etc.

Pick peripheral (heuristic) route

Selective exposure

Persuasive message

Initial attitude and relevant information

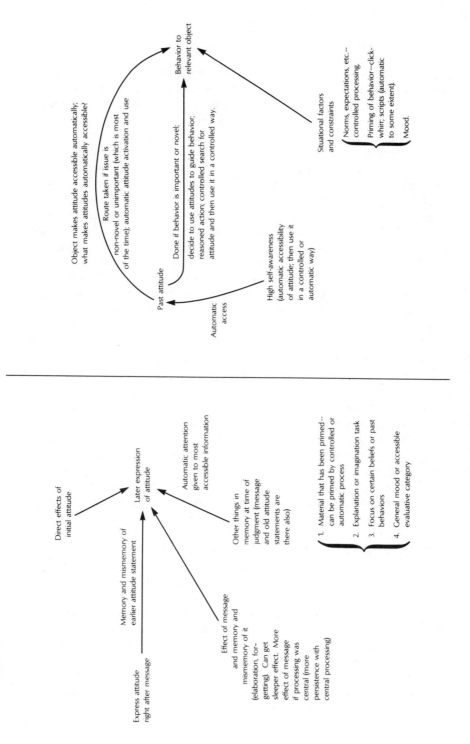

FIG. 3.1. A model of attitude change and expression.

It should be pointed out that this is not, of course, the first time that a cognitive approach to the understanding of the effectiveness of persuasive communications has been adopted. Although much of the work that emerged from Hovland and his colleagues during the 1940s and 1950s was primarily descriptive, the general process implicated by this work highlighted important information processing factors. Hovland understood the attitude change sequence in response to a persuasive message as consisting of three subprocesses—attention, comprehension, and yielding (Hovland, Janis, & Kelley, 1953). These subprocesses clearly involve many of the important factors that are discussed in the present chapter: selective attention, biased interpretation, decision making, etc. McGuire (1968, 1972) later extended this information processing interpretation of persuasion and developed the role of these cognitive processes more systematically. More important, McGuire and his colleagues, as well as other researchers, were able to test empirically many of the assumptions of his six step model (Eagly & Warren, 1976; McGuire & Millman, 1965; Millman, 1968). Many of the more recent approaches (see chapters by Cacioppo & Petty, Chaiken, and Fazio in this volume) have also focused upon cognitive processes in attitude change and expression. Eagly and Chaiken's (1984) recent chapter nicely outlines the various cognitive theories of persuasion that have been developed and tested recently.

In the present chapter, I hope to add to this kind of thinking in several ways. In the first place, I try to discuss the entire sequence of stages beginning with an initial attitude toward an issue as well as issue relevant information, proceeding with selective exposure to a persuasive message, and ending with behavioral expression at a much later point in time. In the second place, I focus on many extra-message factors (e.g., priming, mood) that affect the understanding, interpretation, and cognitive responses to persuasive messages and thus have effects on attitudes and their expression. Third, I concentrate on processes that have been clarified and studied in cognitive and social psychological research only recently (e.g., attentional mechanisms, priming, automatism) and try to indicate the role of these processes in reactions to persuasive communications.

The factors and processes involved in these stages are clearly so extensive and complicated that a single short chapter cannot do justice to them. Just a quick glance at the model outlined in Fig. 3.1 indicates this complexity and may deter the reader from continuing with this chapter. I will thus be able to indicate only briefly what these various factors, processes, and stages involve and to define some of the important issues that will have to be addressed in future thinking and research. Figure 3.1 is not meant to serve as a formal model of the attitude formation and expression process. It is meant only as a schematic summary of the issues and factors involved at each stage. The reader might refer to it while reading the chapter in order to get a better idea of what phase of the process is being discussed and how the overall process moves forward.

EXPOSURE TO THE PERSUASIVE MESSAGE

Individuals may, of course, begin with an initial attitude and initial relevant beliefs about a target topic. On the other hand, the topic may be a totally novel and unfamiliar one. However, even when a topic is novel, it typically can be associated with other issues and topics about which attitudes and beliefs do exist. Thus, when a political figure introduces a brand new defense policy, it will be associated with his/her other defense policy, economic policies, etc. In any case, whether or not attitudes exist prior to exposure to a persuasive communication indicates whether we are dealing with attitude change or attitude formation. Although this has not been a well researched issue in the literature to date, it may represent a quite important distinction. Fazio (1985, this volume) discusses some of the important differences between attitude formation and attitude change.

In terms of exposure to a persuasive message, the individual may or may not have much choice about whether or not to be exposed to any communication. In most laboratory studies, subjects clearly have little choice as they are typically handed a message to read or to listen to. Outside the laboratory, individuals usually have far more freedom in determining whether or not to receive any message, and they can choose the kinds of messages that they will receive. It is here that issues of selective exposure arise. Although selective exposure may depend on many factors (e.g., the amount of time available, the costs of receiving the message, mood, the salience and visibility of the message, etc.), a primary factor will involve the existence of prior attitudes and beliefs. The original dissonance theory formulation (Festinger, 1957) indicated that people will seek out information that is consistent with past attitudes and will avoid attitude inconsistent information. Although this derivation has not always been borne out (Feather, 1963; Freedman, 1965), the issue of selective exposure is indeed an important one. It represents the first point in the process where attentional mechanisms come into play. And it is an important stage in the process. In the absence of seeking out or attending to a persuasive message, the process clearly stops here. Thus, a specification of the factors involved in initial exposure to the communication would represent a significant understanding.

DECIDING HOW TO DEAL WITH THE MESSAGE

In recent years, it has become clear that there are two quite different ways in which a persuasive message is approached—a systematic or central processing route and a peripheral or heuristic processing route. Petty and Cacioppo (1983, 1984; Petty, Cacioppo, & Goldman, 1981) have been largely responsible for defining the distinction between central and peripheral routes to persuasion. A recent chapter (Petty & Cacioppo, 1985) nicely outlines this model. Chaiken and her colleagues have made a similar distinction between systematic vs. heuristic processing (Chaiken, this volume, 1980; Eagly & Chaiken, 1984). Although differences between the central-peripheral and the systematic-heuristic approaches have been identified, for the purposes of this chapter the similarities between these approaches are more important than the differences, and the two will thus be considered together.

In any case, central or systematic processing involves careful, thoughtful, and reasoned consideration of the true merits of the information presented in the message. On the other hand, peripheral or heuristic processing is based on the use of simple rules and simple cues in the persuasion context (e.g., communicator attractiveness or message length) rather than on a scrutiny of the true merits of the information. A good deal of research has demonstrated the utility of this distinction and has shown that different factors determine initial attitude change and subsequent effects when central and systematic as opposed to peripheral and heuristic processing are employed. This research also identifies some of the factors (e.g., motivation, ability, need for cognition, personal involvement, schematicity) that determine which persuasion route will be taken. However, neither Petty and Cacioppo nor Chaiken have discussed in detail the process involved in how we initially come to adopt one route or the other.

One possibility is that this involves a controlled attentional decision. That is, based on existing levels of motivation, interest, resources, etc. an individual may choose in a conscious and attentional way to process the message either centrally or peripherally—or to choose not to process the message at all even though one has been exposed to it. An interesting question is whether this "decision" can be more automatic, involving no attentional resources or conscious decision making. Can people simply "find themselves" processing the message in one way or the other without a prior conscious attentional decision? The answer is probably. Chaiken (this volume) has suggested that there may be cues in persuasive settings that activate heuristic or systematic processing. She suggests that presenting evidence about the reliability of simple heuristic rules might automatically increase the likelihood of using these rules in heuristic processing. For example, subjects exposed to the "expert communicators can be trusted" rule relied on the credibility of the communicator more in their reactions to a subsequent message (Hicks & Chaiken, 1984). Other research demonstrated similar effects for prior exposure to the "length implies strength" rule (Chaiken, Axsom, Hicks, Yates, & Wilson, 1985; Wilson, Axsom, Lee, & Chaiken, 1985).

These findings indicate that prior exposure to a heuristic rule increases the likelihood of subsequently adopting that rule in processing the contents of a message. The same kinds of priming effects might be observable for a bridge player's decision about how to play a particular hand, a chess player's strategy, or a baseball manager's decision about whether to sacrifice bunt or not. Although these effects of prior exposure seem reliable, it is unclear whether the process involves increased accessibility of facts that then carry more weight in a conscious decision-making strategy or whether it is a more automatic process. It is certainly possible that prior exposure to such rules could passively prime these rules outside the level of awareness and lead to their automatic adoption in a subsequent judgment task. LaRue and Olejnik (1980) have demonstrated that the level of moral judgment can be passively primed by prior logic tasks vs. more mindless tasks, and Higgins and Chaires (1980) have shown that general problem-solving approaches can be primed. It is thus clear that priming can affect things far more complex than the accessibility of a single word or a category. Ways of thinking and problem solving can be primed so that they automatically have an advantage or disadvantage in terms of activation and application. In the same way, the adoption of a central or peripheral route for processing a message might be primed. We return to the issues of priming and its effects during discussion of later stages of the social influence process.

In addition, message cues might automatically draw attention to content information and thus initiate central processing or to more peripheral information (e.g., communicator attractiveness) and thus initiate heuristic processing. Chaiken and Eagly (1983) presented subjects with messages in a video, audio, or written format. As a peripheral cue, the communicator was described in either a likable or unlikable way. The peripheral cue was used more with the video and audio messages than with the written message. In these cases, attention would be drawn to communicator likability cues because of their salience and vividness. This selective allocation of attention may then instigate a heuristic process based on simple rule use. Likewise, Pallak (1983) demonstrated that increasing the vividness of the attractiveness of the communicator by showing a clear vs. a blurred photograph enhanced the use of a simple liking-agreement rule in message relevant judgments. In another demonstration, Pallak, Murroni, and Koch (1983) presented emotionally toned or rationally toned messages. The former kind of message may draw attention to communicator attractiveness factors, and rational messages may automatically draw attention to content factors. In fact, peripheral processing was evident with emotionally toned messages, and central processing was used primarily with rationally toned messages. Whether in these studies the allocation of attention to central or peripheral aspects of the message is a conscious controlled process or an automatically instigated process is unclear. However, this difference is an important one and would have implications for attitude change procedures and outcomes. For example, resistance to persuasion would be easier to achieve if the attention allocation process were a conscious and controlled rather than an automatic one.

PROCESSING THE MESSAGE

Having instigated either central or peripheral processing, the message recipient now proceeds to deal with the message according to the appropriate principles and factors. These two routes to persuasion have been adequately described by Petty and Cacioppo (1985) and by Eagly and Chaiken (1984). Thus, only a brief summary is presented here. With central or systematic processing the individual responds to the content of the message, analyzes it, integrates it with past knowledge, and engages in cognitive responses to the message content. There is careful consideration of the information that the reader feels captures the true merits of the attitude position espoused in the message. All cognitive activity is issue relevant. The process is described as controlled and attentive. Initial beliefs and attitudes play an important role in central processing. In fact, central processing is likely to be chosen as the appropriate route when knowledge structures relevant to the issue exist prior to reception of the persuasive message. These knowledge structures will affect cognitive responses to the message and will serve as a framework into which the new message content is compared and integrated.

Prior knowledge structures may even bias the interpretation of the message content. The existence of cognitive structures and the level of schematicity of a recipient for the issue are thus quite important for central processing. For example, Cacioppo, Petty, and Sidera (1982) exposed subjects to a message that was either relevant or irrelevant to a self-schema. Although the conclusion of the message was the same in all cases, schema relevant messages did invoke schematic processing and allowed subjects to cognitively bolster the congruent arguments in the message. In the absence of knowledge structures, simple rules and cues are more likely to be used in response to a message (Srull, 1983; Wood, 1982). In Srull's study, subjects with low knowledge about automobiles were affected in their response to car ads by a mood manipulation. High-knowledge subjects focused on the quality of the message content and were unaffected by the mood manipulation.

Thus, with central processing past knowledge is integrated with message content. This integration leads to an updating of the initial attitude. When central processing is adopted, the main determinant of message impact is the strength of the arguments.

On the other hand, peripheral or heuristic processing involves the use of simple decision rules (e.g., "length equals strength"). There is no diligent and attentive consideration of the pros and cons of the message content. Initial attitudes may not be involved in such processing, and less integration of past beliefs or attitudes with present ideas generated by the message content is achieved with peripheral than with central processing. If these simplifying rules can be used without attention or awareness, heuristic processing may even be described as relatively automatic. Chaiken (this volume) suggests that this is the case. My own view is somewhat different. The use of heuristic principles (Sherman & Corty, 1984; Tversky & Kahneman, 1974) is usually a very attentive and controlled process. The simplicity in using them involves the consideration of a less complex rather than a more complex information base for the decision. This is quite different from using an automatic as opposed to a controlled process. Because the heuristic rule information is simpler to use and to process, less attention is needed of course. But the process itself may be no less controlled than systematic processing.

However, it is true that simpler and less complex responses can be automatized more easily than difficult and more complex responses. Lower order habits get automatized before higher order habits. Thus, heuristic processing certainly has the greater potential for automatization than central processing. And this raises another important point about automatic and controlled processes in response to persuasive communications. Complex tasks such as reading, interpreting, and responding to a persuasive message are clearly achieved by a complex mixture of automatic and attentive responses operating in concert. As Shiffrin (in press) points out, component processes can be either automatic or controlled. We have thusfar discussed two component processes of reading a persuasive message, the "decision" about which processing route to take and the processing route itself once this route is initiated. If the initial decision process is a controlled and attentive one and if the chosen heuristic processing route is automatized, a situation would exist in which an attentive process has triggered an automatic process. Such a sequence is not uncommon. Shiffrin (in press) uses the example of a tennis player consciously and attentively making a shot selection decision. Once that decision is made, however, the shot itself proceeds in an automatic and unattentive manner.

On the other hand, it is possible that the initial "choice" of a central or peripheral route is done automatically as attention is inescapably drawn to one kind of factor or the other. Following this choice, a very controlled and attentive systematic processing procedure may be adopted as message content cues or peripheral cues are weighed and analyzed. In this case, an automatic process would be used to initiate a subsequent attentive process. The sequencing of automatic and attentive processes during message analysis and the complex interplay between these processes will no doubt prove to be important in understanding the attitude change sequence and the factors that might be used to enhance or inhibit such change.

As opposed to central processing, message quality is irrelevant in the use of simplifying heuristic rules. Factors such as message length and communicator credibility are important. In order to employ such heuristic principles, individuals must of course have these relevant rules stored in memory. Not only must they be available, but they must be accessible as well. In addition, there must be information gained from consideration of the message that such rules are applicable. Even if one has decided to use heuristic processing, if no such rules are applicable one might alter the strategy and process the message systematically. Likewise, if one is attempting to process message content systematically but cannot comprehend or integrate it, a change to the use of more easily employed heuristic principles might be adopted. There is evidence that such changes in the mode of processing do occur (Petty, Wells, & Brock, 1976; Wood, Kallgren, & Priesler, 1985). In addition, the use of heuristic or systematic processing is not likely to be pure. For example, heuristic cues such as speaker credibility can lead to biased perception in the processing of and interpretation of message relevant cues.

The key to understanding the effects of a persuasive message involves knowing what information in the message will be attended to, what weights will be given to the various kinds of information, and how the information will be interpreted. The allocation of attention and the interpretation of the information attended to is not a straightforward matter. Nor is it always under the control of the recipient of the message. We have seen that factors such as motivation, ability, need for cognition, personal relevance, etc. determine whether message content or more peripheral cues are likely to attract attention. However, recent experiences of the subject prior to exposure to the message are also likely to have important effects on message processing. Two processes in particular (priming and imagination-explanation) are likely to have important effects on how the message is processed. These are discussed in some detail, and suggestions are made for using these processes to understand the ways in which attitudes change through reading persuasive messages.

Priming

In recent years, priming has been an important technique used by both cognitive and social psychologists to study the processes involved in responses ranging from lexical decision tasks to social judgments, from categorization to attitude expression. In general, priming is a procedure for rendering a specific stimulus, a general category, or a way of thinking more accessible in memory. The primed stimulus, or stimuli closely related in some way, become preactivated and are thus likely to be readily available for subsequent relevant judgment tasks. Differential category accessibility can, of course, represent chronic individual differences (Higgins, King, & Mavin, 1982).

On the other hand, situational activation of categories can also render these categories more accessible. Recent and frequent processing will prime a category and cause it to be relatively accessible in memory (Higgins & King, 1981). This kind of initial activation can be quite automatic and involve little in the way of attentive processing. For example, Bargh has presented stimuli to the unattended ear during a dichotic listening task or tachistoscopically in a visual mode and finds that categories primed in these ways nevertheless have important effects on subsequent evaluations and judgments (Bargh, 1982; Bargh & Pietromonaco, 1982). Alternatively, the initial activation produced by priming can operate through a very controlled and attentive process. Exposure to particular stimuli or events can lead an observer to generate relevant categories consciously.

In any case, once a category is activated through automatic or controlled priming procedures, a process of automatic spreading activation takes place that preactivates targets and associated stimuli for use in lexical decision tasks, impression formation tasks, or attitudinal judgments. Primed categories will determine the speed with which stimuli are processed and will also play a role in the selection of stimuli for further processing.

Primed categories are thought to produce their effects much in the same way that chronically accessible categories do. That is, they exert their influence without conscious direction. As a category is preactivated, ambiguous stimuli will be likely to be interpreted as members of that category. Bruner (1957) discussed these effects of category activation some years ago. Once a category is highly accessible, new stimuli will be identified as members of that category very quickly. In addition, less information is needed before this identification is made, and stimuli that do not actually belong to the activated category become more likely to misidentified as category members. Thus, a ß is likely to be identified as the number 13 if it follows a series of numbers. However, it will be identified as a B if it follows a series of letters. Similarly, social behavior is more likely to be interpreted as reckless if it follows the passive priming of trait terms synonomous with recklessness. However, the same behavior will be interpreted as adventurous if it follows the priming of other terms (Higgins, Rholes, & Jones, 1977; Srull & Wyer, 1979, 1980). Likewise, ambiguous content of a persuasive communication will be interpreted differently dependent upon recently activated categories.

Thus, one important effect of category priming concerns the interpretation and category identification of ambiguous stimuli. And it is this effect that has been primarily investigated in the literature. However, another important effect of priming involves the automatic drawing of attention to certain stimuli or to certain kinds of information. We usually think of automatism as the freeing of attention so that it can be allocated to other tasks. For example, when we are learning to drive, the task commands a lot of attention, and we may not be able to carry on a conversation or generate a grocery list while driving. However, as driving becomes automatized through practice, attention is freed to allow concurrent behavior and thinking.

Shiffrin (in press) has discussed a somewhat different kind of automatism—the possibility that attention itself can become automatized. As subjects practice search procedures involving a consistent set of targets and distractors, this search gets automatized as subjects learn to attend to the targets but to avoid attending to the distractors. If targets and the distractors are suddenly reversed, performance drops well below the initial performance level, and many trials are needed until even this initial performance level is again achieved (Shiffrin & Schneider, 1977). This work has demonstrated that targets come to attract attention automatically (they "jump out" to the subject) and, interestingly, distractors automatically repel attention, rendering them less likely than normal to be processed.

The development of these automatic responses indicates that certain stimuli will be perceived and processed preferentially and inescapably—the receiver cannot control seeing certain stimuli or attending to them. In this sense, the development of an automatic process can bind rather than free attention and can interfere with other attentive processing. Items in our environment are always in competition for attention. This is true for targets and distractors in a search paradigm, different thoughts in memory, or different kinds of items in a persuasive communication. If certain items attract attention preferentially and inescapably, these items will be processed more fully and will play a greater role in any judgment task.

I have suggested that priming a category can lead to automatic and inescapable attention to category relevant stimuli. If so, the priming of content relevant stimuli or more peripheral communicator stimuli can lead to differential attention to these various aspects of a message. Thus, systematic or heuristic processing can be rendered more or less likely through such priming procedures. Alternatively, different aspects of the message content could be made to draw the reader's attention automatically through priming procedures. This could have important effects on the consequences of reading a message. For example, imagine a message about a political candidate where the information in the message is favorable to the candidate with regard to economic policies but is unfavorable with regard to defense policies. Priming one or the other category (by the prior passive presentation of economic terms or defense terms) could lead to the automatic direction of attention to either economic or defense facts with the consequent positive or negative evaluation of the candidate. It is even possible that central or peripheral processing could be primed by a prior task that involved systematic use of information as opposed to simple rule use. When a persuasive message is subsequently read, attention could be automatically drawn to these preactivated kinds of information.

To date, social psychology research on priming has concentrated primarily on its effects on the interpretation of ambiguous stimuli (Higgins & Chaires, 1980, comes closest to demonstrating the effects of passive priming on the direction of attention). However, priming effects on direct attention may be even more important for understanding certain consequences of reading a persuasive message. The aspects of the message that draw the most attention (e.g., message length, certain content, communicator credibility) will obviously determine the effect of the message.

The foregoing discussion indicates that priming can have its effects at several different stages of persuasive message processing. It also demonstrates once again the involvement of both automatic and controlled processes in these stages. In the first stage, a category or way of thinking is made more accessible by the priming procedure. This can occur through automatic activation or through conscious attentive processes. Activation then automatically spreads to other category members. As the message is presented, the heightened accessibility of a category leads to an automatic and inescapable attention to certain aspects of the message and to an automatic interpretation of information in the message in a way that is determined by the primed category. Of course, even though the attention to stimuli and the interpretation of stimuli may be inescapable, the receiver of the message may still be acting on the content in a very controlled and attentive way. Attention to a stimulus may be drawn automatically, but reacting to that stimulus, once attention is drawn, can be highly effortful and controlled. Again, we see the possibility of the initiation of attentive processes by automatic processes and vice versa.

A final point should be made about priming effects. In the work done in cognitive psychology, these effects are generally very short-lived—a matter of milliseconds. However, the effects of priming in social psychology experiments on impression formation (Bargh, 1984; Higgins, Rholes, & Jones, 1977; Srull & Wyer, 1979, 1980) show these effects to be quite long lasting. It may be that the lexical decision tasks used in cognitive psychology experiments are not sensitive enough to detect long lasting changes in memory that result from ''unaware'' primes. It may also be the case that effects of a prime on memory are very short-lived but the effects on production and attentive processes may be much longer lasting. In addition, there are likely to be several different kinds of effects of priming. Neely (1977) has demonstrated that one effect of a prime is the fast automatic activation of semantically related items. However, there is in addition a slower effect of priming that is far more conscious and attentive.

Imagination and Explanation Procedures

Recent work in social psychology has shown that imagining or explaining hypothetical future events renders these events subjectively more probable (Anderson, Lepper, & Ross, 1980; Carroll, 1978; Ross, Lepper, & Hubbard, 1975; Sherman, Skov, Hervitz, & Stock, 1981). The usual interpretation of these effects is that the procedures make certain facts more accessible in memory. When a later judgment is made and relevant facts are accessed, these recently activated thoughts will come to mind quickly and will bias the judgment. Thus, when one is asked to explain a hypothetical success on an anagram task, one will no doubt access information about the self that is consistent with success on such a task (e.g., high verbal S.A.T., a love of games). When one is subsequently asked to judge how one will do on an actual anagram task, these success related facts will come to mind first and will drive the judgment (Sherman et al., 1981).

Unlike priming procedures, imagination-explanation tasks involve a procedure that is clearly attentive and controlled. It is more than the *passive* activation of a category. Rather the subject must think and attend and generate thoughts and details. Also unlike priming, explaining hypothetical outcomes involves the generation of new material and previously unthought ideas. Priming is more concerned with already available material, altering only its accessibility. Imagination and explanation of hypothetical events may lead to the availability of new thoughts and images.

Recent studies (Hirt & Sherman, 1985; Sherman, Zehner, Johnson, & Hirt, 1983) have shown that engaging a subject in a hypothetical explanation task very much affects the way in which the information in a message is processed and used for subsequent evaluations. In this paradigm, subjects are presented with detailed information about two football teams that are scheduled to play each other in a short time. Some subjects are told to read the information with an eye toward explaining a hypothetical victory by one of the teams or the other. These subjects appear to selectively attend to information consistent with the outcome to be explained and to bias their interpretation of certain facts in a way that fits this outcome (e.g., a coaching change by one of the teams can be seen as a good or bad thing depending upon the outcome to be explained). These effects on processing the information in the message are exhibited in subsequent judgment and recall measures. Recall is biased toward facts consistent with the outcome explained, and judgments of the outcome of the game to be played are biased in the direction of the outcome recently explained. Thus, reading a message with the explaining of a hypothetical event as a goal has clear effects on message processing and on subsequent memory for facts and evaluations.

Other subjects in this paradigm were presented with the hypothetical explanation task only after first reading and encoding the information in the message. In this case, selective attention to and biased interpretation of the information in the message on the basis of the explanation task cannot operate. Yet subjects who explain a hypothetical outcome after reading the relevant message content also show subsequent biases in memory for facts in the message as well as biases in judgments of the game's outcome. Only when subjects read the message with instructions to form a general impression of the game and when they have available existing knowledge structures that allow them to form a strong impression of the game can they resist the biasing effects of an explanation task introduced after the message has been read (Hirt & Sherman, 1985). These findings indicate that the effects of explaining hypothetical events are not limited to attention and encoding phases of information processing. Even after the message has been encoded, effects at later stages in processing (e.g., at retrieval or judgment) continue to occur.

Both priming and the introduction of imagination-explanation tasks thus affect the way in which the information contained in a persuasive communication is processed. In addition, these effects appear to take place at various stages of message processing. First, they direct attention to one or another kind of information in the message. They may even determine whether the general processing adopted is systematic or heuristic in nature. Next, they introduce bias into the way in which ambiguous information in the message is interpreted. Moreover, they have effects on the memory for different items in the message. Finally, they appear to have direct effects on the subsequent evaluations and judgments that are relevant to the topic of the message.

It should be pointed out that priming and hypothetical explanation procedures are not merely oddball techniques used by social psychologists in the context of a laboratory experiment—procedures that are unlikely to have any relevance to natural situations involving persuasive messages. On the contrary, recipients of messages never approach these messages with an empty head. Recent thoughts, actions, and judgments are always part of the context of reading the message. Mood, for example, is known to prime certain categories and to affect subsequent responses (Isen & Levin, 1972; Isen, Shalker, Clark, & Karp, 1978). It is thus likely that mood during message processing will focus attention selectively on certain aspects of the message and will bias the interpretation of the facts in the message. Certain categories and ways of thinking are activated—whether by an experimenter or by natural life events and circumstances. Moreover, recipients typically approach the message with some goal. It may not always be the goal of explaining a hypothetical future outcome, but other goals as well will affect attentional and interpretive processes. The context in which a message is received will also have important effects on the interpretation of the message. One of the tenets of social judgment theory (Ostrom, 1970; Sherif & Hovland, 1961) is that the judgment of the position of a message determines its effect; and this judgment is very much affected by the contextual stimuli that will act as anchors during the reception of the message.

The point is that these "extra-message" goals, category activations, contextual cues, etc. may have important effects on the consequences of reading a communication. All relevant factors for effects on attitudes should not be looked for in the message itself or in factors directly related to the message.

ATTITUDE EXPRESSION FOLLOWING MESSAGE RECEPTION

Following message reception and consideration via heuristic or systematic processing, the recipient has presumably formed or changed attitudes toward the target object. In the laboratory, we usually ask subjects at this point in time to indicate their attitude toward the target issue. They must think about their evaluation, consolidate any relevant information, and arrive at a judgment—whether or not they had done this previously while reading the message. Whether this judgment occurs spontaneously as subjects read the message or not is a very important issue. Much recent work has been directed at the question of spontaneous vs. guided consolidation and expression of attitudes, attributions, and impressions (Carlston & Skowronski, 1986; Fazio, 1986; Fazio, Lenn, & Effrein, 1983–1984; Smith & Miller, 1983; and Winter & Uleman, 1984).

It is not yet clear when and under what conditions spontaneous judgments occur, but it is likely that in many cases the very measurement of attitudes does not tap into previously existing evaluations but rather creates these evaluations during the measurement process. The creation of these attitudes may then, of course, have important subsequent effects. When individuals receive persuasive messages in natural settings, no attitude measures are taken following message reception. This fact may account for some of the differences between the findings of attitude change research done in the laboratory (where attitude change is rather easy to achieve) as opposed to survey studies (where attitude change is often difficult to observe; Hovland, 1959). Fazio (1986) discusses many of these issues in his recent chapter.

Given that an individual has been asked to make an attitude judgment soon after the relevant persuasive message has been processed, the question remains concerning what factors affect the judgment at this point. Assuming that the determinants of a judgment are those factors that are most salient and accessible in memory at the time of the judgment, message relevant material could play a major role in the attitude judgment. Whatever aspects of the message were focused on (whether it be content relevant or peripheral cues) and whatever cognitive responses were actively made to the message during processing should still be highly accessible at the time of the judgment. These cognitive responses should be especially accessible because it has been demonstrated that self-generated stimuli become extremely accessible at later points in time (Slamecka & Graf, 1978). We have already seen that stimuli that are focused on during message reception have the greatest effect on the attitude judgment. Content factors are highly related to attitude judgments when central processing has been adopted, and peripheral factors are associated more with attitudinal judgments under heuristic processing.

In addition, the individual's original attitude and beliefs prior to the message may play a direct role in the attitude judgments. We might speculate that this is more likely to occur under heuristic processing than under central or systematic processing. With central processing, the recipient presumably has integrated the old and new information while reading the message content, and any attitude judgment would represent an expression of this integration. The prior attitude of the subject would have already had its effect by directing attention, biasing interpretation of the facts in the message, etc. Under the heuristic processing route, the prior attitude may not have entered into the processing. Rather simple rules were used to arrive at a judgment of the value of the message. However, now at attitude expression time, the individual might consult old attitudes and beliefs about the target topic as well as the heuristically derived conclusions about the message. Thus, with heuristic processing, old attitudes and recent judgments of the message might be integrated at the point in time where attitude judgments are called for. With central processing, the integration of old attitudes and recent message content and interpretation would have occurred at a quite different and an earlier stage in the process.

ATTITUDE EXPRESSION AT A LATER TIME

Although individuals are often asked to express their attitudes immediately after message reception (especially if the experiment was done in a laboratory), they might also be asked to make such an evaluative judgment at a much later point in time. What factors would determine these later judgments? Previous work on the sleeper effect clearly indicates that attitudes measured immediately after message reception may differ substantially from attitudes measured at a later point in time (Hovland & Weiss, 1951). And recently, the conditions leading to these effects and the processes underlying these differences have been identified (Gruder et al., 1978).

At the later point in time, the original message content and other message relevant factors might still be in memory. However, they will not be as salient or accessible as they were immediately following reception of the message. In addition, the previous attitudinal judgment (if one was indeed made) is stored in memory and can be used as a simple and direct basis for a subsequent attitude judgment, independent of any other information that is in memory (Lingle & Ostrom, 1981; Sherman et al., 1983). This distinction between memory-based and impression-based judgment is likely to be an important one in future research. The initial attitude that existed even prior to reception of the message is another potentially available basis for judgment. Finally, as Greenwald (1968) has shown, one must distinguish between the original message content and cues and the subject's cognitive responses to this content. Greenwald demonstrated that cognitive responses were more predictive of subsequent attitude judgments than was memory for message content. It is likely that this advantage for cognitive responses over message factors would increase as the time since reception of the message increases.

An important consideration here is the fact that at a point in time far removed from message reception neither the message content, the peripheral cues surrounding the message, nor the original cognitive responses of the subject are likely to be fully or accurately remembered. Schmidt and R. Sherman (1984) have investigated memory over time for the content of a persuasive communication. They employ Graesser and Nakamura's (1982) schema-copy-plus-tag model to capture the process. This model assumes that, upon reading the message, a subject identifies a relevant schema and enters into memory all schema relevant information (whether or not that information was actually seen in the message). As time passes, the subject becomes increasingly unable to distinguish between actually seen and unseen schema-typical items. In addition, accurate recall for these typical items is higher than recall for schema-atypical items. The point is that to relate *accurate* memory of message content (or cognitive responses to the message) to a subsequent attitudinal judgment is not very meaningful. One should be more concerned with what the subject believes was originally in the message (both accurate and inaccurate items) at the time that the subsequent judgment is rendered.

The subject's level of knowledge (or schematicity) for the topic of the message is likely to be an important factor here—as it was at earlier phases in the process involving choice between a central and peripheral processing route and in biasing the interpretation of the message content when central processing is adopted. As the message is initially processed, the relevant schema is activated if it is available. Subjects with more fully developed knowledge structures are more likely to have these structures activated. This schema activation may be thought of as an instance of categorization and may be initiated automatically. In addition, once the appropriate schema is activated, schema relevant thoughts and embellishments will be generated automatically. When any category is activated, instances of that category and the structure of the category is activated inescapably, probably through a process of spreading activation. Thus, when a subject is presented with the facts $A > B$ and $B > C$, $A > C$ is inescapably generated; and at a later point in time the subject cannot determine which of the relations were given and which were not (Potts, 1972). In the same way, schema consistent facts are inescapably generated once a schema is activated (Cantor & Mischel, 1979; Wyer, 1980).

As indicated previously, changes in memory over time and error intrusions that enter memory can be used to account for the sleeper effect in attitude change research (Gruder et al., 1978). Similarly, M. Ross and his colleagues (Ross, McFarland, Conway, & Zanna, 1983; Ross, McFarland, & Fletcher, 1981) have demonstrated how attitude change can lead to mismemories of the past that can produce changes in subsequent judgments and behavior. We may analyze attitude judgments at a time that is distant from the reception of the message in terms of whether the initial processing of the communication was systematic or heuristic. It should be the case that message relevant factors (content bound in the case of systematic processing and peripheral cues in the case of heuristic processing) and initial cognitive reactions to them will play a bigger role at this later time of judgment when the processing was systematic. This is because such central processing is more extensive and occurs at deeper levels than heuristic processing. This indicates that attitude change following systematic or central processing should be more persistent than attitude change following peripheral processing. Several recent studies have shown this to be true (Chaiken, 1980; Chaiken & Eagly, 1983; Petty, Cacioppo, & Heesacker, 1985). Attitude change thus appears to last longer if it is based on topic relevant thinking, careful and effortful assessment, and self-generated topic-relevant cognitions. One possible reason for this is that the factors responsible for the original attitude judgment have been processed more deeply and will be more accessible at the time of later judgments. Of course, it is also possible that attitude changes achieved through central processing are simply more resistant to subsequent attitude change attempts and are likely to be more persistent for this reason.

Kruglanski (1985), however, argues that central processing may not always lead to more confidently held or more persistent attitudes. He speculates that in certain cases attitudes derived from heuristic processing may be held with extreme confidence and persistence. For example, if a message recipient is strongly identified with the communicator of a message (e.g., a cult member listening to the cult leader), the attractiveness of the source will be the main determinant of attitude change and will lead to very persistent and confidently held attitudes, independent of the quality of the message content. The relative strength and persistence of attitudes derived from Kelman's (1958) processes of identification and internalization (processes that appear to be akin to heuristic and systematic processes) have not yet been fully specified.

We have to this point discussed the roles of the recipient's initial attitude, the message relevant factors and cognitive responses to them, and the attitude judgment following the persuasive message. Other factors are likely to affect subsequent attitude expression as well. Of course, any new information received in the interim between attitude measurments will affect a later judgment. So too will any other attitude relevant process such as mere exposure or classical or operant conditioning procedures. We have already seen how the introduction of hypothetical explanation tasks after message reception can affect subsequent evaluative judgments. The effects of experiences subsequent to message reception can affect later attitude expression either through their impact on the subjects' recall or through reconstruction of the message content or perhaps even in a more direct way.

Aside from attitude relevant experiences, there may be additional factors that are salient and accessible at the time of the later attitude judgments that would have important effects on these judgments. Such factors might include general mood, recently activated categories, or the situational context in which the attitude is measured. Fazio, Powell, and Herr (1983) have recently shown that the priming of general evaluative categories can affect reactions to a target as a result of the accessibility of these evaluative categories. Perhaps one is more likely to respond positively or negatively to any attitudinal inquiry if general positively or negatively toned items have been recently and frequently activated.

TOPIC RELEVANT BEHAVIOR

Up to now we have discussed the message processing and attitude judgment phases. But the most important consequences of reading a persuasive communication no doubt lie in the subsequent behaviors that are adopted with respect to the target of the message. At some point in time, the message recipient will be confronted with the target object or issue and will have to make a behavioral decision. The question is, "What drives this decision and how can we understand the behavior adopted in terms of some of the previous processes that have been discussed?" Of course, much research and theorizing has been devoted to the general issue of attitude-behavior consistency in recent years (see Zanna, Higgins, & Herman [1982] for a recent review). Because this literature has been carefully considered elsewhere (Sherman & Fazio, 1983; Zanna, Higgins, & Herman, 1983), I would prefer to limit the analysis of attitude-behavior relations to discussion of the kinds of processes that have been raised earlier in this chapter.

One issue to consider is the extent of the attitude-behavior relation as a function of whether the persuasive communication was processed centrally or peripherally. For several reasons, it is more likely that attitudes developed through the central or systematic processing route will guide subsequent behavior than will attitudes developed via peripheral or heuristic processing. As indicated earlier, central or systematic processing of message content generally leads to attitudes that are held with more confidence and attitudes that are more resistant to change. This stability will of course increase the correspondence between message derived attitudes and subsequent behavior. In addition, central processing involves a greater depth of processing than does the use of simplifying heuristic principles. This should result in attitudes that are more readily accessible upon exposure to the target issue and thus are more likely to be used in the behavioral decision. Recent research has indicated that conditions that foster high motivation for processing the content of a message or high ability for doing so, conditions that lead to systematic processing, do produce high attitude-behavior correlations (Petty, Cacioppo, & Schumann, 1983; Schumann, Petty, & Cacioppo, 1985). In fact, when peripheral processing is engaged, peripheral cues such as communicator attractiveness enhance liking for the target issue but do not produce a change in behavioral intentions. In addition, people who are high in the need for cognition (Cacioppo & Petty, 1982) and thus are likely to process message content systematically showed greater attitude-behavior consistency in voting than did those who were low in the need for cognition (Cacioppo, Petty, & Rodriguez, 1985). It thus appears that central message processing produces attitudes that are not only more persistent and more resistant to change but in addition are more predictive of subsequent behavior.

Given that attitudes do predict behavior under certain conditions of attitude formation and expression, the important question is how this process occurs. Sherman and Fazio (1983) discuss two general kinds of models to account for attitude-behavior consistency. These models differ in many respects, particularly in terms of whether the process is automatic or involves attention and conscious decision-making.

Fazio, Powell, and Herr (1983) have proposed one such process model of the attitude-behavior relation. The key initial step in this process is the accessing from memory of one's attitude toward the object upon observation of the attitude object. This access is assumed to be automatic and inescapable—a spontaneous association of the object and its evaluative representation upon exposure to the object. Several factors have been shown to determine this automatic attitude accessibility. Prior and repeated expression of the attitude will strengthen the object-evaluation association and increase the likelihood of attitude accessibility (Fazio, Chen, McDonel, & Sherman, 1982). In addition, direct experience with the attitude object is likely to enhance the probability of spontaneous attitude accessibility (Fazio, Powell, & Herr, 1983; Fazio & Zanna, 1981). Attitudes developed through reading a message are probably not as likely to be accessed spontaneously at a later time as are attitudes developed through other procedures such as role-playing or direct experience. However, the more careful consideration of message content and the greater effort involved in central as opposed to peripheral processing make it more likely that subsequent spontaneous activation of attitudes will be achieved following central processing.

Once the attitude is spontaneously accessed upon observation of the relevant object, it will guide perception of that object. This immediate perception will entail selective attention and biased interpretation so that a perception consistent with the accessed attitude is achieved. Based on this perception, a behavioral response to the object will be adopted so that the behavior is likely to be consistent with the attitude that gave rise to the selective perception. Situational cues can also prompt the accessibility of attitudes and thus enhance attitude-behavior consistency (Snyder & Kendzierski, 1982; Snyder & Swann, 1976). It is also possible that increased self-awareness (Wicklund, 1975) can render one's attitudes more accessible. Under conditions of heightened self-awareness (as achieved by such manipulations as looking into a mirror) individuals are in fact more likely to act in accordance with their attitudes (Carver, 1975). Similarly, Abelson (1982) describes various individuating conditions that increase the accessibility of one's attitudes and thereby increase attitude-behavior consistency.

This process of automatic and spontaneous attitude activation is probably the most prevalent process underlying attitude-behavior consistency. A conscious and attentive assessment of one's attitude prior to each and every behavior would be incredibly inefficient and time consuming. Imagine going through a process similar to Ajzen and Fishbein's (1980) reasoned action before engaging in each and every behavioral act. Yet at times we must be more careful and adopt such a reasoned process to be sure that we are making the correct decision. At these times we are likely to actively and attentively generate beliefs about the outcomes of the behavior, combine these beliefs with evaluations of the outcomes, assign weights, and in this conscious and controlled way decide upon an appropriate behavior. Here the process is attentive, although, of course, the attention drawn to particular beliefs or outcomes could be automatically engaged (and effortless). Sherman and Fazio (1983) suggest that such deliberate reasoning processes are activated by the importance of the behavioral decision. The same kinds of factors (high motivation, high ability, self-relevance) that engage systematic and central processing in the reading of a persuasive communication engage reasoned action in behavioral decision-making. In addition, novel behaviors, where prior attitudes cannot be automatically activated, require more controlled and attentive processes.

Most daily behaviors are probably neither sufficiently consequential nor sufficiently novel to induce a careful and controlled analysis. Instead, these behaviors are likely to be adopted in a fairly spontaneous and nonreflective manner. They will be guided by past attitudes if these attitudes are spontaneously activated. If not, the behavior is likely to flow from other factors in the situation that are not attitudinally based (e.g., norms, expectancies, contextual cues). In this case, the behavior will be determined by those features of the immediate situation that are sufficiently salient to influence one's perceptions.

In line with this last point, we must keep in mind that there are other forces on behavior aside from preexistent attitudes. Ajzen and Fishbein (1980) discuss the role of situational constraints such as norms or expectations. Of course, the influence of these factors involves a reasoned and attentive process according to Ajzen and Fishbein. However, it is also possible that situational constraints and expectations may render a definition of the situation in a far more automatic way.

Just as attitude judgments may be affected by thoughts, moods, primed categories, etc. that are salient in one's head at the time of the judgment, so too can behaviors be activated and energized by such factors. Primed categories, previous activities, and contextual cues can indeed guide current behavior. Berkowitz's (1974; Berkowitz & LePage, 1967) work on the effectiveness of subtle cues and previous experiences in guiding aggressive responses is just such an example. More recently Berkowitz (1984) has discussed the role of mass media presentations and articles in priming prosocial and antisocial behavior in the audience.

Certain responses can also be chronically prepotent, as is the case with many phobic responses. In addition, factors that are independent of one's attitudes or beliefs about an object or issue can render certain behavioral responses temporarily more potent. In analyzing compliance and social influence, Cialdini (1985) discusses many examples of agreement sets or "click-whirr" behavioral sequences that make compliance behavior more likely—regardless of the initial attitudes of the individual. Scripted behavior sequences (Abelson, 1976; Bower, Black, & Turner, 1979; Langer & Abelson, 1972) have the same quality. Hornstein and his colleagues (Hornstein, LaKind, Frankel, & Manne, 1975; Holloway, Tucker, & Hornstein, 1977) showed that hearing prosocial or antisocial news items on the radio while "waiting for the experiment to begin" affected subjects' behavior in a Prisoners Dilemma game. Likewise, Wilson and Capitman (1982) demonstrated that passive exposure to certain behavior scripts (e.g., "boy meets girl") made certain interpersonal behaviors more likely in a subsequent social encounter. The work of Isen and her colleagues (Isen & Levin, 1972; Isen et al., 1978) on mood effects on behavior indicates similar kinds of activation effects on behavioral decision making.

Returning for a moment to Fazio et al.'s (1983) model of attitude-behavior consistency, I would like to focus on the importance of the automatic activation of associations as stimuli spontaneously call attention to certain evaluative thoughts or behaviors. I am convinced that this is a critical aspect of human social behavior. Consider our stream of consciousness (or stream of conversation or stream of behavior). Thoughts quickly and spontaneously lead to other thoughts, and words and phrases and sentences and topics quickly lead to other words and topics during conversation. Imagine having to attend to every thought or action and to stop at each point during an interaction to decide what should come next. Fortunately our own thoughts and behaviors spontaneously lead to subsequent thoughts and actions in a way that makes both private thought and social interaction smooth and efficient.

Likewise the ability of external stimuli to call forth associations automatically is very important. As we have seen, this can be achieved by category priming, mood induction, or the spontaneous elicitation of attitudes by the presentation of an object. The attention grabbing quality of stimuli is clearly important in the effectiveness of persuasive communications and the relative importance of different features of the messages. In teaching undergraduate social psychology, I have used the process of automatic associations to explain the consequences of lovers being apart for a period of time (a summer vacation; dual careers in different cities). The question here is whether "absence makes the heart grow fonder" or "out of sight, out of mind." One way to predict which outcome will obtain can be based on the extent to which stimuli in one's environment automatically elicit thoughts of the distant lover. If shared songs, favorite restaurants, and special objects and events spontaneously lead to thoughts of one's lover and if this happens frequently, it is likely that the heart will grow fonder. On the other hand, if the surrounding stimuli do not automatically elicit such thoughts and feelings and they come only after a conscious and controlled decision to think about the other, I am afraid that the relationship is in jeopardy. This would suggest that if separated lovers are in enviroments that contain many automatic reminders of each other, the relationship is likely to survive the separation. If the enviroments are novel and without *automatic* reminders, the couple should at least be sure to send each other plenty of such spontaneous associative stimuli.

Perhaps nowhere is the automatic and inescapable calling forth of attention by stimuli so important as it is in psychopathology. Much of what is considered mental illness can be thought of as inappropriate or counter-productive associations—compulsive thoughts and behaviors, automatic negative interpretations of events and outcomes by depressed clients, anxieties, phobias, etc. These reactions can be characterized as uncontrollable and inescapable, the hallmarks of automatism. The question, then, is how to interfere with these spontaneous associations, thoughts, and behaviors? How do we disautomatize something? Although we now understand something about the processes by which automatic responses develop (Schneider & Shiffrin, 1977; Shiffrin & Dumais, 1981; Shiffrin & Schneider, 1977), we still know very little about how to modify or reverse responses that have become automatic. Certain reflexes can be brought under attentional control. For example, blinking has been modified by introducing attention to foreground stimuli (Anthony & Graham, 1983). However, in general, automatic patterns of behavior are extremely difficult to control. For example, performance on the Stroop task is very difficult to improve (Dyer, 1973). The standard Stroop task requires a subject to name the ink colors in which a series of words are printed. In the control condition, the words do not contain any color names. In the interference condition, the letters spell a color that is different from the ink color in which the word is printed (e.g., RED printed in blue ink). The automatic interference in this condition is difficult to avoid. The standard interpretation of this interference is that the printed name of the color is encoded automatically, despite any attempt by the subject to ignore the printing. This produces a response tendency that conflicts with a different response required to name the ink color.

Is direct weakening and reversal of automatic behavior possible? Many attitude change techniques involve counter-priming or the activation of alternative evaluative associations, and many therapy techniques are similarly designed to break strong and spontaneous cognitive or behavioral associations with stimuli. But, as we know, these responses are quite difficult to control—and they are certainly not changeable by information based arguments (e.g., "There really is nothing to fear from snakes.").

Shiffrin (in press) suggests that some automatic processes may be controllable by attentive means, especially when such attentive processing provides some of the contextual stimuli that trigger the automatic process. By attentively controlling the input to an automatic process, indirect control over the process itself can be achieved. This might suggest that making certain that an individual is attentive to something else when the critical stimulus (the one that automatically elicits the undesirable behavior) appears will solve the problem. When attention to the critical stimulus is limited and the capacity to respond to it is interfered with, perhaps the automatic association will weaken. However, we are of course dealing with automatic and inescapable responses that do not use up capacity. We also know that automatic attention will be drawn to stimuli (e.g., one's own name at a cocktail party) even when one is engrossed in other attention-demanding behavior. And, of course, Bargh (1982; Bargh & Pietromonaco, 1982) has demonstrated how even subliminal exposure to stimuli will automatically prime categories and render certain behaviors prepotent.

The question of disautomatization is quite relevant to issues of attitude stability and change. Fazio (1986) has suggested that attitudes are strengthened and attitude-behavior consistency is assured only when the attitude object automatically calls forth the attitude upon its presentation. Once this automatic association between object and attitude develops, can the attitude ever really change? Can the automatic and spontaneous association be broken? If so, how? In any case, an important question for the future will be how to weaken automatic attention grabbing features and stimuli and how to weaken spontaneous associations as a way of changing attitudes. If this discussion reminds the reader of Staats' (1967) conception of attitudes as classically conditioned and spontaneous responses to stimuli, the similarity is intended. However, the mechanisms suggested in the present chapter for the formation of such attitudes may be quite different from the traditional classical conditioning formation mechanisms. In addition, the present view of attitudes focuses far more on the cognitive components of these attitudes than does the Staats formulation.

CONCLUSIONS AND PERSPECTIVES

All this thinking about the entire sequence of attitude formation, change, expression, and translation into behavior (especially as they occur in response to a persuasive message) requires that we now step back and think a little bit about where this research began, where it has been, where it is at present, and where it will be (or should be) in the future. The modern work on the effectiveness of persuasive messages began of course with Carl Hovland and his colleagues at Yale. The approach of that research endeavor was a "who says what to whom and with what effect" approach. The main goal of the research was simply to identify and to describe communicator, message, and receiver factors that affected the effectiveness of a persuasive communication. The work began with simple designs involving one or two variables at a time, building to more and more variables and higher order interactions until the effects became unwieldy to describe and difficult to comprehend. The work was thus primarily descriptive. In terms of process, the major assumption is that receivers rationally process the information contained in the message. They attend to and comprehend the information in the communication and integrate this information with past beliefs in order to arrive at a decision about whether or not to yield to the message.

The next (and current) generation of research began to be far more process oriented and far more cognitive in its approach. The work already cited by McGuire, Greenwald, Cacioppo and Petty, and Chaiken and Eagly are representative of this "second generational" approach. Several things became clear from this work: (1) The process of attitude change through the presentation of persuasive messages was not entirely a rational process, (2) there was more to the effectiveness of a persuasive communication than attending to and understanding the message content, and (3) there was more than one process route to persuasion.

Another advance of this work over previous research was the increased focus on measures that went beyond the immediate effects of the message on attitudes. Not only was greater interest taken in attitude measures that extended beyond the time immediately following message reception, but the relation between message induced attitudes and subsequent behaviors and judgments began to attract more and more attention. Although process theories of persuasion have begun to abound, these theories are still quite rudimentary. They identify the kinds of information and input that receivers use as they read a message, but they tell us less about the actual cognitive processes involved in acting upon this input.

I believe that the next generation of research should concentrate on the further development of process models at each stage. Fazio (1986) has been systematically developing and testing a process model of the attitude-behavior relation stage. Research has been going on in his laboratory to clarify the various substages (some potentially automatic and some controlled) involved in the determination of behavior from prior attitudes. We need similar specification and empirical testing of all the earlier stages in the process through which attitudes originally form and change. I believe that a key factor in this understanding will be a focus on attentional mechanisms. Throughout this chapter I have indicated the importance of the allocation of attention and the operation of attentive vs. automatic processes. Different stimuli in the message content, in the more peripheral aspects of the message, in the surrounding situation, and in the subject's head all vie and compete for attention. Some of these stimuli automatically draw attention and thus inhibit the allocation of attention to the other factors. Where attention is allocated determines to a large extent the consequences of reading a persuasive communication. Yet we know little about the determinants of attention allocation during message reading. We know little about the automatic and controlled processes involved in this allocation of attention. We know little about the relative importance or the interactive effects of message factors, situational factors, and intraindividual factors in the attentional process. With regard to intraindividual factors, knowledge structures and schemas have been used in explanatory ways to understand the processing of trait relevant information. But less of this work has been done in the area of persuasion. With few exceptions (Cacioppo, Petty, & Sidera, 1982), the role of schemas in attitude change research has not been seriously pursued. Yet cognitive organization and structure obviously play an important role in selective attention to message information, interpretation and encoding of this information, the choice of a central or peripheral persuasion route, memory for and embellishment of message relevant information, and reconstruction of such information in memory at a later point in time. Procedures that affect the accessibility and activation of cognitive structures (e.g., priming, imagination-explanation tasks) must also be understood in terms of their potential role in the persuasion process.

Finally, it is time to begin to integrate the entire sequence in a way such as that outlined in Fig. 3.1. These different phases are not separate and independent but rather are parts of a whole sequence where each previous phase plays an important role in the next phase. I, for one, am finally beginning to feel as though I understand what attitudes are, how they develop and change, and how attitudes get expressed in subsequent judgments and behavior. I used to have categorized in memory the results of hundreds of isolated attitude change studies. I knew how certain factors affected attitudes in each particular study, but I always had the feeling that these were rather specialized findings of limited relevance for understanding what attitudes were in general or how they operated. In the present attempt to look at the "big picture" I believe that important general issues have at least been raised if not yet resolved. And I think that the application of the cognitive principles and process approach to social influence has been largely responsible for this increase in understanding—and I am hopeful that it will continue.

REFERENCES

Abelson, R. P. (1976). Script processing in attitude formation and decision making. In J. S. Carroll & J. W. Payne (Eds.), *Cognition and social behavior*. Hillsdale, NJ: Lawrence Erlbaum Associates.

Abelson, R. P. (1982). Three modes of attitude-behavior consistency. In M. P. Zanna, E. T. Higgins, & C. P. Herman (Eds.), *Consistency in social behavior: The Ontario symposium* (Vol. 2, pp. 131–146). Hillsdale, NJ: Prentice Hall.

Ajzen, I., & Fishbein, M. (1980). *Understanding attitudes and predicting social behavior*. Englewood Cliffs, NJ: Prentice Hall.

Anderson, C. A., Lepper, M. R., & Ross, L. (1980). Perseverance of social theories: The role of explanation in the persistence of discredited information. *Journal of Personality and Social Psychology, 39*, 1037–1049.

Anthony, B. J., & Graham, F. K. (1983). Evidence for sensory-selective set in young infants. *Science, 220*, 742–744.

Bargh, J. A. (1982). Attention and automaticity in the processing of self-relevant information. *Journal of Personality and Social Psychology, 43*, 425–436.

Bargh, J. A. (1984). Automatic and conscious processing of social information. In R. S. Wyer & T. K. Srull (Eds.), *Handbook of social cognition* (Vol. 3, pp. 1–43). Hillsdale, NJ: Lawrence Erlbaum Associates.

Bargh, J. A., & Pietromonaco, P. (1982). Automatic information processing and social perception: The influence of trait information presented outside of conscious awareness on impression formation. *Journal of Personality and Social Psychology, 43*, 437–449.

Berkowitz, L. (1974). Some determinants of impulsive aggression: Role of mediated associations with reinforcements for aggression. *Psychological Review, 81*, 165–176.

Berkowitz, L. (1984). Some effects of thoughts on anti- and prosocial influences of media events: A cognitive-neoassociation analysis. *Psychological Bulletin, 95*, 410–427.

Berkowitz, L., & LePage, A. (1967). Weapons as aggression-eliciting stimuli. *Journal of Personality and Social Psychology, 7*, 202–207.

Bower, G. H., Black, J. B., & Turner, T. J. (1979). Scripts in memory for text. *Cognitive Psychology, 11*, 177–220.

Bruner, J. S. (1957). On perceptual readiness. *Psychological Review, 64*, 123–152.

Cacioppo, J. T., & Petty, R. E. (1982). The need for cognition. *Journal of Personality and Social Psychology, 42*, 116–131.

Cacioppo, J. T., & Petty, R. E. (1985). Central and peripheral routes to persuasion: The role of message repetition. In A. Mitchell & L. Alwitt (Eds.), *Psychological processes and advertising effects*. Hillsdale, NJ: Lawrence Erlbaum Associates.

Cacioppo, J. T., Petty, R. E., & Rodriguez, R. (1985). *Cognitive elaboration, attitude persistence, and behavioral prediction: An individual differences perspective.* Unpublished manuscript, University of Iowa, Iowa City, IA.

Cacioppo, J. T., Petty, R. E., & Sidera, J. (1982). The effects of a salient self-schema on the evaluation of proattitudinal editorials: Top-down versus bottom-up message processing. *Journal of Experimental Social Psychology, 18,* 324–338.

Cantor, N., & Mischel, W. (1979). Prototypes in person perception. In L. Berkowitz (Ed.), *Advances in experimental social psychology* (Vol. 12). New York: Academic Press.

Carlston, D. E., & Skowronski, J. J. (1986). Trait memory and behavior memory: The effects of alternative pathways on impression judgment response times. *Journal of Personality and Social Psychology, 50,* 5–13.

Carroll, J. S. (1978). The effect of imagining an event on expectations for the event: An interpretation in terms of the availability heuristic. *Journal of Experimental Social Psychology, 14,* 88–96.

Carver, C. S. (1975). Physical aggression as a function of objective self-awareness and attitudes toward punishment. *Journal of Experimental Social Psychology, 11,* 510–519.

Chaiken, S. (1980). Heuristic versus systematic information processing and the use of source versus message cues in persuasion. *Journal of Personality and Social Psychology, 39,* 752–766.

Chaiken, S., Axsom, D., Hicks, A. P., Yates, S. M., & Wilson, D. K. (1985). *Priming simple decision rules in persuasion settings.* Unpublished manuscript, Vanderbilt University, Nashville, TN.

Chaiken, S., & Eagly, A. H. (1983). Communication modality as a determinant of persuasion: The role of communicator salience. *Journal of Personality and Social Psychology, 45,* 241–256.

Cialdini, R. B. (1985). *Influence: Science and practice.* Glenview, IL: Scott, Foresman and Company.

Dyer, F. N. (1973). The Stroop phenomenon and its use in the study of perceptual, cognitive and response processes. *Memory & Cognition, 1,* 106–120.

Eagly, A. H., & Chaiken, S. (1984). Cognitive theories of persuasion. In L. Berkowitz (Ed.), *Advances in experimental social psychology* (Vol. 17). New York: Academic Press.

Eagly, A. H., & Warren, R. (1976). Intelligence, comprehension, and opinion change. *Journal of Personality, 44,* 226–242.

Fazio, R. H. (1986). How do attitudes guide behavior? In R. M. Sorrentino & E. T. Higgins (Eds.), *The handbook of motivation and cognition: Foundations of social behavior* (pp. 204–243). New York: Guilford Press.

Fazio, R. H., Chen, J., McDonel, E. C., & Sherman, S. J. (1982). Attitude accessibility, attitude-behavior consistency, and the strength of the object-evaluation association. *Journal of Experimental Social Psychology, 18,* 339–357.

Fazio, R. H., Lenn, T. M., & Effrein, E. A. (1983–1984). Spontaneous attitude formation. *Social Cognition, 2,* 217–234.

Fazio, R. H., Powell, M. C., & Herr, P. M. (1983). Toward a process model of the attitude-behavior relation: Accessing one's attitude upon mere observation of the attitude object. *Journal of Personality and Social Psychology, 44,* 723–735.

Fazio, R. H., & Zanna, M. P. (1981). Direct experience and attitude-behavior consistency. In L. Berkowitz (Ed.), *Advances in experimental social psychology* (Vol. 14, pp. 161–202). New York: Academic Press.

Feather, N. T. (1963). Cognitive dissonance, sensitivity, and evaluation. *Journal of Abnormal and Social Psychology, 66,* 157–164.

Festinger, L. (1957). *A theory of cognitive dissonance.* Stanford, CA: Stanford University Press.

Freedman, J. L. (1965). Preference for dissonant information. *Journal of Personality and Social Psychology, 2,* 287–290.

Graesser, A. C., & Nakamura, G. V. (1982). The impact of a schema on comprehension and memory. *The Psychology of Learning and Memory, 16,* 60–109.

Greenwald, A. G. (1968). Cognitive learning, cognitive response to persuasion, and attitude change. In A. Greenwald, T. Brock, & T. Ostrom (Eds.), *Psychological foundations of attitudes* (pp. 148–170). New York: Academic Press.

Gruder, C. L., Cook, T. D., Hennigan, K. M., Flay, B. R., Alessis, C., & Halamaj, J. (1978). Empirical tests of the absolute sleeper effect predicted from the discounting cue hypothesis. *Journal of Personality and Social Psychology, 36,* 1061–1074.

Hicks, A. P., & Chaiken, S. (1984). *Use of the expertise/agreement heuristic in assessing the validity of a persuasive message.* Unpublished manuscript, Vanderbilt University, Nashville, TN.

Higgins, E. T., & Chaires, W. M. (1980). Accessibility of interrelational constructs: Implications for stimulus encoding and creativity. *Journal of Experimental Social Psychology, 16,* 348–361.

Higgins, E. T., & King, G. A. (1981). Accessibility of social constructs: Information-processing consequences of individual and contextual variability. In N. Cantor & J. F. Kihlstrom (Eds.), *Personality, cognition, and social interaction.* Hillsdale, NJ: Lawrence Erlbaum Associates.

Higgins, E. T., King, G. A., & Mavin, G. H. (1982). Individual construct accessibility and subjective impressions and recall. *Journal of Personality and Social Psychology, 43,* 35–47.

Higgins, E. T., Rholes, W. S., & Jones, C. R. (1977). Category accessibility and impression formation. *Journal of Experimental Social Psychology, 12,* 141–154.

Hirt, E. R., & Sherman, S. J. (1985). The role of prior knowledge in explaining hypothetical events. *Journal of Experimental Social Psychology, 21,* 519–543.

Holloway, S., Tucker, L., & Hornstein, H. A. (1977). The effects of social and nonsocial information on interpersonal behavior of males: The news makes news. *Journal of Personality and Social Psychology, 35,* 514–522.

Hornstein, H. A., LaKind, E., Frankel, G., & Manne, S. (1975). Effects of knowledge about remote social events on prosocial behavior, social conception, and mood. *Journal of Personality and Social Psychology, 32,* 1038–1046.

Hovland, C. I. (1959). Reconciling conflicting results derived from experimental and survey studies of attitude change. *American Psychologist, 14,* 8–17.

Hovland, C. I., Janis, I. L., & Kelley, H. H. (1953). *Communication and persuasion.* New Haven, CT: Yale University Press.

Hovland, C. I., & Weiss, W. (1951). The influence of source credibility on communication effectiveness. *Public Opinion Quarterly, 15,* 635–650.

Isen, A. M., & Levin, P. F. (1972). The effect of feeling good on helping: Cookies and kindness. *Journal of Personality and Social Psychology, 21,* 384–388.

Isen, A. M., Shalker, T. E., Clark, M. S., & Karp, L. (1978). Affect, accessibility of material in behavior, and memory: A cognitive loop? *Journal of Personality and Social Psychology, 36,* 1–12.

Kelman, H. C. (1958). Compliance, identification, and internalization: Three processes of attitude change. *Journal of Conflict Resolution, 2,* 51–60.

Kruglanski, A. W. (1985). *Attitudes as opinions.* Unpublished manuscript, Tel-Aviv University.

Langer, E. J., & Abelson, R. P. (1972). The semantics of asking a favor: How to succeed in getting help without really dying. *Journal of Personality and Social Psychology, 24,* 26–32.

LaRue, A., & Olejnik, A. B. (1980). Cognitive "priming" of principled moral thought. *Personality and Social Psychology Bulletin, 6,* 413–416.

Lingle, J. H., & Ostrom, T. M. (1981). Principles of memory and cognition in attitude formation. In R. E. Petty, T. Ostrom, & T. Brock (Eds.), *Cognitive responses in persuasion.* Hillsdale, NJ: Lawrence Erlbaum Associates.

McGuire, W. J. (1968). Personality and attitude change: An information-processing theory. In A. G. Greenwald, T. C. Brock, & T. M. Ostrom (Eds.), *Psychology foundations of attitudes* (pp. 171–196). New York: Academic Press.

McGuire, W. J. (1972). Attitude change: The information-processing paradigm. In C. G. McClintock (Ed.). *Experimental social psychology.* New York: Holt, Rinehart & Winston.

McGuire, W. J., & Millman, S. (1965). Anticipatory belief lowering following forewarning of a persuasive attack. *Journal of Personality and Social Psychology, 2,* 471–479.

Millman, S. (1968). Anxiety, comprehension, and susceptibility to social influence. *Journal of Personality and Social Psychology, 9,* 251–256.

Neely, J. H. (1977). Semantic priming and retrieval from lexical memory: Roles of inhibitionless spreading activation and limited-capacity attention. *Journal of Experimental Psychology: General, 106,* 226–254.

Ostrom, T. M. (1970). Perspective as a determinant of attitude change. *Journal of Experimental Social Psychology, 6,* 280–292.

Pallak, S. R. (1983). Salience of a communicator's physical attractiveness and persuasion: A heuristic versus systematic processing interpretation. *Social Cognition, 2,* 156–168.

Pallak, S. R., Murroni, E., & Koch, J. (1983). Communicator attractiveness and expertise, emotional versus rational appeals, and persuasion: A heuristic versus systematic processing interpretation. *Social Cognition, 2,* 120–139.

Petty, R. E., & Cacioppo, J. T. (1983). Central and peripheral routes to persuasion: Application to advertising. In L. Percy & A. Woodside (Eds.), *Advertising and consumer psychology* (pp. 3–23). Lexington, MA: Lexington Books, D. C. Heath.

Petty, R. E., & Cacioppo, J. T. (1984). The effects of involvement on responses to argument quantity and quality: Central and peripheral routes to persuasion. *Journal of Personality and Social Psychology, 46,* 69–81.

Petty, R. E., & Cacioppo, J. T. (1985). The elaboration likelihood model of persuasion. In L. Berkowitz (Ed.), *Advances in experimental social psychology* (Vol. 19). New York: Academic Press.

Petty, R. E., Cacioppo, J. T., & Goldman, R. (1981). Personal involvement as a determinant of argument-based persuasion. *Journal of Personality and Social Psychology, 41,* 847–855.

Petty, R. E., Cacioppo, J. T., & Heesacker, M. (1985). *Persistence of persuasion: A test of the elaboration likelihood model.* Unpublished manuscript, University of Missouri, Columbia, MO.

Petty, R. E., Cacioppo, J. T., & Schumann, D. (1983). Central and peripheral routes to advertising effectiveness: The moderating role of involvement. *Journal of Consumer Research, 10,* 134–148.

Petty, R. E., Wells, G. L., & Brock, T. C. (1976). Distraction can enhance or reduce yielding to propaganda: Thought disruption versus effort justification. *Journal of Personality and Social Psychology, 34,* 874–884.

Potts, G. R. (1972). Information processing strategies used in the encoding of linear orderings. *Journal of Verbal Learning and Verbal Behavior, 11,* 727–740.

Ross, L., Lepper, M. R., & Hubbard, M. (1975). Perseverance in self-perception and social perception: Biased attributional processes in the debriefing paradigm. *Journal of Personality and Social Psychology, 32,* 880–892.

Ross, M., McFarland, C., Conway, M., & Zanna, M. P. (1983). Reciprocal relation between attitudes and behavior recall: Committing people to newly formed attitudes. *Journal of Personality and Social Psychology, 45,* 257–267.

Ross, M., McFarland, C., & Fletcher, G. J. O. (1981). The effect of attitude on the recall of personal histories. *Journal of Personality and Social Psychology, 40,* 627–634.

Schmidt, D. F., & Sherman, R. C. (1984). Memory for persuasive messages: A test of a schema-copy-plus-tag model. *Journal of Personality and Social Psychology, 47,* 17–25.

Schneider, W., & Shiffrin, R. M. (1977). Controlled and automatic human information processing: I. Detection, search, and attention. *Psychological Review, 84,* 1–66.

Schumann, D., Petty, R. E., & Cacioppo, J. T. (1985). *Effects of involvement, repetition, and variation on responses to advertisements.* Unpublished manuscript, University of Missouri, Columbia, MO.

Sherif, M., & Hovland, C. I. (1961). *Social judgment: Assimilation and contrast effects in communication and attitude change.* New Haven, CT: Yale University Press.

Sherman, S. J., & Corty, E. (1984). Cognitive heuristics. In R. S. Wyer, Jr. & T. K. Srull (Eds.), *Handbook of social cognition* (Vol. 1, pp. 189–286). Hillsdale, NJ: Lawrence Erlbaum Associates.

Sherman, S. J., & Fazio, R. H. (1983). Parallels between attitudes and traits as predictors of behavior. *Journal of Personality, 51,* 308–345.

Sherman, S. J., Skov, R. B., Hervitz, E. F., & Stock, C. G. (1981). The effects of explaining hypothetical future events: From possibility to probability to actuality and beyond. *Journal of Experimental Social Psychology, 17,* 142–158.

Sherman, S. J., Zehner, K. S., Johnson, J., & Hirt, E. R. (1983). Social explanation: The role of timing, set, and recall on subjective likelihood estimates. *Journal of Personality and Social Psychology, 44,* 1127–1143.

Shiffrin, R. M. (in press). Attention. In R. C. Atkinson, R. J. Herrnstein, G. Lindzey, & R. D. Luce (Eds.) *Stevens' handbook of experimental psychology, 2nd edition.* New York: Wiley.

Shiffrin, R. M., & Dumais, S. T. (1981). The development of automatism. In J. R. Anderson (Ed.), *Cognitive skills and their acquisition.* Hillsdale, NJ: Lawrence Erlbaum Associates.

Shiffrin, R. M., & Schneider, W. (1977). Controlled and automatic human information processing: II. Perceptual learning, automatic attending, and a general theory. *Psychological Review, 84,* 127–190.

Slamecka, N. J., & Graf, P. (1978). The generation effect: Delineation of a phenomenon. *Journal of Experimental Psychology: Human Learning and Memory, 4,* 592–604.

Smith, E. R., & Miller, F. D. (1983). Mediation among the attributional inferences and comprehension processes: Initial findings and a general method. *Journal of Personality and Social Psychology, 44,* 492–505.

Snyder, M., & Kendzierski, D. (1982). Acting on one's attitude: Procedures for linking attitude and behavior. *Journal of Experimental Social Pscyhology, 18,* 165–183.

Snyder, M., & Swann, W. B. (1976). When actions reflect attitudes: The politics of impression management. *Journal of Personality and Social Psychology, 34,* 1034–1042.

Srull, T. K. (1983). The role of prior knowledge in the acquisition, retention, and use of new information. *Advances in Consumer Research, 10,* 572–576.

Srull, T. K., & Wyer, R. S., Jr. (1979). The role of category accessibility in the interpretation of information about persons: Some determinants and implications. *Journal of Personality and Social Psychology, 37,* 1660–1672.

Srull, T. K., & Wyer, R. S., Jr. (1980). Category accessibility and social perception: Some implications for the study of person memory and interpersonal judgments. *Journal of Personality and Social Psychology, 38,* 841–856.

Staats, A. W. (1967). An outline of an integrated learning theory of attitude formation and function. In M. Fishbein (Ed.), *Readings in attitude theory and measurement* (pp. 373–376). New York: John Wiley and Sons, Inc.

Tversky, A., & Kahneman, D. (1974). Judgment under uncertainty: Heuristics and biases. *Science, 185,* 1124–1131.

Wicklund, R. A. (1975). Objective self-awareness. In L. Berkowitz (Ed.), *Advances in experimental social psychology* (Vol. 8). New York: Academic Press, 1975.

Wilson, D. K., Axsom, D., Lee, M., & Chaiken, S. (1985). *Evidence for heuristic processing of persuasive messages.* Paper presented at American Psychological Association Convention, Los Angeles, CA.

Wilson, T. D., & Capitman, J. A. (1982). Effect of script availability on social behavior. *Personality and Social Psychology Bulletin, 8,* 11–19.

Winter, L., & Uleman, J. S. (1984). When are social judgments made? Evidence for the spontaneousness of trait inferences. *Journal of Personality and Social Psychology, 47,* 237–252.

Wood, W. (1982). Retrieval of attitude-relevant information from memory: Effects on susceptibility to persuasion and on intrinsic motivation. *Journal of Personality and Social Psychology, 42,* 798–810.

Wood, W., Kallgren, C., & Priesler, R. (1985). Access to attitude relevant information in memory as a determinant of persuasion. *Journal of Experimental Social Psychology, 21,* 73–85.

Wyer, R. S., Jr. (1980). The acquisition and use of social knowledge: Basic postulates and representative research. *Personality and Social Psychology Bulletin, 6,* 558–573.

Zanna, M. P., Higgins, E. T., & Herman, C. P. (Eds.). (1982). *Consistency in social behavior: The Ontario symposium* (Vol. 2). Hillsdale, NJ: Lawrence Erlbaum Associates.

4 A Functional Approach to Attitudes and Persuasion

Mark Snyder
University of Minnesota

Kenneth G. DeBono
Union College

Reawakening from a period of relative dormancy in the late 1960s and 1970s, interest in persuasion and social influence processes appears to have reemerged in the mid-1980s as an active and productive research domain. Indeed, as the chapters of this volume suggest, researchers from many intellectual perspectives are once again addressing questions concerning the hows and whys of social influence and persuasion. The theories and paradigmatic assumptions guiding present day research in social influence and persuasion, however, are quite different from those that reigned during past peaks of persuasion research (cf. McGuire, 1985). Recent approaches to understanding social influence processes have a distinctly cognitive flavor (e.g., Eagly & Chaiken, 1984). Interest is now focused on the thought processes that occur in persuasion settings and the effects of those thought processes in producing attitude change (cf. Petty & Cacioppo, in press). And, indeed, such interest in cognitive explanations and theories is not unwarranted, as this perspective has proven quite useful in explaining and furthering our understanding of persuasion phenomena as well as in generating intriguing research questions.

However, as much as this approach has stimulated interest in social influence processes, certain seemingly fundamental issues and questions appear not to be given, by this approach, the attention they deserve. A particularly important question that has not been systematically addressed was posed by Smith, Bruner, and White in 1956. They asked the simple, yet intriguing, question "Of what use to people are their opinions?".

By asking such a question, Smith, Bruner, and White, of course, were expressing a concern with the motivational bases of people's attitudes or, in more familiar terms, the functional underpinnings of attitudes (see also Katz, 1960). Functional approaches to the study of attitudes posit that people maintain the attitudes they do because attitudes fulfill certain individualistic needs; attitudes allow individuals to successfully execute specific plans and achieve particular goals.

THE FUNCTIONS OF ATTITUDES

What are the functions of attitudes? Generally, four functions have been proposed (Katz, 1960; Smith et al., 1956). While the precise names of the functions vary across theorists, the general nature of the functions proposed is sufficiently similar to allow for the following taxonomy to be used and yet preserve the contributions of each major theorist. The four functions are:

Ego-defensive. At times, it is posited, people need to protect themselves from accepting truths that are particularly undesirable or threatening. To do so, they may develop attitudes via classic defense mechanisms such as projection or reaction formation. For example, a particularly prejudiced person may repress these feelings through the defense mechanism of reaction formation by forming favorable attitudes toward a very liberal political candidate.

Knowledge/Object Appraisal. People cannot possibly incorporate every detail of information they encounter in their social worlds. Thus, to give meaning to objects, they need to organize this information in an efficient manner. Perhaps the most efficient strategy is to categorize objects and persons on the basis of limited information and use known attributes about that category to make inferences and judgments about the object. For example, attitudes that all professors are liberal and therefore good, or that all New Yorkers are rude and therefore bad, allow the individual to quickly and efficiently arrive at judgments about particular groups and their members.

Value Expressive. Attitudes serving a value expressive function allow the person to express his or her true self: his or her underlying values, dispositions, or personality. For example, a person may support a particular political candidate because that candidate stands for and believes in ideas that the person holds dear. That is, by favoring this candidate, the person is expressing his or her own values.

Social Adjustive. Attitudes may be formed on the basis of how well they allow people to behave in ways appropriate to the various reference groups that comprise their social networks. That is, people may maintain their attitudes because these attitudes allow them to fit into important social situations and to interact smoothly with peers. For example, people may hold the same positive attitude toward the candidate mentioned above, not because by doing so they can express their true inner values, but because most of their friends and other members of important reference groups favor this candidate. By favoring this candidate, then, they can easily fit into, and establish smooth interactions with, peer and reference groups.

The introduction of the functional approach to the study of attitudes and persuasion initially was well received (Kiesler, Collins, & Miller, 1969). Indeed, numerous studies in the late 1950s and early 1960s were conducted to test hypotheses derived from functional theories, with particular interest focused on the ego defensive function (Katz, McClintock, & Sarnoff, 1957; Katz, Sarnoff, & McClintock, 1956; McClintock, 1958; Stotland, Katz, & Patchen, 1959). However, interest in functional theories waned as quickly as it had waxed. The decline in interest in the functional approach is most likely attributable to three sources. The first two sources are more reflections of shifts in research emphasis inherent in the field rather than reflections of anything germane to the functional theories themselves. The late 1960s and early 1970s witnessed a decline of interest in persuasion and persuasion-related phenomena (McGuire, 1985). Reliable persuasion findings were difficult to achieve and findings that did seem robust were often subject to alternative explanations. The literature was replete with inconsistent and nonreplicable findings. Moreover, no general framework or theory appeared capable of incorporating these disparate findings and explanations. As a consequence, interest in persuasion processes, and—by implication—functional theories (at least as they are implicated in persuasion processes) declined.

The late 1960s also marked the emergence of the "cognitive revolution" (Jones, 1985) in personality and social psychology. Beginning with the attribution theories and related approaches to studying social psychological phenomena, the cognitive perspective vaulted to a position of prominence. Indeed, the impact of the cognitive perspective was so great that one of the leading journals in the field (*Journal of Personality and Social Psychology*) began devoting an entire section to reports of research on attitudes and social cognition. Moreover, a new journal (*Social Cognition*) has recently appeared that is home, almost exclusively, to research in social cognition. As a consequence of this cognitive revolution in social psychology, attention to and interest in motivational explanations and theories, and hence, functional theories declined.

Perhaps the most important obstacle contributing to the decline in interest in the functional theories is inherent in the theories themselves. As with any typological approach, a fundamental problem with functional theories is their ability to be empirically validated (Kiesler, Collins, & Miller, 1969). Perhaps the most compelling way to verify a functional approach to the study of attitudes is through a persuasion paradigm. A basic tenet of any functional theory of attitudes and persuasion (e.g., Katz, 1960) is that persuasive messages will be effective to the extent that they address the functional base of the target's attitude. For example, if a person's attitude toward a given issue is serving primarily a social adjustive function, then the most effective message for changing that person's attitude would be one concerning the social appropriateness of that attitude. By contrast, a message suggesting that this particular attitude is not properly expressing a value that the person considers important should have little, if any, impact.

To successfully execute such a program of research, however, the a priori identification of the functional bases of attitudes is necessary. That is, researchers need to know the functional underpinnings of people's attitudes before any persuasive messages are delivered, in order to choose the persuasive message appropriate to an attitude serving that function. To infer the functional bases after observing the effects of different communications is fraught with the dangers of after-the-fact inferences. It is the a priori identification of the functional bases of people's attitudes that has proved to be an especially difficult hurdle to overcome and is most likely the major source of disinterest with the functional theories of attitudes (cf. Lutz, 1981).

IDENTIFYING THE FUNCTIONS OF ATTITUDES

How, then, can the functions of attitudes be identified? One strategy to overcome the difficulties that have plagued the functional approaches is to identify categories of people for whom attitudes may be serving different functions. Such a strategy reflects a larger, global strategy for the study of the links between personality and social behavior. According to this strategy, outlined by Snyder and Ickes (1985) in the chapter on "Personality and Social Behavior" in the recent *Handbook of Social Psychology,* one seeks to identify contrasting categories of people who typically and habitually manifest contrasting behavioral orientations in social situations and interpersonal contexts, with the members of these contrasting categories then serving as subjects for investigation of the processes that account for these contrasting orientations. According to the logic of this strategy, one could hardly study any psychological phenomenon or process in those who rarely or never manifest it.

Thus, by identifying those people who typically manifest the phenomenon or process of concern, one gains access to candidates for investigating the psychology of that phenomenon or process in action. That is, identifying people who typically manifest the phenomenon or process of concern is undertaken, not as an end, but rather as a means toward the end of understanding that phenomenon or process. Viewed from the perspective of this strategy for studying personality and social behavior, to investigate the functional underpinnings of attitudes one would seek to identify contrasting categories of people for whom one might suspect that attitudes are serving different functions. Once identified, members of these categories could then serve as ideal candidates for investigating the functional underpinnings of attitudes, particularly if their differing functional bases is a part of a larger, more generalized syndrome of differing orientations to social situations and interpersonal events.

Are there, then, categories of people for whom attitudes may be serving different functions? Empirical studies and theoretical formulations of the psychological construct of self-monitoring (Snyder, 1974, 1979, 1987) suggest that it may be one construct that can be used to study attitudinal functions. High self-monitoring individuals (identified by their relatively high scores on the Self-Monitoring Scale; Snyder, 1974) typically strive to be the type of person called for by each situation in which they find themselves. They are concerned about, and are adept at, tailoring their behavior to fit social and interpersonal considerations of situational appropriateness (Lippa, 1976). To the extent that the characteristic interpersonal orientation of high self-monitoring individuals is one of fitting themselves into their social circumstances, this interpersonal orientation may also include social attitudes that are formed on the basis of how well they serve the ends of behaving in ways appropriate to the various reference groups that form their social circumstances. As such, the social attitudes of high self-monitoring individuals may, in the language of the functional theories, be serving a *social adjustive* function.

By contrast, low self-monitoring individuals (identified by their relatively low scores on the Self-Monitoring Scale) typically do not attempt to mold their behavior to fit situational and interpersonal considerations of appropriateness (Snyder & Monson, 1975). Rather, these people tend to guide their behavioral choices on the basis of relevant inner sources (such as values, feelings, and dispositions) and are concerned that their behavior in social contexts be accurate reflections of their underlying values, feelings, and dispositions (Snyder & Swann, 1976; Snyder & Tanke, 1976). To the extent that the characteristic interpersonal orientation of low self-monitoring individuals is one of choosing behaviors that accurately reflect and meaningfully communicate their own personal attributes, that interpersonal orientation may also include attitudes formed on the basis of how well they reflect, express, and communicate more fundamental underlying values. As such, the social attitudes of low self-monitoring individuals may, once again in the language of the functional theories, be serving a *value expressive* function.

DIFFERENT FUNCTIONS FOR DIFFERENT PEOPLE

Working with this investigative strategy, DeBono (in press) has used the self-monitoring construct to examine aspects of the social adjustive and value expressive functions of attitudes toward mental illness. College students, known to be either high or low in self-monitoring, learned that the psychology department was sponsoring a "Mental Health Week" during which speakers from all over the country would visit the campus to present lectures and lead discussions in introductory psychology classes on various aspects of mental illness. As preparation for these visits, these students learned that they would hear tapes to familiarize themselves with the topic. They then listened to a tape of (the fictitious) Professor Gregory Stevenson from the University of Nebraska.

Students randomly assigned to the "social adjustive" experimental condition heard Professor Stevenson talk about the results of a survey he had just conducted on the attitudes of college students toward the care, housing, and treatment of the mentally ill, a survey which revealed that 70% of the college students surveyed favored treatment in the state hospitals and institutions, that 23% favored treatment at the community level in half-way houses and the like, and that 7% had no opinion. After discussing the pros and cons of institutionalization and deinstitutionalization, Professor Stevenson concluded by stating that he did not see one position as inherently better than the other and that the debate over the proper place to care for the mentally ill was at a standstill.

Students randomly assigned to the "value expressive" experimental condition heard Professor Stevenson talk about the results of research he had just conducted concerning the particular values that seem to underlie various attitudes toward the care, housing, and treatment of the mentally ill. His research, Professor Stevenson indicated, suggested that the values of loving and responsibility (values that *all* participants in DeBono's study rated relatively highly on the Rokeach [1968] instrumental value survey) appear to underlie favorable attitudes toward the institutionalization of the mentally ill, and that the values of imaginativeness and courageousness (values all participants rated as relatively unimportant to them) appear to underlie favorable attitudes toward the deinstitutionalization of the mentally ill. After describing the pros and cons of institutionalization versus deinstitutionalization, Professor Stevenson concluded by stating that he did not see one position as inherently better than the other and that the debate about the care, housing, and treatment of the mentally ill was at a standstill.

After hearing one or the other tape, all students reported, among other things, their personal attitudes toward the care, housing, and treatment of the mentally ill. The extent to which messages appealing to either a social adjustive function or a value expressive function influenced their attitudes on this issue were, as Fig. 4.1 reveals, very much a reflection of their own self-monitoring propensities. Typically, students in this study were generally favorable toward the deinstitutionalization of the mentally ill before they heard Professor Stevenson's message. In accord with the hypothesized social adjustive function of their attitudes, high self-monitoring students were particularly influenced by the message that played upon social adjustive concerns, reporting attitudes more favorable toward the institutionalization of the mentally ill than after hearing the value expressive message. And, in keeping with the hypothesized value expressive function of their attitudes, low self-monitoring students were more influenced by

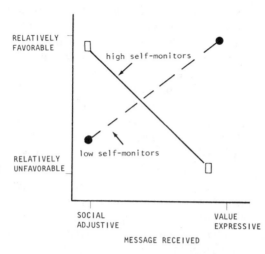

FIG. 4.1. The functional bases of attitudes and persuasion.

the message that addressed itself to value expressive concerns, stating attitudes more favorable toward the institutionalization of the mentally ill than after hearing the social adjustive message.

These results highlight the utility of adopting a functional approach to the study of persuasion and social influence. They suggest that the persuasion settings necessary for successful social influence may indeed need to be very different for different people. That is, people may have different motivational bases for maintaining their attitudes; and, moreover, for a persuasive message to have its maximal impact, these motivations must be identified and addressed. In this context, DeBono's (in press) study suggests that the most compelling persuasive communications will be those directed at the functional underpinnings of relevant attitudes.

APPLYING THE FUNCTIONAL APPROACH: THE PSYCHOLOGY OF ADVERTISING

It is said that there is nothing so practical as a good theory. The present approach to investigating functional approaches to attitudes and persuasion is no exception to this article of faith, which is a part of Kurt Lewin's legacy to psychology (Marrow, 1969). Consider, specifically, that most pervasive form of social influence and persuasion—advertising.

The history of the advertising industry reveals that advertisers seem to belong to two schools, known as the "soft sell" and the "hard sell." Members of the soft sell school typically create ads that appeal to the *images* associated with the use of the product, images that consumers may gain and project by using the product. Adherents to this image-based tradition believe that how a product is packaged by its advertising is as important as the product itself. Typically, the written copy in these ads convey, explicitly or implicitly, the images associated with the use of the product. Rarely, if ever, do these image-oriented ads make any mention of the quality of the product itself.

A landmark case of the image-oriented advertising approach was that for the Arrow shirt collar, an ad campaign that focused not on the product itself but on the image of the man who wore it. Here, the advertisers "created a campaign stressing the accessories and background of the man who wore the product. Instead of picturing the collar by itself, [they] put it around the neck of a stylish young man, impossibly clear of eye, clean of jowl, and square of jaw and surrounded with opulent possessions and women" (Fox, 1984, p. 44). Perhaps the best known contemporary instance of image-oriented advertising is that for Marlboro cigarettes, revolving as it does around the Marlboro man, who projects the rugged masculine image of the man who smokes Marlboro cigarettes.

Members of the hard sell school typically create rather different ads, ones based on claims about the inherent *quality*, abou the intrinsic merit, and about the functional value of the product. Their ads inform the consumer about how good the product is, how well it works, or in the case of things to eat and drink, how good it tastes. Here, it's the "matter not the manner" that counts (Fox, 1984, p. 324). Early on, practitioners of this approach applied their techniques to advertising patent medicines and cure-alls, one of which was Lydia E. Pinkham's Vegetable Compound, advertised with the hard sell claim that it was "a sure cure for all female weaknesses, . . . efficacious and immediate in its effects" (cited in Fox, 1984, p. 141). Recent advertisements for Total cereal, which have emphasized the nutritional benefits of the cereal, as well as ads featuring Pepsi Cola's "Pepsi challenge" taste tests, which have dramatized the supposedly superior taste of Pepsi, clearly are members of the same category of advertising based on claims about product quality.

Without a doubt, these two schools of advertising have flourished throughout the history of the industry and both traditions have produced their share of successful ad campaigns. The fundamental questions to ask, though, are: What is the basis of the effectiveness of either type of advertising? What is it that makes appeals to images and claims about quality succeed in engaging, motivating, and persuading consumers? What are the psychological mechanisms that render each of these strategies successful?

One possibility is that the different advertising strategies are appealing to different functional bases of attitudes. In particular, the soft sell approach, with its appeals to images, may be primarily influencing people for whom attitudes serve a social adjustive function, as its image appeals may allow such people to perceive that a product has the potential to create images appropriate to various social circumstances. By contrast, the hard sell approach may be particularly influential with people for whom attitudes serve a value expressive function. Information about product quality may be readily interpreted by these people in terms of underlying values and other evaluative reactions.

If these conjectures are correct, then people high and low in self-monitoring should be differentially responsive to ads that promise image and to those that feature product quality. In our research, designed to investigate these possibilities (Snyder & DeBono, 1985), we have created ads that, in pictures and words, represented image-based and product-quality messages to consumers. We have created ads for products diverse as coffee and cars, for whiskies and shampoos, and for cigarettes.

In our first study, we created sets of magazine advertisements, each set containing two ads for a particular product. We advertised Canadian Class whisky, Barclay cigarettes, and Irish Mocha Mint coffee. The two ads for each product were identical in all respects save one—the written message or slogan associated with the picture. One message highlighted the image associated with the use of the product whereas the other slogan stressed the product's quality. Here is what went into our ads:

Canadian Club. The picture for this set prominently displayed a bottle of Canadian Club resting on a set of house blueprints. The written copy for the image-oriented advertisement stated "You're not just moving in, you're moving up" and the product-quality advertisement claimed that "When it comes to great taste, everyone draws the same conclusion."

Barclay Cigarettes. Here, the pictorial content depicted a handsome gentleman, about to light up a cigarette, looking into a mirror at his female companion. The woman's hand is shown resting on the gentleman's shoulder. The image-oriented message read "Barclay . . . you can see the difference" and the product-quality message read "Barclay . . . you can taste the difference."

Irish Mocha Mint. For this set, the picture showed a man and a woman relaxing in a candle-lit room, smiling at each other while drinking Irish Mocha Mint coffee. The image-oriented ad promised to "Make a chilly night become a cozy evening with Irish Mocha Mint," and the product-quality ad informed the consumer about "Irish Mocha Mint: A delicious blend of three great flavors—coffee, chocolate, and mint."

We informed participants (all of whom were college students) that, as part of a larger research program, we were studying various ads and that their task would be to help in evaluating the relative merits of these ads. We then presented them, sequentially, with the three sets of ads. After each set, participants filled out a 12-item questionnaire that asked them to compare the two ads along evaluative dimensions. For example, the questionnaire asked "Overall, which ad do you think is better?'', ''Which one appeals to you more?'' and ''Which ad do you think would be more successful?''. With their answers to these questions, we constructed an index of favorability toward the two types of ads.

When we examined their evaluations of our ads, we found that high self-monitoring individuals reacted more favorably to the image-oriented ads than did the low self-monitoring individuals. By contrast, low self-monitoring individuals responded more favorably to the product-quality-oriented ads than did high self-monitoring individuals. Moreover, this pattern of differential favorability was evident for all three products.

Clearly, people high and low in self-monitoring have different evaluative reactions to advertising based on appeals to images and claims about product quality. To determine how generalized these evaluative reactions are, and to begin moving our resarch in the direction of actual consumer behaviors, we next examined the impact of these two modes of advertising on one important feature of consumer behavior. Specifically, in our next study, we sought to determine whether the way a product is advertised would have any effect on how much consumers would be willing to pay for that product. We told participants that, as part of an ongoing research program on advertising, they would respond to a number of ads currently being studied. We then presented them either with three image-oriented ads or with three product-quality-oriented ads (in each case, the same three developed for the first study). After viewing each ad, participants filled out a questionnaire, the critical item of which was ''How much would you be willing to pay for this product?''.

As it happened, what people were willing to pay for these products was very much a function of how these products had been advertised. High self-monitoring individuals were willing to pay more for a product if it was advertised with an image orientation than if it was advertised with a quality orientation; for these people, favorable images were worth money. By contrast, low self-monitoring individuals were willing to pay more for a product if its ad focused on the product's quality rather than its image; for these people, quality was worth paying for.

Our next step, in this series of investigations, took us further into the domain of actual consumer behavior. We sought to determine whether these differing orientations toward advertising extend so far as to influence actual decisions to consume or not consume products based upon information gleaned from advertising. In our next study, we posed as interviewers from a market research firm, and contacted students by telephone to offer them an opportunity to participate in a test marketing study in which they would try out a new shampoo that our client planned to market. In these telephone interviews, we delivered one of two messages, either a message that described the shampoo in terms of the image that its users would project (''The results of recent laboratory tests have indicated that, while compared to other shampoos, this brand usually rates about average in how it cleans your hair, it consistently rates above average in how good it makes your hair look''), or a message that described the shampoo in terms of its quality as a hair-cleaning agent (''The results of recent laboratory tests have indicated that, while compared to other shampoos, this brand usually rates about average in how good it makes your hair look, it consistently rates above average in how clean it gets your hair'').

After hearing one of these two messages, the students expressed their willingness to use the shampoo. High self-monitoring individuals were more willing than low self-monitoring individuals to try the shampoo that would leave their hair looking good, and low self-monitoring individuals were more willing than high self-monitoring individuals to try the shampoo that would leave their hair very clean. Clearly, then, when it came to actual choices to use or not to use this consumer product, high self-monitoring individuals invoked considerations of the images associated with a product (choosing, in this case, to use the shampoo that would make their hair look good, even if it meant that their great-looking hair would be less than perfectly clean) and low self-monitoring individuals responded to attributes of the product's quality in performing its defining functions (choosing, in this case, to use the shampoo that would get their hair very clean, even if their very clean hair would have a less-than-beautiful look).

It seems, then, that we have succeeded in identifying two types of advertising strategies and two types of people who react differentially to these two stratagies (see Fig. 4.2). High self-monitoring individuals react favorably to image-ori-

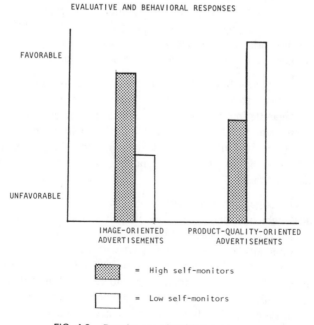

FIG. 4.2.   Reactions to advertising messages.

ented ads, they are willing to pay more money for a product if it is advertised with an image orientation, and they will agree to try a product if it is marketed with an image appeal. By contrast, low self-monitoring individuals react favorably to product quality ads, they are willing to pay more money for a product if its advertisement stresses product quality, and they will agree to try a product if an appeal is made to its quality.

The differential appeal of image-oriented and quality-oriented messages, it should be noted, is not limited to the domain of consumer products. In fact, we have been working with a series of ads whose purpose, rather than encouraging individuals to consume a product, is to encourage people *not* to consume a product, in this case not to smoke (Snyder, DeBono, & Nettle, 1985). We have created three sets of "be a non-smoker" ads, each set containing two ads with the same pictorial content, but differing verbal messages, one with an appeal to image and appearance considerations and one with an appeal to health quality considerations:

The Runner.   In one set of ads, we used a picture of a runner in the Boston Marathon. The image-oriented message appealed to the desirable image of "Be a winner, don't smoke," and the health-quality-oriented message made this claim "Smoking . . . It will take your breath away."

The Couple.   In another set of ads, we used a picture of a man and woman sitting on top of a grassy hill by the ocean. The image-oriented message appealed to romantic allure by saying "Kiss a non-smoker . . . Taste the difference" and the health-quality oriented message hinted about life expectancies by saying "Times like these were meant to last . . . Be a non-smoker."

The Older Brother.   In our third set of ads, we used a picture of a rather pensive looking man, about the right age to be an older brother to students in this study, with a cigarette in his hand. His thoughts, in the image-oriented message were of his appearance: "Bad breath, yellow teeth, smelly clothes . . . Is smoking really worth it?", and in the health-quality-oriented message were of physical consequences of smoking: "Coughing, shortness of breath, sore throat . . . is smoking really worth it?".

When we had college students (virtually all of whom were nonsmokers themselves) indicate which ad in each set was, in their judgment, the better ad, more appealing, more effective, potentially more successful, and so on, high self-monitoring individuals were more impressed with the image-oriented ads and low self-monitoring individuals were more favorably disposed toward the health-quality oriented ads. Moreover, there seems to be some indication that when students choose which ads to use to persuade a fellow student to be a nonsmoker, high self-monitoring individuals feature the image-oriented messages and low self-monitoring individuals feature the health-quality-oriented messages in their persuasive appeals.

How, then, are we to understand the effectiveness of appeals to images and claims about product quality? One basis for such an understanding is provided by the generalized interpersonal orientations characteristic of high and low self-monitoring individuals. That is, the propensity to respond favorably, at the level of evaluative reactions and at the level of behavioral choices, to image-oriented or quality-oriented advertising appeals may be one feature of the larger syndrome of differing cognitive, motivational, and behavioral processes that guide the behavior of high and low self-monitoring individuals in social contexts. The favorable reactions of high self-monitoring individuals to image-based advertising may be yet another manifestation of a chronic striving to be a pragmatic creature of one's situations, to project images appropriate to one's circumstances. Favorable reactions to quality-oriented advertising by low self-monitoring individuals may be yet another manifestation of a continuing quest to be a principled being, with congruence between one's actions and underlying attitudes, values, and dispositions. (For a discussion of criteria for which specific image or quality ads engage particular high or low self-monitoring consumers, see Snyder and DeBono, 1985.)

Not only does the self-monitoring conceptual framework provide a theoretical understanding of the effectiveness of these two types of advertising, but it provides some practical hints as well. It hints that the most potent image-oriented advertisements will be those that most effectively engage social adjustive concerns, ones that convey the message that the images associated with using the advertised products are particularly appropriate ones to project and are images that, if conveyed, will increase the likelihood that one will fit into important life situations. It also hints that the most effective quality-oriented advertisements will be the ones that most successfully activate value expressive concerns by including the message that, by using the advertised products, one will be gaining opportunities to be true to one's own personal attitudes and important values.

Our findings, and our interpretation of them, also provide a new perspective on the two longstanding traditions in the advertising industry—the "soft sell" or image-oriented approach and the "hard sell" or claim-oriented approach. Indeed, it very well may be that these approaches have succeeded, survived, and flourished because each one has managed to appeal to members of one category of consumers. Soft sell, image-oriented advertising campaigns that have worked may have worked because they have succeeded in engaging and motivating the image-making and social adjustive concerns of high self-monitoring consumers. Hard sell, claim-oriented advertising campaigns that have succeeded may have succeeded because they have been effective in engaging and motivating the product-quality and value expressive concerns of low self-monitoring consumers.

THE FUNCTIONAL APPROACH: CHALLENGES AND PROSPECTS

What are the motivational underpinnings of attitudes? This question lies at the heart of the functional approach to the study of attitudes. As we have seen, a fundamental challenge of the functional approach is the a priori identification of the functions being served by specific attitudes for particular people. The approach that we have outlined in this chapter, and the research that it has spawned, together represent one way of meeting that challenge. With a strategy for studying personality and social behavior, we have sought out contrasting categories of people for whom we have theoretical reasons to believe that attitudes are serving different functions. And, we have used these categories of people as vehicles for studying attitudinal functions. In so doing, we have been able to explore not only the dynamics of the functional bases of attitudes, but also their implications for persuasion. Moreover, we have been able to do so both in laboratory and *real life* persuasion settings.

Much of our research has focused on the psychology of advertising and consumer behavior. It has been said that "Advertising is persuasion, and persuasion is . . . an art. Advertising is the art of persuasion" (Bernbach, cited by Fox, 1984, p. 251). Indeed, we have found studies of advertising to be particularly fertile grounds for investigating functional approaches to persuasion. As promising as our findings may be, we must recognize some possible pitfalls in generalizing from advertising as we practiced it in our experiments to advertising as it is practiced within the trade—not to mention generalizing beyond the domain of consumer behavior to persuasion situations in general. Let us examine these possible pitfalls, for they point the way toward some of the challenges still to be met by a functional approach to attitudes and persuasion.

A general challenge facing researchers using the investigative strategy we have proposed is the feasibility of this approach outside of the psychological laboratory. In our research, it was relatively easy to classify participants as high or low in self-monitoring and thereby infer the likely functions of their attitudes. We simply turned to their Self-Monitoring Scale scores collected a few weeks prior to their participation in the research. However, it's not so easy for practitioners, who may not be able to ascertain the self-monitoring status of the targets of their persuasion attempts. For example, theoretically speaking, one could advise a health service official to encourage high self-monitoring individuals to engage in health-related behaviors by informing them of the image enhancing qualities of health behaviors and suggesting that keeping healthy is a socially appropriate behavior. However, practically speaking, such a recommendation would be difficult to implement, given that the only way currently available to ascertain a person's self-monitoring classification is through the use of paper-and-pencil measure, the Self-Monitoring Scale. Although the health service official may be able to collect Self-Monitoring Scale scores (perhaps in an assessment session conducted prior to face-to-face counseling sessions), the problem is even greater for other practitioners. How, for instance, are advertisers to know whether consumers exposed to particular ads they place in magazines, on the radio, or on television are high or low in self-monitoring?

To such concerns, we have two replies. One involves the relations between particular products and the most effective advertising campaigns for them. We suggest that some products (such as cosmetics and wearing apparel) may contribute primarily to one's exterior appearances and public images, thus allowing one to fit into various situations. As such, the natural target population of advertising for such products may be high self-monitoring consumers, who may be particularly likely to look to advertising when choosing products they intend to use for image-making purposes. Thus, advertisers of these products ought to tailor their advertising strategies to the image and appearance concerns of these people. By contrast, other products may contribute primarily to the quality of one's interior well being (such as nutritious foods and beverages) and be useful for what they do rather than what they look like (e.g., appliances and tools). As such, the natural target population of advertising for these products may be low self-monitoring consumers, who may be particularly likely to turn to advertising when choosing products they intend to use for the intrinsic functions they perform. Thus advertisers of these products ought to tailor their advertising strategies to the product quality and product performance concerns of these people.

A second way to leap the hurdles between our laboratory studies and relevant applications is suggested by recent research on the relations between personality and social behavior. This research indicated that people choose to enter and spend time in situations that allow them to act upon their traits, attitudes, and dispositions (Snyder & Ickes, 1985). Therefore, advertisers may be able to identify situations that are most likely to be characteristic of people for whom attitudes are serving specific functions. Once identified, change agents can tailor their persuasive communications to the appropriate functions. For example, given the high self-monitoring concerns with image enhancing qualities of consumer products, might not such people be disposed to subscribe to and read certain magazines (e.g., *Gentlemen's Quarterly, M, Glamour,* and *Vogue*)? Similarly, given the low self-monitoring concern with the quality of consumer products, might not they be disposed to subscribe to and read a different set of magazines (e.g., those featuring product evaluations and test reports such, as *Popular Photography* for camera buffs, *Car and Driver* for car enthusiasts, *Personal Computing* for computer lovers, *Audio* for audiophiles, etc.). If so, then the results of the present studies have a good deal to recommend to the advertiser concerned with choosing "media markets" for optimizing the effectiveness of a persuasive appeal.

While we have dwelled on the utility of adopting a functional approach for understanding advertising as applied persuasion, let us be quick to point out that we believe such an approach to be useful for a theoretical understanding of persuasion processes in general (cf. DeBono, in press). Indeed, we already have seen how persuasive messages concerning the care and treatment of the mentally ill have differential impact on high and low self-monitoring recipients when their arguments are either tailored to social adjustive considerations or are geared to value expressive concerns (DeBono, in press). Yet, there are challenges to be met as we seek further theoretical elaboration of the functional approach to attitudes and persuasion. At this point, only one vehicle for identifying attitudinal functions characteristic of particular categories of people has been documented, and only two functions of attitudes have been explored using this vehicle.

Surely, there are vehicles other than self-monitoring for identifying probable functions of attitudes. Surely, too, some of these vehicles may identify categories of people for whom other functions, such as the ego defensive and the knowledge functions, are characteristically served by their attitudes. We suggest that an investigative strategy of the type we have outlined in this chapter could be used to investigate the role of psychological constructs such as Machiavellianism (Christie & Geis, 1970), need for approval (Crowne & Marlowe, 1964), authoritarianism (Adorno, Frenkel-Brunswik, Levinson, & Sanford, 1950), and need for cognition (Cacioppo & Petty, 1982) in determining the functional bases of individuals' attitudes. Perhaps, research will tell us that people high in need for cognition are particular likely to hold attitudes that serve a knowledge function (although, almost by definition, all attitudes probably serve knowledge functions to some extent, by providing meaning about attitudinal objects), and that the attitudes of people with authoritarian personalities typically serve ego defensive functions, to name but two hypotheses that can be readily explored with this investigative strategy.

As promising as the strategy of identifying particular categories of people to serve as candidates for studying specific functional bases of attitudes may be, we should acknowledge that (at least as we have practiced it) this strategy does rely on *indirect* indicators. The psychological construct of self-monitoring was not developed specifically to characterize attitudinal functions; at its theoretical core, self-monitoring is concerned with attentiveness and responsiveness to situational and dispositional guides to action. Yet, the evidence for its construct validity does suggest that one of the many features of the generalized orientations tapped by the self-monitoring construct is attitudinal functions. Therefore, at the same time as self-monitoring may be an indirect indicator of attitudinal functions, it is an indicator that does allow these differences in attitudinal functions to be placed in the larger psychological context of the generalized interpersonal orientations associated with self-monitoring propensities, and in the larger theoretical framework provided by the entire network of evidence for the construct validity of self-monitoring.

Nevertheless, we recognize a need for direct indicators of attitudinal functions as well. And, in fact, some steps have been taken toward developing a taxonomy of the functional bases of attitudes. Herek (1984), for example, recently used such an approach to categorize the functional bases of people's attitudes toward homosexual men and women. He asked subjects to indicate why they feel as they do toward gay men and lesbians, and to hypothesize about the origins of their feelings. He then analysed the contents of the essays, looking specifically for recurring themes. He was able to reliably identify three functional bases of attitudes (for both his original sample and a later sample): an experiential one, an expressive one, and a defensive one. Moreover, he was able to use the knowledge of the functional bases of people's attitudes to successfully test many hypotheses derived from functional theories.

What, then, are the prospects for functional approaches to attitudes and persuasion? Functional approaches have waxed and waned in the history of research on attitudes and persuasion. Their waxing—as we have seen—seems largely attributable to their success in "asking the right question"; no understanding of attitudes and persuasion could possibly be complete without some understanding of the functions served by attitudes and the role of these functions in the processes of persuasion. Their waning—as we also have seen—seems largely attributable to their inability to meet a fundamental challenge of the functional approach, the challenge of the a priori identification of the functions being served by specific attitudes for particular individuals. The approach that we have outlined in this chapter provides one way of meeting this challenge, and may signal a new waxing. To be sure, and as we are well aware, this approach has its own hurdles to overcome. But, as its first "trial runs" have indicated, this approach does seem to have both theoretical and practical promise. We just may be about to see functional approaches to attitudes, persuasion, and social influence—with all of their potential for theoretical richness and practical utility—awaken from their long winter of hibernation.

ACKNOWLEDGMENTS

Some of the research discussed in this chapter was conducted with the support of National Science Foundation Grant BNS 82-07632 to Mark Snyder. Preparation of this chapter was supported by the Graduate School of the University of Minnesota. We thank Allen M. Omoto and Mark P. Zanna for their helpful comments on the chapter.

Correspondence with Mark Snyder should be addressed to: Department of Psychology, University of Minnesota, 75 East River Road, Minneapolis, Minnesota 55455; with Kenneth G. DeBono, to: Department of Psychology, Union College, Schenectady, New York 12308.

REFERENCES

Adorno, T. W., Frenkel-Brunswik, E., Levinson, D. J., & Sanford, R. N. (1950). *The authoritarian personality*. New York: Harper.

Cacioppo, J. T., & Petty, R. E. (1982). The need for cognition. *Journal of Personality and Social Psychology, 42*, 116–131.

Christie, R., & Geis, F. L. (Eds.). (1970). *Studies in Machiavellianism*. New York: Academic Press.

Crowne, D. P., & Marlowe, D. (1964). *The approval motive: Studies in evaluative dependence*. New York: Wiley.

DeBono, K. G. (in press). Investigating the social adjustive and value expressive functions of attitudes: Implications for persuasion processes. *Journal of Personality and Social Psychology*.

Eagly, A. H., & Chaiken, S. (1984). Cognitive theories of persuasion. In L. Berkowitz (Ed.), *Advances in experimental social psychology*. (Vol. 17). New York: Academic Press.

Fox, S. (1984). *The mirror makers*. New York: Morrow.

Herek, G. M. (1984). *The functions of attitudes: A new approach to an old perspective*. Unpublished manuscript, Yale University, New Haven, CT.

Jones, E. E. (1985). Major developments in social psychology during the past five decades. In G. Lindzey & E. Aronson (Eds.), *The handbook of social psychology* (3rd Ed.). New York: Random House.

Katz, D. (1960). The functional approach to the study of attitudes. *Public Opinion Quarterly, 24*, 163–204.

Katz, D., McClintock, C., & Sarnoff, D. (1957). The measurement of ego defense as related to attitude change. *Journal of Personality, 25*, 465–474.

Katz, D., Sarnoff, D., & McClintock, C. (1956). Ego-defense and attitude change. *Human Relations, 9*, 27–45.

Kiesler, C. A., Collins, B. E., & Miller, N. (1969). *Attitude change: A critical analysis of theoretical approaches*. New York: Wiley.

Lippa, R. (1976). Expressive control and the leakage of dispositional introversion-extraversion during role-playing teaching. *Journal of Personality, 44*, 541–559.

Lutz, R. (1981). A reconceptualization of the functional approach to attitudes. *Research in Marketing, 5*, 165–210.

Marrow, A. J. (1969). *The practical theorist: The life and works of Kurt Lewin*. New York: Basic Books.

McClintock, C. G. (1958). Personality syndromes and attitude change. *Journal of Personality, 26*, 479–593.

McGuire, W. J. (1985). Attitudes and attitude change. In G. Lindzey & E. Aronson (Eds.), *The handbook of social psychology* (3rd Ed.). New York: Random House.

Petty, R. E., & Cacioppo, J. T. (in press). The elaboration likelihood model of persuasion. In L. Berkowitz (Ed.), *Advances in experimental social psychology* (Vol. 19). New York: Academic Press.

Rokeach, M. (1968). *Beliefs, attitudes, and values*. San Francisco: Jossey-Bass.

Smith, M. B., Bruner, S. J., & White, R. W. (1956). *Opinions and personality*. New York: Wiley.

Snyder, M. (1974). The self-monitoring of expressive behavior. *Journal of Personality and Social Psychology, 30*, 526–537.

Snyder, M. (1979). Self-monitoring processes. In L. Berkowitz (Ed.), *Advances in experimental social psychology*. (Vol. 12). New York: Academic Press.

Snyder, M. (in press). Public appearances/Private realities: The psychology of self-monitoring. New York: W. H. Freeman.

Snyder, M., & DeBono, K. G. (1985). Appeals to image and claims about quality: Understanding the psychology of advertising. *Journal of Personality and Social Psychology, 49*, 586–697.

Snyder, M., DeBono, K. G., & Nettle, R. (1985). *Unpublished research*. University of Minnesota, Minneapolis, MN.

Snyder, M., & Ickes, W. (1985). Personality and social behavior. In G. Lindzey & E. Aronson (Eds.), *The handbook of social psychology* (3rd Ed.). New York: Random House.

Snyder, M. & Monson, T. C. (1975). Persons, situations, and the control of social behavior. *Journal of Personality and Social Psychology, 32*, 637–644.

Snyder, M. & Swann, W. B., Jr. (1976). When actions reflect attitudes: The politics of impression management. *Journal of Personality and Social Psychology, 34,* 1034–1042.

Snyder, M. & Tanke, E. D. (1976). Behavior and attitude: Some people are more consistent than others. *Journal of Personality, 44,* 510–517.

Stotland, E., Katz, D., & Patchen, M. (1959). The reduction of prejudice through the arousal of self-insight. *Journal of Personality, 27,* 507–531.

II
COMPLIANCE AND CONFORMITY

5 Self-Perception Theory: A Current Perspective

Russell H. Fazio
Indiana University

It is now some 20 years since Bem first proposed self-perception theory (Bem, 1965). Elegantly simple, this theory argued that attitudes were inferences stemming from observation of one's behavior. The theory immediately captured the attention of social psychologists. It generated a great deal of research unique to the theoretical perspective. Furthermore, because self-perception theory was presented as an alternative to dissonance theory, it instigated theoretical and empirical controversy that, I believe, benefitted the field enormously. Finally, coinciding as it did with the rise of the attributional perspective in social psychology, the introduction of the theory linked such attributional processes to the domain of attitudes.

The present chapter reviews briefly this central and important theory and provides an update of where the theory stands at this point in time. In particular, I focus upon recent empirical advancements stemming from my own and others' research that have provided answers (or at least clues) regarding some longstanding questions about self-perception processes. Finally, I conclude by discussing some of the more general implications of what has been learned about self-perception processes for attitudes and social influence.

Bem's initial theoretical statements stemmed from a Skinnerian radical behaviorist perspective involving a somewhat mysterious language of "mands" and "tacts"—terminology that has befuddled many a psychology major. Nevertheless, as intimated a moment ago, the simplicity of self-perception theory is part of its elegance. By 1972, the theory had taken on more of an attributional perspective, and Bem was able to summarize the theory very simply. "Individuals come to 'know' their own attitudes, emotions, and other internal states partially by inferring them from observations of their own overt behavior and/or the circumstances in which this behavior occurs" (Bem, 1972, p. 2). Given that the situational cues indicate that the behavior was not manded, i.e., attributable to some external force, one's attitude can be inferred directly from the behavior via an implicit self-selection rule, "what must my attitude be if I am willing to behave in this fashion in this situation?"

Such self-observation is by no means the only manner by which individuals may form attitudes. However, the theory suggests that overt behavior and the situational cues surrounding that behavior provide the individual with a clear indication of his or her attitude toward the object in question. In fact, a second postulate of the theory even more directly points to the critical role of behavior by suggesting a partial equivalence between self and interpersonal perception. "To the extent that internal cues are weak, ambiguous, or uninterpretable, the individual is functionally in the same position as an outside observer, an observer who must necessarily rely upon those same external cues to infer the individual's inner states" (Bem, 1972, p. 2).

Very early on, it became evident that self-perception theory had the potential to serve as a viable alternative to cognitive dissonance theory. For years, the field was embroiled in a controversy as to which perspective provided the most appropriate account of attitude change following the performance of freely-chosen counterattitudinal action. This is not the time to review the controversy. It will suffice to note that empirical investigations that focused on the role of arousal proved supportive of the dissonance theory claim that arousal is critical to the attitude change process in such situations (see Fazio & Cooper, 1983, for a recent review of this work). Ironically, then, self-perception theory no longer appears an adequate alternative to dissonance theory.

Yet, as Fazio, Zanna, and Cooper (1977) tried to point out, self-perception theory remains useful. It is supported by much independent evidence that is beyond the domain of dissonance theory. It has much to say about one process by which attitudes are formed and how at least some types of attitudes are modified by inference from behavior that is not markedly discrepant from initial attitudes (e.g., Kiesler, Nisbett, & Zanna, 1969). Furthermore, the theory provides a viable interpretation of a number of social influence phenomena. Self-perception processes are central to the interpretation of the foot-in-the-door phenomena, i.e., people's greater likelihood of compliance with a large request when that request has been preceded by a less demanding act of compliance (e.g., Freedman & Fraser, 1966; Uranowitz, 1975). Self-perception theory also provides a viable account of the overjustification effect, i.e., the undermining of intrinsic interest in an activity that stems from the perception that one has engaged in the activity only as a means of reaching some desirable end (e.g., Lepper, Greene, & Nisbett, 1973; Ross, 1975). Furthermore, self-perception processes have been shown to be relevant to such diverse topics as interpersonal attraction (e.g., Seligman, Fazio, & Zanna, 1980) and pain perception (e.g., Bandler, Madaras, & Bem, 1968; Corah & Boffa, 1970). Thus, although it is no longer as capable of addressing some phenomena as it was once believed to, the theory remains a powerful conceptual framework.

Having briefly reviewed self-perception theory in a historical perspective, let me now turn to some research that concerns a series of questions that are not addressed in Bem's theoretical statements. The consideration of three such matters will permit the desired updating of self-perception theory. (1) What prompts self-perception? That is, what motivates individuals to form attitudes via a self-inference process? (2) From what behavioral evidence are individuals willing to draw attitudinal inferences? In particular, is one's failure to engage in behavior regarded as attitudinally informative as overt performance? (3) What can be discerned about the status of the attitude before and after an individual's having engaged in a self-perception process? As we shall see, recent research on these three questions serves to clarify ambiguities that are not addressed by the original theoretical statements and to document previously unsubstantiated aspects of self-perception theory.

THE MOTIVATION FOR ATTITUDE FORMATION

Bem speaks of individuals *coming to "know"* their attitudes via a self-perception process. The first question to be addressed centers upon this phrase "come to know." Why do people want to know? What motivates people to self-perceive, i.e., to undertake a self-perception analysis so as to form attitudes?

Bem's theoretical statements are fairly mute with respect to this issue. Indeed, the only relevant statement I could find is "self-perception theory lacks any motivational construct other than an implicit assumption that individuals are willing to answer inquiries concerning their internal states" (Bem, 1972, p. 44). Thus, the implication is that it is a need to respond to a verbal inquiry that motivates people to undertake a self-perception analysis. There is in fact a great deal of evidence to suggest that people engage in self-perception when faced with an inquiry about their attitudes (e.g., Kiesler et al., 1969; Salancik & Conway, 1975). They consider recent and/or salient behavior that they have performed and infer their attitude via an implicit self-selection rule. But, is a verbal inquiry the only inducement to self-perceive?

Actually, this question can be addressed at a far more general level. When do individuals naturally and spontaneously form attitudes? That is, what situational factors prompt individuals to reflect upon their behavior, integrate whatever information they have about the attitude object, or do whatever, to develop an attitude? In discussing the functional value of attitudes, theorists have argued that attitudes serve to organize and structure a rather chaotic universe of objects, i.e., an object appraisal or knowledge function. An attitude is thought to provide, according to Smith, Bruner, and White (1956), "a ready aid in 'sizing up' objects and events in the environment" (p. 41). The obvious implication is that individuals might form attitudes when it is functional for them to do so. Any situational cue that suggests that it might be useful to have a "ready aid" may prompt immediate attitude formation.

Two such cues were examined in a recent pair of experiments conducted by Fazio, Lenn, and Effrein (1984): (1) an expectation of future questioning about the attitude object and (2) an expectation of future interaction with the attitude object. In order to be capable of responding more effectively to anticipated queries about the object or to interact more effectively with the object in the future, individuals may find it useful to form attitudes in the immediate situation, rather than to delay attitude formation until the later situation.

The major difficulty that had to be overcome to test these hypotheses concerned an appropriate methodology. How could we discern whether individuals had spontaneously formed attitudes following their perception of a cue that implied that it would be functional to do so? The logic underlying our methodology involves the use of response time and an experimental design that includes two critical comparison conditions. All subjects are first introduced to a set of novel attitude objects. One group of subjects, the consolidation condition, is forced to form attitudes toward the object by our giving them an attitude scale to complete. Another group, the no consolidation condition, receives neither the attitude scale nor a cue of any sort. These two conditions constitute the comparison conditions to which reference was made earlier.

The dependent measure involves subjects' latency of response to inquiries about their attitudes toward the objects. How quickly can individuals tell us that they like or dislike some object? Previous research has observed a difference between latencies in consolidation and no consolidation conditions (e.g., Fazio, Chen, McDonel, & Sherman, 1982). Just as one would expect, people who had been forced to form attitudes out of the need to complete a traditional attitude scale responded faster than those who had not received this same prompt. Apparently, those in a no consolidation condition did not spontaneously engage in the cognitive work necessary to form attitudes. At minimum, whatever steps they did take in this regard were not as complete as what subjects in a consolidation condition did when responding to the attitude scale.

The critical issue is where a cue condition falls in terms of response latency. Do subjects not forced to consolidate but given a cue implying that it may be functional to form attitudes display response times equivalent to those in the consolidation condition or to those in the no consolidation condition? If the pattern is such that latencies in the cue condition are equivalent to latencies in the consolidation condition but faster than latencies in the no consolidation condition, then the cue must have been sufficient to prompt attitude formation. If, on the other hand, the pattern of latencies indicate that the cue condition is equivalent to the no consolidation condition and slower than the consolidation condition, then the cue did not prompt spontaneous attitude formation. By comparing latencies within a cue condition to latencies within consolidation and no consolidation conditions, then, it should be possible to discern whether the cue was sufficient to prompt attitude formation.

This is precisely what we did in two experiments. In each, subjects first worked in a 15 minute free-play setting with five types of novel intellectual puzzles that presumably were to form part of an aptitude test that was being developed. Consolidation and no consolidation conditions were created, along with a cue condition. In Experiment 1, the cue involved an expectation of future questioning. Subjects were briefly warned about a second major part of the experiment and were then told: "Basically, though, Dr. Clark, one of the psychologists who is involved in preparing the test items, would like to speak to you. He's very interested in discussing the puzzles with you and each of the other participants on an individual basis. In this way, he can find out about your reactions to each of the five types of puzzles." In Experiment 2, the cue involved future interaction with the attitude object and again forewarned the subject of a second major part to the experiment. Presumably, we wanted to determine whether the aptitude test could be prepared for computer administration. Subjects were told "We will give you 10 minutes of computer time and allow you to instruct the computer as to which type of puzzles you wish to see and work on. The computer will allow you to work on any of the types of puzzles that you want." Essentially, then, the cue was intended to imply that, in order to make one's selections on the computer efficiently, it might be useful to form attitudes toward the various puzzle types.[1]

The latency data from both experiments indicated that each cue successfully prompted spontaneous attitude formation. The data are presented here in terms of the differences in response time for the target puzzles vs. some filler puzzles, mazes and crosswords, that we could be confident subjects had already formed attitudes toward.[2] A positive score indicates that the subject responded more quickly on the target trials than on the filler trials. In each experiment, the mean latency in the no consolidation condition is significantly slower than those in either the consolidation or the cue conditions, which do not differ reliably from one another. Thus, the pattern suggests that each cue, an expectation of future questioning about the attitude object in Experiment 1 and an expectation of future interaction with the object in Experiment 2, was sufficient to induce attitude formation. Instead of waiting until the subsequent situation when they would

---

[1]In both experiments, two cue conditions were included, one in which the cue was delivered before the free-play behavior and one in which it was delivered after free-play. The timing of the cue had no discernible impact in either experiment. The means listed in Table 5.1 for the cue conditions are averages collapsed across timing. See Fazio et al. (1984) for a more detailed presentation of the data.

[2]Parenthetically, there are a number of reasons to believe that the use of such filler trials is absolutely essential in such response time research. Fazio et al. (1984) provide a lengthy discussion of the value of filler latencies in guiding interpretation of the data.

actually face questioning or the need to make behavioral decisions, individuals who received a cue formed their attitudes immediately. (See Table 5.1.)

The findings suggest that any cue implying functionality would produce this same effect. The implication for self-perception processes is clear. Apparently, individuals would bother to reflect upon their behavior and infer an underlying disposition when they have received a direct inquiry concerning their attitudes or when they have perceived a cue implying that it may be functional to form attitudes. Indeed, in each of the above experiments there was some indication that attitudes may have been formed, at least in part, via a self-perception process involving inference from behavior. Within-subject correlations between behavior toward the puzzles during the introductory free-play period and subsequently expressed attitudes averaged .48 and .45 in Experiments 1 and 2, respectively. Of course, it is not possible to determine whether attitudes were inferred from the behavior or whether attitudes and behavior were commonly dependent upon various features of the stimuli. Nevertheless, the findings suggest that individuals undertake the effort involved in developing attitudes, be it via information integration, self-inference, or any other cognitive process, only when they perceive that it might be functional to have stored in memory "a ready aid to 'size up' objects" (Smith et al., 1956, p. 41).

One conceivably fruitful way of conceptualizing the sort of situations that may motivate such spontaneous attitude formation is provided by Kruglanski's theory of lay epistemology (Kruglanski, in press; Kruglanski & Freund, 1983). In a fashion that parallels attitude theorists' discussion of the knowledge (Katz, 1960) or object appraisal (Smith et al., 1956) function that attitudes serve, Kruglanski considers the motivational construct "need for structure." This motivation refers to a "need to have some knowledge on a given topic, any knowledge as opposed to confusion and ambiguity" (Kruglanski & Freund, 1983, p. 450). Situational pressure to form a clear opinion, make a decision, execute an action, or the like is thought to engender a need for structure. Although not limited to attitude formation, these notions are clearly relevant to the situational

TABLE 5.1
Mean Differences in Response Latency
for Target vs. Filler Items

	Experiment	
Condition	1	2
Consolidation	$.21_a$	$.50_a$
Cue	$.64_a$	$.22_a$
No Consolidation	-1.04_b	$-.60_b$

Note. The more positive the score, the faster the latency on target trials relative to filler trials. Within each column, means not sharing a common subscript differ significantly.

cues that have the potential to prompt attitude formation. Furthermore, they are embedded in the context of a theory that also considers how the fear of reaching an invalid conclusion might affect the diligence of the process by which the needed structure (i.e., attitude, in the present discussion) is developed. Thus, the theory of lay epistemology may provide a useful framework for further consideration of the issue of why and when people bother to form attitudes.

With respect to self-perception processes, the following general proposition can be offered. Any situation that creates a need for structure regarding some novel attitude object will induce individuals to consider any behavior that they might have performed relevant to the attitude obect so as to infer an attitude. Such a need may emanate from a direct inquiry regarding one's evaluation of the object, from an expectation of a future inquiry, or from the prospect of having to engage in some future action with respect to the attitude object.

Of course, such functional need merely creates the motivation to form an attitude. The attitude may be formed solely via inference from behavior. Alternatively, the attitude may stem from some other process or from conceivably multiple processes of which inference from behavior might be but one component. The extent to which a self-perception process serves as the single or primary mode of attitude formation in any given situation is apt to depend on a number of factors, including how diagnostic and relevant individuals view any behavior that they have performed and the extent to which they are apprenhensive about reaching an invalid judgment (Kruglanski, in press; Taylor, 1975). Also relevant is the availability of sources of knowledge concerning one's attitude other than one's behavior. For example, research by Tybout and Scott (1983) suggests that the availability of immediate sensory data (in this case, taste) at the time that attitude formation is initiated can obviate reliance upon a process of inferring attitude from behavior. Subjects were less likely to infer an attitude on the basis of having chosen to sample the product in a situation that involved the presence or absence of a financial incentive for doing so, when they had tasted the product immediately after making the choice. Further research is needed to identify factors that determine whether attitude formation will occur primarily via a self-perception process.

THE ABSENCE VERSUS PRESENCE OF BEHAVIOR

The second question that I raise concerns the evidential basis from which it is that individuals are willing to draw an attitudinal inference. Self-perception theory speaks of individuals inferring attitudes "from observations of their own overt behavior." Just how *overt* need the behavior be?

It has clearly been established that individuals do infer attitudes, under appropriate circumstances, from their performance of a behavior. It has also been demonstrated that an overt refusal to perform a given behavior can serve as input to a self-perception process. For example, both Zanna (1972) and Harvey & Mills (1971) examined attitude change as a function of a subject's decisions *not* to alter a speech they were to deliver. Such refusals to behave did affect subsequently expressed attitudes. Both an overtly performed behavior and a refusal to behave are active behaviors involving readily observable sets of responses.

Are individuals as rational as all this appears? Frequently, it is the case that we do not refuse to behave, but simply fail to behave, i.e., fail to take advantage of an opportunity to behave. According to the logic of Bem's theory, failures to behave, or nonbehaviors as I refer to such instances, should be as useful and as informative about one's attitude as overt behavior. Provided there are no constraining external forces, a nonbehavior should be a good indication of one's internal state.

Although nonbehaviors should logically be useful for self-inference, recent work suggests that people may have a blind spot when it comes to such nonbehaviors. Both humans and animals seem to have difficulty in processing negative information and in using nonoccurrences as positive cues for making judgments or solving problems (e.g., Jenkins & Sainsbury, 1970; Newman, Wolff, & Hearst, 1980). That is, it is far easier to learn a discrimination, solve a problem, or the like, when the presence of a feature serves as the signal of a positive outcome than when the absence of a feature serves as the positive signal. This phenomenon has been referred to as the feature-positive effect.

In order to investigate the feature-positive effect in the self-perception process, Fazio, Sherman, and Herr (1982) conducted an experiment using a procedure modeled after one of Bem's (1965) early experiments. Subjects were shown a set of cartoons that they had rated as neutral in an earlier session. They were asked to decide whether each was "very funny" or "very unfunny." After making each dichotomous judgment, the subjects provided a scalar rating of the degree to which the cartoon was funny. The manner in which subjects expressed their initial dichotomous judgment was manipulated. Some subjects, the single-response/funny condition, indicated their categorization of a cartoon as "very funny" by making an active behavioral response (e.g., pressing a button or blowing a whistle). Unfunniness was indicated only by the absence of this response. Other subjects, the single-response/unfunny condition, indicated "very unfunny" by the active behavior and used the absence of a response to indicate funniness. In a two-response control condition, subjects indicated both categorizations by the performance of an active behavior, e.g., pressing a button for funny cartoons and blowing a whistle for cartoons judged to be unfunny.[3]

---

[3]Two control conditions were included in this experiment and are described fully in the original report (Fazio et al., 1982). In one, subjects made two different responses for cartoons judged to be funny or unfunny (e.g., blowing a whistle in one case and pressing a button in the other). In the other, subjects made two similar responses (i.e., pressing one button in one case and another button in the other case). It is the former control condition that is reported in Table 5.2 for the actor experiment. Only this control condition was employed in the observer experiment.

The analysis focused on the extremity of subjects' final scalar ratings of the cartoons. The results supported the existence of a feature-positive effect in the self-perception process (see the left column of Table 5.2). Relative to the control condition, subjects in the single response conditions made more extreme attitudinal inferences from their judgmental behaviors than from their judgmental nonbehaviors. Logically, of course, there should be no difference in the information value of the behavior vs. nonbehavior in this situation. Both were freely chosen and indicated a certain evaluation. Yet the absence of a response was treated as less informative.

We recently completed what Bem would refer to as an "interpersonal simulation" of this study (Fazio, Sherman, & Howell, 1985). Observer subjects viewed videotapes of an actor indicating her categorization of each cartoon. The videotapes were constructed so as to correspond to the three conditions used in the previous experiment. After each trial, the observer subject estimated the actor's attitude toward the cartoon in question. Once again, the findings revealed a feature-positive effect (see the right column of Table 5.2). Observers made more extreme inferences when the actor's judgment involved the active performance of a behavior than when it involved the absence of a behavior.

Thus, for both actors and observers, when estimating their own or another's attitudes, respectively, what one does not do matters less than what one does. Attitudinal inferences from the occurrence of behavior tend to be more extreme than inferences from equivalently informative nonoccurrences of behavior.

This feature-positive effect in the attitude inference process appears to be yet another example of perceivers' sensitivity to the salience of information. There is much evidence to indicate that salience and vividness are important in attribution processes (e.g., Pryor & Kriss, 1977; Reyes, Thompson, & Bower, 1980; Taylor & Fiske, 1978). Furthermore, within the context of self-perception processes, Salancik (1974) found that the salience of behaviors implying that one's participation in a course was due to intrinsic versus extrinsic reasons affected subjects' inferences about their attitudes toward the course. Similarly, Seligman et al. (1980) found the salience of intrinsically versus extrinsically motivated be-

TABLE 5.2
Mean Differences in Polarization for
Funny vs. Unfunny Cartoons

	Experiment	
Condition	Actors	Observers
Single Response/Funny	-0.87_a	4.49_a
Two Responses	-4.23_{ab}	-0.22_a
Single Response/Unfunny	-10.32_b	-6.75_b

Note. The more positive the score, the greater the attitude polarization for cartoons judged funny than the polarization for cartoons judged unfunny. Within each column, means not sharing a common subscript differ significantly.

haviors to affect dating couples' reports of the level of attraction that the two members of the couple felt toward one another. Also, Ross (1975) has documented the importance of salience of the expected reward to the overjustification effect; reward led to the inference of less intrinsic interest in the activity only when the reward was made salient. In the same way, nonbehaviors may not be as salient as overt actions. As a result, nonbehaviors are less likely to be used as a basis for judgment.

STATUS OF THE ATTITUDE PRIOR
TO SELF-PERCEPTION

The third question that I wish to address concerns Bem's proviso regarding internal cues. The self-perception postulate stipulates that attitudinal inference from behavior occurs "to the extent that internal cues are weak, ambiguous, or uninterpretable." It was this postulate, of course, that was the early focus on the controversy between dissonance and self-perception theories. Salience of initial attitude was critical to the interpretation of findings from interpersonal simulations (see Bem, 1968; Jones, Linder, Kiesler, Zanna, & Brehm, 1968). In addition, many so-called "crucial" experiments employed a manipulation of salience of initial attitudes in order to test the appropriateness of the two competing explanations (e.g., Ross & Shulman, 1973; Snyder & Ebbesen, 1972).

Despite all this attention, there existed until recently little or no direct evidence to support the self-perception postulate. However, it now seems clear that self-perception processes are limited, as Bem had suggested, to cases in which individuals lack a strong initial attitude. Fazio (1981) conducted an experiment that manipulated salience of initial attitude within the context of an overjustification experiment. Children engaged in a target activity with or without the promise of reward for doing so. Half the children were shown a photograph, taken in an earlier session, of themselves freely engaging in the target activity. The photo was intended to remind the children of their intrinsic interest in the task. Just as predicted by the self-perception postulate, expected reward decreased subsequent intrinsic interest only when initial attitudes were relatively nonsalient. The intrinsic interest of those children who were shown their photographs was not undermined by expected reward.

The strongest evidence for the self-perception postulate is found in an excellent study by Chaiken & Baldwin (1981). In order to document the moderating impact of internal cues, these investigators employed a procedure developed by Salancik & Conway (1975). In a clever test of self-perception theory, Salancik & Conway had varied the salience of subjects' past proreligious or antireligious behaviors by means of a linguistic device. In the proreligious condition, proreligious behaviors were paired with the adverb "on occasion" and antireligious behaviors with the adverb "frequently," so as to induce subjects to recall having performed more pro than antireligious behaviors. The pairings of the adverbs and the religious behaviors were reversed in the antireligious condition. Subsequently, subjects for whom proreligious behaviors had been made salient expressed more positive attitudes toward being religious than did subjects for whom antireligious behaviors had been made salient.

Chaiken and Baldwin (1981) varied the salience of proecology or antiecology behaviors in a similar manner. However, they observed the effect found by Salancik and Conway only for subjects whose initial attitudes could be considered weak. Attitudinal strength was operationalized by assessing the consistency between affective and cognitive measures of the attitude. Only subjects characterized by relatively low affective-cognitive consistency displayed evidence of having undergone a self-perception process.

Apparently, subjects whose attitudes were marked by high affective-cognitive consistency were able to "read" the internal cue and did not need to rely upon salient behavior to draw an attitudinal inference. I prefer to interpret these findings (and this is consistent with the thrust of the authors' discussion of the results) as indicating that the attitudes of some subjects were sufficiently strong that they could be accessed directly from memory when the subjects were requested to express their attitudes. If an individual's attitude toward some object involves a strong association between the object and his or her evaluation of that object, then he or she can activate the attitude directly from memory. This capability lessens any need to construct an attitude "on the spot" by inference from current or salient behavior.

Evidence consistent with this reasoning is provided by some recent research by Wood (1982). Using an overjustification paradigm, Wood induced some subjects to agree to prepare proattitudinal persuasive messages in return for monetary payment. Other subjects committed themselves to the same task but were not led to expect any reward for doing so. Final attitudes were found to be more favorable in the no reward than in the reward condition. However, this "undermining" of initial attitude was restricted to a specific group of subjects—those who might be said to have an attitude characterized by relatively low accessibility. In a preliminary session, subjects had been asked to list beliefs about the attitude topic and behaviors that they had performed relevant to the issue. In each case, they did so under a 2-minute time limit, and the number of items listed served as the index of accessibility of attitude-relevant information. Those subjects who listed relatively few items, especially those who listed relatively few behaviors, were susceptible to the means-end contingency implied by the expected reward. However, those who were capable of retrieving many items of information displayed no evidence of having drawn an attitudinal inference from their externally induced behavior.

This finding provides further substantiation regarding the applicability of self-perception processes only to cases involving weak internal cues. In addition, to the extent that the listing measure can be regarded as an indicant of the accessibility of the attitude, and not as solely sensitive to the amount of relevant information (belief or behavioral) that the individual possesses, this experiment illustrates the importance of attitude accessibility. The accessibility of the attitude from memory may determine whether individuals will infer attitudes from recently performed behavior.

STATUS OF THE ATTITUDE FOLLOWING
SELF-PERCEPTION

Given that a highly accessible attitude obviates reliance upon an inferential process, a question arises concerning the outcome of a self-perception process. Once a self-inference from behavior is made, is the resultant attitude still weak, ambiguous, or uninterpretable? Although the initial attitude may be relatively weak and, hence, the individual may, like an observer, be forced to rely upon observable behavior to infer what his/her attitude might be, will such self-inference serve to strengthen the attitude? One's answer to this question depends to a large extent on one's view of attitudes. It is unfortunate that self-perception theory has been associated with a view of attitudes as epiphenomena, i.e., momentary after-the-fact explanations for behavior. Within this perspective, attitudinal expressions have been considered constructions made on the basis of whatever behavior and contextual information happens to be salient, implying that no strong, relatively enduring, internal disposition exists. However, this epiphenomenal view of attitudes is by no means necessitated by the assumptions and logic of self-perception theory. The theoretical proviso regarding weak internal cues itself suggests that strong internal evaluations can exist and the research by Chaiken and Baldwin (1981) and Wood (1982) provides substantiation for this point.

Recently, Fazio, Herr, and Olney (1984) examined the subsequent accessibility of an attitude inferred via a self-perception process. Because self-perception theory indicates that not all behavior is such that it can serve as input to self-perception process, we manipulated the nature of the behavior in question and then examined the accessibility of the resultant attitude. In each of two experiments, the aim was to compare attitude accessibility in a condition that was conducive to the inference of an attitude from behavior to attitude accessibility in a condition that was not. The first experiment involved religious behaviors. Subjects completed a lengthy inventory that listed behaviors relevant to religion (e.g., attending services, praying before meals) by checking those behavioral items that they had performed. Some subjects completed this inventory with respect to a time frame of the past year. Because the subjects were college students, it was assumed that the behaviors would have been freely chosen. Other subjects completed the inventory with respect to their childhood on the assumption that the behaviors would have been required by parents and family. The recent and unmanded nature of the behaviors reviewed in the Adult Review condition make them a more appropriate basis for self-inference than are the behaviors reviewed in the Childhood Review condition, which are both more distant in time and manded. A third group of subjects in a No Review condition did not complete the behavioral inventory. In the conditions that are of relevance here, the subjects were then forced to consolidate their attitudes by the need to complete a measure of their attitudes toward religion. Importantly, the distributions of attitudes in the three conditions were equivalent to one another. Thus, the manipulation did not produce changes in attitude extremity, but as we will see shortly, it did affect the accessibility of the attitude from memory.

In order to measure attitude accessibility, all subjects then participated in a response time task involving a number of trials inquiring about attitudes toward a variety of issues, including two trials regarding religion. Each trial involved the presentation of an attitude issue followed by an evaluative adjective, e.g., "Being Religious: Good?" Subjects responded by pressing a yes or a no button, and the time interval between trial onset and the response was automatically recorded. Before the data are described, it should be mentioned that we have used response latency as a measure of attitude accessibility in a number of experiments (e.g., Fazio et al., 1982; Powell & Fazio, 1984). Furthermore, there is now evidence to indicate that such latency of response to an attitudinal inquiry is an approximation of the likelihood that an individual's attitude will be activated automatically upon his or her encountering the attitude object (Fazio, Sanbonmatsu, Powell, & Kardes, 1986).

The latency data within the religion study were very clear. As predicted, response latencies were significantly faster for subjects in the Adult Review condition than for subjects in each of the other two conditions, who displayed equivalent latencies. Thus, the opportunity to review recent, unmanded behaviors strengthened the attitude in the sense of enhancing its accessibility from memory.

In a second experiment testing this hypothesis, subjects were induced to perform a new behavior, rather than recall previous behaviors, under manded or unmanded conditions. We employed the induced compliance procedure. The actual behavior that subjects were committed to perform was held constant but the conditions under which it was performed served to make it more or less appropriate as a basis for attitudinal inference. Attitudes toward tuition increases served as the target issue. Subjects first participated in a response time task involving both target and filler trials, which provided pre-experimental latency data. They then completed a latitudes scale so that we could identify which of nine statements varying in their support of tuition increases each subject found most acceptable. In an ostensibly separate experiment, some subjects were then committed to writing an essay regarding tuition increases. Subjects were randomly assigned to one of three conditions: (1) a high choice condition in which the subject freely chose to write the essay, (2) a low choice condition, or (3) a control condition in which no mention of an essay was made. In order to ensure that actual change in attitude extremity would not occur, the position that subjects in each essay condition supported was the position that the subject had earlier deemed most acceptable. This procedure did in fact prevent the occurrence of any change in attitude extremity.

Following the manipulation, all subjects completed a scale measuring attitudes toward tuition increases so as to ensure that the high choice subjects engaged in the necessary self-perception process and consolidated their attitudes. All subjects then participated in the response time task a second time. The data pattern was just as predicted. High choice subjects displayed greater reductions from pre to post assessment in response latencies on tuition items than either the low choice or control subjects. As in the earlier experiment, this effect was observed despite equivalence in terms of the extremity of attitude scores across the conditions.

These data provide converging evidence from two very different experiments regarding the accessibility of attitudes following the consideration or the performance of unmanded behavior. Apparently, just as Bem's self-perception theory assumes, freely-performed behavior is viewed as highly reflective of one's attitude toward the object in question. Consequently, the actor in such a case can strongly associate the evaluation implied by the behavior with the attitude object, producing an attitude that is highly accessible from memory. It is somewhat ironic that an individual's undergoing what is described as a radical behaviorist process has the outcome of strengthening the attitude, making it more of an accessible, internal cue and, hence, lessening the need to rely upon a similar process in the future.

The findings suggest that an attitude resulting from a self-perception process does not appear to have the ephemeral qualities implied by an epiphenomenal view. The available literature provides additional evidence to corroborate this notion. Attitudes based on behavioral inference appear more apt to guide later behavior than attitudes not so based (see Fazio & Zanna, 1981, for a review of the relevant evidence). For example, in a particularly relevant investigation, Zanna, Olson, and Fazio (1981) ran an experimental condition similar to the unmanded condition of the religion study on attitude accessibility. Within this experimental condition, college students indicated which of a long list of religious behaviors they had performed in the past year before indicating their attitude toward being religious. One month later subjects provided self-reports concerning religious behaviors performed during the interim period. Within the experimental condition, a condition conducive to self-perception, the attitudes expressed were more predictive of the later behavior than within a control condition. This finding suggests that the more a reported attitude is the result of an inference from one's relevant prior behavior, the more effectively it predicts subsequent behavior.

Yet another indication of the strength of attitudes inferred from behavior is provided by Kiesler's (1971) work on commitment. For example, in an experiment that was very similar at an operational level to our study on the accessibility of attitudes toward tuition increases, Kiesler and Sakumura (1966) focused on the resistance of an attitude to counterpersuasion. Subjects who had freely chosen to deliver an attitude-congruent speech for little monetary payment (in other words, unmanded behavior) were less persuaded by a subsequent message than were subjects who delivered the speech for a greater payment (in other words, manded behavior) or subjects who had engaged in no behavior at all. Ross, McFarland, Conway, and Zanna (1983) also examined resistance to persuasion and found that inducing subjects to recall attitudinally relevant behaviors enhanced the likelihood that attitudes would be maintained in the face of an attack.

Interestingly, a recent and successful intervention program, which was intended to change children's attitudes about media violence, can be viewed as having taken advantage of the power of attitudinal inference from behavior (Huesmann, Eron, Klein, Brice, & Fischer, 1983). The children were induced to adopt an attitude that watching television violence is harmful by having them compose, and read before a video camera, speeches supporting this view. Not only was the desired attitude successfully induced, but it persisted over time. A posttest questionnaire administered 2 to 3 months later revealed an effect of the intervention. Furthermore, this newly adopted attitude was accompanied by a significant reduction in the children's tendency to behave aggressively, as measured by peer ratings collected some four months after the intervention.

In sum, then, attitudes inferred from behavior display remarkable strength. I would suggest that this occurs because people recognize that their own unmanded behaviors are a highly reliable and relevant indication of their attitudes, just as they do when, as observers, they heavily weigh another's behavior in considering the dispositions that the target person might possess (Amabile & Kabat, 1982). This is in fact the core assumption of Bem's self-perception theory. The research that has been reviewed provides evidence regarding the validity of the assumption. The enhanced attitudinal "strength" that has been found to follow from the opportunity to infer attitudes from behavior suggests that individuals do indeed regard behavioral information as highly diagnostic. This perceived diagnosticity leads to the development of an attitude that involves a strong association between the attitude object and its evaluation, an association that is highly accessible from memory. It may be this very accessibility that enhances the resistance of the attitude to attack and the extent to which it is likely to guide later behavior.

SUMMARY: SELF-PERCEPTION THEORY NOW

In just a few words, where is self-perception theory now, some 20 years after it was proposed? Elliot Aronson once wrote: research "continues to clarify, specify, and strengthen the applicability of the conceptual statement by establishing clear boundaries. The theory seems to have survived its brash infancy and tempestuous adolescence. It has now matured into a much tighter conceptual scheme that accounts for an important set of human social behaviors" (Aronson, 1978, pp. 219–220). The subject of that comment was cognitive dissonance theory. Yet, I believe that it is also pertinent to self-perception theory. It is not that the theory itself has been modified in drastic manner. Even the loss of the radical behaviorist language is more of a change in exposition than a change in substance (Bem, 1972). Instead, research over the years has served to clarify and, as a result, restrict the domain of the theory.

The theory is no longer an alternative to dissonance theory; it does not appear applicable to the domain of behaviors that are markedly discrepant from individuals' initial attitudes, i.e., those within the latitude of rejection. Furthermore, given the current evidence, it appears that self-perception theory may be more relevant to the issue of attitude *formation* than attitude *change*. Self-perception processes, just as intimated by Bem, are limited to instances in which the individual possesses a weak internal cue. This proviso can be conceptualized as the lack of an attitude that is readily accessible from memory. One of the consequences of undergoing a self-perception process is the formation of an attitude characterized by enhanced accessibility, thus lessening the need to undergo a similar process in the future. Finally, people would appear to undergo such a process when they have engaged in some relevant behavior and perceive some functionality to developing an attitude that summarizes their evaluative reactions to the attitude object.

General Implications

As a final comment, I would like to discuss what I see as important implications of the work I have described in the context of self-perception theory for social influence and attitudes in general. A number of years ago, both Hovland (1959) and Converse (1970) attempted to reconcile differences that had been observed between survey and laboratory research on attitude change. In so doing, they each, but Converse in particular, focused upon a distinction between attitudes and nonattitudes. The attitude/nonattitude distinction centered upon the observation that a person may respond to an item on an attitude survey, even though that particular attitude does not really "exist" in any a priori fashion for the individual. The attitude issue may be one the individual has not even considered prior to administration of the attitude survey. Apparently, then, a traditional attitude measure can "create" an attitude where none initially existed.

This point is well-documented by the first experiments that were presented on spontaneous attitude formation (Fazio et al., 1984). Recall the difference that was observed between consolidation and no consolidation conditions. It is conceivable that subjects in the no consolidation condition did engage in some cognitive work relevant to attitude formation, and possibly even developed poorly articulated and inaccessible attitudes. Whatever steps they did take in this regard, however, were clearly not as complete as the cognitive work done by subjects who were forced to respond to the attitude scale. This then is one important methodological implication. We should be aware that our attitude scales are not instruments on which subjects passively report a necessarily preexisting attitude. Instead, the instrument may have consequences for the very attitude it seeks to assess.

More important, the research that has been discussed points to the need to be aware of the status of the individual's attitude. Within the self-perception context, we see this illustrated very well. Nonexistent or relatively inaccessible attitudes are more amenable to self-perception processes than are accessible attitudes. Indeed, the construct of attitude accessibility provides a way of further conceptualizing the attitude/nonattitude distinction. It is not a dichotomy that exists, but instead a continuum, ranging from a nonattitude, to an existing but not readily accessible attitude, to a highly accessible attitude that is capable of being activated from memory automatically (Shiffrin & Schneider, 1977) when the individual encounters or hears mention of the attitude object. (See Fazio et al., 1986, for further discussion of this continuum.)

The "state of the attitude" with respect to this attitude/nonattitude continuum is a very important construct in need of more attention than it has received thus far. Not all participants in a social influence investigation necessarily possess pre-existing attitudes toward the target issue. Even those who do may not possess an attitude that involves a sufficiently strong association between the attitude object and the evaluation to allow for automatic activation of the attitude when the object is encountered. Yet, the existence or the lack of an accessible attitude may greatly affect how new information is interpreted. One only has to consider the case of two individuals—one of whom holds a highly accessible attitude capable of being activated automatically upon mention of a product and another who holds no preexisting attitude—to recognize the value of the construct. It is difficult to imagine that two such people would "receive" the same message when exposed to an advertisement for the product. Only the latter, relatively "open-minded" individual is apt to be affected by the persuasion attempt. If such is the case in many studies of attitude, then, as Converse (1970) noted, it should be kept in mind that the results have implications not for attitude change but for attitude formation. Furthermore, the question then arises as to what social influence strategies might be effective in terms of producing attitude change and how they might differ from those that affect only attitude formation.

It is toward such issues that consideration of the attitude/nonattitude continuum forces attention. In the present discussion, we have seen how the state of the attitude both determines the likelihood of a self-perception process being undertaken and how it is affected by a self-perception process. The lower the status of the attitude, the more people rely upon self-inference from behavior.

The outcome of such self-observation is an enhancement of the status of the attitude. Thus, self-perception theory provides an excellent illustration of the value of considering initial position along the attitude/nonattitude continuum.

Research on attitude-behavior consistency similarly has benefited from consideration of the attitude/nonattitude continuum. A number of investigations have identified qualities of the attitude itself that, independent of the extremity of the attitude, appear to determine the extent to which the attitude influences later behavior. The confidence with which the attitude is held (Fazio & Zanna, 1978; Sample & Warland, 1973) and the consistency between affective and cognitive components of an attitude (Norman, 1975) serve as examples of this approach. Each of the attitude qualities that has been identified as a moderator of the relation can be viewed as a means of positioning a given individual's attitude along the attitude/nonattitude continuum. Indeed, Fazio (1986) has suggested that they all may be related to the accessibility of the attitude from memory and has proposed that the automatic activation of attitude from memory upon an individual's encountering the attitude object is a critical step in the process by which attitudes guide behavior. A recent investigation of the 1984 presidential election yielded evidence indicating that the accessibility of attitudes toward Reagan (i.e., position along the attitude/nonattitude continuum) moderated the relation between those attitudes, as measured nearly four months prior to the election, and later voting behavior (Fazio & Williams, in press).

There is reason to believe that it may prove similarly valuable to consider the attitude/nonattitude continuum in the context of persuasion. For example, the Kiesler and Sakumura (1966) study implies that the state of the attitude determines the likelihood of persuasion. Subjects who underwent a procedure that later research has shown to enhance attitude accessibility were less likely to change their attitudes in response to a persuasive communication than control subjects.

More recently, Wood (1982) employed the listing measure described earlier in an investigation of persuasion. The recipients of a counterattitudinal message were less likely to change their attitudes if they previously had been capable of listing many attitude-relevant items in a limited time interval than if they had listed relatively few (see also Wood, Kallgren, & Preisler, 1985). Subjects may have listed few items either because they lacked information about the attitude topic (and, hence, conceivably lacked attitudes) or because they had difficulty retrieving whatever relevant belief and behavioral information they did possess (possibly indicating pre-existing but relatively inaccessible attitudes). Either way, the position of these subjects on the attitude/nonattitude continuum would appear to be closer to the nonattitude end than would the position of subjects who were able to list many items in the limited time provided. Provided that the listing measure can be considered to reflect position along the attitude/nonattitude continuum in this way, the finding illustrates the relevance of the attitude/nonattitude continuum to persuasion. The more an individual can be characterized as possessing a pre-existing attitude that is highly accessible from memory, the less susceptible the individual is to counterpersuasion.

Further evidence consistent with this proposition is provided by Fazio & Williams' (in press) investigation of the presidential election. The accessibility of attitudes toward Reagan was found to moderate the relation between attitudes and judgments of the performance of the candidates in the nationally televised presidential and vice-presidential debates. Individuals with highly accessible attitudes displayed more evidence of having selectively processed the debates, implying that only individuals with relatively less accessible attitudes were in a position to have their attitudinal stances modified by the information that became available during the course of the debates.

The general implication is that the state of the attitude may determine what it is that people perceive and process in a persuasive communciation, how well they counterargue, and their cognitive responses. In general, the state of the attitude may affect the likelihood that persuasion or social influence will be successful. As one theory that explicitly recognizes the importance of the attitude/nonattitude continuum, self-perception theory should serve as a useful reminder that some of what has been traditionally viewed as theory and research concerning attitude *change* may be more accurately portrayed as concerning attitude *formation*. The challenge for the future may be to understand, as was the case for self-perception theory, the extent to which models of social influence and persuasion might be limited to particular domains within the attitude/nonattitude continuum.

ACKNOWLEDGMENT

Preparation of this chapter was supported by Grant MH 38832 from the National Institute of Mental Health. The author thanks Daryl Bem, Steven Sherman, Mark Snyder, and Mark Zanna for their helpful comments on an earlier draft.

REFERENCES

Amabile, T. M., & Kabat, L. G. (1982). When self-descriptions contradict behavior: Actions do speak louder than words. *Social Cognition, 1,* 311–335.

Aronson, E. (1978). The theory of cognitive dissonance: A current perspective. In L. Berkowitz (Ed.), *Cognitive theories in social psychology* (pp. 215–220). New York: Academic Press.

Bandler, R. J., Madaras, G. R., & Bem, D. J. (1968). Self-observation as a source of pain. *Journal of Personality and Social Psychology, 9,* 205–209.

Bem, D. J. (1965). An experimental analysis of self-persuasion. *Journal of Experimental Social Psychology, 1,* 199–218.

Bem, D. J. (1968). The epistemological status of interpersonal simulations: A reply to Jones, Linder, Kiesler, Zanna, and Brehm. *Journal of Experimental Social Psychology, 4,* 270–274.

Bem. D. J. (1972). Self-perception theory. In L. Berkowitz (Ed.), *Advances in experimental social psychology* (Vol. 6, pp. 1–62). New York: Academic Press.

Chaiken, S., & Baldwin, M. W. (1981). Affective-cognitive consistency and the effect of salient behavioral information on the self-perception of attitudes. *Journal of Personality and Social Psychology, 41*, 1–12.

Converse, P. E. (1970). Attitudes and non-attitudes: Continuation of a dialogue. In E. R. Tufte (Ed.), *The quantitative analysis of social problems* (pp. 168–189). Reading, MA: Addison-Wesley.

Corah, N. L., & Boffa, J. (1970). Perceived control, self-observation, and response to aversive stimulation. *Journal of Personality and Social Psychology, 16*, 1–4.

Fazio, R. H. (1981). On the self-perception explanation of the overjustification effect: The role of salience of initial attitude. *Journal of Experimental Social Psychology, 17*, 417–426.

Fazio, R. H. (1986). How do attitudes guide behavior? In R. M. Sorrentino & E. T. Higgins (Eds.), *The handbook of motivation and cognition: Foundations of social behavior* (pp. 204–243). New York: Guilford Press.

Fazio, R. H., Chen, J., McDonel, E. C., & Sherman, S. J. (1982). Attitude accessibility, attitude-behavior consistency, and the strength of the object-evaluation association. *Journal of Experimental Social Psychology, 18*, 339–357.

Fazio, R. H., & Cooper, J. (1983). Arousal in the dissonance process. In J. T. Cacioppo & R. E. Petty (Eds.), *Social psychophysiology* (pp. 122–152). New York: Guilford Press.

Fazio, R. H., Herr, P. M., & Olney, T. J. (1984). Attitude accessibility following a self-perception process. *Journal of Personality and Social Psychology, 47*, 277–286.

Fazio, R. H., Lenn, T. M., & Effrein, E. A. (1984). Spontaneous attitude formation. *Social Cognition, 2*, 217–234.

Fazio, R. H., Sanbonmatsu, D. M., Powell, M. C., & Kardes, F. R. (1986). On the automatic activation of attitudes. *Journal of Personality and Social Psychology, 50*, 229–238.

Fazio, R. H., Sherman, S. J., & Herr, P. M. (1982). The feature-positive effect in the self-perception process: Does not doing matter as much as doing? *Journal of Personality and Social Psychology, 42*, 404–411.

Fazio, R. H., Sherman, S. J., & Howell, J. (1985). *The feature-positive effect in observers' attribution of attitudes to actors.* Unpublished data.

Fazio, R. H., & Williams, C. J. (in press). Attitude accessibility as a moderator of the attitude-perception and attitude-behavior relations: An investigation of the 1984 presidential election. *Journal of Personality and Social Psychology.*

Fazio, R. H., & Zanna, M. P. (1978). Attitudinal qualities relating to the strength of the attitude-behavior relationship. *Journal of Experimental Social Psychology, 14*, 398–408.

Fazio, R. H., & Zanna, M. P. (1981). Direct experience and attitude-behavior consistency. In L. Berkowitz (Ed.), *Advances in experimental social psychology* (Vol. 14, pp. 162–202). New York: Academic Press.

Fazio, R. H., Zanna, M. P., & Cooper, J. (1977). Dissonance and self-perception: An integrative view of each theory's proper domain of application. *Journal of Experimental Social Psychology, 13*, 464–479.

Freedman, J. L., & Fraser, S. C. (1966). Compliance without pressure: The foot-in-the-door technique. *Journal of Personality and Social Psychology, 4*, 195–202.

Harvey, J., & Mills, J. (1971). Effect of an opportunity to revoke a counterattitudinal action upon attitude change. *Journal of Personality and Social Psychology, 18*, 201–209.

Hovland, C. I. (1959). Reconciling conflicting results derived from experimental and survey of attitude change. *American Psychologist, 14*, 8–17.

Huesmann, L. R., Eron, L. D., Klein, R., Brice, P., & Fischer, P. (1983). Mitigating the imitation of aggressive behaviors by changing children's attitudes about media violence. *Journal of Personality and Social Psychology, 44*, 899–910.

Jenkins, H. M., & Sainsbury, R. S. (1970). Discrimination learning with the distinctive feature on positive or negative trials. In D. Mostofsky (Ed.), *Attention: Contemporary theory and analysis*. New York: Appleton-Century-Crofts.

Jones, R. A., Linder, D. E., Kiesler, C., Zanna, M., & Brehm. J. W. (1968). Internal states or external stimuli: Observers' attitude judgments and the dissonance theory—self-persuasion controversy. *Journal of Experimental Social Psychology, 4,* 247–269.

Katz, D. (1960). The functional approach to the study of attitudes. *Public Opinion Quarterly, 24,* 163–204.

Kiesler, C. A. (1971). *The psychology of commitment*. New York: Academic Press.

Kiesler, C. A., Nisbett, R. E.,& Zanna, M. P. (1969). On inferring one's belief from one's behavior. *Journal of Personality and Social Psychology, 11,* 321–327.

Kiesler, C. A., & Sakumura, J. (1966). A test of a model for commitment. *Journal of Personality and Social Psychology, 3,* 349–353.

Kruglanski, A. W. (in press). *Basic processes in social cognition: A theory of lay epistemology*. New York: Plenum.

Kruglanski, A. W., & Freund, T. (1983). The freezing and unfreezing of lay-inferences: Effects on impressional primacy, ethnic stereotyping, and numerical anchoring. *Journal of Experimental Social Psychology, 19,* 448–468.

Lepper, M. R., Greene, D., & Nisbett, R. E. (1973). Undermining children's intrinsic interest with extrinsic reward. *Journal of Personality and Social Psychology, 28,* 129–137.

Newman, J., Wolff, W. T., & Hearst, E. (1980). The feature-positive effect in adult human subjects. *Journal of Experimental Psychology: Human Learning and Memory, 6,* 630–650.

Norman, R. (1975). Affective-cognitive consistency, attitudes, conformity, and behavior. *Journal of Personality and Social Psychology, 32,* 83–91.

Powell, M. C., & Fazio, R. H. (1984) Attitude accessibility as a function of repeated attitudinal expression. *Personality and Social Psychology Bulletin, 10,* 139–148.

Pryor, J. B., & Kriss, M. (1977). The cognitive dynamics of salience in the attribution process. *Journal of Personality and Social Psychology, 35,* 49–55.

Reyes, R. M., Thompson, W. C., & Bower, G. H. (1980). Judgmental biases resulting from differing availabilities of arguments. *Journal of Personality and Social Psychology, 39,* 2–12.

Ross, M. (1975). Salience of reward and intrinsic motivation. *Journal of Personality and Social Psychology, 32,* 245–254.

Ross, M., McFarland, C., Conway, M., & Zanna, M. P. (1983). Reciprocal relation between attitudes and behavior recall: Committing people to newly formed attitudes. *Journal of Personality and Social Psychology, 45,* 257–267.

Ross, M., & Shulman, R. F. (1973). Increasing the salience of initial attitudes: Dissonance versus self-perception theory. *Journal of Personality and Social Psychology, 28,* 138–144.

Salancik, G. R. (1974). Inference of one's attitude from behavior recalled under linguistically manipulated cognitive sets. *Journal of Experimental Social Psychology, 10,* 415–427.

Salancik, G. R., & Conway, M. (1975). Attitude inferences from salient and relevant cognitive content about behavior. *Journal of Personality and Social Psychology, 32,* 829–840.

Sample, J., & Warland, R. (1973). Attitude and prediction of behavior. *Social Forces, 51,* 292–304.

Seligman, C., Fazio, R. H., & Zanna, M. P. (1980). Effects of salience of extrinsic rewards on liking and loving. *Journal of Personality and Social Psychology, 38,* 453–460.

Shiffrin, R. M., & Schneider, W. (1977). Controlled and automatic human information processing: II. Perceptual learning, automatic attending, and a general theory. *Psychological Review, 84,* 127–190.

Smith, M. B., Bruner, J. S., & White, R. W. (1956). *Opinions and personality*. New York: Wiley.

Snyder, M., & Ebbesen, E. (1972). Dissonance awareness: A test of dissonance theory versus self-perception theory. *Journal of Experimental Social Psychology, 8,* 502–517.

Taylor, S. E. (1975). On inferring one's attitudes from one's behavior: Some delimiting conditions. *Journal of Personality and Social Psychology, 31,* 126–131.

Taylor, S. E., & Fiske, S. T. (1978). Salience, attention, and attribution: Top of the head phenomena. In L. Berkowitz (Ed.), *Advances in experimental social psychology* (Vol. 11). New York: Academic Press.

Tybout, A. M., & Scott, C. A. (1983). Availability of well-defined internal knowledge and the attitude formation process: Information aggregation versus self-perception. *Journal of Personality and Social Psychology, 44,* 474–491.

Uranowitz, S. W. (1975). Helping and self-attributions: A field experiment. *Journal of Personality and Social Psychology, 31,* 852–854.

Wood, W. (1982). Retrieval of attitude-relevant information from memory: Effects on susceptibility of persuasion and on intrinsic motivation. *Journal of Personality and Social Psychology, 42,* 798–810.

Wood, W., Kallgren, C. A., & Priesler, R. M. (1985). Access to attitude-relevant information in memory as a determinant of persuasion: The role of message attributes. *Journal of Experimental Social Psychology, 21,* 73–85.

Zanna, M. P. (1972). Inference of belief from rejection of an alternative action. *Representative Research in Social Psychology, 3,* 85–95.

Zanna, M. P., Olson, J. M., & Fazio, R. H. (1981). Self-perception and attitude-behavior consistency. *Personality and Social Psychology Bulletin, 7,* 252–256.

The Effects of Collective Actions on The Attitudes of Individual Group Members: A Dissonance Analysis

Mark P. Zanna
Gerald N. Sande
University of Waterloo

Several of the chapters in this volume have examined attitude change processes in the context of persuasive communications. Over the past 25 years, however, social psychologists have determined that an effective way of changing a person's attitude is not necessarily to present a persuasive communication, but instead to commit the person to a behavior that goes against his or her current beliefs. After numerous studies designed to determine the boundary conditions as well as the underlying mediating processes of this phenomenon, it seems fair to say that there is reasonable agreement about the boundary conditions: People must feel responsible for producing aversive consequences that often follow from counterattitudinal behavior.

While the two major theories which attempt to account for this effect, Festinger's (1957) cognitive dissonance theory and Bem's (1972) self-perception theory, generally agree on these conditions, they do propose different mediating processes. Dissonance theory suggests that attitude change occurs as a means of reducing the unpleasant tension state produced by feeling responsible for behavior that produces aversive consequences. In contrast, self-perception theory suggests that individuals simply infer that they hold the attitude implied by their behavior, taking into account, of course, the context in which the behavior is performed. Thus, whereas dissonance theory holds that we are rationalizing beasts, self-perception theory views us as rational, information-processing animals.

Recent work (Fazio, Zanna, & Cooper, 1977) indicates that dissonance processes are operative for attitude change following clearly discrepant or counterattitudinal behavior while self-perception processes best account for attitude change which follows the performance of behavior that is generally consistent with an individual's initial beliefs.

While we would maintain that this research on the behavior-attitude relation has advanced our understanding a great deal, one procedural fact in all this work has recently captured our attention. Primarily for the sake of simplicity and control, virtually all of the research has investigated individuals acting alone. That is, experimenters have attempted to induce only isolated individuals to behave counterattitudinally.

In an attempt to extend this research in a more truly *social* psychological direction, we have begun to look at the social context in which an individual engages in counterattitudinal behavior, and, hence, potentially experiences dissonance. It is not difficult to imagine circumstances in which behaviors performed in conjunction with others might arouse cognitive dissonance. In fact, given the pressure in groups toward uniformity of behavior, counterattitudinal actions or the performance of insincere roles are likely events. For example, adolescents are frequently subject to peer pressure to engage in behavior which might initially be counterattitudinal, such as dropping out of school, starting to smoke, taking drugs, etc. Similarly, members of formal organizations are subject to "role stress" which results from pressures arising within the group, e.g., organizational role constraints, to act in a manner inconsistent with their personal values. These examples raise interesting questions for research. Will individuals acting as members of groups experience cognitive dissonance in the same manner as has been demonstrated for individuals acting alone? If so, will this dissonance be reduced by means of post-behavioral attitude change?

At the outset, three interesting possibilities were considered. First, it is possible that individuals might experience *more* dissonance (and change their attitudes more) in group situations. For example, if subjects induced to write a counterattitudinal policy statement believe that "three heads are better than one," they might also believe that the counterattitudinal essay written by the group is more persuasive than the essay of a single subject. If so, they are likely to believe their behavior will produce more aversive consequences and, as previous research suggests, they will experience more dissonance.

On the other hand, individuals might experience *less* dissonance in groups. Recent research has demonstrated that individuals often put less energy or effort into their work in groups than when acting alone. This phenomenon has been referred to as the "social loafing" effect (cf. Latane, Williams, & Harkins, 1979; Petty, Harkins, & Williams, 1980). Perhaps dissonance might motivate group subjects to loaf even more than usual, since a "poor effort" might allow subjects to conclude either that they really didn't (much) engage in the counterattitudinal behavior in the first place, or that the consequences of the collective action weren't so aversive after all.

Finally, and perhaps more theoretically interesting, individuals behaving counterattitudinally in a group context might experience the *same*, or even *more*, dissonance but change their attitudes *less* than individuals acting alone. This follows from the fact that group members have a viable avenue of dissonance reduction not available to individuals. They can diffuse responsibility for their action and its aversive consequences to the other group members, and as a result, avoid having to change their attitudes.

That group members will diffuse responsibility for potentially costly behaviors has been clearly demonstrated by Mynatt and Sherman (1975). In that study, groups and individuals were induced to give advice to a target person. When this advice led to failure, group members assumed less responsibility for the consequences of their advice than did individual subjects. In the domain of helping behavior, Latane and Darley (1970), Latane and Rodin (1969) and others have shown that people in groups are much less likely to assume personal responsibility for helping a victim than are solitary bystanders.

Since it is generally accepted that attitude change is one of the more effortful and "costly" means of coping with dissonance (Zanna & Aziza, 1976), to the extent that diffusion of responsibility is available as an avenue of dissonance reduction, it was expected that group members would employ this option and, compared to individuals experiencing dissonance alone, manifest little postbehavioral attitude change. With these theoretical considerations in mind, a series of studies was conducted to determine how dissonance-motivated processes mediate the effects of collective actions on the attitudes of individual group members.

EXPERIMENT 1: THE INDUCED COMPLIANCE STUDY

Method. As part of what was ostensibly a study on "brainstorming," 109 subjects acting alone or in same-gender groups of three were induced under conditions of high or low choice to write essays advocating a counterattitudinal point of view. Subjects in the Low Choice conditions were simply assigned to their essay topic. Subjects in the High Choice conditions were given several opportunities to discontinue their participation once they had been informed about the essay topic (only two subjects dropped out). The choice manipulation was carried out before subjects in the Group conditions were assembled into triads.

All subjects were first given time to think about and list possible counterattitudinal arguments in isolation. Subjects in the Alone conditions were then simply asked to write an essay based on these arguments. In contrast, subjects in the Group conditions came together in groups of three to discuss their arguments and decide which points ought to be included in the group's essay. When the group decided on a point, each member of the group recorded it on his or her own copy of the group's essay. All subjects were led to believe that their actions

TABLE 6.1
Experiment 1: Mean Attitude Change Scores

Decision	Context	
Freedom	Alone	Group
High Choice	1.64	.90
Low Choice	.24	1.47

Note. Survey control mean equals .30. Cell n's range from 24 to 29.

might have aversive consequences in that the essays were to be submitted to a relevant policy-making committee on campus.

Once the essays were completed, each subject, in isolation, completed a posttest measure of their attitudes (a pretest had been taken several weeks earlier in the context of an unrelated study) and, for group members, perceptions of who was primarily responsible for the group's essay.[1]

Results.   Preliminary hierarchical analysis of variance indicated there were no main effects or interactions due to groups, so the individual group member was treated as the unit of analysis.

Responses to a measure of perceived choice confirmed the effectiveness of our choice manipulation. High Choice subjects perceived more choice ($M = 9.86$, on an 11-point scale) than did Low Choice subjects ($M = 6.87$), regardless of whether subjects were acting alone or in groups, $F(1,100) = 36.33, p < .001$.

Analysis of variance of the attitude change measure indicated, as expected, that the interaction between the Choice and the Alone/Group variables was highly reliable, $F(1,99) = 11.58, p < .001$ (see Table 6.1). The form of this interaction can be summarized as follows.

Among the subjects in the Alone conditions the basic dissonance effect was replicated. These subjects displayed more behavior-consistent attitude change following *freely* performed counterattitudinal behavior. Not only was there significantly more attitude change in the Alone/High Choice condition than the Alone/Low Choice condition, $t(49) = 2.81, p < .01$, only subjects in the High Choice condition differed reliably from the survey control (in which subjects merely returned to the laboratory to fill out the attitude questionnaire), $t(43) = 2.48, p < .03$.

---

[1]Actually, two replications were performed. In the first, male subjects wrote essays advocating government cutbacks in university funding; in the second, female subjects wrote essays advocating government cutbacks in daycare centre funding. Preliminary analyses of the main attitude change results indicated there were no effects for Replications, so the results will be presented collapsing across this factor. The perceived responsibility measure was included only in Replication 2.

Unexpectedly, subjects in the Low Choice/Group condition also displayed significant attitude change relative to the survey control, $t(45) = 2.19, p < .05$. However, this change does not seem to be due to dissonance processes. First, these Low Choice/Group subjects didn't perceive much choice, $M = 6.64$, on a 11 - point scale, and certainly perceived themselves to have had no more choice than did low choice subjects acting alone, $M = 7.13, t < 1$. Second, perceived responsibility, which, theoretically speaking, ought to mediate dissonance-produced attitude change was uncorrelated with attitude change for these subjects, $r(16) = -.08$, n.s.

Although we cannot be certain, attitude change in the Low Choice/Group condition does not seem to be due to persuasion processes, in that these subjects, when asked, did not indicate that they were exposed to any new ideas during the group discussion. Rather, attitude change seems to be due to processes of social comparison and/or public accountability. We infer that social comparison processes were important for these Low Choice subjects from two facts. First, these subjects were apparently susceptible to the so-called "fundamental attribution error" (Ross, 1977). Their estimates of their fellow group members' attitudes ($M = 4.31$ on a 9-point scale) indicated that, compared to the High Choice/Group subjects ($M = 2.52$), these Low Choice/Group subjects believed the other group members' actions in constructing the essay actually reflected their real attitudes, $t(33) = 3.18, p < .01$. Second, this belief correlated strongly with attitude change, $r(16) = .75, p < .001$.

We infer that public accountability processes were important because these subjects appeared to believe that their fellow group members were susceptible to the fundamental attribution error. In response to the question, "What do the other group members think your attitude is?", these Low Choice/Group subjects made estimates ($M = 5.56$ on a 9-point scale) more congruent with the point of view expressed in the essay than did High Choice/Group subjects ($M = 3.06$), $t(33) = 3.79, p < .01$. This estimate also correlated highly with attitude change, $r(16) = .55, p < .01$. It seems, then, that Low Choice/Group members may have changed their attitudes to bring them into line with what they perceived to be the attitudes of their colleagues and/or the actions they thought they were being held accountable for by their colleagues.[2]

High Choice/Group subjects changed their attitudes less, but not significantly less, than subjects experiencing dissonance alone. To be precise, .90 is not different from 1.64 (nor is it different from .30). However, there is no indication that High Choice/Group subjects experienced less dissonance than High

---

[2]It is interesting that although attributions of attitude-behavior consistency should have been more feasible in the *high choice* groups (Jones & Harris, 1967), these subjects apparently made no such inferences. Possibly, these subjects were so inwardly focused in an attempt to resolve their intrapsychic experience of dissonance that they paid little attention to more externally oriented attribution processes.

Choice/Alone subjects. Further analyses suggested that group members may have, in fact, experienced *more* dissonance than subjects acting alone.

On measures of perceived effort and involvement (Petty, Harkins, & Williams, 1980), High Choice/Group subjects ($M = 7.53$) reported that they "loafed" somewhat less than subjects in both the High Choice/Alone condition ($M = 6.87$), $t(29) = 1.90$, $p < .07$, and the Low Choice/Group condition ($M = 6.78$), $t(34) = 1.85$, $p < .07$. Thus, High Choice/Group subjects did not engage in social loafing in order to avoid feeling responsible for their counterattitudinal actions. Further, they do seem to believe that "three heads are better than one." They rated their essays as more persuasive than did High Choice subjects acting alone, $M = 7.65$ vs. $M = 5.93$, $t(30) = 2.22$, $p < .05$. Thus, it seems that more dissonance was aroused in the group conditions because subjects in this condition appeared to expend more effort on a counterattitudinal task which they believed would produce more aversive consequences. Despite these conditions, there was slightly less, rather than more attitude change.[3]

Following a procedure developed by Ross and Sicoly (1979), we asked each group member to indicate how responsible each group member was, including himself or herself, for the final group product. Thus, subjects could be classified as either egocentrically biased (taking more credit for the construction of the essay than their fellow group members gave them), or altercentrically biased (taking less responsibility than others gave them). It is apparent that diffusion of responsibility was not as ubiquitous as had been anticipated. Only 40% of the High Choice/Group condition members took less responsibility than was given to them by their fellow group members.[4] In contrast, only 10% of the Low Choice/Group condition members assumed less responsibility than the others assigned to them, showing that the egocentric bias phenomenon demonstrated by Ross and Sicoly (1979) is especially "alive and well" under these circumstances.

The final question we asked was: Did the subjects who diffused responsibility (the altercentrically biased subjects) change their attitudes less than subjects who did not diffuse responsibility (the egocentrically biased subjects)? In fact, this is exactly what happened. Altercentric subjects did not change their attitudes, $M = .48$, while egocentric subjects, $M = 1.97$, showed significantly more attitude change compared to the survey controls, $t(26) = 2.38$, $p < .05$. These subjects even changed slightly (but not significantly) more than subjects in the High

---

[3]It is of interest to note that our measures of perceived effort and perceived persuasiveness seem to be reasonably valid correlates of dissonance arousal in that each correlated with attitude change in the High Choice/Alone condition (r's(25) = .38, .33, respectively, $p < .05$, in each case), though not in the High Choice/Group condition (r's(27) = .03, .18, respectively).

[4]One procedural reason for this may be that perceived responsibility was assessed immediately after the interaction. Delayed assessment, e.g., one week after the interaction, might have resulted in an increased diffusion of responsibility (cf. Burger & Rodman, 1983).

Choice/Alone condition. It should be noted that the altercentric and egocentric subjects apparently did not differ in the amount of dissonance they experienced; they were virtually identical on our measures of perceived choice, effort, and persuasiveness of the essay.

So, while our initial expectations that all (or most) of the subjects experiencing dissonance in groups would diffuse responsibility was not confirmed, the results do support the notion that diffusing responsibility to other group members is a viable avenue of dissonance reduction in groups.[5] It appears that individuals behaving counterattitudinally as members of a group experienced more dissonance than those acting alone, and that group members who assumed responsibility for their actions changed their attitudes, while those who diffused responsibility to others did not.

Encouraged by these initial findings, and cognizant of the fact that not everyone seems inclined to diffuse responsibility to fellow group members, we decided next to explore the role of personality variables which ought to moderate the diffusion of responsibility effect. While several personality dimensions are of potential interest, one appears to be directly relevant to our present concerns: A predisposition to assume or deny personal responsibility for the consequences of one's actions. According to Schwartz (1977, p. 230), Responsibility Denial is "the individual tendency to accept rationales for denying responsibility for the consequences of one's behavior." This trait is "measured by agreement with or rejection of a set of 28 items which mention or allude to actions with interpersonal consequences and provide rationales for ascribing [some] responsibility for the actions and/or their consequences away from the actor" (Schwartz, 1977, p. 257).

Responsibility Denial has been shown to relate to several behaviors in the helping domain. Most relevant to our research is the study reported by Schwartz and Clausen (1970), which demonstrated that the classic bystander intervention effect (in Schwartz and Clausen's case, less helping, as a function of group size, for a person experiencing a nervous seizure) held only for those who tended to accept rationales for denying responsibility. Presumably this is because the high Responsibility Denial subjects diffused responsibility for helping onto the other bystanders. In our next study, then, we decided to test the notion that individuals high on the dimension of Responsibility Denial would be less likely to change their attitudes following dissonance-producing actions in groups.

---

[5]In a somewhat similar dissertation study Mynatt (1976, experiment 3) found less attitude change in High Choice groups than in a High Choice/Alone condition, although he found no relation between perceived responsibility and attitude change. However, Mynatt's procedure differs from ours in ways that may have attenuated perceived responsibility. The interaction between group members was minimal (and may be better considered as coaction). Further, choice was not manipulated on an individual basis prior to the formation of the group. As a result, all subjects perceived very low levels of personal responsibility for their actions.

This study had a second purpose as well. We very much wanted to extend our research effort to the other classic dissonance paradigm, the so-called "free-choice" or decision-making paradigm, since it is our intuition that this paradigm is more prototypical of the dissonance experience in the group context. As members of formal and informal groups we are often required to participate in the making of collective decisions that are consequential for ourselves and others. Especially when members of organizations are required to participate in decisions which have aversive consequences, for example, deciding which employees to lay off, dissonance is likely to be aroused.

EXPERIMENT 2: THE FREE-CHOICE STUDY

Method. One hundred and fifty-five subjects acting alone or in groups of three were induced to consider the merits and shortcomings of two applicants to an attractive, new student housing project. In the Decision (or high dissonance) condition, subjects actually made what they perceived to be a consequential decision concerning the fate of two applicants by recommending to the housing authorities that one applicant be accepted and one be rejected. In the No Decision (or low dissonance) condition, subjects engaged in a similar assessment of the candidates, but for a different purpose. These subjects provided feedback about the quantity and quality of information in the application packages, ostensibly so that the housing authority could assure the fairest procedures would be used to select students for this scarce and rather attractive resource.

Once the decision was made (or the feedback was decided upon), all subjects, in isolation, were asked to anonymously rate seven applicants, including the two candidates they had intensively scrutinized. Following past dissonance research, the difference in evaluation between the applicant chosen and the applicant rejected constituted the measure of attitude change.

We went to considerable lengths to convince our subjects that they were making a consequential decision that would affect other people's important, real world outcomes. First, subjects were not recruited for a psychology experiment. Instead they were recruited for a market research project ostensibly conducted by a firm that was in the process of designing a new cooperative residence for students. Since it was important that our subjects believe their advice would be taken seriously and would have consequences, subjects were told that they were being recruited because their housing experience at university made them ideally suited to provide advice on a cooperative residence project. During an initial phone conversation, potential subjects were asked if they were currently living in dormitories or off campus. No matter how they answered, subjects were told that the company was seeking the opinion and advice of students in similar living circumstances. The cover story was enhanced by running the experiment at a location other than the psychology building and by having the experimenter

TABLE 6.2
Experiment 2: Mean Differential Evaluation Scores of Recommended
and Rejected Applicants

Decision	Personality/Context			
Condition	Deniers		Ascribers	
	Alone	Group	Alone	Group
Decision	5.47	3.05	2.51	4.30
No Decision	2.71	3.67	2.96	3.65

Note. Survey control means equals 3.21. Cell n's range from 14 to 25.

dressed in business attire. Finally, the materials included professionally prepared applications and actual architectural plans for the residence. This procedure proved to be very convincing. When the experimenter suggested that the company felt it was only fair to get student input on who should actually get to live in this highly desirable residence, subjects agreed heartily. Debriefing revealed that the subjects believed they were participating in a real and consequential task.

Results.[6]   Subjects, who filled out the Schwartz (1977) Ascription of Responsibility scale on a separate occasion, were split at the median into groups of Responsibility Deniers and Ascribers. A two (Decisions vs. No Decision) by two (Group vs. Alone) by two (Deniers vs. Ascribers) analysis of variance of the attitude change measure indicated that the three-variable interaction was reliable, $F(1,175) = 4.93$, $p < .05$. The form of this interaction is depicted in Table 6.2.

The results for the Responsibility Deniers were exactly as expected. In the Alone condition these subjects show the basic dissonance effect, more spreading apart of alternatives (in this case, greater differential evaluation of the two housing applicants) following a consequential decision. Indeed, Responsibility Deniers changed their attitudes more in the Alone/Decision condition than in either the Alone/No Decision condition, $t(175) = 3.14$, $p < .01$, or the Survey Control (in which subjects, n = 29, once again, merely filled out our attitude measure), $t(175) = 2.57$, $p < .02$.

---

[6]Actually, two replications were performed. In the first, male subjects completed the dependent measures immediately following their deliberations, as described in the text; in the second, female subjects completed these measures in a second, individual session approximately one week later. A preliminary analysis indicated that the pattern of results was virtually identical across the two replications (all interaction F's involving the Replication factor were less than one). Not surprisingly, overall, there was more attitude change in the first ($M = 4.27$) as compared to the second ($M = 3.08$) replication, $F (1,175) = 5.50$, $p < .05$). Therefore, the results will be presented collapsed across the replication factor for ease of presentation.

When the Group condition is compared with the Alone condition, it can be seen that Responsibility Deniers changed their attitudes less when the decision was made by a group, $t(175) = 2.75, p < .01$. In fact, taking the Survey Control as the baseline, these subjects, who were expected to reduce dissonance in this situation by diffusing responsibility to their fellow group members did not, in fact, change their attitudes at all, $t < 1$.

Responsibility Ascribers, who exhibit a predisposition to assume responsibility for the consequences of their actions, show a markedly different pattern of results. Interestingly, but unexpectedly, when alone, these subjects do not exhibit any evidence of changing their attitudes following a consequential decision. Perhaps these subjects, who naturally accept responsibility for their actions, have less of a need to justify their decisions.

In contrast, there is some indication that these subjects do seem to change their attitudes more in the group context, perhaps due to social influence processes, although this trend is only marginally significant (main effect for the Alone vs. Group variable for the Responsibility Ascribers, $F(1,175) = 3.12, p < .10$).

Overall, these results support the notion that diffusion of responsibility is a viable avenue of dissonance reduction following collective actions, at least, in this case, for those with a predisposition to deny responsibility for the consequences of those actions.

Two important aspects of our decision-making study ought to be noted: (1) for the first time, at least to our knowledge, dissonance theory has been extended to decisions which influence the fate of others rather than the self, and (2) the group itself (in contrast to an experimenter) exerted the sort of conformity pressure that led to compliance on the part of individual group members. We believe both of these aspects of our procedure simulate an important prototypical situation where dissonance is often experienced in the real world. Hopefully, research using this sort of paradigm will be informative about the conditions under which public compliance (or conformity) turns into private acceptance.

GENERAL DISCUSSION

This research exemplifies the complicated task one faces when investigating group contexts, in which different psychological processes can co-occur and interact. As we were quickly reminded in our first, induced-compliance experiment, dissonance is hardly the only social influence process operative in groups. Subjects not experiencing dissonance not only succumbed to the fundamental attribution error themselves, but acted as if they realized that their fellow group members were also susceptible to this bias. As a consequence of these beliefs their attitudes were apparently influenced.

Nevertheless, our initial results have encouraged us to speculate upon those situational (in addition, to individual difference) variables that might determine whether or not responsibility is diffused or attitudes are changed following dissonance-producing collective actions. Of particular interest, we would like to consider group, interpersonal and intergroup characteristics.

For example, group size and group structure are characteristics that may well influence one's opportunity to diffuse responsibility. It might be expected that members of larger groups will be more likely to resolve dissonance by diffusing responsibility, presumably because the extent of one's relative contributions to the group product is less clearcut in larger groups. Group structure is of interest not only because different positions in a group are naturally associated with different levels of responsibility for group performance, but also because it may be easier to diffuse responsibility from some positions than from others. It may be very difficult for group leaders to deny the fact that "the buck stops" with them. On the other hand, those occupying low-status positions may have little need to diffuse responsibility because they are, in reality, least responsible for the group product. Interestingly, it may be those who occupy the middle-level positions of organizations, for example, advisers or assistants to group leaders, whose contributions are the most ambiguous. When collective actions do not arouse dissonance, these individuals may exaggerate their responsibility, believing themselves to be the "power behind the throne." When dissonance is aroused, however, they can convince themselves they are mere underlings, not really responsible at all for much of what goes on.

An interpersonal variable that should impact on the responsibility diffusion process is the individual's commitment to the group. Increased commitment ought to lead to less diffusion. There are several potential ways of manipulating commitment to the group and, therefore, influencing the probability that responsibility will be diffused. For example, the greater the cohesiveness of the group (Back, 1951), the less likely a group member will be to diffuse responsibility. A related hypothesis is that the ongoing relationships among group members will affect the tendency to diffuse responsibility. For example, diffusion may be less likely to occur in groups composed of friends than in groups composed of strangers (cf. Latane & Rodin, 1969). We are particularly interested in a related determinant of commitment to the group, group interdependence (Kelly & Thibaut, 1978). Quite apart from whether or not an individual likes and/or respects fellow group members, he or she may be more or less dependent upon them for the attainment of some desired outcome. We propose that greater group interdependence will lead to less diffusion.

An intergroup variable that should determine the ease with which diffusion can occur is public accountability. In many cases individual group members are called upon to justify the actions of the group. In an organizational context, for example, individual members of a policymaking committee may be held personally accountable for the consequences of the group's decisions. To the extent that one expects to be held personally accountable for the group's action, diffusion of responsibility may be less available as an avenue of dissonance reduction. Public accountability is also of interest in cases where the individual is called upon to justify, after the fact, a collective action for which he or she either diffused responsibility or did not initially feel responsible. This kind of *post hoc* induction of accountability leads to the possibility of retroactive arousal of dissonance, which cannot easily be reduced by diffusing responsibility. Under these circumstances one might discover delayed attitude change, where none was initially observed.

In conclusion, while the present research has demonstrated that diffusion of responsibility to other group members is a viable alternative to attitude change as an avenue of dissonance reduction, at least for some individuals in some circumstances, the results of both studies suggest a number of factors which ought to moderate the acceptance and diffusion of responsibility for dissonance-producing collective actions. Thus, it appears that group actions represent a particularly interesting context in which to study the relation between attitude change and diffusion of responsibility.

ACKNOWLEDGMENTS

We wish to thank Robert Croyle and Russell Fazio for their comments on earlier drafts of the chapter. The research reported in this chapter was supported by a grant from the Social Sciences and Humanities Research Council of Canada. Correspondence can be sent to Mark P. Zanna, Department of Psychology, University of Waterloo, Waterloo, Ontario, Canada N2L 3G1.

REFERENCES

Back, K. W. (1951). Influence through social communication. *Journal of Abnormal and Social Psychology, 46,* 9–23.
Bem, D. (1972). Self-perception theory. In L. Berkowitz (Ed.). *Advances in Experimental Social Psychology* (Vol. 6, pp. 1–62). New York: Academic Press.
Burger, J. M., & Rodman, J. L. (1983). Attributions of responsibility for group tasks: The egocentric bias and the actor-observer difference. *Journal of Personality and Social Psychology, 45,* 1232–1242.
Fazio, R. H., Zanna, M. P., & Cooper, J. (1977). Dissonance and self-perception: An integrative view of each theory's proper domain of application. *Journal of Experimental Social Psychology, 13,* 464–479.
Festinger, L. (1957). *A theory of cognitive dissonance.* Stanford, CA: Stanford University Press.
Jones, E. E., & Harris, V. A. (1967). The attribution of attitudes. *Journal of Experimental Social Psychology, 3,* 1–24.
Kelley, H. H., & Thibaut, J. W. (1978). *Interpersonal relations: A theory of interdependence.* New York: Wiley.

Latane, B., & Darley, J. M. (1970). *The unresponsive bystander: Why doesn't he help?* Englewood Cliffs, NJ: Prentice-Hall.

Latane, B., & Rodin, J. (1969). A lady in distress: Inhibiting effects of friends and strangers on bystander intervention. *Journal of Experimental Social Psychology, 5,* 189–202.

Latane, B., Williams, K., & Harkins, S. (1979). Many hands make light the work: The causes and consequences of social loafing. *Journal of Personality and Social Psychology, 37,* 822–832.

Mynatt, C. (1976). *The diffusion of responsibility hypothesis: A theoretical analysis and an empirical test.* Unpublished doctoral dissertation, Indiana University.

Mynatt, C., & Sherman, S. J. (1975). Responsibility attribution in groups and individuals: A direct test of the diffusion of responsibility hypothesis. *Journal of Personality and Social Psychology, 32,* 1111–1118.

Petty, R. E., Harkins, S. G.. & Williams, K. D. (1980). The effects of group diffusion of cognitive effort on attitudes: An information-processing view. *Journal of Personality and Social Psychology, 38,* 81–92.

Ross, L. (1977). The intuitive psychologist and his shortcomings: Distortions in the attribution process. In L. Berkowitz (Ed.), *Advances in Experimental Social Psychology* (Vol. 10). New York: Academic Press.

Ross, M., & Sicoly, F. (1979). Egocentric biases in availability and attribution. *Journal of Personality and Social Psychology, 37,* 322–336.

Schwartz, S. H. (1977). Normative influences on altruism. In L. Berkowitz (Ed.), *Advances in Experimental Social Psychology* (Vol. 10, pp. 221–279). New York: Academic Press.

Schwartz, S. H., & Clausen, G. (1970). Responsibility, norms, and helping in an emergency. *Journal of Personality and Social Psychology, 16,* 299–310.

Zanna, M. P., & Aziza, C. (1976). On the interaction of repression-sensitization and attention in resolving cognitive dissonance. *Journal of Personality, 44,* 577–593.

7 Compliance Principles of Compliance Professionals: Psychologists of Necessity

Robert B. Cialdini
Arizona State University

For a long time, I have had a professional interest in the subject of compliance, which can be defined as action that is taken only because it has been requested. That interest has focused on two related questions: Which are the most powerful compliance tactics and principles, and why do they work so well? The first of the questions is concerned, of course, with the identification of effective strategies, while the second is concerned with their conceptual mediation.

At the beginning of my investigations, I made a pair of natural errors for someone trained like me in the tradition of experimental social psychology. First, I put the cart before the horse and began examining issues of conceptual mediation before I had properly identified what was important enough to study. Second, I confused reliability with potency.

I believe I was led to both errors by my choice of initial research settings: the controlled, laboratory experiment. Controlled experimentation offers a marvelous context for addressing such issues as whether an effect is real (i.e., reliable) and which theoretical account best explains it. But this approach does a poor job of identifying effects that are sufficiently powerful or prevalent in the course of natural behavior or warrant our attention. That is, because the best designed experiments (1) eliminate or control away all sources of influence except the one under study and (2) possess highly sensitive measurement techniques, they can register ecologically trivial effects. What's more, these effects, that may be so small as to never appear when extraneous factors are allowed to vary naturally, can be replicated repeatedly in the antiseptic environment of the controlled, laboratory experiment, giving the mistaken impression of power.

When the implications of the foregoing analysis struck me, I recognized that my approach to the study of compliance had been wrongheaded to that point. I had started with two questions, Which are the most powerful compliance tactics and principles, and Why are they so effective? By using controlled experimental procedures to answer both, I was answering neither. This was so because such procedures do not properly address the issue of real power. Therefore, it was wholly possible that I was spending my time studying the reliability and conceptual mediation of effects that were epiphenomena of my research setting—and that's all.[1]

Some other way than rigorous experimentation had to be found, then, to identify the major influences on the compliance process. The one I chose was participant observation, in which the researcher infiltrates the group to be studied and becomes a spy of sorts to gain insights from the inside—a research strategy I knew virtually nothing about, save my graduate school reading of *When Prophesy Fails* (Festinger, Riecken, & Schachter, 1956). The approach was the provence of other social sciences. So, I began to read, with benefit, into the literatures of anthropology and sociology where participant observational methods had been developed and honed.

Another choice I made was to focus my participant observations not so much on the targets of influence as on the practitioners—those individuals whose profession it is to influence others to comply. That choice was based on what strikes me as the inescapable upshot of a logic akin to that of natural selection. Because their economic livelihoods are at stake, compliance professionals who use powerful compliance procedures will survive, flourish, and, consequently, pass these procedures on (somewhat like genes) to succeeding generations (e.g., trainees); those who use ineffective procedures, on the other hand, will either drop them or will wither away. Thus, over time and over a wide range of naturally occurring compliance settings, the most effective practices, based on the most powerful and adaptive principles of social influence, will rise, concentrate, and persist.

The lesson was clear: To find the most powerful compliance tactics and principles in our society, I should determine from the inside what the compliance professionals did, based on the largest sample of naturally occurring compliance settings I could access. I spent nearly 3 years in the endeavor, taking training in a variety of sales organizations (encyclopedia, portrait photography, fire alarm, automobile, insurance, etc.), infiltrating a pair of advertising agencies and a pair of fundraising organizations, talking to recruiters, public relations specialists, lobbyists, and police bunco-squad officers. In the process, I tried to watch for

---

[1]I hope that I will not be misunderstood as believing that an experimental approach is inappropriate for the study of compliance action, as that is hardly the case. I mean only to suggest that it is more properly suited to answering questions of the reliability and conceptual mediation of effects that have been identified by other means to be worthy of such inquiry. Readers interested in a fuller discussion of the interplay between experimental and nonexperimental methods in this regard may wish to refer to Cialdini (1980).

overarching compliance principles. It was important to resist the temptation to look for such general principles in any one specific form, time, profession, or practitioner. Instead, it was the pervasiveness of a principle across these dimension that would be most instructive, according to the natural-selection-like logic described earlier. Consequently, I developed an informal "transcendency index" on which to rate the principles I saw in use. The index consisted of ratings derived from four test questions:

Does the principle transcend forms? A truly general influence on the compliance process is likely to appear in a multitude of versions and variations. Therefore, principles that appeared in numerous tactical forms were given high marks by this criterion. For example, one principle scoring well in this regard was commitment/consistency, which serves as the basis for a variety of frequently employed compliance techniques (bait and switch, foot-in-the-door, four walls, low-ball, building agreements, etc.), each of which works by generating an initial commitment in the target person that is logically consistent with compliance with a subsequent, related request.

Does the principle transcend professions? By the earlier-described logic, the fundamental principles governing the influence process will have risen to prominence in all long-standing influence professions. What's more, the practices that activate those principles will have been carried by practitioners migrating from one influence profession to another. Consequently, the principles in use across the widest range of the professions I sampled were assigned "star" character here. The principle of social validation scored highest in this category.

Does the principle transcend practitioners? Principles that can be engaged effectively by most practitioners are sufficiently powerful and general to sustain their effects through the many differences in style, appearance, and experience of practitioners. So, if within a given profession (e.g., public relations) a certain principle (e.g., reciprocity) was employed almost universally by members of the profession, it was graded higher in my scoring system.

Does the principle transcend eras? Some practices have a history of success; they are traditional (e.g., appeals to scarcity). Those principles that have stood the test of time, that have survived the vagaries of fads, trends, Zeitgeists and changing economic conditions are to be considered noteworthy by my system. These are the principles that seem to engage persisting features of the human condition.

Which are the transcendant principles of influence by virtue of my analysis? I counted six that stood out from the rest. For experimental social psychologists, there won't be any big surprises on the list. All the principles have been investigated and found effective in social psychological experimentation. Still, there are some notable absences of traditional effects within our literature. For instance, the systematic use of primacy/recency effects seemed nonexistant in my sample. I saw no evidence that situations were being arranged by practitioners to take advantage of primacy/recency influences. In a related vein, there are other principles which we have spent less time and effort investigating than is commensurate with their degree of use (e.g., scarcity).

After nearly 3 years of collecting compliance techniques and assessing their pervasiveness, I ended this initial stage to do some structuring. It was quite evident that many of the common tactics I had observed clustered into groups. More importantly, each group seemed to illuminate one of a very few major rules that people use to determine when to comply. Most of these rules were of the rule-of-thumb variety (cf. Chaiken, this volume). In each case, the rule could be seen as stemming from a fundamental social psychological principle, through which the rule acquired its power to influence behavior. In each case, as well, the rule was apparently triggered by a specific grouping of compliance tactics. The most notable thing about the rules for me was that they all governed in classic heuristic form, providing behavioral direction on the basis of a single, highly diagnostic stimulus feature (or two) of the situation rather than on the basis of a more complete analysis of the situation's relevant information. I found it fascinating that, in the most persuasive compliance tactics I observed, each contained one of those single stimulus features.

Although a more detailed account is available (Cialdini, 1985), the material below offers a summary of the results of my investigations. It is organized around the supraordinate social psychological principles that appear from my evidence to be most implicated in naturally occurring compliance. The heuristic rule that derives from each principle is also discussed, as is a brief sample of common trigger tactics that activate the rule. Additionally, the treatment of each principle includes an attempt to offer experimental data relative to the relevant hows and whys of the compliance process.

Before presenting results, a sizeable *caveat* is in order. My survey of compliance practices, ratings of their pervasiveness, and interpretation of the implications are all—my training makes me shudder at the word—subjective. No matter how careful and thorough I tried to be, the practices I observed were seen only through my eyes and registered through the filter of my expectations and previous experience. Furthermore, the settings I chose to investigate were neither exhaustive nor random, being, instead, those that allowed easy access in the two cities where I lived during the time, Phoenix and San Diego (although a few settings were sampled in Chicago, Las Vegas, and Columbus, Ohio). Therefore, the judgments of tactic prevalence—on which most of what follows is based— must be seen as those of one person, made in a moderately large but not necessarily representative set of compliance contexts.

THE PRINCIPLES, THE HEURISTICS, AND SOME TRIGGER TACTICS

The commitment/Consistency Principle

Social psychological theorists have repeatedly noted that most people possess a strong desire to be consistent within their attitudes, beliefs, words, and deeds. Several of the most prominent of these theorists have incorporated the "strain" for consistency into their perspectives on important areas of human behavior, assigning it the role of prime motivator (e.g., Festinger, 1957; Heider, 1958; Newcomb, 1953). Recently, recognition has grown concerning a somewhat different type of consistency drive than the private, intrapersonal variety that concerned the early theorists. The desire to *appear* consistent is currently seen as having substantial influence over much human action as well (Baumeister, 1982; Tedeschi, 1981). According to this view, the appearance of personal consistency is a socially desirable thing, and individuals will be consistent with their prior pronouncements and actions to project a positive public image.

It is not difficult to understand why the tendency to look and be consistent is so strong. First, good personal consistency is highly valued by other members of the society, whereas poor such consistency is negatively valued. The former is commonly associated with such positive traits as stability, honesty, and intellectual strength. The latter, on the other hand, is often seen as indicative of such desirable traits as indecisiveness, confusion, weakness of will, deceitfulness. or even mental illness. Second, aside from its effect on public image, generally consistent conduct provides a reasonable and gainful orientation to the world. Most of the time, we will be better off if our approach to the world is well-laced with consistency. Without it our lives would be difficult, erratic, and disjointed. Finally, good personal consistency provides a valuable shortcut through the density of modern life. Once we have made up our minds about an issue or have decided how to act in a given situation, we no longer have to process all of the relevant information when subsequently confronted with the same (or highly similar) issue or situation. All we need do is recall the earlier decision and respond consistently with it. The advantage of such a shortcut should not be minimized. It allows us a convenient, relatively effortless method of dealing with our complex environments that make severe demands on our mental energies and capacities. What's more, provided that the first decision was made in a thoughtful fashion and that nothing has changed drastically, we will probably be correct in our subsequent decisions by simply using consistency as the sole guideline.

In keeping with the above reasons, people frequently respond to compliance requests in a rather unthinking fashion (Langer, 1978) that is characterized by automatic consistency with a previous commitment. A heuristic that governs such situations can be worded as follows:

After committing oneself to a position, one should be more willing to comply with requests for behaviors that are consistent with that position. Thus, the pressure for consistency is engaged through the act of commitment. A variety of strategies may be used to produce the instigating commitment. Certain of these do so by asking for initial agreements that are quite small but nonetheless effective in stimulating later agreement with related, larger requests. One such start-small-and-build strategy is called the four walls technique. As far as I know it has never been experimentally investigated. Yet, it is a frequent practice of door-to-door salespeople, who use it primarily to gain permission to enter a customer's home. I first encountered it while training as an encyclopedia salesman. The technique consists of asking four questions to which the customer will be very likely to answer yes. To be consistent with the previous answers, the customer must then say yes to the crucial final question. In the encyclopedia sales situation I infiltrated, the technique proceeded as follows: *First wall,* Do you feel that a good education is important to your children? *Second wall,* Do you think that a child who does his or her homework well will get a better education? *Third wall,* Don't you agree that a good set of reference books will help a child do well on homework assignments? *Fourth wall,* Well, then, it sounds like you'll want to hear about this fine set of encyclopedias I have to offer at an excellent price. May I come in?

A similar start-small procedure is embodied in the much more researched foot-in-the-door technique. A solicitor using this technique will first ask for a small favor that is virtually certain to be granted. The initial compliance is then followed by a request for a larger, *related* favor. It has been found repeatedly that people who have agreed to the initial, small favor are more willing to do the larger one (cf. Beaman, Cole, Preston, Klentz, & Steblay, 1983; DeJong, 1979 for reviews), seemingly to be consistent with the implication of the initial action.

Other, more unsavory techniques induce a commitment to an item and then remove the inducements that generated the commitment. Remarkably, the commitment frequently remains. For example, the bait and switch procedure is used by some retailers who may advertise certain merchandise (e.g., a room of furniture) at a special low price. When the customer arrives to take advantage of the special, he or she finds the merchandise to be of low quality or sold out. However, because customers have by now made an active commitment to getting new furniture at that particular store, they are more willing to agree to examine and, consequently to buy, higher priced merchandise there. A similar strategy is employed by car dealers in the low-ball technique, which proceeds by obtaining a commitment to an action and *then* increasing the costs of performing the action. The automobile salesperson who "throws the low-ball" induces the customer to decide to buy a particular model car by offering a low price on the car or an inflated one on the customer's trade-in. After the decision has been made (and, at times, after the commitment is enhanced by allowing the customer to arrange financing, take the car home overnight, etc.), something happens to remove the reason the customer decided to buy. Perhaps a price calculation error is found, or the used car assessor disallows the inflated trade-in figure. By this time, though, many customers have experienced an internal commitment to that specific automobile and proceed with the purchase. Experimental research (Burger & Petty, 1981; Cialdini, Cacioppo, Bassett, & Miller , 1978) has documented the effectiveness of this tactic in settings beyond automobile sales. On the conceptual level, this research indicates that the tactic is effective primarily when used by a single requester and when the initial commitment is freely made.

A unitary feature of these procedures (and others like them) is the induction of a commitment that is consistent with a later action desired by the compliance professional. The strain for consistency then takes over to compel performance of the desired behavior. In distinctive heuristic fashion, all that is necessary for enhanced compliance is the single stimulus feature of a proper commitment, even when the reasons for that commitment are rendered irrelevant or are eliminated. Of course, not all behaviors constitute "proper commitments." However, there is research evidence suggesting the types of commitments that lead to consistent future responding. The present context does not allow sufficient space for a thorough discussion of that evidence. Nonetheless, I would argue that a fair summary of the research literature is that a commitment is likely to be maximally effective in producing consistent future behavior to the extent that it is active (Bem, 1967), effortful (Aronson & Mills, 1959), public (Deutsch & Gerard, 1955) and viewed as internally motivated (i.e., uncoerced, Freedman, 1965).

The Reciprocity Principle

According to the sociologist Alvin Gouldner (1960), who made an extensive review of the subject, every human society abides by a norm for reciprocation that directs us to provide to others the sort of behaviors they have provided us. By virtue of the norm of reciprocation, we are *obligated* to the future repayment of favors, gifts, invitations, and the like. A widely shared feeling of future obligation made an enormous difference in human social evolution because it meant that one person could give something (e.g., food, energy, care) to another with confidence that it was not being lost. For the first time in evolutionary history, one individual could give away any of a variety of resources without actually giving them away. The result was the lowering of the natural inhibitions against transactions that must be begun by one person providing personal resources to another. Thus, a person could provide help, gifts, defense, or trade goods to others in the group knowing that, when the time came, he or she could count on their repayment. Sophisticated and coordinated systems of gift-giving, defense, and trade became possible, bringing immense benefit to the societies that possessed them. With such clearly adaptive consequences for the culture, it is not surprising that the norm for reciprocation is so deeply implanted in us by the process of socialization we all undergo.

By working to help ensure fairness in exchanges between people, the norm strengthens the society. But beacuse it is so thoroughly ingrained, it acquires a heuristic status, at times directing us to behave in a mindless manner that results in unfair exchanges—with ourselves on the short end. The reciprocity heuristic for compliance can be worded as follows:

One should be more willing to comply with a request to the extent that the compliance constitutes a reciprocation of behavior. Under this general rule, then, people will sometimes be willing to return a favor with a larger favor (e.g., Regan, 1971). A number of sales and fundraising tactics use this factor to advantage. The compliance professional initially gives something to the target person, thereby causing the target to be more likely to give something in return. Often, this "something in return" is worth much more than the initiating favor.

The unsolicited gift, accompanied by a request for a donation, is a commonly used technique that employs the norm for reciprocation. One example experienced by many people is the Hare Krishna solicitor who gives the unwary passerby a book or a flower and then asks for a donation. Other organizations send free gifts through the mail; legitimate and less-than-legitimate missionary and disabled veterans organizations often employ this highly effective device. These organizations count on the fact that most people will not go to the trouble of returning the gift and will feel uncomfortable about keeping it without reciprocating in some way. The organizations also count on the willingness of people to send a contribution that is larger than the cost of gift they received.

Retail stores and services also make use of the powerful social pressure for reciprocation in their sales techniques. It is not uncommon to find exterminating companies that offer free home inspections. These companies bargain on the fact that, once confronted with the knowledge that a home is infested with termites, the consumer will not delay action until he or she has done some comparison shopping. A customer who feels indebted to a particular company will buy its services to repay the favor of a free examination. Certain companies, knowing that the customer is unlikely to comparison shop, have been known to raise the quoted price of extermination above normal for those who have requested a "free" inspection.

One extremely successful technique incorporating the reciprocation norm is used by the Amway Corporation. A housewife will be given a tray of products to try at her leisure for a particular period of time. The products often are provided in half-full bottles, but enough is provided to allow the customer to test it. After using a portion of one or two of these products, the consumer often feels obligated to buy at least something—often the majority of the products on the tray. When the Amway representative returns to collect the products—still in partially full bottles—the customer puts in her order. The same tray, replenished as necessary, is then passed on to the next customer, who in turn feels obligated to reciprocate the favor.

A variation of the norm for reciprocation of favors is that for reciprocation of concessions. A reciprocal concessions procedure (or door-in-the-face technique) for inducing compliance has been documented by Cialdini et al. (1975). When one bargaining party retreats from an initial demand to a second, smaller one, social conventions require the other party to reciprocate that concession. However, if the first party intentionally begins with a request much greater than that which is actually desired, when it is rejected, he or she may make a compliance-enhancing retreat to the level of request that was really wanted in the first place. This tactic often is used in appliance sales: The salesman starts with a large request of the consumer by offering the top of the line. When this request is refused, the salesperson appears to retreat by making a concession and offering a lower priced product. The customer feels a pressure to meet the salesperson halfway by agreeing to buy the lower priced product, which may still be more expensive than the one he or she meant to at the outset.

This reciprocal concessions strategy also can be successfully used for charitable solicitations. Cialdini and Ascani (1976) used this technique in soliciting blood donors. They first requested a person's involvement in a long-term donor program. When that request was refused, the solicitor made a smaller request for a one-time donation. This pattern of a large request (that is refused) followed by a smaller request significantly increased compliance with the smaller request, as compared to a control condition of people who were asked only to perform the smaller, one-time favor (50% vs. 32% compliance rate).

The Social Validation Principle

People frequently use the beliefs, attitudes and actions of others, particularly similar others, as a standard of comparison against which to evaluate the correctness of their own beliefs, attitudes and actions (cf. Festinger, 1954). Thus, it is common for individuals to decide on appropriate behaviors for themselves in a given situation by searching for information as to how similar others have behaved or are behaving (e.g., Latané & Darley, 1970; Schachter & Singer, 1962). Powerful modeling effects of similar others have been found in both adults and children in such diverse activities as altruism (e.g., Hornstein, Fisch, & Holmes, 1968), phobia remission (e.g., Bandura & Menlove, 1968) and suicide (Phillips, 1974).

Normally, the tendency to see an action as more appropriate when like others are doing it works quite well. As a rule, we will make fewer mistakes by acting in accord with social evidence than contrary to it. As such, social validation allows us another convenient shortcut. By processing what similar people do, we can usually decide what we should do, with a minimum of additional effort. When this reliance on social evidence alone becomes automatic, however, we can find ourselves behaving in objectively inappropriate ways. For example, research indicates (e.g., Cupchik & Leventhal, 1974) that people rate comedy funnier and laugh more and longer at it when the sound of others' laughter is present, even when it is known that the others' laughter is on a manufactured laugh track! As regards compliance, the social validation heuristic can be worded as follows:

One should be more willing to comply with a request for behavior to the degree that similar others are or have been performing it. Charity and other-nonprofit organizations frequently make use of social validation information to encourage people to donate. It is typical for the master of ceremonies at a telethon to read incessantly from a handful of pledge cards. The pledges are structured to represent a cross-section of the viewing public so that all may have evidence of the similarity of contributors. The message being communicated to the holdouts is clear, "Look at all the people like you who have decided to give; it must be the correct thing to do." Church collection plates (as well as bartender's tip jars) are often "salted" beforehand with folding money to provide social validation for the donation of sizeable amounts. Evangelical preachers are known to seed their audiences with "ringers," who are rehearsed to come forward at a specified time to give witness and offerings. Research by Reingen (1982) has demonstrated that individuals shown lists of prior contributors are more likely to donate to charity; further, the longer the list the greater the effect.

Social validation techniques are also used extensively by profitmaking organizations. Advertisers love to inform us that a product is the "largest selling" or "fastest growing" because they do not have to convince us directly that the product is good, they need only imply that many others think so, which seems proof enough. Salespeople are trained to spice their presentations with numerous accounts of other individuals who have purchased the product. When such individuals will testify in writing to the product's effectiveness, these testimonials are collected and prominently displayed. At the height of the disco craze, certain club owners counterfeited a brand of social validation for the club's quality by creating long waiting lines utside when there was plenty of room inside.

The Authority Principle

Legitimately constituted authorities are extremely influential persons (e.g., Aronson, Turner, & Carlsmith, 1963; Milgram, 1974). Whether they have acquired their positions through knowledge, talent, or fortune, their positions bespeak of superior information and power. For each of us this has always been the case. Early on, these people (e.g., parents, teachers) knew more than us, and we found that taking their advice proved beneficial—partly because of their greater wisdom and partly because they controlled our rewards and punishments. As adults, the authority figures have changed to employers, judges, police officers and the like, but the benefits associated with doing as they say have not. For most people, then, conforming to the dictates of authority figures produces genuine practical advantages. Consequently, it makes great sense to comply with the wishes of properly constituted authorities. It makes so much sense, in fact, that people often do so when it makes no sense at all.

This paradox is, of course, the same one that attends all of the major compliance principles. When a principle normally counsels correctly, there is a tendency to respond according to it in an unthinking fashion that leads to errors. In the instance of the authority principal, the compliance heuristic can be worded as follows:

One should be more willing to follow the suggestions of an individual who is a legitimate authority. Authorities may be seen as falling into two categories: authorities with regard to the specific situation and more general authorities. Compliance practitioners employ techniques that seek to benefit from the power invested in authority figures of both types. In the case of authority relevant to a specific situation, we can note how often advertisers inform their audiences of the level of expertise of product manufacturers (e.g., "Fashionable Men's Clothiers since 1841." "Babies are our business, our only business."). At times, the expertise associated with a product has been more symbolic than substantive, for instance, when actors in television commercials wore physician's white coats to recommend a product. In one famous Sanka commercial, the actor involved, Robert Young, did not need a white coat, as his prior identity as a TV doctor (Marcus Welby, M.D.) provided the medical connection. It is instructive that the mere symbols of a physician's expertise and authority are enough to trip the heuristic mechanism that governs authority influence. One of the most prominent of these symbols, the bare title "Dr.," has been shown to be devestatingly effective as a compliance device among trained hospital personnel. In what may be the most frightening study I know, a group of physicians and nurses conducted an experiment that documented the dangerous degree of blind obedience that 95% of hospital nurses accorded to an individual whom they had never met, but who had claimed in a phone call to be a doctor (Hofling, Brotzman, Dalrymple, Graves, & Pierce, 1966).

In the case of influence that generalizes outside of a specific situation, the impact of authority (real and symbolic) appears equally impressive. For instance, Bickman (1974) found that, when wearing a security guard's uniform, a requester could produce more compliance with requests (e.g., to pick up a paper bag on the street, to stand on the other side of a Bus Stop sign) that were irrelevant to a security guard's domain of authority. Less blatant in its connotation than a uniform, but nonetheless effective, is another kind of attire that has traditionally bespoken of authority status in our culture—the well-tailored business suit. It, also, can mediate influence. Take as evidence the results of a study by Lefkowitz, Blake, and Mouton (1955) who found that three and a half times as many people were willing to follow a jaywalker into traffic when he wore a suit and tie versus a work shirt and trousers. Con artists frequently make use of the influence inherent in authority attire. For example, a gambit called the bank examiner scheme depends heavily on the automatic deference most people assign to authority figures, or those merely dressed as such. Using the two uniforms of authority we have already mentioned, a business suit and guard's outfit, the con begins when a man dressed in a conservative three-piece business suit appears at the home of a likely victim and identifies himself as an official of the victim's bank. The victim is told of suspected irregularities in the transactions handled by one particular teller and is asked to help trap the teller by drawing out all of his or her savings. After doing so, the victim is to give the money to a uniformed bank guard waiting outside, who will then return it to the proper account. Often, the appearance of the "bank examiner" and uniformed "guard" are so impressive that the victim never thinks to check on their authenticity and proceeds with the requested action.

The Scarcity Principle

As opportunities, and the items they contain, become more scarce, they are perceived as more valuable. There seem to be two major reasons why, for the things we can have, scarcity increases attractiveness. First, it is normally the case that what is less available *is* more valuable. Precious metals and stones, for instance, are precious (in both major meanings of the word) precisely because of their limited supply. The fundamental relationship between supply and assigned worth appears so commonly that an item's availability can be taken as an indication of its quality. Consequently, it frequently is so taken, automatically. Research by Worchel, Lee, and Adewole (1975) has provided data concerning how and when an item's scarcity affects its perceived value. They found that cookies were rated as more desirable, more attractive to consumers, and more costly when they were scarce rather than abundant. Furthermore, the effect was greater when the scarcity replaced previous abundance, and when it was caused by a social demand. Other research and theorizing by Brock and Fromkin has suggested that in addition to commodities, limited access to information makes the information more desirable—and more influential (Brock, 1968). A recent test of Brock and Fromkin's thinking by one of my students found good support in a business setting. Wholesale beef buyers who were told of an impending imported beef shortage purchased significantly more beef when they were informed that the shortage information came from certain "exclusive" contacts that the importer had (Knishinsky, 1982). Apparently, the fact that the news was itself scarce made it more valued and persuasive.

A second reason that increasing scarcity leads to increasing attraction is that, as things become less available, the freedom to have them decreases. According to Brehm's reactance theory (Brehm & Brehm, 1981), the loss of free access to an item increases the drive to have it. Thus, when increasing scarcity limits prior access to something, reactance will be generated, causing individuals to want and try to possess the thing more than before. Much laboratory evidence exists to support reactance theory predictions (cf. Brehm & Brehm, 1981). In addition, some support has been found in naturally occurring settings. For example, Mazis (1975) showed that newly limited access to a certain type of detergent enhanced its attractiveness for customers. As regards compliance, the scarcity heuristic could be worded as follows:

One should want to try to secure those opportunities that are scarce. With the scarcity principle operating powerfully on the worth assigned to things, it should not be surprising that compliance professionals have a variety of techniques designed to convert this power to compliance. Probably the most frequently used such technique I witnessed was the limited number (or Standing Room Only) tactic in which the customer is informed that membership opportunities, products, or services exist in a limited supply that cannot be guaranteed to last for long. In some instances I observed, the limited number information was true; in others it was not. In each case, however, the intent was to convince prospects of an item's scarcity and thereby increase its immediate worth in their eyes. At one appliance store where I worked, it was not uncommon for salespeople to raise the value of a particular sale item for a customer by announcing that "the last one has just been sold, and I'm sure we have no more in the back; however, I can check with our other store and, if I can get it for you at the sale price, would you like to buy it?" In this way, customers were induced to make a commitment at a time when the scarcity principle would render the merchandise most attractive. Many of our customers agreed eagerly and were uniformly pleased (even relieved) when the salesperson invariably reported that, yes, the other store location still had one in stock.

Related to the limited number tactic is the "deadline" technique in which an official time limit is placed on the customer's opportunity to get what is being offered. Newspaper ads abound with admonitions to the customer regarding the folly of delay: "Last three days." "Limited time offer." "One week only sale." etc. One rather single-minded movie advertiser managed to load three separate appeals to the scarcity heuristic into just five words of copy in a newspaper ad I recently saw. It read, "Exclusive, limited engagement, ends soon." The purest form of a decision deadline—right now—occurs in a variant of the deadline technique in which customers are told that, unless they make an immediate purchase decision, they will have to buy the item at a higher price or they will not be able to purchase it at all. I found this tactic used in numerous compliance settings. A large child photography company urges parents to buy as many poses and copies as they can afford because "stocking limitations force us to burn the unsold pictures of your children within 24 hours." A prospective health club member or automobile buyer might learn that the deal offered by the salesperson is good for that one time; should the customer leave the premises the deal is off. One home vacuum cleaner company instructed me as a trainee to claim to prospects that "I have so many other people to see that I have the time to visit a family only once. It's company policy that even if you decide later that you want this machine, I can't come back and sell it to you.'' For anyone who thought about it carefully, this was nonsense; the company and its representatives are in the business of making sales, and any customer who called for another visit would be accommodated gladly. The real purpose of the can't-come-back-again claim was to evoke the scarcity heuristic.

Recall that in the Worchel et al. (1975) study scarcity was most effective when it was produced by social demand. This finding highlights the importance of competition in the pursuit of limited resources. We want a scarce item even more when in competition for it. Advertisers often try to commission this tendency in their behalf. In their ads, we see crowds pressing against the doors of a store prior to the start of a sale; we watch a flock of hands quickly deplete a supermarket shelf of a product; etc. There is much more to such images than the idea of ordinary social validation. The message is not just that the product is good because other people think so, but, as well, that we are in direct competition with those people for it. Real estate agents are taught to convey a similar idea to hesitant customers. A realtor trying to sell a house to a fence-sitting prospect sometimes will call with news of another potential buyer (real or fabricated) who has seen the house, liked it, and is scheduled to return the following day to talk about terms. The tactic, called in some circles "goosing them off the fence,'' works by turning a hesitant prospect into a competitor for a scarce resource.

The Friendship/Liking Principle

A fact of social interaction that hardly needs belaboring is that people are favorably inclined toward those they know and like. A compliance heuristic consequence of this tendency could be worded as follows:

One should be more willing to comply with the requests of friends or other liked individuals. Compliance professionals make use of the tendency to comply more readily to the requests of friends by enlisting the friends of prospects in the request presentation. The clearest illustration of this strategy that I know is the home party concept, made prominent by the Tupperware Corporation but now used to sell everything from cookware to lingerie. In the case of Tupperware, the real compliance-inducing power of the party comes from a particular arrangement that trades on friendship. The true request to purchase the product does not come from the stranger who is the company sales representative; it comes from a friend to every person in the room. Usually, it is a woman who has called her friends together for the product demonstration in her home and who, everyone knows, makes a profit from each piece sold at the party. In this fashion, the company arranges for their customers to buy from and for a friend rather than an unknown salesperson. Of course, other compliance practitioners also recognize the increased pressure to say yes to a friend. Charity organizations prefer to have volunteers canvass for donations close to their homes. They understand how much more difficult it is to turn down a charity request when it comes from a friend or neighbor. Other compliance professionals have found that the friend need not be present to be affective; often, the mention of the friend's name is sufficient and, consequently, friendship referral systems are common in direct sales.

But, what do compliance professionals do when the already-formed liking or friendship is not present for them to employ? Here, the professionals' strategy is quite direct: They first get their customers to like them. Tactics designed to generate liking occur in a variety of forms that cluster around certain factors that have been shown by research to increase liking: similarity, praise, cooperation, and physical attraction.

Similarity of attitude (e.g., Byrne, 1971) or background (e.g., Stotland & Patchen, 1961) can increase liking. Consequently, compliance professionals often point to (or manufacture) similarities between themselves and target persons before making a request. Car salespeople, for example, are trained to look for evidence of a prospect's background and hobbies while examining the trade-in car. Similarity of dress is another way to induce liking, probably because it provides a basis for assumptions about other more important areas of similarity, such as opinions and values. For instance, in a study done on peace marchers in the early 1970s (Suedfeld, Bochner, & Matas, 1971), subjects were significantly more likely to sign the petition of a similarly dressed requester, and to do so without reading it. This latter finding once again suggests the automatic and mindless (Langer, 1978) quality of much compliance that is triggered by a single cue, in this case, similarity of dress.

Praise and other forms of positive estimation also stimulate liking (e.g., Byrne & Rhamey, 1965). The actor Maclain Stevenson once described how his wife tricked him into marriage: "She said she liked me." Although designed for a laugh, the remark is as much instructive as humorous. The simple information that someone fancies us can be a bewitchingly effective device for producing return liking and willing compliance. Although there are limits to our gullibility—especially when we can be sure that the flatterer's intent is manipulative (Jones & Wortman, 1973)—we tend as a rule to believe praise and to like those who provide it. Evidence for the power of praise on liking comes from a study (Drachman, de Carufel, & Insko, 1978) in which men received personal comments from someone who needed a favor from them. Some of the men got only positive comments, some only negative comments, and some got a mixture of good and bad. There were three interesting findings. First, the evaluator who offered only praise was liked best. Second, this was so even though the men fully realized that the flatterer stood to gain from their liking of him. Finally, unlike the other types of comments, pure praise did not have to be accurate to work. Compliments produced just as much liking for the flatterer when they were untrue as when they were true.

It is for such reasons that direct salespeople are educated in the art of praise. A potential customer's home, clothes, car, taste, etc. are all frequent targets for compliments. One famous compliance practitioner, Joe Girard who was named the "World's Greatest Salesman" by the *Guinness Book of World Records* for his phenomenal car sales record, made an extensive (and expensive) habit of statements of positive evaluation. Each month he sent every one of his over 13,000 former customers a holiday greeting card containing a personal message. The holiday greeting changed from month to month ("Happy New Year" or "Happy Thanksgiving" etc.), but the message printed on the face of the card never varied. It read, "I like you." As Joe explained in an interview, "There's nothing else on the card. Nothing but my name. I'm just telling 'em that I like 'em." The process of sending over 150,000 "I like you" cards per year seems very costly. Could it be worth the expense? Joe Girard thinks so; and someone who sold an average of five cars and trucks every day he worked deserves our attention on the topic of compliance.

Cooperation is another factor that has been shown to enhance positive feelings and behavior (cf. Aronson, Bridgeman, & Geffner, 1978; Cook, 1978). Those who cooperate toward the achievement of a common goal are more favorable and helpful to each other as a consequence. That is why compliance professionals frequently strive to be perceived as cooperating partners with a target person. Automobile sales managers frequently set themselves as "villains" so that the salesperson can "do battle" in the customer's behalf. The cooperative, pulling-together kind of relationship that is consequently produced between the salesperson and customer naturally leads to a desirable form of liking that promotes sales. A related technique is employed by police interrogation officers to induce a suspect to confess to a crime. Called "good cop/bad cop," the tactic begins when a pair of interrogators confronts a suspect with vastly different styles. One officer (bad cop) takes a harsh, hard approach and pretends to try to bully the suspect into confessing. He then leaves the suspect alone with a second officer (good cop) who takes a soft, conciliatory approach. Good cop tries to convince the suspect that he does not approve of bad cop's style nor methods and that he is allied with the suspect against bad cop. If he will only confess, good cop will work with the suspect to see that he gets fair treatment from the judicial system and that bad cop's threats of severe punishment will go unrealized. This cooperative orientation is often effective in winning trust and confessions from the suspect.

Finally, physical attraction and its effect on liking have long been acknowledged as producing an advantage in social interaction. Recent research findings indicate, however, that the advantage may have been sorely underestimated. There appears to be a "halo" effect for physical appearance that generalizes to such favorable trait perceptions as talent, kindness, honesty, and intelligence (e.g., Dion, Berscheid, & Walster, 1972; Rich, 1975). As a consequence, attractive individuals are more persuasive both in terms of changing attitudes

(Chaiken, 1979) and getting what they request (Benson, Karabenic, & Lerner, 1976). For instance, a study of the 1974 Canadian Federal elections found that attractive candidates received more than 2 ½ times the votes of unattractive ones (Efran & Patterson, 1976). Equally impressive results seem to obtain in the judicial system. In a Pennsylvania study, researchers rated the physical attractiveness of 74 separate male defendants at the start of their criminal trials. When, much later, the researchers checked the results of these cases via court records, they found that the better-looking men received significantly lighter sentences. In fact, the attractive defendants were twice as likely to avoid incarceration as the unattractive defendants (Stewart, 1980). When viewed in the light of such powerful effects, it is not surprising that extremely attractive models are employed to promote products and services, that sales trainers frequently include appearance and grooming tips in their presentations, nor that, commonly, con men are handsome and con women pretty.

CONCLUSION

It is my belief the six foregoing principles are used ubiquitously by compliance professionals because they spur compliance when it is wholly appropriate. That is, for most of us it makes sense to comply because we feel obligated or committed or because similar people are doing so or because a legitimate authority or liked friend has urged it. It is also my belief, however, that these principles normally work so well in counseling us as to when compliance makes sense that they can spur compliance when it makes no sense at all. The six principles cue automatic, heuristic compliance. When we encounter one or another of these cues we can usually stop processing all the relevant information in a considered fashion and count on the principle alone to steer us correctly. Here is the point at which heuristic responding becomes a simultaneous blessing and bane. It is a blessing because it is economical; we can respond to just one piece of information and usually be right. It's a bane because it produces decisions based on only a single piece of the available information (e.g., an authority says so); and no single piece of evidence can ever substitute for considered analysis.

The danger of using the single-piece-of-normally-reliable-evidence approach can be seen in the account of a meeting between a television talk show host, Joe Pine, known for his caustic, antagonistic interview style, and Frank Zappa, the rock musician. It was at a time in the 1960s when very long hair on males was still novel and controversial. When Zappa appeared as a guest on Pine's show, the following exchange occurred:

Pine: I guess your long hair makes you a girl.
Zappa: I guess your wooden leg makes you a table.

I have been impressed by how the changing form and accelerating pace of modern life is likely to make us more frequent users of heuristic decision-making techniques—we simply don't have the time or cognitive capacity anymore for a fully considered assessment of all the information in the various decision situations we face. The consequence of any increased reliance on a single-usually-reliable-piece-of-information approach, however, is an increased vulnerability to the kind of mistake made by Joe Pine. When such errors are made in the presence of clever individuals like Frank Zappa, those mistakes can be exploited to make us look foolish or much worse.

REFERENCES

Aronson, E., & Mills, J. (1959). The effect of severity of initiation on liking for a group. *Journal of Abnormal and Social Psychology, 59,* 177–181.

Aronson, E., Bridgeman, D. L., & Geffner, R. (1978). The effects of a cooperative classroom structure on student's behavior and attitudes. In D. Bar-Tal & L. Saxe (Eds.), *Social psychology of education: Theory and research.* Washington, D.C.

Aronson, E., Turner, J. A., & Carlsmith, J. M. (1963). Communicator credibility and communication discrepancy as a determinant of opinion change. *Journal of Abnormal and Social Psychology, 67,* 31–36.

Bandura, A., & Menlove, F. L. (1968). Factors determining vicarious extinction of avoidance of behavior through symbolic modeling. *Journal of Personality and Social Psychology, 8,* 99–108.

Baumeister, R. F. (1982). A self-presentational view of social phenomena. *Psychological Bulletin, 91,* 3–26.

Beaman. A. L., Cole, C. M., Preston, M., Klentz, B., & Steblay, N. H. (1983). A meta-analysis of fifteen years of foot-in-the-door research. *Personality and Social Psychology Bulletin, 9,* 181–196.

Bem, D. J. (1967). Self-perception: An alternative interpretation of cognitive dissonance phenomena. *Psychological Review, 74,* 183–200.

Benson, P. L., Karabenic, S. A., & Lerner, R. A. (1976). Pretty pleases: The effects of physical attractiveness on race, sex, and receiving help. *Journal of Experimental Social Psychology, 12,* 409–415.

Bickman, L. (1974). The social power of a uniform. *Journal of Applied Psychology, 4,* 47–61.

Brehm, S. S., & Brehm, J. (1981). *Psychological reactance.* New York: Academic Press.

Brock, T. C. (1968). Implications of commodity theory for value change. In A. G. Greenwald, T. C. Brock, & T. M. Ostrom (Eds.), *Psychological foundations of attitudes.* New York: Academic Press.

Burger, J. M., & Petty, R. E. (1981). The low-ball technique: Task of person commitment. *Journal of Personality and Social Psychology, 40,* 492–500.

Byrne, D. (1971). *The attraction paradigm.* New York: Academic Press.

Byrne, D., & Rhamey, R. (1965). Magnitude of positive and negative reinforcements as a determinant of attraction. *Journal of Personality and Social Psychology, 2,* 884–889.

Chaiken, S. (1979). Communicator physical attractiveness and persuasion. *Journal of Personality and Social Psychology, 37,* 1387–1397.

Cialdini, R. B. (1985). *Influence: Science and practice.* Glenview, IL: Soctt, Foresman.

Cialdini, R. B. (1980). Full-cycle social psychology. In L. Bickman (Ed.), *Applied Social Psychology Annual* (Vol. 1). Beverly Hills, CA: Sage.

Cialdini, R. B., & Ascani, K. (1976). Test of a concession procedure for inducing verbal, behavioral, and further compliance with a request to give blood. *Journal of Applied Psychology, 61,* 295–300.

Cialdini, R. B., Cacioppo, J. T., Bassett, R., & Miller, J. A. (1978). Low-ball procedure for producing compliance: Commitment then cost. *Journal of Personality and Social Psychology, 36,* 463–476.

Cialdini, R. B., Vincent, J. E., Lewis, S. K., Catalan, J., Wheeler, D., & Darby, B. L. (1975). Reciprocal concessions procedure for inducing compliance: The door-in-the-face technique. *Journal of Personality and Social Psychology, 31,* 206–215.

Cook, S. W. (1978). Interpersonal and attitudinal outcomes in cooperating interracial groups. *Journal of Research and Development in Education, 12,* 28–38.

Cupchik, G. C., & Leventhal, H. (1974). Consistency between expressive behavior and the evaluation of humerous stimuli: The role of sex and self-observation. *Journal of Personality and Social Psychology, 30,* 429–442.

DeJong, W. (1979). An examination of self-perception mediation on the foot-in-the-door effect. *Journal of Personality and Social Psychology, 37,* 2221–2239.

Dion, K., Berscheid, E., & Walster, E. (1972). What is beautiful is good. *Journal of Personality and Social Psychology, 24,* 285–290.

Deutsch, M., & Gerard, H. B. (1955). A study of normative and individual judgments. *Journal of Abnormal and Social Psychology, 51,* 629–636.

Drachman, D., deCarufel, A., & Insko, C. A. (1978). The extra-credit effect in interpersonal attraction. *Journal of Experimental Social Psychology, 14,* 458–467.

Efran, M. G., & Patterson, E. W. J. (1976). *The politics of appearance.* Unpublished manuscript, University of Toronto.

Festinger, L. (1954). A theory of social comparison processes. *Human Relations, 2,* 117–140.

Festinger, L. (1957). *A theory of cognitive dissonance.* Stanford, CA: Stanford University Press.

Festinger, L., Reicken, H. W., & Schachter, S. (1956). *When prophecy fails.* Minneapolis: University of Minnesota Press.

Freedman, J. L. (1965). Long-term behavioral effects of cognitive dissonance. *Journal of Experimental Social Psychology, 1,* 145–155.

Gouldner, A. W. (1960). The norm of reciprocity. *American Sociological Review, 25,* 161–178.

Heider, F. (1958). *The psychology of interpersonal relations.* New York: Wiley.

Hofling, C. K., Brotzman, E., Dalrymple, S., Graves, N., & Pierce, C. M. (1966). An experimental study in nurse-physician relationships. *Journal of Nervous and Mental Disease, 3,* 177–180.

Hornstein, H. A., Fisch, E., & Holmes, M. (1968). Influence of model's feeling about his behavior and his relevance as a comparison other on observer's helping behavior. *Journal of Personality and Social Psychology, 10,* 222–226.

Jones, E. E., & Wortman, C. (1973). *Ingratiation: An attributional approach.* Morristown, NJ: General Learning Press.

Knishinsky, A. (1982). *The effects of scarcity of material and exclusivity of information on industrial buyer perceived risk in provoking purchase decisions.* Doctoral dissertation, Arizona State University.

Langer, E. (1978). Rethinking the role of thought in social interaction. In J. Harvey, W. Ickes. & R. Kidd (Eds.), *New directions in attribution research* (Vol. 2). Hillsdale, NJ: Lawrence Erlbaum Associates.

Latané B., & Darley, J. M. (1970). *The unresponsive bystander: Why doesn't he help?* New York: Appleton-Century-Crofts.

Lefkowitz, M., Blake, R. R., & Mouton, J. S. (1955). Status factors in pedestrian violation of traffic signals. *Journal of Abnormal and Social Psychology, 51,* 704–706.

Mazis, M. B. (1975). Antipollution measures and psychological reactance theory: A field experiment. *Journal of Personality and Social Psychology, 31,* 654–666.

Milgram, S. (1974). *Obedience to authority.* New York: Harper.

Newcomb, T. M. (1953). An approach to the study of communicative acts. *Psychological Review, 60*, 393–404.

Phillips, D. P. (1974). The influence of suggestion of suicide: Substantive and theoretical implications of the Werther effect. *American Sociological Review, 39*, 340–354.

Regan, D. T. (1971). Effects of a favor and liking on compliance. *Journal of Experimental Social Psychology, 7*, 627–639.

Reingen, D. H. (1982). Test of a list procedure for inducing compliance with a request to donate money. *Journal of Applied Psychology, 67*, 110–118.

Rich, J. (1975). Effects of children's physical attractiveness on teacher's evaluations. *Journal of Educational Psychology, 67*, 599–607.

Schachter, S., & Singer, J. E. (1962). Cognitive, social, and physiological determinants of emotional states. *Psychological Review, 69*, 379–399.

Stewart, J. E. (1980). Defendant's attractiveness as a factor in the outcome of trials. *Journal of Applied Social Psychology, 10*, 348–361.

Stotland, E., & Patchen, M. (1961). Identification and change in predudice and authoritarianism. *Journal of Abnormal and Social Psychology, 62*, 250–256.

Suedfeld, P., Bochner, S., & Matas, C. (1971). Petitioner's attire and petition signing by peace demonstrators: A field experiment. *Journal of Applied Social Psychology, 1*, 278–283.

Tedeschi, J. T. (1981). (Ed.). *Impression management theory and social psychological research.* New York: Academic Press.

Worchel, S., Lee, J., & Adewole, A. (1975). Effects of supply and demand on ratings of object value. *Journal of Personality and Social Psychology, 32*, 906–914.

8

Goals and Strategies of Persuasion: A Cognitive Schema for Understanding Social Events

Brendan Gail Rule
Gay L. Bisanz
University of Alberta

A persuasive attempt is one of the most familiar events that occurs in our everyday life. We know that people spend a great deal of time trying to get others to act in desired ways. Indeed, it has been suggested by several researchers that the most essential social skills to acquire are those that enable "people to get others to think, feel or do what they want them to" (e.g., Weinstein, 1969, p. 753). Communicative acts designed to achieve these goals involve social problem-solving skills, the success of which has been viewed as an index of social competence (reviewed by Rubin & Borwick, 1983). At least one important component of these skills is a person's naive psychology or beliefs about the most effective tactics for persuading others (Finley & Humphreys, 1974; Heider, 1958). Our chapter examines the nature and organization of knowledge about these tactics.

A person's naive psychology about the relevant tactics used to achieve various goals can be conceptualized as a social knowledge structure or schema. When people observe a compliance-gaining interaction between two other people in real life, on TV, or as described in a story, it is assumed that their knowledge about how to persuade others will affect their interpretation of the events. And indeed, their understanding and memory for the observed events may in turn affect their subsequent attitudes and behavior. In addition, a persuasion schema may operate as a cognitive system that affects the behavior of an actor in a problem solving endeavor where the goal is to generate a series of communicative messages that will get someone to do something. For both the actor and the observer, the schema will serve as a guide to the encoding, storage, and retrieval of information related to this domain (Bartlett, 1932; Fiske & Taylor, 1983; Paul, 1969). The goal of the theorist is to specify the nature of the schema in sufficient detail to enable specific predictions about how the schema will affect these cognitive processes.

Despite the importance accorded to persuasion tactics in the social world by developmental, social and clinical psychologists, relatively little theory and research has been accomplished in this area. The purpose of this chapter is to provide an overview of a cognitive analysis of knowledge of persuasion as it relates to the behavior of members of a dyad. The term persuasion, rather than compliance, is used because it corresponds to the vocabulary used in cognitive and developmental research and also seems to reflect more common lay terminology.

In our model, we suggest that the cognitive representation or schema for this domain consists of at least twelve common goals, such as obtaining an object, getting assistance, and changing an attitude. These goals can be achieved by fifteen strategies that are ordered, so that failure to achieve a goal by one method leads to selection of a strategy usually occurring later in the sequence. Our focus has been on the specification of the knowledge *observers* would use to interpret the behavior of others' attempts to persuade because our initial goal is to understand how readers or listeners comprehend the actions of characters in stories. We assume that the schema serves as a guide to processing information in this domain by its effect on comprehension, understanding and memory for persuasive events described in narratives.

In making this assumption, our work can be seen as part of ongoing work in cognitive psychology and artificial intelligence, one goal of which is to develop models of how human observers interpret human events, especially purposeful action sequences (e.g., Abbott, Black, & Smith, 1985; Black & Bower, 1980; Bower, 1978; Bower, Black, & Turner, 1979; Bruce & Newman, 1978; Omanson, 1982; Schank, 1975; Schank & Abelson, 1977; Trabasso, Secco, & Van Den Broek, 1984; Warren, Nicholas, & Trabasso, 1979). Such models must include knowledge systems that embody both "naive psychology" and "naive physics" (e.g., Schank & Abelson, 1977; Trabasso, Secco, & Van Den Broek, 1984). Although the ideas and constructs about persuasion that we will discuss have been developed in the narrative tradition, where the focus is on event understanding, theories of comprehension or understanding are certainly relevant to recent studies in social psychology and communication research concerned with how individual (actors) *generate* persuasive appeals and how those appeals influence other people. Related knowledge, if not the same knowledge systems, must be involved.

Our chapter consists of several sections. In the first section, we review and evaluate major approaches in the communication literature and social psychology dealing with the persuasion strategies reportedly used by individuals in their own attempts to gain compliance. Because these data pertain only to an actor's perception of his or her own persuasion techniques, rather than to an observer's view of others' persuasion strategies, they are useful primarily for (1) the development of, and comparison with, our work and (2) the preparation of our stimulus materials for information processing studies. In the second section, we present a cognitive analysis of knowledge about persuasion derived from Schank and Abelson's work (1977). We then discuss the data from studies we have conducted to examine the assumptions of their theory and to extend their work. In the third section, we propose a reconceptualization of the issues based on our research and provide an example of how we can test the information-processing aspects of our model. In the fourth section we reflect upon the significance of this research in relation to trends in cognitive and social psychology.

REVIEW OF MAJOR TRENDS IN EXTANT RESEARCH

The history of interest in interpersonal persuasion techniques is long and emanates from diverse-theoretical traditions. Some of the early speculations are seen in work by a radical-behaviorist, (Skinner, 1953), a sociologist (Parsons, 1963), social psychologists (French & Raven, 1960), and an organizational psychologist (Etzioni, 1961). Despite this historical and theoretical interest, it is only recently that there has been active research in the area.

A. *Taxonomies Based on Individuals' Perceptions of Their Own Strategies.* In one recent approach to this problem, investigators have examined the types of strategies reported by individuals in their attempts to persuade others. Several criticisms have been leveled against this research on both conceptual and methodological grounds. In some studies, a deductive approach has been employed as a means to develop taxonomies of the persuasive strategies used by individuals (e.g., Marwell & Schmitt, 1967). The emerging taxonomies included reward, punishment, expertise, activation of personal commitment, and socially acceptable or unacceptable strategies. The validity of this approach has been questioned, largely because the strategies were deduced from extant theories of social influence rather than from actual encounters. Few strategies are included that are relevant to those socialized to be less assertive (Johnson, 1975). As a consequence, the extent to which the taxonomies are exhaustive or even representative of the persuasive strategies available to an individual is uncertain (See Falbo, 1977; Falbo & Peplau, 1980; Johnson, 1975; Tedeschi, Schlenker & Lindskold, 1972; Wiseman & Schenck-Hamlin, 1981). Furthermore, although some researchers have suggested that affect and power relations influence tactics (Falbo & Peplau, 1980; Wood, Weinstein, & Parker, 1967), the effects of such situational variables on strategy choice are in question. When situational variables were unconfounded with the specific message used to represent a given strategy (Jackson & Backus, 1982), their effects on tactics were eliminated.

Given these difficulties, other investigators (Cody, McLaughlin, & Jordan, 1980; Cody, McLaughlin, & Schneider, 1981; Falbo, 1977; Falbo & Peplau,

1980; Schenck-Hamlin, Wiseman, & Georgacarako, 1982; Wiseman & Schenck-Hamlin, 1981) have used an inductive approach, asking participants to generate strategies they would use to persuade others. Participants have been asked to generate strategies under differing conditions. These have ranged from children pretending to persuade a parent to buy a puppy (e.g., Clark & Delia, 1976) to undergraduates writing an essay on "How I Get My Way" (e.g., Falbo, 1977). Methods of grouping specific messages into strategy types have varied from relying on the intuition of expert coders (e.g., Falbo, 1977) to relying on a conceptual framework relevant to the specific issue under investigation (e.g., Clark & Delia, 1976). The nature and range of strategy types included in the taxonomies that result from this research have differed especially with the application of scaling or factor analytic techniques. For example, using multidimensional scaling techniques, Cody (1982) identified clusters of deescalation vs. termination, and positive tone vs. negative identity management whereas Falbo (1977) identified rational vs. irrational strategies and direct vs. indirect strategies. And, although the data from these studies suggest that situational variables, such as intimacy and perceived resistance to persuasion, may effect strategy choice, the data collectively illustrate the difficulties of conducting research outside the limiting assumptions of a theoretical framework.

   B. Situational Analysis.   In another approach to the problem, some investigators (Forgas, 1976; Magnussen, 1971; Wish & Kaplan, 1977) have attempted situational analyses in which they ask for similarity ratings for communication episodes in everyday encounters involving persuasion. Statistical procedures are then applied to discover the dimensions of similarity underlying these episodes. However, the dimensions identified differ among studies. For example, Wish and Kaplan (1977) identified dimensions labeled as cooperative vs. competitive, intense vs. superficial, dominance vs. equality, formal vs. informal and task vs. nontask-oriented while Forgas reported a perceived intimacy and a self-confidence dimension for housewives and an involvement, pleasantries and know how to behave dimension for students. These differences may be the result of differing labels attached to the dimensions and/or the use of different types of analyses (multidimensional scaling, factor analysis, cluster analysis). It may also be that the events or episodes rated in these studies differ unsystematically on many variables, such as perceived resistance to compliance and personal benefits to the persuader, factors that have been identified as important to strategy selection in other research.
   Considering these major approaches in the extant research, there is no emergent consensus about the cognitive invariants that affect strategy choice in a given situation either in terms of the nature of strategy types considered by an individual or factors that affect strategy choice. Clearly, progress in the area would be optimized by research that embedded the broader vision of the induc-

tive approach within the context of a theoretical framework whose limiting assumptions have testable psychological implications. The goal of our work is to develop an approach to persuasion that has these advantages.

A COGNITIVE APPROACH

Schank and Abelson's Theory

The most detailed analysis of knowledge about persuasion within a cognitive framework to date has occurred in the area of artificial intelligence. Schank and Abelson identified a "persuade package" as being essential to understanding the behavior of characters in stories (for empirical data relevant to this claim, see Bisanz, 1982). Although their theory is about the process of story understanding, the ideas and constructs embodied in it provide the basis of a general theory about how observers understand human interactions. Within their framework, understanding human actions is a two-part process that consists of ascertaining an individual's goal and the particular method being used to achieve that goal. Schank and Abelson also make a number of assumptions about the nature and organization of the goals and methods that constitute knowledge about persuasion. First, they suggest that the number of goals associated with the use of the persuasion schema is a small finite set; Second, they assume that these goals are all linked to the use of a standard set of methods; Third, if these methods fail, they assume that additional methods (referred to as auxiliary methods) may be tried. Finally, Schank and Abelson assume that use of the standard methods is ordered so that once an initial method is selected and fails, the individual will select a strategy further down in the sequence.

Because Schank and Abelson did not provide empirical support for their ideas, the purpose of the research we report in this section was to examine their assumptions and extend their work. In two studies we asked individuals "what" and "how" questions designed to examine Schank and Abelson's assumptions about the goals and strategies involved in persuasive attempts. In two further studies, we examined the ordering assumption. We are using as our model research that has tested the effects of well-articulated theories of specific schemata on information processing and memory (e.g., Bower et al., 1979; Graesser, 1981; Mandler & Goodman, 1982). Within this tradition, methodologies like those employed in our research—open-ended questions and rating of schematic elements—are commonly used in determining the nature and organization of a schema. However, we want to stress that the studies presented here are merely a first step. They must be followed by research designed to assess the psychological validity of the knowledge structure outlined in this paper (cf. Mandler & Goodman, 1982; Wiseman & Schenck-Hamlin, 1981), which will be the subject of our third section.

OUR RESEARCH[1]

Study 1

Because it has been suggested that people's goals would vary depending upon the relationship between the persuader and the target individual, participants in this first study were asked to indicate what kinds of things people persuade their friends, fathers and enemies to do. These targets embodied the affective (friends vs. enemies) and power (friends vs. father) dimensions of relationships, although the latter pair is confounded with respect to affect.

Schank and Abelson identified only four goals as being related to the use of compliance-gaining strategies. These are shown in the top part of Table 8.1. They are: to acquire information, to acquire a physical object, to get power or authority to do something, and to get someone to do something for you. Based on the literature, we anticipated that there would be additional goals in that small finite set, including attempts to change someone's opinion, to get someone to go somewhere, to get someone to buy or sell something, and to get someone to change a role relationship. These are shown in the middle section of Table 8.1.

Our method involved giving 32 men and 32 women booklets containing the general question: "What kinds of things do people persuade other people to do?" One half of the subjects were then asked the same question about friends and fathers and the other half about friends and enemies. Each time subjects were asked to list as many responses as they could think of. The experimenter explained that the purpose of the study was to elicit information about people's knowledge of persuasion.

We found that 23% of the responses were classifiable using the four goals suggested by Schank and Abelson, 71% were classifiable using those goals plus the four goals we suggested, and 95% using additional goals that emerged through examination of the data. In the bottom portion of Table 8.1, the additional goals are described with the percentage of responses encompassed by each goal cited in parentheses.

To determine whether goals varied with the target individual, the percentage of responses generated for each goal was used to assign goals a rank for each target. The goal with the highest percentage of responses was assigned a 1 and the lowest a 12. The ranks and percentages are shown in Table 8.2. A Kendall's W, a rank coefficient of concordance for multiple samples, was calculated separately for each group of targets. There was a highly significant degree of similarity between the ranks.

From this study we drew several conclusions about knowledge of persuasion. First, although we had anticipated differences, both the nature of the goals

---

[1]For a detailed account of Studies 1 and 2, see Rule, Bisanz, and Kohn (1985). The more complete account of the data collected in Study 3 appears in this chapter.

TABLE 8.1
Taxonomy of Goals

Persuader's (P's) Goal	Definition	Example
Schank & Abelson		
Information (1.2)[a]	to acquire information from the target person (T)	to get advice on how to act
Object (12.8)	to acquire a physical object from T	lend them (P) their (T's) notes for a class they (P) missed
Permission (2.1)	to get power or authority from T to do something	you ask them to let you stay out later
Agency (7.0)	to get T to do something for P	to run to the store on an errand for them (P)
Rule, Bisanz, & Cohn		
Opinion (13.9)	to change T's opinion	to change his (T's) attitude toward school
Activity (28.4)	to get T to go somewhere or do something	to go out for the evening and relax
Ownership (3.5)	to get T to buy what P is selling or get T to sell something to P	to buy their (a particular manufacturer's) brand
Relationship (2.5)	to get T to change an existing role relationship	to get married
Data		
Habit (7.4)	to get T to change a personal habit or characteristic	to quit drinking, smoking, or using drugs
Assist (8.0)	to get T to help P do something	helping them (P) to do their homework
Third-party (1.2)	to get T to help or harm a third party	to do volunteer work for charity
Harm (7.2)	to get T do do something that will be self-harmful	to commit crimes

[a]Percentage of responses classifiable with each goal. From Rule, Bisanz, and Kohn (1985). Anatomy of a persuasion schema: Targets, goals, and strategies. *Journal of Personality and Social Psychology*, 1985, *48*, No. 5. Copyright (1985). Reproduced by permission of the American Psychological Association.

generated and the ranks reflecting frequency of generation showed a surprising degree of similarity across targets. These findings could be taken as strong evidence for Schank and Abelson's notion of a finite set of goals associated with methods of persuasion. However, we would point out that two of our four targets (friend and father) involved close personal relationships. If we had chosen targets from more distant relationships (e.g., sales people) there may have been larger differences.

Second, our data provided evidence that, although methods of persuasion can be applied to disliked persons, an enemy is a unusual target, one that falls outside the normal boundaries of application for this schema. We conclude this because subjects generated fewer responses for this target and the responses were qualita-

TABLE 8.2
Ranks for Each Goal and Target

Goal	People	Friends	Fathers	Enemies
Knowledge	12 (0.8)	8 (1.9)	11 (0.4)	11 (0.0)
Object	6 (7.4)	5 (10.1)	1 (34.4)	6 (2.7)
Permission	11 (1.0)	12 (0.0)	2 (14.9)	11 (0.0)
Agency	4 (9.4)	6 (7.9)	8 (4.0)	4 (5.3)
Opinion	2 (16.7)	2 (16.7)	4 (10.6)	2 (18.7)
Activity	1 (34.5)	1 (37.4)	3 (13.3)	3 (16.5)
Ownership	5 (9.3)	10 (0.3)	10 (1.0)	11 (0.0)
Relationship	10 (1.4)	7 (2.1)	7 (5.0)	5 (4.6)
Habit	3 (9.6)	4 (11.4)	5 (7.9)	9 (0.8)
Assist	7 (5.9)	3 (11.6)	6 (7.3)	8 (1.0)
Third-party	9 (1.6)	11 (0.2)	9 (1.2)	7 (1.6)
Harm	8 (2.5)	9 (0.4)	12 (0.0)	1 (48.7)

Note. Rank order is noted on the left of the mean percentage of responses noted in parentheses. The ranks for "people" and "friends"
shown here are pooled across samples. From Rule, Bisanz, and Kohn
(1985). Anatomy of a persuasion schema: Targets, goals, and strategies.
Journal of Personality and Social Psychology, 1985, *48*, No. 5. Copyright
(1985). Reproduced by permission of the American Psychological Association.

tively different and impoverished compared to those for other targets. As a
consequence, we excluded this target from subsequent studies.

Finally, the ability to classify 95% of the responses generated using our
taxonomy of goals could be taken as further evidence that goals related to the
persuasion schema constitute a small finite set. In drawing this conclusion,
however, one must also acknowledge that the set is larger than that suggested by
Schank and Abelson. If one looks at both the nature of the goals added to the
taxonomy as a result of the data collected and the frequency of occurrence of
goals especially with respect to the "other people" and "enemies" targets, it
seemed to us that the goals were more closely related to the type of target
individual than Schank and Abelson's assumption would imply. Rather than
accepting their assumption, we suggest it may be more useful to conceptualize
the data in a different way. We suggest that the set of goals may be finite with
respect to a given role relationship. For example, using goals that account for
more than 5% of subjects' responses as a rough index, it can be seen in Table 8.2
that the goals of object, opinion, activity, habit, and assist are common to both
friends and fathers. These targets are distinguished in that individuals commonly
want permission to do something from their father but they want a friend to do
something for them. In order to understand and evaluate the persuasive attempts
that occur in stories or daily interaction we must identify the finite sets of
normatively-appropriate goals associated with different role relationships.

Study 2

In Study 2, we focused on the assumption that a standard set of methods exists.
According to Schank and Abelson, the standard methods associated with goals of

the persuasion schema are: ask, invoke a theme (i.e., remind the individual or an existing interpersonal or role relationship), inform of a personal reason, bargain for an object, bargain for a favor, and finally threaten. Examples are given in the first portion of Table 8.3. If consent cannot be obtained using those methods, it is assumed that auxiliary methods will be used to force consent and the auxiliary methods will differ according to the nature of the goal. For example, Schank and Abelson suggest the auxiliary methods for acquiring a physical object are "steal" and "overpower" and for getting power or authority are "usurp" and "going overhead."

In our view, however, additional standard methods may include invoking altruism, moral principles and social norms. These latter methods make reference to aspects of the larger social arena in which the dyadic interaction is taking place. Examples are given in the middle portion of Table 8.3. The purpose of this second study was to test the Schank and Abelson assumption about methods by asking subjects how they persuade their friends or fathers for several goals. Evidence consistent with this assumption would be obtained by a finding that a relatively small set of methods encompassed the majority of responses generated by subjects over goals and targets. The remaining responses should be auxiliary methods that vary with the nature of the desired goal.

The goals suggested by Schank and Abelson and the five other most frequently generated goals in Study 1 were the focus of investigation. Seventy-four subjects participated. Half were asked to list all the ways that people can get their friends to achieve each goal. For the other half the target was fathers. Subjects were instructed to "Begin by listing the approach that you think would be tried first, then list the approach that you think would be tried next given the first approach fails, and so on. Keep going until you've listed all the ways you can think of. Include all methods, even those that you yourself do not approve of. Number your methods in the order that you think they would be tried."

In order to examine whether the goals of the persuasion schema are associated with a standard set of methods, we classified responses using the taxonomy presented in Table 8.3. Methods additional to those suggested by Schank and Abelson are needed to classify responses. For the nine goals the percentage of responses classifiable ranged from 94 to 100%. However, the set of methods identified encompasses virtually all of the responses generated for each goal summed over targets. Subjects reported others using methods related to physical and social force infrequently enough that it was not really possible to examine Schank and Abelson's auxiliary method assumption. We simply grouped these methods under "force" in Table 8.3.

The major issue addressed in this study was whether the goals of the persuasion schema are associated with a standard set of methods. We concluded that they are, but, as shown in Table 8.3, the set is larger than that suggested by Schank and Abelson.

Recall that in Study 1 rather than assuming that goals associated with a persuasion schema constitute a small finite set in some absolute sense we sug-

TABLE 8.3
Taxonomy of Methods

Persuader's (P's) Method*	Percentage	Definition	Example
Schank & Abelson			
Ask (Directly or Indirectly)	18.5	P asks directly or by a method like hinting for T's cooperation. No reason is given.	P casually mentions the topic so that T is not aware that P is fishing for the information. (Example of Indirect asking.)
Invoke Role Relationship (Invoke a Theme)	1.6	Mention of an existing role relationship is used to elicit cooperation.	P says T isn't a true friend if s/he won't give in to P.
Inform Personal Reason	12.6	A personal reason is given relevant to P or T to elicit cooperation. It is a selfish appeal.	P tells T how much he needs the object.
Bargain Object	5.1	Offering a highly desired physical object (could be money) in exchange for cooperation. Could be called bribe.	P offers to pay T.
Bargain Favor	7.1	Offering or collecting on a favor in exchange for cooperation.	P offers to do something else in return.
Threaten	8.6	Indicating the negative consequences of not cooperating.	P threatens to reveal some deep dark embarrassing secret about T to someone special.
Force	4.3	P overpowers T physically or goes over T's head socially.	P hits T, grabs the object, and runs.

Rule, Bisanz, & Kohn

Invoke Altruism	3.7	A reason is given for coopera-tion that expresses an unselfish interest in the welfare of others or T.	P tells T that T's habit bothers other people or is bad for T's health.
Invoke Norm	2.4	An appeal is made to a social norm to elicit cooperation.	P tells T that the item is the _in_ thing; everyone has one.
Invoke Moral Principle	0.8	An appeal is made to a moral value to elicit cooperation.	P convinces T that T would be doing the "right" thing.
Data			
Invoke Personal Expertise	9.4	P provides facts or evidence intended to elicit T's coop-eration.	P shows T results of buying it (e.g., car - shows low mileage, how it'll save money on public transporta-tion).
Butter-up	3.9	Before asking, P attempts to make T feel wonderful or im-portant.	P tells T how nice T looks today and asks if T has lost some weight.
Criticize	7.3	Before asking, P attacks T on a personal level - making T feel terrible or insignificant.	P says "You're so lazy - you never want to do anything."
Emotional Appeals	10.8	Examples include begging, crying, tantrums, etc., designed to elicit T's cooperation.	P sulks, hoping T will feel guilty.
Deceive	4.1	P misleads T to elicit coopera-tion.	P lies to T about the cir-cumstances.

*Interrater reliability was 89.4%. T = target of persuasion. From Rule, Bisanz, and Kohn (1985). Anatomy of a persuasion schema: Targets, goals, and strategies. _Journal of Personality and Social Psychology_, 1985, _48_, No. 5. Copyright (1985). Reproduced by permission of the American Psychological Association.

gested that the set might be finite with respect to a given role relationship. In contrast, here we are willing to accept Schank and Abelson's assumption. We do so, in part, because the strategies we identified by asking people to think about the tactics used by other people correspond well to those reported by investigators using an inductive approach, asking participants to think about their own strategies (see previous discussion). The other part is attributed to some tentative conclusions we reached after comparing the data from the first two studies. Namely, the goals one person can maintain with respect to another individual are potentially limitless and restricted only by the resources (including role relationships) that each individual controls. However, the set of strategies, while larger than Schank and Abelson suggested, can be readily enumerated. In fact, some strategies—ask, hint, bargain, threaten, butter-up, criticize, deceive—are so commonly recognized that they have acquired verbal labels that are readily understood. There is nothing equivalent in the domain of goals.

Study 3

The final assumption we examined was that once an initial strategy is selected the application of subsequent strategies follows an order; however, that order is not rigid in that the persuader might skip some methods. The application order Schank and Abelson propose on logical grounds is the one mentioned earlier, outlined in Table 8.3. However, it seemed to us that simply asking and more self-oriented strategies such as giving a personal reason or invoking personal expertise, may occur earlier followed by strategies that refer to dyadic interactions, such as bargaining for a favor or making reference to an existing relationship, and finally followed by strategies that invoke social principles, such as appeals to norms, or altruism, or moral reasoning. The latter order of elicitation is similar to the developmental stages of egocentrism, reciprocity and subjective moral reasoning (Piaget, 1965). We hypothesized that cognitively and morally mature adults may follow this sequence both because this may reflect the order in which it is learned and because it saves the potentially most effective yet socially more desirable appeals as a last resort. Appeals to social principles are potentially more effective because of the force of the social contract. If they are used too much and too readily, however, their effectiveness may diminish. When these strategies fail, or are deficient because of individual differences or situational constraints, more aggressive strategies may occur. No previous research has examined an ordering hypothesis.

Initially, we attempted to examine these hypotheses using the sequences of strategies generated by subjects in Study 2. Unfortunately, there are methodological difficulties in analyzing the organizational structure of lists where the number of items recalled (or in this case, generated) varies for each subject (see for example, Pellegrino & Hubert, 1982). As a consequence, in this third study, we asked subjects to rank order their use of the whole set of strategies identified in Study 2 for two targets and nine goals. With this method, we risk asking subjects to rank order certain methods they may have *skipped* given a particular goal and target. This could add "noise" to the ranks for any particular goal and target. However, an examination of the ordered list derived from summing across targets and goals should provide a very clear picture of the empirical order of the whole set. This order can then be compared to the orders hypothesized by Schank and Abelson and ourselves.

We also examined order for males and females because some studies on subjects reported use of their own strategies have found sex differences (e.g., Falbo & Peplau, 1980; Michener & Schwertfeger, 1972). However, given that our instructions were designed to evaluate a general, culturally shared schema, we did not expect to find such differences.

Finally, we asked subjects to indicate their approval of the methods they had ranked to determine whether strategies that invoke social principles were indeed more approved than some of the methods utilized earlier in the sequence and all of the methods applied later.

Our method was as follows. A simple name and brief description of each method was listed on a sheet of paper. Sixty-men and 60 women were presented different random orders of this list. For half of the subjects the target individual was father, for the other half it was friend. Subjects were given situations embodying each of the nine goals used in Study 2. They were asked to rank each method from 1 to 15 in the order that people in general would use each method in the situation described. After ranking the methods, they were instructed to indicate how much they would approve of each method if they saw it being used by a person in the situation described, using a scale where 1 was "strongly disapprove" and 9 was "strongly approve."

Table 8.4 displays the rank order of use for each method summed across targets, goals, and sex as well as the mean approval rating and its relative ranking. A Kendall's W on the summed ranks for use indicated that there was an extremely high degree of concordance for males and females, thus we pooled over sex in subsequent analyses. In addition, Kendall's W's showed extremely high concordance for these ranks for goals pooled over targets and also for the ranks for the two types of targets pooled over goals.

To test Schank and Abelson's ideas about the order of methods used, we examined responses of "ask," "invoke role relationship," "give a personal reason," "bargain object," "bargain favor," and "threaten." The upper portion of Table 8.5 presents the mean rank values and their rank orders. It can be seen from inspection that their expectations were only weakly supported by the rank ordering of the methods.

According to our views, participants were expected to report the order of methods as ask, give self-oriented reasons, give dyadic-oriented reasons, invoke social principles and then to use negative tactics in that order. The lower portion of Table 8.5 presents the mean ranks and rank orders of responses in these categories. Our expectations about order received strong support. In addition, approval for the methods paralleled the order of use except that strategies that

TABLE 8.4
Mean Rank and Rank Order of Methods and Approval Ratings

Method	Mean Rank of Methods Use	Rank Order	Mean Approval Ratings	Rank Order
Ask	2.4	1	8.49	1
Personal Expertise	4.1	2	8.18	2
Personal Benefit	5.3	3	6.96	3
Invoke Role Relationship	6.5	5	4.85	9
Bargain Favor	6.6	6	5.92	5
Norm	6.8	7	5.57	7
Moral Principle	7.1	8	5.77	6
Altruism	7.5	9	6.43	4
Butter-up	5.5	4	5.05	8
Bargain Object	8.7	10	4.76	10
Emotional Appeal	9.8	11	3.48	11
Personal Criticism	10.9	12	2.68	12
Deceive	11.5	13	1.98	13
Threaten	12.8	14	1.69	14
Force	14.6	15	1.17	15

Note. Methods are clustered in the table consistent with the ordering hypothesis that we propose.

TABLE 8.5
Mean Rank and Rank Order for Methods and Approval Ratings
(Schank and Abelson Vs. Rule, Bisanz, and Kohn)

Method	Mean Rank of Methods Used	Rank Order	Mean Approval Ratings	Rank Order
Schank & Abelson				
Ask	2.4	1		
Invoke Role Relationship	6.5	3		
Give Personal	5.3	2		
Reason	8.7	5		
Bargain Object		4		
Bargain Favor	6.6	6		
Threaten	12.8	7		
Force	14.6			
Rule, Bisanz, & Kohn				
Ask	2.4	1	8.5	1
Self-Oriented	4.7	2	7.6	2
Dyad-Oriented	6.6	3	5.4	4
Principle	7.1	4	5.9	3
Negative	10.5	5	3.0	5

invoke social principles as a group were more highly approved than dyad oriented strategies (see Table 8.5).

From this study we can draw three further conclusions about knowledge of persuasion. First, as Schank and Abelson suggested, the methods do appear to be ordered. However, the order is more consistent with the developmental trend we proposed than the order they suggested. Inspection of the values in Table 8.4 for order of use of all 15 met shows that only "butter-up" occurred earlier in the sequence than was expected.

Recall, however, that this order was derived by classifying persuasive strategies in terms of stages of development in moral reasoning. Confirmation of the order raises the issue of the relationship between stages in moral reasoning and the acquisition of knowledge about how to persuade others. It now also becomes important to determine the relationship between ordering in the general schema examined in this paper and the actual sequence of acquisition of methods in development. Although we have assumed that the order hypothesized follows, in part, a developmental sequence, we have no evidence in this study about the order in which it is actually acquired.

Second, both men and women reported virtually identical ordering along these dimensions. The failure to find sex differences corresponds to earlier literature in the persuasion domain (see Eagly, 1978). Our failure to find greater differences is consistent with our lack of theoretical basis for expecting gender differences in general schemata.

Third, the approval ratings provide evidence that, in addition to developmental factors, social desirability of methods as well as potency may influence the order of method application. We say this with some caution, however, in that, as shown in Table 8.4, there was some overlap in the desirability of dyad-oriented strategies and those that invoke social principles.

In addition, several observations of relevance to social psychologists can be made about these methods. For example, in addition to the factors discussed so far as determining the order of strategy use, another factor may involve the perceived costs or negative consequences associated with using a given strategy. In addition, logical necessity may play a role in the order of use: Some methods may preclude the use of other methods, e.g., if a threat fails to gain compliance, an appeal to altruistic norms is unlikely to be effective. These possibilities can be examined in subsequent research. Moreover, it would be interesting to determine the frequency with which these methods are actually used, as well as to examine the relative effectiveness of each method. Finally, these methods do not conform to those reported in the compliance literature. Techniques such as "door-in-the-face" or "foot-in-the-door" were never mentioned by our subjects. It may be that the latter strategies are commonly found in exchanges between compliance professionals and their targets (see Cialdini, this volume), but are unusual in the context of more mundane interpersonal exchanges of the type we have been investigating.

Study 4

The fourth study was designed to further explore whether there are gender differences in general schemata. In Study 3 we asked whether men and women rank methods differently when instructed to think of the order that *people in general* would use the methods. There was no difference in the reactions of men and women. In Study 4, we asked men and women to think of *men in general* and *women in general* as they ranked the methods. The data are shown in Table 8.6, along with the rankings obtained in Study 3 broken down by sex.

Perhaps the first aspect of the data to notice is the clear similarity of the ranks generated by men and women in Study 3 with respect to the strategies used by people in general. The pooled ranks presented in Table 8.4 are indeed representative. The second aspect of the data to notice is the similarities of the rankings obtained in the two studies are more notable than the differences. For example, agreement between the ranks generated by women for people and men are highly similar. Some disagreement is seen in comparing these sets of ranks to those generated by women thinking about the strategies used by women; women see women as appealing to altruism earlier and bargaining for a favor later in the sequence. By comparison, men's rankings show more variability. The ranks generated by men for people and men are identical except in the categories we referred to earlier as ''dyad-oriented'' and ''social principles.'' Here men see men as appealing to moral principles and altruism earlier and resorting to appeals to role relationships and norms later than when they were ranking strategies with respect to their use by people in general. They see women appealing to norms later as well. Thus in general, men view themselves as employing more socially approved methods earlier in the sequence (refer to approval ratings in Table 8.4). The most striking differences, however, are in comparing the rankings generated by men for people and women. The differences center around negative strategies. Men see women as using the butter up strategy much earlier (second) in the sequence. Less striking, but still notable, is the perception women will be deceptive before being personally critical. However, if the sets of ranks were pooled over category type, as they were in Table 8.5, each set would support the developmental trend we suggested.

Since gender can affect expectations about behavior (e.g., Greenglass, 1982), examining the effects of gender on individuals' expectations about the likely sequence of application of persuasive strategies provides a good index of how robust that sequence may be. Based on the data obtained in Study 4, it is possible to conclude that the gender of an individual observing sequences of persuasive attempts affects, to some degree, expectations about the likely sequences of strategies employed. More striking, however, are the common expectations of men and women about the likely order of strategy use. These commonalities make us optimistic about the possibility of demonstrating the effects of the persuasion schema on aspects of information processing and memory.

TABLE 8.6

Mean Rank and Rank Order of Methods for Men and Women for Three Types of Persuaders

	Women's Rankings						Men's Rankings					
	People (Study 3)		Men (Study 4)		Women (Study 4)		People (Study 3)		Men (Study 4)		Women (Study 4)	
Method	M Rank	Rank Order	M Rank	Rank Order	M Rank	Rank Order	M Rank	Rank Order	M Rank	Rank Order	M Rank	Rank Order
Ask	2.8	1	2.4	1	2.5	1	2.1	1	2.2	1	3.1	1
Self-Oriented												
Personal Expertise	4.0	2	3.8	2	3.7	2	4.1	2	4.0	2	5.3	3
Personal Benefit	5.4	3	5.2	3	4.8	3	5.2	3	5.1	3	5.4	4
Dyad-Oriented												
Role Relationship	6.6	6.5	6.6	5.5	6.2	5	6.4	5	7.5	8	6.5	5
Bargain Favor	6.5	5	6.6	5.5	7.1	9	6.6	6	6.6	5	6.7	6
Social Principles												
Norm	6.6	6.5	7.2	7	6.7	6.5	7.0	7	7.4	9	7.6	9
Moral Principle	7.1	8	7.3	8	6.9	8	7.1	8	6.7	6	7.0	7
Altruism	7.5	9	7.9	9	6.7	6.5	7.5	9	7.0	7	7.2	8
Negative												
Butter-up	5.5	4	5.8	4	5.5	4	5.5	4	6.2	4	4.9	2
Bargain Object	8.9	10	8.6	10	9.2	10	8.4	10	8.5	10	9.3	10.5
Emotional Appeal	9.6	11	10.2	11	10.0	11	10.0	11	10.5	11	9.3	10.5
Personal Criticism	10.8	12	10.7	12	11.2	12	10.9	12	10.7	12	10.7	13
Deceive	11.8	13	11.2	13	11.8	13	11.3	13	11.1	13	10.5	12
Threaten	12.6	14	12.3	14	12.9	14	13.0	14	12.6	14	12.2	14
Force	14.4	15	14.3	15	14.7	15	14.7	15	14.4	15	14.3	15

OUR CONCLUSIONS AND MODEL

Although the data from these studies generally confirm the structure of the cognitive representation proposed by Schank and Abelson, the specific content does not. First, although the goals associated with knowledge about persuasion may constitute a finite set, that set is larger than they proposed. In fact, the set of goals may be finite with regard to a given role relationship.

Second, goals do seem to be linked to a standard set of methods that are ordered. However, the number of strategies in the set is larger than suggested by Schank and Abelson and its ordering differs from the one they proposed. We propose that the order of methods is based, in part, on a developmental sequence, from self-oriented to social oriented tactics. We also suggest that perceived potency and social desirability may also be factors that contribute to the order of use.

Third, there was only marginal support for their assumption that auxiliary methods will be tried if standard methods fail. Perhaps appeals to authority may be more likely to occur in hierarchically organized formal structures. For example, Kipnis and Schmidt (1985) provide examples of different strategies used by managers vs. couples with the former going to authority persons. Consequently, Schank and Abelson's assumption may have to be modified to accommodate these restrictions.

At this stage, we have provided an initial set of data suggesting that we have identified some aspects of the knowledge representation in this domain. This structure undoubtedly reflects the cultural stereotype of persuasion strategies. In order to test our assumptions further, research must follow several lines. First, it is necessary to examine whether the set of goals is indeed finite with regard to a given role relationship. Because we have examined affectively positive and intimate targets, our next studies should vary disliked targets and neutral strangers, such as salesmen. Second, although our data confirmed that the sequence of methods was ordered according to our developmental hypothesis, we have not provided evidence regarding the development of these strategies per se. We are currently planning developmental studies that would address this issue.

While we think it is important to extend our data on aspects of how the knowledge base per se is organized, we have sufficient data to begin to address the issue of the psychological reality of the persuasion schema. The central question here concerns whether the persuasion schema functions as do other schemata (e.g., Bower, Black, & Turner, 1979) in guiding the processing of information as reflected in recall and recognition of social interactions as observed in real life, narrative or visual media presentations. To this end, we have initiated research on memory.

For example, one of the first steps in demonstrating the psychological validity of an ordered schema such as ours is to examine how reading a story where events are described in-order versus out of order affects memory. Past research has illustrated that stories presented in canonical order are remembered more accurately than those out of order (e.g., Mandler, 1978; Stein & Nezworski, 1978). In the latter case, the inaccuracy of recall reflects memory errors toward the canonical order. This presumably reflects the effect of a story schema on encoding and retrieval. To assess this in our research, we presented stories with characters who attempt to reach goals, such as asking for help in a chemistry laboratory, using tactics representing our five ordered categories of strategies: ask, self-oriented, personal appeals, dyadic-oriented appeals, appeals to social principles and negative appeals. Readers were presented scenarios where the sequences of persuasive strategies employed were in canonical or random order. In developing the scenarios we relied on the variables reported in communication literature as important in eliciting different strategies. We suggested earlier that cost to the persuader, resistance of the persuadee and affective relation between the persuader and persuadee were determinants of strategy type. If this is so, we wanted to control on these variables in our stimuli. Pilot work varying different levels of such variables confirmed our manipulations. If we are correct in assuming that one important aspect of the persuasion schema is strategy ordering, then our memory data should parallel the results obtained with story schemata.

Preliminary analyses of these data provide evidence that receiving stories about a sequence of persuasive attempts in canonical order does indeed enhance memory for the order of events relative to other orders. However, there also appear to be points of difference between the way this schema and a story schema operate. Other studies are planned to assess the psychological validity of the persuasion schema as well, including one that examines how the schema affects reading time for sentences in stories about compliance-gaining interactions.

FINAL REMARKS

In the introduction to this chapter we asserted that recent theories of event understanding developed in the narrative tradition in cognitive psychology and artificial intelligence were relevant to social psychologists interested in the persuasive messages generated by individuals and the effects of those messages on other people. Presumably the same or related knowledge structures are critical to our understanding of both types of phenomena. Yet investigators working in the narrative tradition have placed high priority on specifying the structure and organization of cognition. Surprisingly little work of this type has been done by social psychologists.

This state of affairs is surprising because, even when behaviorism made the study of mental life taboo in experimental psychology, cognition was of central concern to social psychologists. This historic importance of cognition is illustrated by Lewin's cognitive motivation theory (see Deutsch, 1954 for a review), Festinger's theory of cognitive dissonance (see Zajonc, 1968 for a review) and

Heider's (1958) attribution theory. However, despite its centrality, none of these theories embodies a conception of cognition precise and sufficient enough to relate the workings of the mind to overt behavior. Instead, behavioristic orientations in the field as a whole led social psychologists away from elaborations of cognitive theory to extensions of these theories through a search for behavioral effects. Lacking were the precise characterizations of the knowledge and cognitive processes that would unify our understanding of these effects.

Today social psychologists once again are embarking on the study of social cognition, only this time greater attention is being given to the nature of cognitive representations, an issue that Scheerer argued, as early as 1954, should be *the* subject of study for cognitive social psychologists. This is happening at a time when cognitive psychologists are beginning to realize that "studies of story understanding and recall are bringing memory research closer to topics of personality and social psychology" (Bower, 1978, p. 230).

Just as recognition of these common interests brought a social and a cognitive psychologist together to collaborate on the research discussed in this paper, it is our hope that greater recognition of common interests by cognitive and social psychologists generally will forge an alliance that will result in more powerful theories of both the actor in, and observer of, human interactions. Certainly one implicit goal of both our research and this chapter has been to raise awareness of the rich potential for this alliance.

ACKNOWLEDGMENT

Preparation of this chapter and the authors' research was facilitated by grants to the authors from the Natural Sciences and Engineering Research Council of Canada.

REFERENCES

Abbott, V., Black, J. B., & Smith, E. E. (1985). The representation of scripts in memory. *Journal of Memory and Language, 24,* 179–199.

Bartlett, F. C. (1932). *Remembering: A study in experimental and social psychology.* Cambridge, England: Cambridge University Press.

Bisanz, G. L. (1982). Knowledge of persuasion and story comprehension: Developmental changes in expectations. *Discourse Processes, 5,* 245–277.

Black, J. B., & Bower, G. H. (1980). Story understanding as problem solving. *Poetics, 9,* 223–250.

Bower, G. H. (1978). Experiments on story comprehension and recall. *Discourse Processes, 1,* 211–231.

Bower, G. H., Black, J. B., & Turner, T. J. (1979). Scripts in memory for text. *Cognitive Psychology, 11,* 177–220.

Bruce, B., & Newman, D. (1978). Interacting plans. *Cognitive Science, 2,* 195–234.

Clark, R. A., & Delia, J. G. (1976). The development of functional persuasive skills in childhood and early adolescence. *Child Development, 47,* 1008–1014.

Cody, M. J. (1982). A typology of disengagement strategies and an examination of the role intimacy, reactions to inequity and relational problems play in strategy selection, *Communication Monographs, 49,* 148–170.

Cody, M. J., McLaughlin, M. L., & Jordan, W. J. (1980). A multi-dimensional scaling of three sets of compliance gaining strategies. *Communication Quarterly, 28,* 34–46.

Cody, M. J., McLaughlin, M. L., & Schneider, M. J. (1981). The impact of intimacy and relational consequences on the selection of interpersonal persuasion tactics: A reanalysis. *Communication Quarterly, 29,* 91–106.

Deutsch, M. (1954). Field theory in social psychology. In G. Lindzey (Ed.), *Handbook of Social Psychology, 1.* Reading, MA: Addison-Wesley.

Eagly, A. H. (1978). Sex differences in influenceability. *Psychological Bulletin, 85,* 86–115.

Etzioni, A. (1961). *A Comparative Analysis of Complex Organizations,* New York: The Free Press.

Falbo, T. (1977). Multidimensional scaling of power strategies. *Journal of Personality and Social Psychology, 35,* 537–547.

Falbo, T., & Peplau, L. A. (1980). Power strategies in intimate relationships. *Journal of Personality and Social Psychology, 38,* 618–628.

Finley, G. E., & Humphreys, C. A. (1974). Naive psychology and the development of persuasive appeal in girls. *Canadian Journal of Behavioural Sciences, 6,* 75–80.

Fiske, S. T., & Taylor, S. E. (1983). *Social cognition.* Reading, MA: Addison-Wesley.

Forgas, J. P. (1976). The perception of social episodes: Categorical and dimensional representations in two different social milieus. *Journal of Personality and Social Psychology, 34,* 199–209.

French, J. R. P., Jr., & Raven, B. (1960). The bases of social power. In D. Cartwright & A. Zander (Eds.), *Group dynamics,* New York: Harper and Row, 607–623.

Graesser, A. C. (1981). *Prose comprehension: Beyond the word.* New York: Springer-Verlag.

Greenglass, E. R. (1982). *A world of difference: Gender roles in perspective.* New York: Wiley.

Heider, F. (1958). *The psychology of interpersonal relations.* New York: Wiley.

Jackson, S., & Backus, D. (1982). Are compliance-gaining strategies dependent on situational variables? *Central States Speech Journal, 33,* 469–479.

Johnson, P. (1975). Woman and power: Toward a theory of effectiveness. *Journal of Social Issues, 32,* 99–110.

Kipnis, D., & Schmidt, S. (1985, April). The language of persuasion. *Psychology Today,* 40–48.

Magnusson, D. (1971). An analysis of situational dimensions. *Perceptual and Motor Skills, 32,* 851–867.

Mandler, J. M. (1978). A code in a node: The use of a story schema in retrieval. *Discourse Processes, 1,* 14–35.

Mandler, J. M., & Goodman, M. S. (1982). On the psychological validity of story structure. *Journal of Verbal Learning and Verbal Behavior, 21,* 507–523.

Marwell, G., & Schmitt, D. R. (1967). Dimensions of Compliance-gaining behavior: An empirical analysis, *Sociometry, 30,* 350–364.

Michener, H. A., & Schwertfeger, M. (1972). Liking as a determinant of power tactic preference, *Sociometry, 35,* 190–202.

Omanson, R. C. (1982). An analysis of narrative: Identifying central, supportive, and distracting content. *Discourse Processes, 5,* 195–224.

Parsons, T. (1963). On the concept of influence. *The Public Opinion Quarterly, 27,* 37–62.

Paul, I. H. (1967). The concept of schema in memory theory. In R. R. Holt (Ed.), Motives and thought: Psychoanalytic essays in honor of David Rapoport. *Psychological Issues,* Vol. V, No. 2–3, Monograph 18–19. New York: International Universities Press.

Piaget, J. (1965). (Ed.). *The moral judgment of the child.* New York: The Free Press.

Pellegrino, J. W., & Hubert, L. J. (1982). The analysis of organization and structure in free recall. In C. R. Puff (Ed.), *Handbook of research methods in human memory and cognition* (pp. 129–172). New York: Academic Press.

Rubin, K. H., & Borwick, D. (1983). The communicative skills of children who vary with regard to sociability. In H. E. Sypher & J. L. Applegate (Eds.), *Understanding interpersonal communication: Social cognitive and strategic processes in children and adults.* Beverly Hills: Sage Publications.

Rule, B. G., Bisanz, G. L., & Kohn, M. (1985). Anatomy of a persuasion schema: Targets, goals and strategies. *Journal of Personality and Social Psychology: Attitudes and Cognition, 48,* 1127–1140.

Schank, R. C. (1975). The structure of episodes in memory. In D. G. Bobrow & A. Collins (Eds.), *Representation and understanding: Studies in Cognitive Science.* New York: Academic Press.

Schank, R., & Abelson, R. (1977). *Scripts, plans, goals and understanding.* Hillsdale, NJ: Lawrence Erlbaum Associates.

Scheerer, M. (1954). Cognitive theory. In G. Lindzey (Ed.), *Handbook of Social Psychology, 1.* Reading, MA: Addison-Wesley.

Schenck-Hamlin, W., Wiseman, R. L., & Georgacarakos, T. N. (1982). A model of properties of compliance-gaining strategies. *Communication Quarterly, 30,* 92–100.

Skinner, B. F. (1953). Science and human behavior, New York: Macmillan.

Stein, N. L., & Nezworski, T. (1978). The effects of organization and instructional set on story memory. *Discourse Processes, 1,* 177–194.

Tedeschi, J. T., Schlenker, B. R., & Lindskold, S. (1972). The exercise of power and influence: The source of influence processes. J. T. Tedeschi, (Ed.), *Social influence processes.* Chicago: Aldine.

Trabasso, T., Secco, T., & Van Den Broek, D. (1984). In H. Mandl, N. L. Stein & T. Trabasso. (Eds.), *Learning and comprehension of text.* Hillsdale, NJ: Lawrence Erlbaum Associates.

Warren, W. H., Nicholas, D. W., & Trabasso, T. (1979). Event chains and inferences in understanding narratives. In R. O. Freedle (Ed.), *New directions in discourse processing.* Hillsdale, NJ: Lawrence Erlbaum Associates.

Weinstein, E. A. (1969). *The development of interpersonal competence.* In D. A. Goslin (Ed.), *Handbook of socialization theory and research.* Chicago: Rand-McNally.

Wiseman, R. L., & Schenck-Hamlin, W. (1981). A multidimensional scaling validation of an inductively-derived set of compliance-gaining strategies. *Communication Monographs, 48,* 251–270.

Wish, M., & Kaplan, S. J. (1977). Towards an implicit theory of interpersonal communication. *Sociometry, 40,* 234–246.

Wood, R., Weinstein, E. A., & Parker, T. B. (1967). Children's interpersonal tactics. *Sociological Inquiry, 37,* 129–138.

Zajonc, R. B. (1968). Cognitive theories in social psychology. In G. Lindzey & E. Aronson (Eds.), *Handbook of social psychology, 1.* Reading, MA: Addison-Wesley.

9

Majority and Minority Influence: A Social Impact Analysis

Sharon Wolf
California State University at Long Beach

A vast amount of research on conformity over the past 35 years has documented the pervasive influence of the group on the individual and of the majority on the minority (for reviews, see Allen, 1965; Kiesler & Kiesler, 1969). This research has viewed the minority as the passive recipient of influence pressures from a larger and more powerful majority. Traditional explanations of the social influence process, derived within this context, have focused on the minority's dependence upon the majority either for information or for material and psychological benefits that the majority can provide (Deutsch & Gerard, 1955; Jones & Gerard, 1967). From this perspective, the minority is an unlikely source of social influence. The majority's superior size, status, and power afford it a better basis for establishing social reality (Festinger, 1950) and greater resources for rewarding those who adopt its viewpoint.

Over the past 15 years, however, an impressive amount of evidence has accumulated showing that minorities need not be the passive recipients of influence pressure, that they may, through the influence process, actively bring about the modification and change of group norms (for reviews, see Levine, 1980; Moscovici, 1976; Mugny, 1982). This recent research on innovation poses a challenge to traditional explanations of the social influence process. Models based on the greater resources of the majority seem inadequate to account for influence produced by a numerically disadvantaged and relatively powerless minority.

The demonstration that minorities may be sources as well as targets of influence has raised important issues in the social influence literature. What are the psychological processes by which influence operates? Are these processes the same for majorities and minorities (a single-process viewpoint) or are different explanatory frameworks for the two forms of influence (a dual-process viewpoint) necessary? Several theoretical analyses of majority and minority influence have recently appeared in the literature, some arguing in favor of a single process (Doms, 1983; Latané & Wolf, 1981; Tanford & Penrod, 1984; Wolf & Latané, 1985), others arguing in favor of a dual process (Maass & Clark, 1984; Moscovici, 1980; Mugny, 1982; Nemeth, this volume; Papastamou, 1983). A number of empirical studies have addressed this issue explicitly, with mixed results (Aebischer, Hewstone, & Henderson, 1984; Doms & Van Avermaet, 1980; Maass & Clark, 1983; Moscovici & Doms, 1982; Moscovici & Lage, 1976; Moscovici & Personnaz, 1980; Mugny, 1974–75; Mugny, 1976; Nemeth & Wachtler, 1983; Personnaz, 1981; Wolf, 1985a; Wolf & Latané, 1983).

Proponents of a dual-process viewpoint argue that majority and minority influence are qualitatively different phenomena, involving different underlying mechanisms. Attempts to demonstrate a dual process have led in two research directions. One avenue of research has attempted to show that the two forms of influence are differentially affected by variations in antecedent conditions. Conformity has long been thought to be mediated by variables that affect members' dependence upon the group for information or for group-mediated rewards (Deutsch & Gerard, 1955; Jones & Gerard, 1967). Innovation, on the other hand, has been thought to be mediated by variables that affect inferences made about the minority's commitment to its position. Behavioral styles that imply confidence and unwillingness to compromise, such as consistency, enhance minority influence (Moscovici & Faucheux, 1972; Moscovici & Lage, 1976; Moscovici, Lage, & Naffrechoux, 1969; Nemeth, Swedlund, & Kanki, 1974).

One line of evidence in favor of a dual process, then, would demonstrate that majority influence is mediated primarily by dependence variables, whereas minority influence is mediated primarily by behavioral style variables. This line of evidence has relied almost exclusively on comparisons across studies. As Doms (1983; Doms & Van Avermaet, 1980) noted, conformity and innovation paradigms are fundamentally different, making cross-study comparison tenuous. In the conformity paradigm, a single subject confronts a group of confederates. Changes in the subject's judgment can be attributed, with reasonable confidence, to the behavior of the confederates. In the innovation paradigm, on the other hand, a group of subjects confronts one or two confederates. These subjects are exposed not only to the influence of the confederates but also to the reactions of the other subjects. Changes in a subject's judgment may be due to the confederates, the other subjects, or both. Evidence along this line, then, has been weak.

A second avenue of research has attempted to show that majority and minority influence produce different consequences, indicative of different underlying processes. Moscovici (1980) proposed that majorities produce compliance, a superficial and transient response to situational pressures, whereas minorities produce conversion, a relatively permanent restructuring of opinion. The compliance-conversion distinction is not simply a difference in public and private responding. Conversion takes place on an "indirect, latent level, leading on the whole to an acceptance that may be so deep that the subject is not even aware of it" (p. 216). Latent influence, which may elude awareness and self-control, must be assessed by measures that are indirect and unobtrusive.

Evidence in favor of a dual process, then, would demonstrate that majorities have their greatest impact on manifest or behavioral responses, whereas minorities have theirs on the latent level underlying the manifest response. Support for this proposition comes from a series of studies investigating perceptual after-images (Moscovici & Personnaz, 1980; Personnaz, 1981). Subjects viewing blue slides were exposed to the influence of a confederate who labeled the slides "green." Latent influence was measured by subjects' judgments of the after-image perceived on the white screen following exposure to each slide. When the confederate represented a majority viewpoint, subjects reported seeing an after-image close to the complement of blue (i.e., yellow) but when the confederate represented a minority viewpoint, subjects reported seeing an after-image closer to the complement of green (i.e., red). However, Doms and Van Avermaet (1980) failed to replicate this result using the same paradigm. Further, research by Sorrentino, King, and Leo (1980) demonstrated that the perceptual shift could have been due simply to heightened attention to the stimulus rather than to the effects of social influence. The slides contained some green wavelengths and thus the perception of red hues in the after-image was veridical. Evidence along this second line, then, has also been weak. We return to a discussion of latent influence later in this chapter.

Five years ago, Bibb Latané and I (Latané & Wolf, 1981) attempted to bring the majority and minority influence literature under one conceptual umbrella by analyzing the social influence situation from the perspective of Latané's (1981) new social impact theory. We argued that majority and minority influence are most parsimoniously viewed as potential outcomes of a single process, mediated by a common set of variables. We proposed that influence by either a majority or a minority will be a multiplicative function of the strength, immediacy, and number of its members.

Our arguments were supported primarily by reanalyses of existing studies of social influence that were not originally designed to test predictions of our model. Thus important propositions of the model were untested. Since our analysis was published, we have conducted a number of experiments to test hypotheses explicitly derived from the theory. At the same time, several criticisms of the theory have appeared in the literature and alternative models have been proposed.

My plan in the present chapter is to review the basic principles of social impact theory, as they apply to the social influence situation, and to review the recent empirical support for the theory. Then I address some of the criticisms that have been proposed. The most important criticism is that the theory is merely descriptive and ignores the psychological processes by which social influence operates. I argue that these processes enter into the social impact formulation as determinants of source strength, one of the central variables of the theory.

SOCIAL IMPACT THEORY

Social impact is defined as any of the great variety of changes, physiological, emotional, attitudinal, or behavioral, that occur in an individual as a result of the real, imagined, or implied presence of other individuals (Latané, 1981). These effects are described in terms of social force fields, analogous to the physical force fields that govern the transmission of light, sound, and gravity. Latané (1981) has identified two different types of force fields, with two general laws determining the total amount of impact experienced by a target individual in each.

Social Force Fields

In a multiplicative force field, the individual is the lone target of social forces coming from some number of source persons. Three variables determine the combined impact of the sources on the target: their strength (status, power, abilities, etc.), their immediacy to the target (proximity in time or space), and the number of source persons present. These variables are hypothesized to combine multiplicatively so that in this case, Impact = $f(SIN)$, where S, I, and N are the strength, immediacy, and number of sources. Increases in any of the three variables should produce a corresponding increase in impact and, as the multiplicative relationship implies, the effect of any one variable should be greater the greater the value of the other variables.

Further, the theory proposes that the effect of an increase in the number of sources is not linear; rather it is a power function, with each additional source producing a smaller increment in impact than the previous one. This principle of marginally decreasing impact is expressed, Impact = sN^t, where s is a scaling constant reflecting the impact of a single source and t is an exponent with a value of less than one. This formula implies that impact should grow as some root of the number of source persons.

In a divisive force field, the individual stands with others as the target of social forces coming from outside the group. In this case, impact is diffused or divided among the target individuals, with each individual feeling less impact than he or she would if alone. As the strength, immediacy, or number of individuals in the target group increases, the impact of an external source on the individual should decrease so that in this case, Impact = $f(1/SIN)$. The effect of an increase in the number of persons in the target group is again hypothesized to be a power function, with each additional target producing a smaller decrease in impact than the previous one. In this case, Impact = sN^{-t}, reflecting the divisive nature of the force field.

The Social Influence Situation

Latané and Wolf (1981) have described the social influence situation in terms of a generalized social force field in which the forces impinging on a target person are experienced as pressure to adopt the suggested opinion. Social impact theory does not offer predictions with respect to the response level (public, private, or latent) on which this impact will be expressed. All three forms of influence should, theoretically, conform to the general laws of the theory.

There are two ways to view the force field from the perspective of the individual target. In one case, the individual may view himself or herself as the lone recipient of influence pressures from other people. This perspective would be likely if the individual were a newcomer to the group, if he or she had no initial opinion or was neutral on the issue in question, or if he or she were simply the observer of an interaction between other people. This individual would be in a multiplicative force field.

The most frequent instances of a multiplicative force field in the social influence literature are situations in which a single individual confronts a unanimous majority (e.g., Asch 1951, 1952, 1956; Gerard, Wilhelmy, & Conolley, 1968). In these situations, all of the social forces impinging on the individual act together to create pressure to conform to the majority viewpoint. Social impact theory proposes that the magnitude of conformity will be a multiplicative function of the number of majority members and the amount of impact generated by each of them. As majority size increases, conformity should increase as a power function, with the largest differences in conformity being associated with the first few majority members.

Less common instances of a multiplicative force field in the literature are situations in which an independent individual, who is a member of neither the majority nor the minority, confronts others who are divided on the issue in question (e.g., Davis & Latané, cited in Latané & Wolf, 1981; Maass & Clark, 1983; Wolf & Latané, 1983). In this case, the individual is exposed simultaneously to two social forces. The force of the larger faction creates pressure to adopt the majority position, whereas the force of the smaller faction creates pressure to adopt the minority position. According to social impact theory, the magnitude of each force will be a multiplicative function of the strength, immediacy and number of faction members. Latané and Wolf (1981) have proposed that the resultant impact experienced by this target individual will be a function of the majority's impact *minus* that of the minority, or Impact = f(SIN majority − SIN minority). All else being equal, conformity to the majority position should increase as a power function of majority size and decrease as a power function of minority size.

In the second case, the individual may view himself or herself as a member of either the majority or the minority and the target of forces coming from the other faction. In this case, the individual will be in both a multiplicative and a divisive force field. The influence of the opposing group will be direct. The influence of the individual's own group will be indirect, in the form of a diffusion of impact by the opposing faction. Latané and Wolf (1981) have proposed that the impact experienced by this individual will be a function of the impact of the opposing group *divided* by the impact of the individual's own group, or Impact = f(SIN opposing group/SIN own group). All else being equal, influence by the opposing group should increase as a direct power function of the size of the opposing group and decrease as an inverse power function of the size of the individual's own group.

It may be noted, however, that the analogy to physical force fields seems to break down in the case of divisive force fields. The physical impact of light, sound, or gravity on an individual is not diminished by the presence of other people. Thus, it is not clear that social impact should simply be diffused or divided among people in the target group. It seems more plausible that each individual's capacity to resist influence from outside the group is increased by the knowledge that other people share his or her opinion. Rather than the indirect role of diffusing impact, suggested by Latané (1981), it seems more likely that other members of the target group play a direct role of providing social support (Allen, 1975; Doms, 1983; Doms & Van Avermaet, 1985).

In summary, social impact theory offers a general framework by which to understand the influence of majorities and minorities. Both forms of influence are viewed as potential outcomes of a single process mediated by a common set of variables. Influence by either a majority or a minority will be a multiplicative function of the strength, immediacy and number of its members. Further, social impact theory distinguishes between the impact experienced by participants in an interaction between a majority and a minority and the impact experienced by observers of that interaction. For both participants and observers, it offers precise predictions with respect to the simultaneous influence of majorities and minorities and the relative magnitude of their effects.

Empirical Support

Majority and Minority Size.   The first study to simultaneously vary majority and minority size was conducted in the context of an experiment on social influence and person perception. Davis and Latané (cited in Latané & Wolf, 1981) asked subjects to integrate information from several sources in order to form a coherent impression of a target person. Each of up to 24 different persons who knew the target person gave a one-word trait description, either positive or negative, and subjects were asked to report how much they would like the person described on a scale from -100 to $+100$. Each subject rated 216 different target persons, each described by 0 to 24 different people, with a combination of 0 to 12 extremely positive and 0 to 12 extremely negative adjectives listed on a single page.

As expected, ratings of the target persons were substantially affected by the number of positive and negative descriptions. Considering those cases in which people gave either all positive or all negative descriptions, the change in liking from a no-influence baseline increased systematically with the number of trait descriptions and the first few descriptions had the greatest impact. The power function, Impact $= 22N^{.49}$, accounts for 99% of the variance in means, implying that the first person giving a description increased or decreased liking for the target person by 22 percentage points and that impact grew as the square root of the number of people giving descriptions.

When individuals were exposed to both positive and negative influences at the same time, the data suggest that they simply subtracted the lesser influence from the greater to form their resultant impression, as shown in Fig. 9.1. Holding the number of negative descriptions constant, an increase in the number of people giving positive descriptions led to very regular increases in the favorability of the final impression. Similarly, holding the number of people giving positive de-

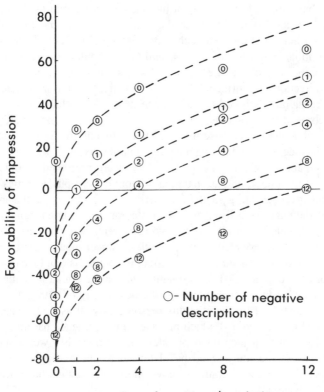

FIG. 9.1. Favorability of impression as a function of number of positive and negative descriptions. (Figure from "The Social Impact of Majorities and Minorities" by Bibb Latané and Sharon Wolf (1981), *Psychological Review, 88,* 438–453. Copyright (1981) by the American Psychological Association. Reprinted by permission.)

scriptions constant, an increase in the number of people giving negative descriptions led to systematic decreases in the favorability of the final impression.

Consistent with social impact theory, the data from this experiment suggest that both majority size and minority size are related to influence by a power function. Further, these data support the proposition that when exposed to the simultaneous influence of a majority and a minority, conformity to the majority position by an independent target will be a function of the majority's impact *minus* that of the minority.

Majority and Minority Size and Strength.   In a second study, designed to test the proposed multiplicative relations, majority and minority strength were varied in addition to majority and minority size (Wolf & Latané, 1983). Subjects were exposed to the restaurant preferences (both likes and dislikes) of two groups of 12 stimulus persons, consisting of both highly expert individuals and individuals with little basis for making restaurant judgments. By integrating the information provided, subjects could determine the number of high- and low-expert individuals who liked and disliked each restaurant. Six levels of majority-minority size (unanimous majorities of 1, 2, 4, and 6, and holding majority size at four, opposing minorities of 1 and 2), two levels of strength (high and low expertise) and two directions of influence (positive and negative) were created, with a different restaurant assigned to each of the 24 experimental conditions.

Subjects read two booklets. One described 12 male college students in Los Angeles, while the other described 12 male students in Seattle. Information about each student, including the manipulation of expertise, was provided at the top of a separate page. High-expert students were portrayed as older, having lived in the city longer, and as engaging in more off-campus activities than low-expert students, suggesting greater familiarity with restaurants in the area. At the bottom of the page were listed the two restaurants the student reportedly liked best in Los Angeles (Seattle) and the two restaurants he liked least. By integrating the information provided in each booklet, subjects could determine the distribution of opinions concerning each restaurant. Subjects rated the restaurants at the end of each booklet. Asked to imagine that eating dinner at home would be rated 20, they made relative ratings of the desirability of eating at each of the restaurants mentioned by the stimulus persons, as well as four restaurants that had not been mentioned and which provided a no-influence baseline. Although subjects recorded their judgments privately, in writing, they were asked to sign their booklets so that they could be identified by the experimenter. Thus the judgments reflected public conformity which may or may not have been accompanied by private acceptance.

The study tested five hypotheses derived from social impact theory:

1. Majority influence would increase as a power function of majority size;
2. majority influence would increase with increases in majority strength;
3. majority size and strength would interact, such that strength would have a more pronounced effect as majority size increased;

4. holding majority size constant, minority influence would increase as a power function of minority size;

5. strength would be a more important determinant of majority influence than minority influence.

This latter effect was predicted because strength is assumed to be multiplicatively related to the number of influence sources and majorities are, by definition, more numerous.

Unexpectedly, negative information about the restaurants, whether provided by a majority or by a minority, had no effect on subjects' restaurant preferences. Therefore, the hypotheses could be tested only in the positive information conditions, where social influence was clearly obtained. Under those conditions, the number and strength of influence sources affected influence largely as predicted.

Majority influence increased systematically with increases in majority size, as shown in Fig. 9.2. The power function, Impact $= 1.75N^{.20}$, accounts for 99% of the variance in means, revealing that the first few majority members had the

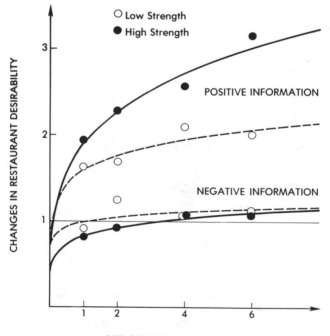

SIZE OF UNANIMOUS MAJORITY

FIG. 9.2. Size and strength of unanimous majority on ratings of restaurant desirability as a function of positive and negative information. (Figure from "Majority and Minority Influence on Restaurant Preferences" by Sharon Wolf and Bibb Latané (1983), *Journal of Personality and Social Psychology, 45,* 282–292. Copyright (1983) by the American Psychological Association. Reprinted by permission.)

greatest impact and that influence increased as the fifth root of majority size. Further, majority influence increased with increases in majority strength, especially as majority size increased. Minority influence also increased with increases in minority size, as predicted, but, as can be seen in Fig. 9.3, there was no evidence of a negatively accelerating function. Finally, where majority influence was obtained, it was strongly affected by majority strength; where minority influence was obtained, on the other hand, it was unaffected by minority strength. Taken together, these data provide support for the hypothesis that strength is a more important determinant of majority influence than minority influence.

Where social influence was obtained, then, the data were generally consistent with the predictions of social impact theory, particularly in the majority conditions. Minority influence did not increase as a power function of minority size nor did it increase with increases in minority strength, as predicted. However, with only two levels of minority size, it is difficult to estimate the form of these relations. Minority strength would be expected to play a greater role with in-

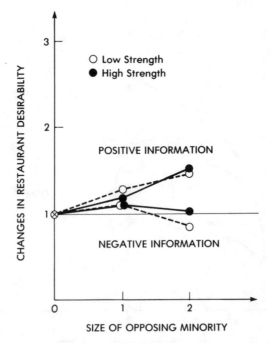

FIG. 9.3.   Size and strength of opposing minority, against a majority of four, on ratings of restaurant desirability as a function of positive and negative information. (Figure from ''Majority and Minority Influence on Restaurant Preferences'' by Sharon Wolf and Bibb Latané (1983), *Journal of Personality and Social Psychology, 45,* 282–292. Copyright (1983) by the American Psychological Association. Reprinted by permission.)

creases in minority size beyond two. A more surprising aspect of the data is that so little influence was obtained when the sources provided negative information. This may have been due to the sequential presentation of information about the restaurants. As the number of individuals who mentioned a given restaurant increased, the number of exposures to the name of the restaurant increased as well. It is possible, therefore, that mere exposure (Zajonc, 1968) increased the attractiveness of the frequently disliked restaurants, diminishing the impact of the negative information.

This study, along with the Davis and Latané study, provides support for the general propositions of social impact theory concerning the number and strength of sources of social influence. It may be noted, however, that both studies used within-subject designs where each subject was exposed to all of the experimental conditions. In a recent paper, Mullen (1985) pointed out that such designs are conducive to eliciting responses guided by demand characteristics. It may be obvious to experimental subjects, as it is to social impact theorists, that larger numbers of high strength sources will have more impact. Although it seems unlikely that subjects would surmise the precise form of the predicted interaction of number and strength and especially the power function relating number of sources to their impact, it is possible that the results of these studies depended on an implicit comparison of experimental conditions by the subjects. It seemed desirable, therefore, to replicate the effects of number and strength of sources in a study using a between-subjects design.

Number and Strength of Courtroom Witnesses.   In a series of three experiments, each using a between-subjects design, Wolf and Bugaj (1985) investigated the effects of the number and strength of witnesses for the prosecution and defense in a simulated courtroom trial. A social impact theory analysis of the courtroom situation would view the prosecution and defense as separate influence forces, the magnitude of each being a multiplicative function of the strength, immediacy, and number of influence sources (i.e., witnesses). The resultant force on jurors should be a simple function of the difference in impact imparted by each faction. Judgments of the defendant's guilt should increase as a power function of the number of prosecution witnesses and decrease as a power function of the number of witnesses for the defense.

In all three experiments, subjects playing the role of mock jurors read a transcript of a court trial containing a case summary, opening statements by the prosecution and defense lawyers (each consisting of five, prescaled arguments, equated in terms of their strength), and instructions by the judge. In Experiments 1 and 3, the transcript also contained statements by some number of witnesses. All of the witnesses in a given transcript testified for the same side, either the prosecution or the defense. The testimony of each witness was built around a single prescaled argument and was presented in the context of an examination of the witness by an attorney.

The first experiment varied the number of witnesses whose testimony was presented (one, two, or four), witness strength (high- or low-occupational status), and the direction of influence (pro-prosecution or pro-defense). A no-witness control condition was also run. The primary measure asked subjects to judge the defendant on a 21-point scale ranging from "definitely innocent" to "definitely guilty." Subjects recorded their responses anonymously and thus the data reflect influence on a private level.

In the absence of testimony from the witnesses the case was clearly ambiguous, with guilt judgments averaging near the center of the scale ($M = 10.57$). In the experimental conditions, perceptions of the defendant's guilt increased systematically with increases in the number of prosecution witnesses and decreased systematically with increases in the number of witnesses for the defense, as illustrated in Fig. 9.4. For both the prosecution and the defense, a power function with an exponent of less than one does a good job of describing the relationship

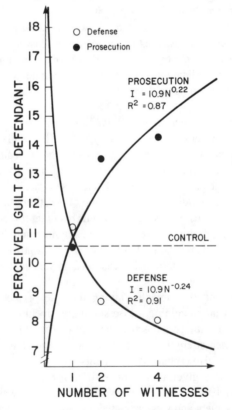

FIG. 9.4 Ratings of the defendant's guilt as a function of the number of prosecution and defense witnesses, with data presented in antilogarithmic units.

between the number of witnesses and their influence, accounting for 87 and 91% of the variance in means, respectively. The parameters of these empirically-derived functions (from the formula Impact = sN^t) are strikingly similar. For both the prosecution and the defense, influence appears to grow as about the fourth root of the number of witnesses, with the first witness having the largest impact. Surprisingly, the manipulation of witness strength did not significantly affect guilt judgments, although it did lead to differential perceptions of the witnesses' trustworthiness.

The results of this experiment replicated the effect for number of influence sources found in the restaurant preference study but not the effect for source strength nor the strength by number interaction. Further, the results provided only equivocal support for the effect of number because each additional witness provided new, relevant information. Social impact theory would predict increases in influence with increases in the number of witnesses independent of the informational value of their testimony. The purpose of Experiments 2 and 3 was to determine if the amount and quality of the information presented rather than the number of influence sources per se could have accounted for the findings of the first experiment.

The procedure of the second experiment was the same as the first, except that no witnesses were presented. Rather, the prescaled arguments around which the witnesses' testimony was built were embedded in the opening statements of the prosecution and defense lawyers. Thus, the number of additional arguments (one, two, or four) and the direction of influence (pro-prosecution or pro-defense) were varied, while the number of influence sources was held constant. Briefly, there was no effect for the number of additional arguments on subjects' guilt ratings, suggesting that the number of sources to whom the testimony was attributed in Experiment 1 was a more critical determinant of influence than the informational content of that testimony. One could argue, however, that since the arguments were added to the original five arguments included in the lawyers' opening statements, the effect of increasing the amount of information reached an asymptote, rendering further increments in the number of arguments ineffective.

If the informational value of the testimony were responsible for the findings of Experiment 1, variations in the strength of that testimony (i.e., the quality of the arguments presented) should affect subjects' judgments of guilt. In Experiment 3, the strength of evidence presented by the witnesses (strong or weak) was varied in addition to number of witnesses (one or four), witness strength (high or low status), and direction of influence (pro-prosecution or pro-defense). The procedure was the same as in Experiment 1, except that half of the witness statements contained strong, high-quality arguments and half contained weak, low-quality arguments.

Although subjects found the strong arguments to be more "convincing" and "satisfying" than the weak arguments, the strength of evidence did not significantly affect their judgments of the defendant's guilt nor did the strength of evidence interact with any of the other variables. The means for the guilt judgments, collapsed across strength of evidence, are presented in Table 9.1. Consistent with the predictions of social impact theory and with the findings of the restaurant preference study, subjects' guilt ratings proved to be a multiplicative function of the number of witnesses, witness strength (status), and the direction of influence. Inspection of the means indicates that high-strength witnesses were more influential than low-strength witnesses only when there were four of them. When there was but a single witness, variations in witness strength had little effect.

Taken together, these experiments suggest that the persuasive impact of courtroom witnesses is largely a function of their strength and number rather than of the content of the testimony they present. That subjects were influenced by superficial characteristics of the sources of influence (i.e., their number and occupational status) rather than by the quality of their messages suggests that subjects may have been processing information in a heuristic rather than a systematic mode (see the chapter by Chaiken in this volume). These findings, derived from experiments using between-subjects designs, demonstrate further that the effects of source strength and number do not depend on a comparison of experimental conditions by the subjects and are not likely to be simply the result of demand characteristics.

The studies on person perception, restaurant preference, and witness testimony provide support for the general propositions of social impact theory in situations in which a lone individual is the target of influence from other people. The degree of influence observed in these studies is somewhat surprising, considering that the influence sources were not physically present and the value of the immediacy variable was low. However, unlike traditional studies of social influence, the subjects in these studies had no preconceived opinions on the experimental issues and were probably more amenable to influence. The social forces operating in these situations were entirely informational. These studies

TABLE 9.1
Mean Ratings of the Defendant's Guilt

Number of Witnesses	Witness Status	Direction of Evidence	
		Proprosecution	Prodefense
1	low	10.77	9.05
	high	10.22	10.22
4	low	11.05	7.95
	high	12.82	6.60

Note. Responses were scored from 0 to 20. A higher score represents judgments of greater guilt. The mean of the control group was 9.95.

utilized information-integration tasks, which simulated the process of information acquisition and opinion formation rather than opinion change. Thus the findings may not be applicable to situations in which individuals initially hold strong opinions or to situations in which group pressure is a necessary component of influence (Festinger, 1950).

Majority and Minority Influence in a Group Context   A fourth study was conducted to test predictions of social impact theory in the context of a simulated group interaction (Wolf, 1985a). This study provided a direct comparison between majority and minority influence and assessed the relative effects of a dependence variable, group cohesiveness, and a behavioral style variable, consistency, on both forms of influence. Both group cohesiveness and consistency are strength variables in the social impact formulation. The theory does not specify a priori when these variables will affect influence. It does specify, however, that if either variable affects influence, the effect of that variable will be greater for majorities than minorities, because of the proposed multiplicative relation between strength and number.

Female subjects, led to believe that they were interacting in groups of four, were asked to decide upon an amount of compensation to be awarded to the plaintiff in a civil suit. They deliberated on the case by means of an exchange of notes, so that the distribution of opinions in the group, as perceived by each subject, could be controlled by the experimenter. The facts of the case were weighted to encourage an initial judgment between 15 and 45 thousand dollars. The influence source, ostensibly one of the group members, advocated a minimal award of $5,000 throughout their interaction. For half of the subjects, this judgment reflected a majority position in the group; the reported judgments of the other two group members were $2,000 and $7,000. Thus, these subjects found themselves in a minority of one confronted by a majority of three. For the other subjects, the $5,000 judgment reflected a minority position in the group; the judgments of the other two group members were $3,000 higher and $2,000 lower than the subject's own judgment. Thus, these subjects found themselves in a majority of three confronted by a minority of one.

Two levels of group cohesiveness were created by providing subjects with false feedback about the degree of interpersonal attraction in the group. Subjects in high-cohesive groups learned that the group members had rated one another quite positively on a first impression rating questionnaire, whereas subjects in low-cohesive groups learned that the first impression ratings were negative. Additionally, the behavioral style of the influence source was varied. For half of the subjects, the influence source maintained her position consistently, with confidence and conviction, throughout the interaction. For the other subjects, she expressed some uncertainty on the final exchange of notes ("I thought $5,000 was appropriate but now I'm not so sure").

Following the group interaction, subjects indicated their final compensation judgment on an anonymous measure. Influence on a manifest level was measured by the change in this judgment from before to after the group interaction, with movement in the direction of a decreased award reflecting the influence of the source. Two additional measures were included to assess influence in an indirect and unobtrusive manner. Both before and after the group interaction, subjects indicated the maximum and minimum compensation awards that they would find acceptable. The difference between the maximum and minimum award was presumed to reflect the subject's latitude of acceptance (Sherif & Hovland, 1961). Zaleska (1980) had suggested that latent influence might be detected by an increase in the subjects' latitude of acceptance. Second, subjects rated the value of money in a novel context (the penalty value of fines and the utility value to a plaintiff of compensation awards). However, no differential influence effects for majorities and minorities were found on either of the secondary measures.

Results on the measure of manifest influence are presented in Table 9.2. Not surprisingly, subjects were more influenced when the influence source was a member of the majority (an average reduction of $10,940) than when she was a member of the minority (an average reduction of $5,460). Further, more influence was produced in highly cohesive groups than in groups that were less cohesive. Finally, the majority-minority status of the influence source interacted with group cohesiveness. Consistent with the predictions of social impact theory, the cohesiveness manipulation had a much greater impact in the majority than in the minority source conditions. Although the manipulation of behavioral style resulted in differential perceptions of the confidence and willingness to compromise displayed by the influence source, no effects for that variable were found on social influence.

The results of this study support the predictions of social impact theory, in particular, and a single-process model of social influence, in general. Consistent

TABLE 9.2
Means for Manifest Influence

Type of Group Behavioral Style	Influence Source	
	Majority	Minority
High Cohesive		
High Consistent	-11.75	-6.62
Low Consistent	-19.00	-5.17
Low Cohesive		
High Consistent	-7.38	-6.33
Low Consistent	-5.54	-3.71

Note. A negative score indicates movement in the direction advocated by the influence source. Responses were scored in thousands of dollars. Thus, a change of -11.75 represents an average reduction of $11,750.

with the proposed effect of number, majorities were more influential than minorities. Consistent with the proposed effect of strength, more influence was produced under conditions of high- than low-group cohesiveness. Finally, consistent with the predicted interaction of strength and number, cohesiveness proved to be a more important determinant of majority than minority influence. Further, both majority and minority influence were affected by the same strength variable, cohesiveness; neither was affected by the behavioral style of the influence source. There was no evidence to suggest that minorities have their strongest impact on a different (latent) level. These results provide further support for the predictions of social impact theory in a situation in which subjects held an initial opinion on the experimental issue and in which group pressures were operating.

Social impact theory, however, would not have permitted a priori predictions for the relative importance of group cohesiveness compared to behavioral style. The main effect for cohesiveness is consistent with the earlier speculation of Wolf (1979) that both conformity and innovation are mediated by dependence. A dependence model, however, would not have predicted the interaction of cohesiveness with the majority-minority status of the source. A combination of the dependence and social impact models appears to provide the most complete account of the data. The dependence model suggested that cohesiveness was the relevant strength variable; the social impact model specified the multiplicative relation between that variable and the number of influence sources.

Summary

Social impact theory has received support from four studies that compared majority and minority influence in a single experimental context and that were designed explicitly to test predictions derived from the theory. The data from these studies are consistent with the propositions that both majority and minority influence vary as a power function of the number of influence sources, that both majority and minority influence vary with variations in the strength of the influence sources (whether strength is operationalized as expertise, occupational status, or attractiveness), that strength and number interact, such that strength has a greater effect the greater the number of influence sources, and that consequently, strength is a more important determinant of majority than minority influence. The general laws of social impact theory applied both to situations of opinion formation and to situations of opinion change. In the former, the subject held no initial opinion on the experimental issue and was merely an observer of the interaction between a majority and a minority; in the latter, the subject held an initial opinion and was a member of one of the factions. Yet, despite the apparent support for social impact theory as a general model of social influence, several criticisms of the theory have recently been raised and alternative models have been proposed in the literature.

ALTERNATIVE MODELS

Social Influence Model

Tanford and Penrod (1984) have recently argued that social impact theory fails to fully incorporate source and target effects into one analysis, that it cannot account for some findings in the literature concerning majority and minority size, that it fails to place a limit on the amount of influence that can be obtained, and that it does not take into account features of the experimental situation nor individual differences in the target that may affect susceptibility to influence. They have proposed an alternative, social influence model (SIM), designed to address these perceived shortcomings of social impact theory.

Actually, the two models share a number of features in common. Both propose that majority and minority influence operate by the same process and that social influence is primarily a function of the number of sources and targets of influence. For SIM, however, the relationship of number to influence is not a power function but an S-shaped growth curve; influence is minimal with a single source, accelerates with the addition of the second source, reaches an inflection point with the addition of the third source, and then decelerates. Both models propose that influence will level off as the number of sources increases, but only SIM places a ceiling on the amount of influence that can be obtained. Finally, SIM omits the immediacy and strength variables of social impact theory, but includes other parameters, such as features of the experimental context (e.g., type of group, type of task, type of response measure, consistency of the source) and individual differences in resistance to persuasion. From a meta-analysis of a selected group of studies on conformity, deviant rejection, and minority influence, Tanford and Penrod concluded that SIM provided a better account of the data than social impact theory.

We would argue that social impact theory can indeed incorporate source and target effects into a single analysis. In fact, it offers two different combinations of source and target effects, depending on the nature of the particular force field in which the target finds himself or herself. In one analysis, the target of influence actively disagrees with the source. In this case, Impact = f(SIN source group/SIN target group). This is quite similar to the analysis proposed by Tanford and Penrod. In the second analysis, the target neither agrees nor disagrees with the source. In this case, Impact = f(SIN majority − SIN minority). Tanford and Penrod do not offer predictions for this situation and, in fact, studies of opinion formation were excluded from their meta-analysis. One advantage of social impact theory is that it can be applied whatever the initial opinion of the target.

The S-shaped growth curve was postulated by SIM in order to account for two findings in the literature concerning majority and minority size that contradict the predictions of social impact theory. First, early studies by Asch (1951, 1952, 1956) revealed a very different relationship between majority size and conformity from that predicted by social impact theory. Asch found that majorities of one and two produced very little conformity, conformity was greatest when the majority consisted of three individuals, and increases in majority size beyond three did not lead to increasing amounts of conformity. Second, Moscovici and Lage (1976) found that whereas a minority of two individuals was influential, a minority of one produced no influence at all. Social impact theory predicts that the first person in the force field will have the greatest impact, However, both the Asch and the Moscovici and Lage studies utilized perceptual judgment tasks, with an unambiguous stimulus that was judged erroneously by the influence source. In such situations, it is likely that subjects required a substantial amount of social pressure before they were able to overcome their resistance to making counter-factual judgments. Consistent with Lewin's (1947; Coch & French, 1948) conceptualization of the social influence process, it is possible that the first one or two sources provided the pressure necessary to remove counter-forces and to bring the subjects to a yielding threshold. A single influence source produces considerably more influence when ambiguous stimuli are used (Nemeth & Wachtler, 1974; Wolf, 1979, 1985a).

SIM places a ceiling on the amount of influence that can be obtained. Tanford and Penrod restricted their analysis to situations in which "total" influence was possible. The concept of "total" influence makes sense when influence is measured as a dichotomous (conform-not conform) variable. In this case, influence is defined either as percentage of conforming responses or as percentage of conforming subjects. The concept does not seem to apply to situations in which individuals can become more extreme in their opinions or more confident with respect to them. Any model, including social impact theory, would predict an asymptote when "total" influence is reached.

SIM omits the variables of strength and immediacy, but includes a number of other parameters that can be incorporated into the model. Tanford and Penrod do not offer a theoretical rationale for the inclusion of one set of predictor variables as opposed to the other, making their model somewhat speculative. Strength and immediacy are included in social impact theory by analogy to their role in physical force fields. It is interesting to note, however, that of the additional parameters included in their meta-analysis, source consistency, a strength variable, was the most potent predictor of influence. A large literature on the effects of source characteristics, beyond consistency, attests to their importance as mediators of social influence (e.g., Chaiken, 1986; Eagly, 1983). As the results of the studies on restaurant preference, witness testimony, and jury decision making have demonstrated, social impact theory gains considerable predictive power from the inclusion of strength and, particularly, the strength by number interaction.

Self-Attention Model

Mullen (1983) has offered a more serious criticism of social impact theory that has also been raised by Maass and Clark (1984). As Latané and Wolf (1981) noted, social impact theory offers general laws that determine the amount of impact when it occurs, but does not detail the specific mechanisms by which social impact is transmitted. The theory is by nature a posteriori and descriptive, to a neglect of the psychological processes involved.

The self-attention model proposed by Mullen offers a more process-oriented approach to conceptualizing the effects of the group on the individual. The focus of this model is on heterogeneous groups within which at least two subgroups can be identified (even if one of the subgroups consists of only a single individual). According to this model, individuals become more self-attentive as the relative size of their subgroup decreases. The consequence of increased self-attention is an attempt to match behavior to salient behavioral standards, as they are perceived by the individual. The magnitude of self-attention and consequent matching-to-standards is determined by the Other-Total Ratio. As the size of the individual's subgroup decreases or the size of the opposing subgroup increases, the Other-Total Ratio increases. The individual becomes more self-attentive and increases his or her attempts to match to behavioral standards. Note that the Other-Total Ratio, like the principle of marginally decreasing impact in social impact theory, describes a negatively accelerating power function between the number of sources (i.e., others) and their impact, with each additional "other" having less impact than the previous one.

From meta-analyses of a large sample of studies, Mullen demonstrated increases in self-attention with increases in the Other-Total Ratio and corresponding increases in conformity and prosocial behavior and decreases in social loafing and antisocial behavior. Of interest here is his analysis of the conformity situation. Holding group size constant, as the size of the individual's subgroup decreases or the opposing subgroup increases, the individual should become more self-attentive and increase attempts to match to standards. Conversely, as the size of the individual's subgroup increases or the size of the opposing subgroup decreases, the individual should become less self-attentive and decrease attempts to match to standards.

The question, of course, is whose behavioral standards will be salient for the individual. Implicit in Mullen's analysis of the conformity situation is the assumption that the group norm, as defined by the majority viewpoint, is the salient behavioral standard for the subject. Conformity by a minority individual to the majority viewpoint thus increases with increases in majority size or with decreases in minority size. It is not clear, however, that the majority viewpoint will always be viewed as the behavioral standard by subjects in the minority. In fact,

Mullen's analysis suggests that the focus of attention in the group, for both the majority and the minority, will be on the minority viewpoint. The smaller faction in the group becomes the focus of attention, the figure against the ground, in Mullen's analysis. Because attention in the group will be directed to the smaller minority, perhaps its viewpoint will become the salient standard. An interesting implication of this analysis is that minority influence should decrease with increases in minority size, as the minority loses visibility and its viewpoint becomes less salient. This prediction would be consistent with the argument of Moscovici and Faucheux (1972) and Nemeth, Wachtler, and Endicott (1977), that the minority loses some of its stylistic advantage as its size. increases. However, this prediction has not been confirmed by any of the studies that have varied minority size (Davis & Latané, cited in Latané & Wolf, 1981; Moscovici & Lage, 1976; Nemeth, Wachtler, & Endicott, 1977; Wolf & Latané, 1983). Although Nemeth et al. (1977) found that minorities were perceived as less confident as their size increased, larger minorities were nevertheless more influential.

Summary

Both social impact theory and the alternative social influence model proposed by Tanford and Penrod offer descriptive accounts of influence produced by majorities and minorities, although neither attempts to explain the processes by which social influence operates. The self-attention model proposed by Mullen makes one attempt to explicate the psychological mechanism by which group members affect one another. However, Mullen's theoretical analysis did not extend to minority influence and his inability to specify behavioral standards a priori makes his account of the influence situation highly speculative. Nevertheless, his argument that the mechanisms underlying impact should be explored more thoroughly is well-taken.

Social impact theory is a meta-theory, providing only general rules that determine the magnitude of impact when it occurs, and is most useful when combined with specific theories relevant to each area of application (Latané & Wolf, 1981, p. 449). It is the contention of the present chapter that informational and normative dependence are the processes by which social influence operates and that, when combined with social impact theory, offer the most complete account of influence phenomena. A dependence model of influence specifies which components of the strength variable will be important in a given influence situation; the social impact model specifies the multiplicative relation of strength, immediacy and number. Psychological processes enter into the social impact formulation, then, as determinants of the components and magnitude of the strength variable.

DETERMINANTS OF STRENGTH

In an earlier paper (Wolf, 1979), I argued that minority influence, like majority influence, is mediated by informational and normative dependence (Deutsch & Gerard, 1955). Informational dependence exists when an individual relies on others for information about the environment or its meaning; the motivational basis of influence in this case is the individual's need to establish the validity of his or her perceptions, judgments, or opinions. Normative dependence exists when an individual relies on others for the direct satisfaction of needs; the motivational basis of influence in this case is the individual's desire to obtain positive outcomes, such as social approval, and to avoid negative outcomes, such as rejection. Informational influence, because the goal is to assess reality, tends to result in an internalized acceptance of an influence attempt. Normative influence, because the goal is to achieve harmonious relations with others, tends to result in public compliance which may or may not be accompanied by private acceptance.

Majorities are at an advantage with respect to both processes. Their numerical superiority provides a stronger consensus for establishing truth and affords them greater control over material and social resources. In fact, Moscovici (1976) argued that because minorities lack those characteristics (e.g., power, status, perceived expertise) that would make others dependent on them, dependence models of influence cannot explain minority influence.

I would argue that the type of influence, informational or normative, is defined not by the attributes of the influence source but rather by the needs of the target. Of course, informational and normative needs may be created in the target by attributes of the influence source (e.g., an expert source might arouse informational needs). But they may also be created by attributes of the influence situation (e.g., stimulus ambiguity or task difficulty might arouse informational needs). The needs of the target determine which components of the strength variable will be prominent in a given influence situation. When informational concerns are aroused in the target, ability, task competence, and expertise of the source will be the most important components. When normative concerns are aroused in the target, power, status, and attractiveness will be more important determinants of source strength.

The introduction of a minority viewpoint in a group may be sufficient to arouse informational concerns in other group members. Prior to the introduction of the minority opinion there is a group norm which, because it is as yet unchallenged, group members accept as the only viable position. The minority increases the diversity of responses in the group, creating a need to search for information to reconcile the difference of opinion. At this point, the consistency and confidence of the minority may become important components of its strength, leading other group members to regard it as an expert and trustworthy source of information. In this case, we would expect minority influence to be detected on private measures and to generalize to related measures.

Minorities are less likely to arouse normative needs, where those needs do not already exist, and there is little evidence in the literature that minorities produce influence motivated entirely by normative concerns. Two studies (Wolf, 1979, 1985a) found more minority influence under conditions of high than low group cohesiveness, suggesting that minority influence attempts are more effective when normative concerns are raised experimentally. However, in both studies the judgmental task was ambiguous and the majority members in the group were presented as wavering in their judgments. Thus, informational needs were undoubtedly aroused in the subjects as well. Consistent with the conjecture that informational concerns were operating, influence in both studies was manifested on private measures.

In contrast to minorities, majorities derive their strength from many sources: their control over resources, power, status, and attractiveness, as well as their ability, task competence and expertise. Majorities arouse and respond to both normative and informational concerns. When the basis of their influence is normative, their influence is more likely to be detected on public than on private measures. When the basis of their influence is informational, their influence should be detected on private measures and should generalize to related measures as well.

A recent study by Insko, Smith, Alicke, Wade, and Taylor (1985) supports the argument that the effect of number of sources on influence is mediated both by the concern with being right, or informational influence, and by the concern with being liked, or normative influence. They had subjects judge the color of each of a series of green-blue disks as being closer to green or to blue in an Asch-type conformity setting. Subjects made their judgments after being exposed to the judgments of either one or four confederates. To assess the effects of the concern with being right, they led half the subjects to believe that there was an objectively-determined correct judgment for each slide and half to believe that the correct judgment could not be objectively determined. To assess the effects of the concern with being liked, they had half the subjects announce their judgments aloud and half record their judgments in private. Not surprisingly, the results confirmed the greater influence of the larger majority. More importantly, majority size interacted with both the determined-undetermined variable and the public-private variable. The effects of both variables were more pronounced in the larger majority-size conditions. The interactions provide strong evidence that the effect of number of sources on influence is mediated by both informational and normative influence.

Summary

Social impact theory is clearly a theory of majority rule (Latané & Wolf, 1981). It suggests that minorities will produce social influence less often than majorities and that when they do produce influence, it will be smaller in magnitude. Minorities derive their strength primarily from perceived expertise and competence, perhaps inferred from the consistency and confidence with which they present their viewpoints. Thus, minorities are most likely to be influential when others are informationally dependent and their influence is likely to persist on private measures and to generalize to related issues. Majorities derive their strength from many sources and will be influential when others are either normatively dependent or informationally dependent. Thus, their influence will sometimes be found only on public measures and sometimes will generalize to private and to related measures as well.

This analysis suggests that one process, dependence, is sufficient to explain influence by either a majority or a minority and that, when combined with the general laws of social impact theory, offers the most complete account of social influence phenomena. The dependence of the target determines the components and magnitude of source strength; strength combines multiplicatively with number and immediacy to determine the overall impact of the source. The implications of this analysis, however, are somewhat different for minorities than for majorities. Because of the proposed multiplicative relation of strength and number, minorities need relatively more strength to have an impact. This suggests that minorities may have to work particularly hard to convince others of their truth. But when they are successful, their influence is likely to be internalized and to persist over time.

CONCLUDING REMARKS

The foregoing analysis has implications for how important concepts in the social influence literature are defined. Much of the argument about whether a single-process model is sufficient to explain influence by both majorities and minorities or whether a dual-process model is necessary may be reduced to a difference in how key concepts are defined by researchers in both camps.

Definitions of Majority and Minority.   A major impediment to communication among social influence researchers is that we do not all share a common definition of the majority or minority status of an influence source (Wolf, 1985b). Some researchers define majority and minority primarily in terms of the relative number of individuals holding a given position on an issue within the experimental group (e.g., Doms, 1983; Latané & Wolf, 1981; Nemeth, Wachtler, & Endicott, 1977; Tanford & Penrod, 1984). It is interesting to note that these researchers, with the exception of Nemeth, have also been the major proponents of a single-process model of social influence. Other researchers define majority and minority in terms of social or political ingroups and out-groups (e.g., Aebischer et al., 1984; Maass, Clark, & Haberkorn, 1982), dominant cultural norms, political ideology, and economic, political, or military power (e.g., Moscovici, 1976; Mugny, 1982; Papastamou, 1983). In Moscovici's (1985) most recent statement on minority influence, he argued that minorities must be defined jointly by two characteristics: their numerical inferiority and the antinomic, or nonnormative, nature of the position they advocate (p. 38). For these researchers, who are interestingly the major proponents of a dual-process model of social influence, the majority or minority status of an influence source, is determined jointly by number, strength, and the content of the position espoused.

Social impact theory treats number, strength, and content of position as three separate and distinct variables, with the number variable determining the majority or minority status of the influence source. Frequently, numbers go hand-in-hand with strength and immediacy and we tend to think of large, powerful, visibly present majorities and small, weak, covert minorities. Historically, however, there have been resourceful, highly visible minorities and powerless, distant majorities (Allen, 1985). By treating strength, immediacy, and number as conceptually distinct, social impact theory allows for these possibilities. Social impact theory is concerned essentially with sources and targets of social influence; the content of an advocated position is not considered within the scope of the theory (Latané & Wolf, 1981). One advantage of the theory is that it can be applied whatever the content of the position advocated.

Definitions of Influence.   A second impediment to communication among social influence researchers is that we do not all share a common definition of influence. Proponents of a dual-process model have suggested that social influence may be manifested on any of three response levels: public, private or latent. The public level corresponds to compliance, or public yielding without private acceptance. The private level corresponds to internalization, or private acceptance with or without public yielding. The public-private distinction has had a long history in the social influence literature (Allen, 1965). Latent influence, which presumably differs from both public and private responding, is a new concept in the field. Moscovici (1980) has argued that minorities have an advantage over majorities on this response level, indicating that different processes underlie their influence. Moscovici has not offered a clear, operational definition of latent influence and it is difficult to know what features must be present in a measure of the concept. He has suggested, however, that the latent influence of minorities may be detected by their greater influence on private than on public measures. Several studies have shown that minority influence tends to be detected on private measures (Maass & Clark, 1983; Wolf, 1979, 1985a) and to generalize to different, but related, measures (Moscovici & Lage, 1976; Moscovici, Lage, & Naffrechoux, 1972; Mugny, 1974–75, 1976; Nemeth & Wachtler, 1974; Wolf, 1979); majority influence results most often only in public compliance (Allen, 1965). This pattern would be expected if minority influence is mediated primarily by informational dependence, whereas majority influence is mediated frequently by normative dependence. Studies employing the chromatic after-image as measures of latent influence (Moscovici & Personnaz, 1980; Personnaz, 1981) would offer stronger support for the phenomenon but, as was mentioned earlier, the results have not held up to replication (Doms & Van Avermaet, 1980; Sorrentino, King, & Leo, 1980). Influence on a latent level, by either a majority or a minority, has not been well established in the literature.

Recently, Nemeth (this volume; Nemeth & Wachtler, 1983) argued that the definition of social influence should be broadened to include consequences beyond movement toward or the adoption of an advocated position. She argued that important goals of influence are to stimulate creativity and to raise the quality of group decision-making, by promoting a better search for information, a fuller consideration of alternatives, and so forth. She argued further that the representation of a minority viewpoint in a group promotes such forms of influence.

These potential contributions of the minority to the group merit further consideration. However, rather than add to confusion in the social influence literature, by extending the concept of influence beyond changes in opinion or behavior, I would prefer to view them as "contributions" rather than as forms of influence. Given a traditional definition of influence, the present analysis suggests only that minority opinions are relatively unlikely to prevail. It does not imply that minorities make no other contributions to the group, such as stimulating creative and thoughtful solutions to problems. The work of Janis (1982) on the value of minority dissent in preventing groupthink and of Nemeth and Wachtler (1983) on the role of minorities in promoting creativity clearly shows that they do.

ACKNOWLEDGMENT

I am grateful to Charlan Nemeth and Mark Zanna for insightful comments on an earlier draft of this chapter.

REFERENCES

Aebischer, V., Hewstone, M., & Henderson, M. (1984). Minority influence and musical preference: Innovation by conversion not coercion. *European Journal of Social Psychology, 14*, 23–33.

Allen, V. L. (1965). Situational factors in conformity. In L. Berkowitz (Ed.), *Advances in experimental social psychology*, (Vol. 2, pp. 133–175). New York: Academic Press.

Allen, V. L. (1975). Social support for nonconformity. In L. Berkowitz (Ed.), *Advances in experimental social psychology*, (Vol. 8, pp. 1–43). New York: Academic Press.

Allen, V. L. (1985). Infra-group, intra-group and inter-group: Construing levels of organisation in social influence. In S. Moscovici, G. Mugny, & E. Van Avermaet (Eds.), *Perspectives on minority influence* (pp. 217–238). Cambridge: Cambridge University Press.

Asch, S. E. (1951). Effects of group pressure upon the modification and distortion of judgments. In H. Guetzkow (Ed.), *Groups, leadership and men* (Reprinted in 1963, pp. 177–190). Pittsburgh, PA: Carnegie Press.

Asch, S. E. (1952). *Social psychology*. Englewood Cliffs, NJ: Prentice-Hall.

Asch, S. E. (1956). Studies of independence and conformity: A minority of one against a unanimous majority. *Psychological Monographs, 70*, Whole No. 416.

Chaiken, S. (1986). Physical appearance variables and social influence. In C. P. Herman, E. T. Higgins, & M. P. Zanna (Eds.), *Appearance and social behavior: The Ontario Symposium*, (Vol. 3). Hillsdale, NJ: Lawrence Erlbaum Associates.

Coch, L., & French, J. R. P., Jr. (1948). Overcoming resistance to change. *Human Relations, 11*, 512–532.

Deutsch, M., & Gerard, H. B. (1955). A study of normative and informational social influences upon individual judgment. *Journal of Abnormal and Social Psychology, 51*, 629–636.

Doms, M. (1983). The minority influence effect: An alternative approach. In W. Doise and S. Moscovici (Eds.), *Current issues in European social psychology* (Vol. 1,pp. 1–32). Cambridge: Cambridge University Press.

Doms, M., & Van Avermaet, E. (1980). Majority influence, minority influence and conversion behavior: A replication. *Journal of Experimental Social Psychology, 16*, 283–292.

Doms, M., & Van Avermaet, E. (1985). Social support and minority influence: The innovation effect reconsidered. In S. Moscovici, G. Mugny, & E. Van Avermaet (Eds.), *Perspectives on minority influence* (pp. 53–74). Cambridge: Cambridge University Press.

Eagly, A. H. (1983). *Who says so? The processing of communicator cues in persuasion.* Paper presented at the meeting of the Eastern Psychological Association, Philadelphia.

Festinger, L. (1950). Informal social communication. *Psychological Review, 57*, 271–282.

Gerard, H. B., Wilhelmy, R. A., & Conolley, E. S. (1968). Conformity and group size. *Journal of Personality and Social Psychology, 8*, 79–82.

Insko, C. A., Smith, R. H., Alicke, M. D., Wade, J., & Taylor, S. (1985). Conformity and group size: The concern with being right and the concern with being liked. *Personality and Social Psychology Bulletin, 11*, 41–50.

Janis, I. L. (1982). *Victims of groupthink*. Boston: Houghton Mifflin.

Jones, E. E., & Gerard, H. B. (1967). *Foundations of social psychology*. New York: Wiley.

Kiesler, C. A., & Kiesler, S. B. (1969). *Conformity*. Reading, MA: Addison-Wesley.

Latané, B. (1981). The psychology of social impact. *American Psychologist, 36*, 343–356.

Latané, B., & Wolf, S. (1981). The social impact of majorities and minorities. *Psychological Review, 88*, 438–453.

Levine, J. M. (1980). Reaction to opinion deviance in small groups. In P. B. Paulus (Ed.), *Psychology of group influence* (pp. 375–429). Hillsdale, NJ: Lawrence Erlbaum Associates.

Lewin, K. (1947). Group decision and social change. In T. M. Newcomb & E. L. Hartley (Eds.), *Readings in social psychology* (pp. 330–344). New York: Holt, Rinehart, & Winston.

Maass, A., & Clark, R. D. (1983). Internalization versus compliance: Differential processes underlying minority influence and conformity. *European Journal of Social Psychology, 13*, 45–55.

Maass, A., & Clark, R. D. (1984). Hidden impact of minorities: Fifteen years of minority influence research. *Psychological Bulletin, 95*, 428–450.

Maass, A., Clark, R. D., & Haberkorn, G. (1982). The effects of differential ascribed category membership and norms on minority influence. *European Journal of Social Psychology, 12*, 89–104.

Moscovici, S. (1976). *Social influence and social change.* London: Academic Press.

Moscovici, S. (1980). Toward a theory of conversion behavior. In L. Berkowitz (Ed.), *Advances in experimental social psychology* (Vol. 13, pp. 209–239). New York: Academic Press.

Moscovici, S. (1985). Innovation and minority influence. In S. Moscovici, G. Mugny, & E. Van Avermaet (Eds.), *Perspectives on minority influence* (pp. 201–215). Cambridge: Cambridge University Press.

Moscovici, S., & Doms, M. (1982). Compliance and conversion in a situation of sensory deprivation. *Basic and Applied Social Psychology, 3,* 81–94.

Moscovici, S., & Faucheux, C. (1972). Social influence, conformity bias, and the study of active minorities. In L. Berkowitz (Ed.), *Advances in experimental social psychology* (Vol. 6, pp. 149–202). New York: Academic Press.

Moscovici, S., & Lage, E. (1976). Studies in social influence III: Majority versus minority influence in a group. *European Journal of Social Psychology, 6,* 149–174.

Moscovici, S., Lage, E., & Naffrechoux, M. (1969). Influence of a consistent minority on the responses of a majority in a color perception task. *Sociometry, 32,* 365–379.

Moscovici, S., & Personnaz, B. (1980). Studies in social influence V: Minority influence and conversion behavior in a perceptual task. *Journal of Experimental Social Psychology, 16,* 270–282.

Mugny, G. (1974–75). Majorité et minorité: Le niveau de leur influence. *Bulletin de Psychologie, 28,* 831–835.

Mugny, G. (1976). Quelle influence majoritaire? Quelle influence minoritaire? *Revue Suisse de Psychologie Pure et Appliquée, 4,* 255–268.

Mugny, G. (1982). *The power of minorities.* London: Academic Press.

Mullen, B. (1983). Operationalizing the effect of the group on the individual: A self-attention perspective. *Journal of Experimental Social Psychology, 19,* 295–322.

Mullen, B. (1985). Strength and immediacy of sources: A meta-analytic evaluation of the forgotten elements of social impact theory. *Journal of Personality and Social Psychology, 48,* 1458–1466.

Nemeth, C., Swedlund, M., & Kanki, B. (1974). Patterning of the minority's responses and their influence on the majority. *European Journal of Social Psychology, 4,* 53–65.

Nemeth, C., & Wachtler, J. (1974). Creating the perceptions of consistency and confidence: A necessary condition for minority influence. *Sociometry, 37,* 529–540.

Nemeth, C., & Wachtler, J. (1983). Creative problem solving as a result of majority vs minority influence. *European Journal of Social Psychology, 13,* 45–55.

Nemeth, C., Wachtler, J., & Endicott, J. (1977). Increasing the size of the minority: Some gains and some losses. *European Journal of Social Psychology, 7,* 15–27.

Papastamou, S. (1983). Strategies of minority and majority influence. In W. Doise and S. Moscovici (Eds.), *Current issues in European social psychology* (Vol. 1, pp. 33–83). Cambridge: Cambridge University Press.

Personnaz, B. (1981). Study in social influence using the spectrometer method: Dynamics of the phenomena of conversion and covertness in perceptual responses. *European Journal of Social Psychology, 11,* 431–438.

Sherif, M., & Hovland, C. (1961). *Social judgment.* New Haven, CT: Yale University Press.

Sorrentino, R.M., King, G., & Leo, G. (1980). The influence of the minority on perception: A note on a possible alternative explanation. *Journal of Experimental Social Psychology, 16,* 293–301.

Tanford, S., & Penrod, S. (1984). Social influence model: A formal integration of research on majority and minority influence processes. *Psychological Bulletin, 95,* 189–225.

Wolf, S. (1979). Behavioural style and group cohesiveness as sources of minority influence. *European Journal of Social Psychology, 9,* 381–395.

Wolf, S. (1985a). The manifest and latent influence of majorities and minorities. *Journal of Personality and Social Psychology, 48,* 899–908.

Wolf, S. (1985b). Old issues, new perspectives. *Contemporary Psychology, 30,* 706–707.

Wolf, S., & Bugaj, A. M. (1985). *The social impact of courtroom witnesses.* Unpublished manuscript.

Wolf, S., & Latané, B. (1983). Majority and minority influence on restaurant preferences. *Journal of Personality and Social Psychology, 45,* 282–292.

Wolf, S., & Latané, B. (1985). Conformity, innovation and the psychosocial law. In S. Moscovici, G. Mugny, & E. Van Avermaet (Eds.), *Perspectives on minority influence* (pp. 201–215). Cambridge: Cambridge University Press.

Zajonc, R. B. (1968). Attitudinal effects of mere exposure. *Journal of Personality and Social Psychology Monograph, 9,* (2, Pt. 2).

Zaleska, M. (1980). *Quelques résultats et reflexions sur les rapports entre l'influence observée et des tendences latentes.* Paper presented at the International Symposium on Social Influence Processes, Barcelona, Spain.

10 Influence Processes, Problem Solving and Creativity

Charlan J. Nemeth
University of California, Berkeley

Social influence can be defined as broadly as "direct or indirect effects of one person on another" (Stang & Wrightsman, 1981, p. 47). However, its usual textbook treatment is confined to specific forms of influence, in particular, conformity, imitation, and persuasion. More important for the thesis of this paper is the fact that social influence tends to be operationalized in terms of *movement to the position advocated.* Thus, Kiesler and Kiesler (1969) define conformity as a "change in behavior or belief *toward a group* as a result of real or imagined group pressure" (p. 2). Baron and Byrne (1984) emphasize influence as altering subjects' "behavior, attitudes, or feelings in *ways we desire*" (p. 248). The italics are mine.

In our recent research on influence exerted by minorities, we have been forced to consider influence in broader terms. Minorities, to be sure, rarely *prevail* (Tanford & Penrod, 1984). Direct movement to the minority's views occurs on statistically few occasions. Private movement to the position advocated is seen more frequently (Moscovici, Lage, & Naffrechoux, 1969; Nemeth & Wachtler, 1983). However, more importantly, we have recent evidence that the conflict engendered by persistent minority opinions leads to a reassessment of the situation, to the detection of novel and correct solutions, and to thinking in more original ways. As such, we have come to recognize the importance of minority influence on the ways people think about an issue and about the quality of their decision making. Let us briefly summarize some important findings from the literature on minority influence and its comparisons with influence processes initiated by a majority of individuals.

MINORITY INFLUENCE

Many of the early studies in minority influence focused on the bidirectionality of influence and were designed as a corrective to the then prevailing emphasis on the conformity process. We had argued (Moscovici & Nemeth, 1974) that studies on conformity portrayed the minority or individual as a passive agent, one who could say "yes" or "no" to the position offered by the majority. Since the majority consisted of paid confederates who were trained to give preprogramed judgments, influence of the minority on the majority could not be studied. Thus, one considered whether individuals "conformed" or remained "independent." Independence meant maintenance of one's original position and was evidenced by a resistance to the influence attempts of the majority. The fact that the minority could have an alternative set of answers, ones that they would defend and argue, and ones that could ultimately prevail, was not considered.

As a result of the preceding emphasis, our early studies tended to focus on the "other direction" of influence, namely that exerted by the minority on the majority. We had a minority of individuals (2 of 6) say they saw "green" when the stimulus was blue (Moscovici et al., 1969; Nemeth et al., 1974) or we had a minority (1 of 5) favor $3,000 compensation when the majority favored $15,000 (Nemeth & Wachtler, 1974). In these studies, we learned a good deal. We learned the importance of consistency of position for the minority to prevail (Moscovici et al., 1969). We learned the importance of behavioral acts of confidence, e.g., taking the head seat at a rectangular table, for minority influence (Nemeth & Wachtler, 1974). We learned that consistency is defined in terms of patterning of judgments rather than repetition and that the perception of consistency and confidence appeared important for the influence of the minority position (Nemeth, Swedlund, & Kanki, 1974). However, we emphasized movement to the minority position; we focused on *prevailing* just as the studies on conformity had done. It is when we compared the influence exerted by a majority vs. a minority that some interesting distinctions began to emerge.

First, most studies on conformity show more direct influence than those on minority influence. By and large, individuals move to the majority position more than a minority position. Further, individuals may move on early trials or in early minutes of discussion when a majority of individuals offers an opposing position. Minorities posing an alternative position rarely find movement to their position in early trials or early moments of discussion. *If* minority influence occurs, it tends to manifest itself later and it usually takes the form that one person from the majority "breaks" and others follow. There is a "snowball" or "group effect" (Nemeth, Swedlund, & Kanki, 1974).

Perhaps more importantly, the influence of the minority appears to be latent. One can find numerous examples of majority influence where the manifest/direct level is strong and the latent/indirect level is weak or nonexistent (Allen, 1965).

Minority influence, however, tends to be stronger at the latent level. Consider the first experimental study on this issue by Moscovici et al. (1969). In that study, a minority of two individuals judged blue slides to be "green." The control groups (and the majority of four naive subjects) saw the slides accurately; they were "blue." When the minority was consistent (they said "green" on every trial), direct influence was small but significant. Individuals reported seeing "green" on 8.42% of the trials. However, measures of latent influence were more dramatic. After the public setting, Moscovici et al. asked subjects to place a series of "green/blue" stimulus cards into piles of "green" or "blue." Subjects exposed to that consistent minority view of "green" called stimuli "green" that control subjects would call "blue." Thirty seven out of the 40 subjects showed this pattern.

In a simulated jury deliberation, Nemeth and Wachtler (1974) had a confederate argue for $3,000 compensation when the others (four subjects) favored an average of $15,000 for a plaintiff suffering a personal injury. In one condition, when the confederate *chose* the head seat at the table, he was quite influential. However, he was influential at a latent level rather than a manifest level. Subjects did not move to his position during the deliberation. However, when determining appropriate compensation on another personal injury case, they gave significantly less compensation than a control. In another study simulating jury decision making on personal injury cases, Nemeth and Brilmayer (1986) found little movement to the minority's position in the public setting or in writing at the end of the deliberation. However, significant influence was found on a series of "new" personal injury cases, some of which were similar to the case discussed and others which differed in important respects. Other researchers (e.g., Mugny & Papastamou, 1976) report similar findings. Influence by the minority is often greater on indirect items (not specifically mentioned by the minority) than on direct items. (See generally Maass & Clark, 1984).

Some provocative yet problematic results come from a study by Moscovici and Personnaz (1980) who offered evidence that the latent change wrought by the minority may even extend to the perceptual level. In their study, naive subjects were exposed to a majority or minority who consistently judged the blue slides to be "green." When the influence source was a minority, there is evidence that subjects report an after-image consistent with "green," rather than "blue," that is, they move in the direction of pink rather than yellow. In two replications, however, such provocative results are questioned. Doms and Van Avermaet (1980) report such results for both the majority and the minority influence conditions while Sorrentino, King, and Leo (1980) report no significant differences between majority and minority influence sources. With internal analyses, however, the latter authors found evidence for the fact that subjects reporting suspicion showed the "after'image effect." These authors reasoned that suspicion led to greater attention to the properties of the stimulus and thus to perceptions of the after image.

THEORETICAL FORMULATIONS AND EMPIRICAL EVIDENCE

The asymmetry of findings between influence exerted by a majority vs. a minority has been considered by several theorists. In 1976 (Nemeth, 1976, later published as Nemeth and Wachtler, 1983), we suggested that people exposed to influence attempts from a majority tend to reduce the world of alternatives to two: that proposed by the majority and that held by themselves. They assume that the majority is correct and they encounter a great deal of stress when confronting an opposing majority view. Thus, the exercise is to decide which is correct but the range of consideration would tend to be a decision between the two alternatives. By contrast, we assumed that stress would be much less under a minority influence situation. Since individuals in the majority initially *assume* the minority must be incorrect, they come to question this assumption only in the light of persistence on the part of the minority. Even so, the question becomes how can they be so sure and yet so wrong but the consideration of these issues leads to a greater perusal of the stimulus situation, particularly those aspects not suggested by the minority. In the process, we hypothesized, they may come to detect new solutions or aspects of the situation that otherwise would have gone undetected by them. Although clearly speculative, we basically argued that influence by the majority limits the range of considerations while influence by a minority expands them.

Some experimental support for such a hypothesis was found in the study cited in Nemeth (1976) and Nemeth and Wachtler (1983). In that study we showed subjects a series of slides containing a standard and 6 comparison figures. Subjects were asked to name all the comparison figures that contained the standard (see Fig. 10.1). The task involved "embedded figures." One of the comparison figures was "easy" (R in the example). A pretest on 128 subjects showed that 77% saw that it contained the standard. The other figures were difficult. Pretest-

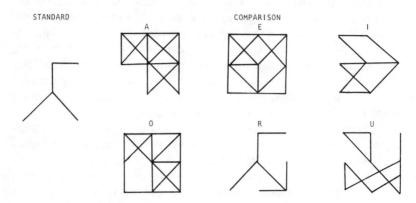

FIG. 10.1.   Sample stimulus used in Nemeth and Wachtler, 1983.

ing showed that less than 15% judged a difficult figure as containing the standard. In the experimental conditions, either a majority (4 confederates in a group of 6) or a minority (2 confederates in a group of 6) said that the figure was embedded in the "easy" as well as in one other comparison figure. This judgment was either correct or incorrect, depending on the condition—that is, the other comparison figure did indeed contain the standard or it did not. The other 4 figures were created such that 2 were correct and 2 were incorrect. The results showed that the majority was more successful in getting subjects to adopt the proposed position. In other words, subjects followed the confederates exactly. In the illustration, the confederates said the figure was contained in A and R. Subjects were more willing to say A and R if the source of influence was a majority rather than a minority. Correctness was relatively unimportant. In the example, both "A" and "R" are correct (it is sideways in "A"). Had "A" been incorrect, subjects would have "followed" as much.

By contrast, subjects exposed to the minority judgment were more likely to find novel solutions that *were correct*. They were less likely to *follow* the minority, i.e., they were less likely to say "A" and "R" in the example. However, they were more likely to see the figure in "E" and/or "O" (which are correct). Importantly, they were not guessing. While those exposed to the minority view of "A" and "R" were likely to find the standard embedded in "E" and/or "O" (which are correct), they were not likely to judge the figure as embedded in "I" and/or "U" (which are incorrect). As hypothesized, subjects also reported being under more stress in the majority than in the minority conditions.

The above findings lent some credence to the notion that persistent minority views, while less likely to *prevail*, are likely to be influential in that they foster an examination of the stimulus situation that allows for the detection of correct solutions. Thus, we would argue that the presence of dissenting views held by a minority can provide a creative contribution to decision making groups.

A similar and yet different perspective has been offered by Moscovici (1980). He, for example, argues that social pressure creates tension but the way of removing oneself from that tension is different if the source is a majority rather than a minority. He argues that change in the *public* realm is easier for those faced with a majority since change in the private realm would cause a perception of lack of individuality. Movement in the private realm should be easier for those facing a consistent minority since people are unwilling to become deviants "even if they have adopted a deviant point of view" (p. 216). Thus, one gets more direct influence by majorities and more indirect influence by minorities.

In the present formulation, we are not so much concerned with the distinction between public and private change. Rather, we hypothesize that the amount and nature of the cognitive work should be different when the influence source is a minority rather than a majority. The Nemeth (1976; Nemeth & Wachtler, 1983) study illustrated that subjects were detecting *novel* solutions when faced with a minority position while they were *following* the solutions proposed by the majority. We hypothesized that the range of considerations was greater for subjects exposed to the minority than the majority. Thus, they considered solutions not suggested by the influence source and ones that they would not have normally considered themselves. We also assume that more cognitive work was involved in finding these solutions.

This notion that minority influence stimulates more cognitive work *and* that this "work" is spent on a broader range of considerations *and* this tends to lead to the detection of correct solutions has received some recent support.

In one study, we (Nemeth & Kwan, 1985a) exposed subjects to the series of "blue" slides; they were asked to indicate its color and its perceived brightness. Subjects were paired with a confederate who said that she saw "green" on every trial. However, subjects were given information presumably based on previous studies that "green" was a majority or a minority response. In one condition, subjects learned that nearly 80% responded "green" to these slides and 20% responded "blue" (majority condition) or that 80% responded "blue" and 20% responded "green" (minority condition). Subsequent to this experimental setting, subjects were asked to give word associations to the stimulus words of "blue" and "green." Each word was repeated 7 times and the associations were scored for uniqueness using the Minnesota word association norms (Postman & Keppel, 1970). Results showed that subjects exposed to the opposing minority view gave more associations to the stimulus words and those words were more unique relative to the majority condition or the control. Subjects gave more words and gave highly infrequent words. Thus, for example, a subject in the minority condition might associate the word "sad" to the word "blue" while a subject in the majority condition might associate "sky" to the word "blue."

In the second study (Nemeth & Kwan, 1986), we concerned ourselves with the production of correct solutions in a typical creativity task, i.e. the solving of anagrams. Subjects were shown a letter string, for example, "tDOGe." With very short exposure times, subjects tend to see the word "DOG" first. It is the word formed by the capital letters from left to right. In groups of 4, subjects were led to believe that three people saw "DOG" but that one person saw "GOD," that is, the reversal of the capital letters. This was the "minority" condition. In the "majority" condition, subjects were told that three people saw "GOD" and one saw "DOG." Each thought the latter was herself. Five such letter strings were presented with the alternative viewpoint being the same, i.e., a reversal of capital letters by either a majority or minority of one's group. Subjects were then shown 10 letter strings consisting of the 5 experimental "strings" plus 5 ones seen for the first time. They were instructed to write down all the words they could make from each letter string.

Results showed that subjects exposed to a *minority* who offered an opposing position found more correct solutions. They made more words from the letter strings than those in the majority condition or the control. In fact, there is some evidence that those exposed to the *majority* who offered the alternative viewpoint followed that majority but at the expense of the other solutions. As shown in Table 10.1, subjects in the majority condition used a "backward" strategy more than did the control but they tended to use the "forward" strategy *less* often. The total number of words created was quite similar between the majority condition and the control but the form of the majority influence, much like that found in the Nemeth and Wachtler (1983) study, showed a tendency for "prevailing" or direct following. By contrast, those exposed to the minority did not find solutions of one type. They utilized the forward, backward and mixed strategies of combining letters. As a result, they found more solutions overall.

RELATED LITERATURE

While this is not the place for a careful examination of the work on problem solving, creativity, and groupthink, it is clear that such literatures have emphasized the debilitating consequences of convergent thought and of premature closure. In the literature on creativity, it is clear that divergence rather than convergence of thought processes is inherent in the definition. Watson (1928), for example, refers to "shifting about until a new pattern is hit upon" (p. 198). Guilford (1956) and Mednick (1962) emphasize the importance of flexibility of the search among ideas and associations. In the problem-solving literature, the culprit is often "set," a tendency to adopt an inappropriate "dominant" solution. The classic experiment by Luchins (1942), for example, showed this phenomenon with "water jar" problems. Individuals were asked to find 100 gallons by using containers holding 21, 127 and 3 gallons respectively. This, and other problems to follow, could all be solved by the formula $B - A - 2C$ (127−21−6). When these individuals were then asked to find 20 gallons from 23, 49 and 3 gallon containers, they tended to use the same formula (49−23−6) to arrive at the correct answer. However, they neglected to see the easier solution of $A - C$ (23−3) because they tended to use the dominant rather than the best formula.

In Janis and Mann's (1977) work on decision making, they argue that good group decision making involves a search for information and examination (and reexamination) of alternative positions. While they too have come to the conclusion that dissent is useful to keep the options open, to allow for such examination and reexamination, we would argue that it is not the *presence* of dissent, but

TABLE 10.1
Percentage of Correct Words Detected

	Minority	Majority	Control
Forward sequence	28.7	25.7	28.2
Backward sequence	24.9	22.3	15.0
Mixed sequence	13.3	10.8	11.3

Adopted from Nemeth and Kwan (1985b).

rather the conflict created by persistent maintenance of a dissenting position that fosters the reappraisal considered so valuable in the decision-making process. (See Nemeth, 1986 for a fuller discussion).

APPLICATIONS

Such an analysis has applied importance. Let us consider, for a moment, decision-making groups such as juries. Most countries want community representation. At the same time, there have been expressions of fear that not all persons are capable of the onerous duties of jury service (Cornish, 1968; Van Dyke, 1970). Whether by statute or by procedure, certain categories of persons have either been excluded or underrepresented. These tend to be the nonwhite, the female, the very young and the very old, the highly and the lowly educated (see generally Nemeth, 1980; Saks & Hastie, 1978). This "middle" bias can be found in most countries and has been aptly characterized by Lord Devlin as "male, middle aged, middle minded and middle class" (Pope, 1961, fn 10). With such relative homogeneity, we assume that dissent tends to be underrepresented.

Even if a dissenting view is present, procedural rules used by a number of countries tends to limit the effective voicing of such dissent. The allowance of nonunanimity and the reduction in size of juries, for examples, have been linked to the effective suppression of dissenting minority views (Nemeth, 1977; Saks & Hastie, 1978). A minority view is less likely to have an ally and is thus more likely to conform to the majority (Asch, 1956). Deliberations tend to be shortened (Saks & Hastie, 1978) and there is less "robust conflict" (Nemeth, 1977) under such procedural rules.

In France, this takes an exaggerated form in that three judges deliberate *with* nine laymen where only 8 of the 12 votes are needed for conviction. In an analysis of those historical trends, we (Nemeth, 1984) have argued that the effective expression of dissent aids the jury in its deliberation in that one would expect attention to more facts, a consideration of more alternatives and more careful examination of those alternatives. To be sure, evidence on this issue is sparse. However, the two studies previously mentioned are supportive of this line of reasoning.

In summary, we argue that influence processes emanating from a majority rather than a minority source are quite different and that they have implications for the quality of decision making. If one simply construes influence from the point of view of direct movement to the position proposed, it is clear that majorities exert more "influence" than do minorities. Within that restricted domain, there is more influence with more numbers. However, such an approach underestimates the influence of the minority and tends to obscure the impact of dissenting minority views. The available research reveals that the processes of influence emanating from a majority vs a minority differ in terms of the initial assumptions and the relationship between public and private change. What we have recently proposed (Nemeth, 1986) and consider to be the most important, however, is the possibility that the conflict engendered by persistent minority views aids the decision-making process. It appears to cause a more active consideration of the stimuli and, importantly, it tends to foster the detection of correct solutions.

Philosophers such as John Stuart Mill have argued against the suppression of dissent, even if it is wrong. In his treatise, *On Liberty* (1879), he defends this as a principle in and of itself. However, he also assumes that the allowance of diversity, variety and choice, as well as the airing of differing views provide a mechanism for the detection of truth and for the vitality of that truth. Our experiments lend support for these notions. "Truth" does not necessarily win out and it certainly is not the case that the truths posed by a minority will necessarily be accepted. However, it does appear that the confrontation with minority views, *even* if they are wrong, leads to more "cognitive work." People tend to think in more original ways and detect solutions that otherwise would have gone undetected. From this perspective, the dissent permitted and even encouraged in democratic institutions may be a mechanism for clarification, thought, and ultimately, justice.

REFERENCES

Allen, V. L. (1965). Situational factors in conformity. In L. Berkowitz (Ed.), *Advances in experimental social psychology*. New York: Academic Press.

Baron, R. A., & Byrne, D. (1984). *Social psychology*. Boston, MA: Allyn & Bacon.

Cornish, W. R. (1968). *The jury*. London: Penguin Press.

Doms, M., & Van Avermaet, E. (1980). Majority influence, minority influence and conversion behavior: a replication. *Journal of Experimental Social Psychology, 16,* 283–292.

Ghiselin, B. (1963). Ultimate criteria for two levels of creativity. In C. Taylor & F. Barron (Eds.), *Scientific creativity: Its recognition and development* (pp. 30–43). New York: Wiley.

Guilford, J. P. (1956). The structure of intellect. *Psychological Bulletin, 33,* 267–293.

Janis, I. L., & Mann, L. (1977). *Decision making*. New York: The Free Press.

Kiesler, C. A., & Kiesler, S. B. (1969). *Conformity*. Reading, MA: Addison-Wesley.

Luchins, A. S. (1942). Mechanization in problem solving—the effect of Einstellung. *Psychological Monographs* 54 (whole no. 248).

Maass, A., & Clark, R. D. (1984). The hidden impact of minorities: Fifteen years of minority influence research. *Psychological Bulletin, 95,* 428–450.

Mednick, S. (1962). The associative basis of the creative process. *Psychological Review, 69,* 220–232.

Mill, J. S. (1979). *On liberty*. New York: Penguin Books. (First published 1859.)

Moscovici, S. (1980). Toward a theory of conversion behavior. In L. Berkowitz (Ed.), *Advances in experimental social psychology, Volume 13* (pp. 209–239). New York: Academic Press.

Moscovici, S., Lage, E., & Naffrechoux, M. (1969). Influence of a consistent minority on the responses of a majority in a color perception task. *Sociometry, 32,* 365–380.

Moscovici, S., & Nemeth, C. (1974). Social influence II: Minority influence. In C. Nemeth (Ed.), *Social psychology: Classic and contemporary integrations*. Chicago: Rand McNally.

Moscovici, S., & Personnaz, B. (1980). Studies in social influence V: Minority influence and conversion behavior in a perceptual task. *Journal of Experimental Social Psychology, 16*, 270–82.

Mugny, G., & Papastamou, S. (1976). A propos de "credit idiosyncratique" chez Hollander: Conformisme initial ou negociation? *Bulletin de Psychologie XXIX, 325:18*, 970–976.

Nemeth, C. (1976, August). *A comparison between conformity and minority influence*. Paper presented to International Congress of Psychology. Paris, France.

Nemeth, C. (1977). Interactions between jurors as a function of majority *v* unanimity decision rules. *Journal of Applied Social Psychology, 7*, 38–56.

Nemeth, C. (1980). Jury trials: Psychology and law. *Advances in Experimental Social Psychology, 14*, 309–367.

Nemeth, C. (1984). Processus de groupe et jurys: Les Etats-Unis et la France. In S. Moscovici (Ed.), *Psychologie sociale*. (pp 229–251) Paris: Presses Universitaires de France.

Nemeth, C. (1986). Differential contributions of majority and minority influence. *Psychological Review, 93*, 23–32.

Nemeth, C., & Brilmayer, A. (1986). *Negotiation vs. influence. European Journal of Social Psychology*, in press.

Nemeth, C., & Kwan, J. (1985). Originality of word associations as a function of majority vs. minority influence processes. *Social Psychology Quarterly, 48*, 277–282.

Nemeth, C., & Kwan, J. (1986). Minority influence, divergent thinking and the detection of correct solutions. *Journal of Applied Social Psychology*, in press.

Nemeth, C., Swedlund, M., & Kanki, B. (1974). Patterning of the minority's responses and their influence on the majority. *European Journal of Social Psychology, 4*, 53–64.

Nemeth, C., & Wachtler, J. (1974). Creating the perceptions of consistency and confidence: A necessary condition for minority influence. *Sociometry, 37*, 529–540.

Nemeth, C., & Wachtler, J. (1983). Creative problem solving as a result of majority vs. minority influence. *European Journal of Social Psychology, 13*, 45–55.

Pope, J. (1961). The jury. *Texas Law Review, 39*, 426–448.

Postman, C., & Keppel, G. (1970). *Norms or word associations*. New York: Academic Press.

Saks, M. J., & Hastie, R. (1978). *Social psychology in court*. New York: Van Nostrand Reinhold.

Sorrentino, R. M., King, G., & Leo, G. (1980). The influence of the minority on perception: a note on a possible alternative explanation. *Journal of Experimental Social Psychology, 16*, 293–301.

Stang, D. J., & Wrightsman, L. S. (1981). *Dictionary of social behavior and social research methods*. Monterey, CA: Brooks Cole.

Tanford, S., & Penrod, S. (1984). Social influence model: A formal integration of research on majority and minority influence processes. *Psychological Bulletin, 95*, 189–225.

Van Dyke, J. M. (1970). The jury as a political institution. *Center Magazine*, 17–26.

Watson, J. (1928). *Behaviorism*. London: Kegan Paul.

11

Information and Affective Value: A Case for the Study of Individual Differences and Social Influence

Richard M. Sorrentino
Rodney D. Hancock
The University of Western Ontario

In this chapter we argue that it is time for those who study social influence to return to examination of the relevance of individual differences for research and theory. We believe we have pinpointed important underlying dimensions to social influence and can show how these dimensions relate to personality and vice versa. Given our analysis we argue that it will be a mistake for future theorists and researchers to ignore relevant dimensions of individual differences.

Over the past decade, those involved in our research program have spent considerable time, effort, and thought devoted to elucidating the important underlying dimensions of achievement behavior. We now believe we have accomplished this goal. These underlying dimensions are directly related to individual differences in affective and information value (see Sorrentino & Short, 1986). Raynor and McFarlin (1986) first used these terms to point out that a person engages in an activity in order to feel good (affective value) and to find out (information value). To the extent that an activity will lead to a positive affective state and/or provide information to the individual about his or her self or environment, the person will be motivated to engage in that activity. We, in turn, have gone on to demonstrate that individual differences in both information value and affective value systematically affect achievement behavior (see Sorrentino & Hewitt, 1984; Sorrentino & Short, 1986; Sorrentino, Short, & Raynor, 1984). We argued, first, that neither the original theory of achievement motivation (Atkinson, 1964; Atkinson & Raynor, 1974), which took primarily an affective view (e.g., pride in accomplishment, fear of failure), nor alternative approaches (e.g., Trope, 1975; Weiner, 1972) which advocated cognitive information seeking, were correct. Rather both affect and information about the self or the environment are important determinants of achievement behavior. Second, individual differences in affective value (in this case, achievement-related motives) and information value (i.e., uncertainty orientation) interact with situational variables (e.g., probability of succeeding, relevance to future goals, uncertainty of the outcome) in determining behavior.[1]

Although it would be inappropriate to dwell on these findings here, we have digressed to this point because we see a striking parallel between what we were attempting to do in the achievement area and what could and possibly should be done in the area of social influence. The bridge between the two areas stems from an important distinction evident in one of the first major subareas of study in social influence, conformity. As most students in social psychology are aware, Sherif (1935) demonstrated that in an ambiguous situation (the autokinetic effect) people will conform to the judgment of a group, and Asch (1951) went on to show that even in a totally unambiguous situation (line judgments) conformity to the group also occurs. In distinguishing between these two types of processes, Deutsch and Gerard (1955) discuss informational conformity vs. normative demands. The first has to do with the group serving as a source of social reality; the latter has to do with conformity to the group's norm in order to maintain membership in the group. In the Sherif (1935) study, then, subjects were most likely conforming for reasons related to what we call information value, that is the group was providing the subject with information as to the possible true nature of the stimulus. In the Asch (1951) study, however, subjects were conforming for reasons related to affective value; they were increasing their chances of being liked or avoiding chances of being rejected by the other group members.

The connection between the underlying dimensions for achievement and for social influence may now be clear. The distinction between information value and affective value is important for both areas. As we did in the achievement area, we hope to demonstrate that an investigation of individual differences in these two dimensions may also be fruitful for the area of social influence. The important individual difference variable related to information value is what we call uncertainty orientation. The individual difference variable related to affective value is the affiliation motive. The former variable has only recently been developed. The latter variable has been around a long time but never clearly understood.[2] Because uncertainty orientation is a relatively new variable and most of the research has been devoted to the achievement area, we can only offer a good deal of speculation as to its role in social influence at this point. With this in mind, let us look at some of the research and speculation that exists for both

---

[1]Up to this point theorists had attributed information value goals to achievement motivation, arguing that success-oriented persons were higher in the desire for self-assessment (e.g., Trope, 1975) or curiosity (e.g., Heckhausen, 1968).

[2]At this point we believe that there are many affective individual difference variables also related to social influence (e.g., self monitoring, machiavellianism, power motivation, social desirability), but uncertainty orientation (or those similar conceptually, e.g., need for cognition, dogmatism, authoritarianism) may be the only important information variable.

information and affective value; then, let us return to our claim that individual differences should be incorporated into theories of social influence.

UNCERTAINTY ORIENTATION

The information variable we have identified is what we call uncertainty orientation (see Sorrentino & Short, 1986). It is concerned with how one orients him or herself toward the uncertainty concerning the self or the environment. It is cognitive in nature and has much to do with what many have called cognitive information seeking. What may be of greatest importance to the contemporary study of social influence, however, is that this variable also has a great deal to do with maintenance of the status quo. In other words, it appears that there are in fact persons who would like to keep things the way they are. These persons are not interested in finding out new information about themselves or the world. They also may not conduct causal searches in their attempts to form attributions, could care less about socially comparing themselves with others, and may not "give a hoot" for resolving inconsistencies between such things as the self and behavior, two cognitions, or what have you. Indeed such persons (these are people we call certainty-oriented) will go out of their way *not* to perform activities such as these (people who go out of their way to do such things are people we call uncertainty-oriented). As we pointed out earlier, our research program has been primarily concerned with uncertainty orientation in the domain of achievement behavior (e.g., Sorrentino et al., 1984; Sorrentino & Hewitt, 1984; Sorrentino & Short, 1986). Hence, much of what we have to say in terms of social influence remains conjecture for the time being. We do believe we know enough about the variable, however, to point out what could be some interesting effects in future research on social influence.

A Theory of Uncertainty Orientation

The prototype for uncertainty orientation comes from Rokeach's "*The Open and Closed Mind.*" For Rokeach (1960), one must distinguish between types of people on a continuum ranging from gestalt types on one end to psychoanalytic types on the other. The former were characterized by the need for a cognitive framework to know and understand, whereas the latter were characterized by the need to ward off threatening aspects of reality (Rokeach, 1960, p. 67). Although this harks back to Freudian notions regarding basic trust and mistrust of the world (with the open-minded person passing successfully through the oral stage and seeking out the new world, and the closed-minded person still fixated, hanging on to mommy's skirts and daddy's coattails—or vice versa), it is also not unlike current notions of cognitive schema or category accessibility (Higgins & King, 1981; Markus, 1977). Rokeach (1960) argues that the open-minded person possesses a cognitive belief system oriented toward new beliefs and/or information, whereas the close-minded person possesses a belief system oriented toward familiar and/or predictable events. We might think of these orientations as general schemas, one a schema for information related to uncertainty about the self or the environment, the other, a schema for information related to certainty about the self or the environment. For uncertainty-oriented persons, situations of uncertainty are highly accessible. For certainty-oriented persons, situations of certainty are highly accessible.

An important point we make throughout this chapter (see also Sorrentino & Short, 1986) is that cognitive theories in general stress the uncertainty oriented type to the relative (or absolute) neglect of the certainty oriented type. This is most unfortunate given that the majority of the adult population is probably more of the latter.

Uncertainty Orientation as Positive Information Value

As stated previously, Raynor and McFarlin (1986) make an important distinction between two types of value, information value and affective value. Basically, it is the distinction between finding out versus feeling good. To the extent that one or both of these opportunities exist in a given situation, the person will be motivated to undertake that activity. In an achievement situation, so the reasoning goes, if a person can find out about his or her ability, and feel good about succeeding at the activity, he or she will be highly motivated to undertake that activity. Similarly, in a conformity situation, if the person is relying on the group to find out about the stimulus and hopes to establish friendly relations by conforming, then that person will be highly likely to conform.

We believe now that uncertainty orientation is primarily concerned with information value. The uncertainty-oriented person seeks to *attain* clarity about his or her self or environment (Raynor & McFarlin's self vs. behavioral systems). Certainty-orientation is also concerned with information value, but in terms of *maintaining* clarity about the self or the environment.[3]

Now, what we are saying is that it is the uncertainty-oriented person who is akin to Rokeach's (1960) gestalt type. It is he or she who will search for meaning, making sense out of his or her environment, and seek out new or novel situations. The certainty-oriented person is akin to the psychoanalytic type,

---

[3]In order to assess one's uncertainty orientation, a resultant uncertainty orientation score is obtained from two component measures. The first is a projective measure we call *n* Uncertainty (Fredrick, Sorrentino, & Hewitt, 1985), the second is a measure of authoritarianism (Byrne & Lamberth, 1971). The *n* Uncertainty measure is based on one's concern about uncertainty regarding the self or the environment, whereas authoritarianism deals with endorsement of traditional beliefs and values, as well as rejection of new ideas or beliefs (see Sorrentino, Short, & Raynor, 1984). These scores are transformed into Z-scores and the authoritarianism Z-score is then subtracted from the *n* Uncertainty Z-score. Subjects whose resultant Z-score falls within the upper tertile of scores are considered uncertainty-oriented. Those in the lower tertile are considered certainty-oriented.

maintaining information value by adhering to situations that are not confusing or uncertain in the first place. This person was at first an enigma to us until we realized that we too thought of every one as more or less a gestalt type. But the certainty-oriented person simply isn't interested in finding out anything new about his or her self or the environment.

A case in point is our replication of one of two studies done by Trope (1979). Trope set out to demonstrate that people will prefer to find out about their ability regardless of whether the outcome is positive or negative. In his study, people in one group (Ascending condition) were led to believe that they did not have low ability on a test of a new ability, but it was uncertain whether they had intermediate or high ability. In another group (Descending condition), people were led to believe that they did not have high ability, but it was uncertain whether they had low or intermediate ability. When given the opportunity to construct a further test made up of items of their choice, subjects in both conditions were more likely to choose test items which would resolve this uncertainty. Hence, Trope (1979) found, as predicted, that subjects were more likely to choose uncertainty reducing items than other items regardless of whether the items would indicate high or low ability.

Although this is an ingenious experiment, from our perspective it relates only to the uncertainty-oriented person. Certainty-oriented persons would probably not choose such items as they would then have to engage in a situation where uncertainty or confusion with regard to their ability abounds. Figure 11.1 shows

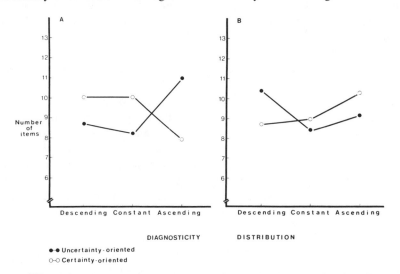

FIG. 11.1. Mean number of items chosen from each subtest as a function of uncertainty orientation (uncertainty-oriented vs. certainty-oriented) and conditions (A = ascending, B = descending). From Sorrentino & Hewitt (1984). The uncertainty reducing properties of achievement tasks revisited. *Journal of Personality and Social Psychology*, *47*, 884–889. Copyright 1984 by the American Psychological Association. Adapted by permission.

the results of our replication of Trope's (1979) study. Subjects who knew that they did not have low ability, but were uncertain whether they were of intermediate or high ability are in the Ascending condition of Fig. 11.1. Subjects who knew they did not have high ability but were uncertain whether they had intermediate or low ability are in the Descending condition. These subjects were given the opportunity to take a further test of that ability. The test was divided into three subtests and subjects could choose as many items as they wished from the three subtests, up to a total of 28 items. Subjects were then shown charts where it was evident that one of the subtests would reduce uncertainty about their ability (Ascending portion of diagnosticity distribution for Ascending condition, Descending portion for Descending condition in Fig. 11.1).

Note that, as we expected, the tendency to choose items most diagnostic of their ability (i.e., ascending subtest items in the Ascending condition, descending subtest items in the Descending condition) was shown only by the uncertainty-oriented group. Indeed, the certainty-oriented group appears to have actually avoided diagnostic items in both conditions. Here we see, then, persons choosing not to engage in an uncertain situation (i.e., take another test where they are uncertain about their ability), even though they could eventually resolve this uncertainty by so doing. They simply were not interested in being placed in a situation uncertainty-oriented or gestalt types would. The certainty-oriented person simply does not act like a "normal" person. More on this later.

In our research program to date, we have run several laboratory and field studies where support for our view of uncertainty orientation has accumulated. It does appear to be an individual difference variable in construct accessibility for certain vs. uncertain cognitive domains (King, 1980, 1983), and uncertainty-oriented persons do seem to have a preference for uncertain outcomes whereas certainty-oriented persons select outcomes of greater certainty (Hewitt & Sorrentino, in preparation; Sorrentino & Hewitt, 1984). Hewitt and Sorrentino (in preparation) have recently shown that this preference extends to games of chance and skill. In addition, in several studies we have shown complex interactions of uncertainty orientation with achievement-related motives and situational determinants that vary the certainty of the outcome (see Sorrentino, Short, & Raynor, 1984). This includes a recent study (Sorrentino & Roney, in press) demonstrating that Trope's (1982) finding that persons will work harder and perform better on a diagnostic than a nondiagnostic task is qualified by an interaction of task diagnosticity with uncertainty-orientation and achievement-related motives.

Implications of Uncertainty Orientation for Social Influence

There are several obvious implications of uncertainty orientation for the study of social influence, particularly for those which deal with information value. Elsewhere (Sorrentino & Short, 1986), we try to demonstrate that uncertainty orientation is critical for research and theory not only on achievement behavior but also on other forms of social behavior such as self-assessment, social comparison, self-concept discrepancies, and risk taking. As well, we see uncertainty orientation as directly relevant to the information value side of social influence. This is due to what is perhaps the key difference between the uncertainty-oriented and the certainty-oriented person. The former is what we call process oriented, the latter is outcome oriented (see Raynor, McFarlin, Zubek, & Sorrentino, in preparation). The uncertainty-oriented person engages in thoughtful processing of information related to the issue. The certainty-oriented person seeks only the solution, without conscious, active processing of the available information. Illustrative of this point, we shall briefly discuss central and peripheral routes to persuasion (Cacioppo & Petty, this volume), the heuristic model of persuasion (Chaiken, this volume; Eagly & Chaiken, in press), and a few other processes related to information value.

Central and Peripheral Routes to Persuasion.   In their chapter, Cacioppo and Petty (this volume) discuss the two basic routes to persuasion as being: (1) thoughtful consideration of arguments central to the issue; and (2) peripheral cues in, and simple decisional rules evoked by, the persuasion situation. We would argue that uncertainty-oriented people will be more prone to the former route, whereas certainty-oriented people will be most susceptible to the latter. That is, persons who seek to attain clarity about the self or environment would be most likely to select the central route; persons who are not interested in finding out about themselves or the environment would be influenced by peripheral routes. Such a predisposition should lead to interesting interactions with what Petty and Cacioppo (1984) have already discovered. For example, the finding that under high personal relevance, attitudes were influenced more by the quality of the arguments (a central route) than the expertise of the source (a peripheral route) should hold for uncertainty-oriented persons but should be the *reverse* for certainty-oriented persons. The greater the personal relevance, the *more* the certainty-oriented person should rely on peripheral characteristics such as expertise of the source, whereas uncertainty-oriented persons would rely on thoughtful consideration of the arguments central to the issue.

This brings to mind Rokeach's example of how open and closed minded communists and facists processed the Warsaw Pact agreement between Stalin and Hitler. The open-minded persons on both sides were in state of shock as the two underlying philosophies do not readily fit together. "Thus, some Communists, when confronted with the demand that they change their beliefs about Communist collaboration with the Nazis, saw implications for changing other beliefs about the theory and practice of communism. Sometimes it led to disillusionment and defection, and sometimes to a qualitatively different view of the nature of communism so that it was still acceptable" (Rokeach, 1960, p. 727). Closed-minded persons, however, had no problem with what their respective experts did. "To go back to an example we have used before, some Communists were observed to change their beliefs about Communist collaboration with the Nazis immediately following the announcement of the Hitler-Stalin pact in 1939. When asked for their reason for doing so, such persons were typically evasive until they could learn the reason for themselves from the next morning's *Daily Worker* or through some other party channel" (Rokeach, 1960, p. 227). They simply shifted their beliefs to be in line with those of their leaders. Hence, a highly relevant issue accentuated selection of either central or peripheral processing *depending* upon the uncertainty-orientation of the individual.

Another example of the possibility of an interaction between uncertainty orientation, routes to persuasion, and involvement would be the study of Petty and Cacioppo (1984) dealing with the number of arguments vs. the cogency of arguments. The investigators found that the number of arguments were less important and cogency more important under high as opposed to low involvement. Whereas, uncertainty-oriented persons would be more likely to choose cogency rather than number of arguments under high as opposed to low involvement, certainty-oriented persons would be more susceptible to quantity than cogency under high than low involvement. Bear in mind that we are saying that the more relevant a situation becomes to individuals, the more susceptible people will be to routes of persuasion to which they are predisposed. Uncertainty-oriented persons will seek to resolve uncertainty via a central route. Certainty-oriented persons will seek to find solutions without processing information, via a peripheral route.

As an aside, perhaps the reason why Petty and Cacioppo (1984) found an overall effect for number of arguments on persuasion is that their samples were predominantly uncertainty-oriented; one would expect college students to be more uncertainty-oriented than the lay population. Finally, we note with great interest that Cacioppo and Petty have developed a measure they call need for cognition (Cacioppo, Petty, & Morris, 1983). Using this measure, these authors have found that those high in need for cognition are more responsive to quality of arguments than those low in need for cognition. Unfortunately, our recent research (see below) indicates that this measure has little in common with our measure of uncertainty orientation, as we might have expected.

Heuristic Model of Persuasion.   The heuristic model of persuasion (Chaiken, this volume; Eagly & Chaiken, in press) is similarly a candidate for individual differences in information value. This model asserts that many persuasion cues are often processed by means of simple schemas or decision rules. According to Chaiken (this volume) without fully processing the semantic content of persuasive argumentation (or cognitively elaborating on such argumentation), people may, for example, agree more with long (vs. short) messages containing many (vs. few) arguments, or with communications delivered by expert (vs. inexpert) sources. This is quite similar to peripheral vs. central routes. Thus, to the extent that heuristic processes maintain clarity about the environment (sans information processing), we would expect that certainty-oriented persons are more susceptible to those cues than to cues that require more systematic processing. We should also expect uncertainty orientation to affect systematically predictions made by these authors. For example, in the research reported by Chaiken (1980), findings supporting the idea that high involvement leads message recipients to employ a systematic information processing strategy in which message-based cognitions mediate persuasion, may hold only for uncertainty-oriented persons. For certainty-oriented persons, high involvement could lead to even greater reliance on heuristic processing strategies. In addition, the finding that content-mediated opinion change shows greater persistence than source-mediated opinion change may be reversed for the certainty-oriented group (e.g., for certainty-oriented fascists, Hitler's message may persist far beyond any opposing content-mediated message). Interestingly, it appears that while Cacioppo and Petty may be theorizing mainly about our uncertainty-oriented person, Chaiken may be theorizing somewhat more about our certainty-oriented person. Certainty-oriented persons, then, are probably those most likely to employ "folk" heuristics and the kinds of heuristic biases evident in the decision making literature (see Tversky & Kahneman, 1973).

Attitude-behavior Consistency.   The issue of central vs. peripheral, simple heuristic vs. systematic, emerges as controlled vs. automatic processing in the attitudes literature (see Fazio, 1986). In support of automatic processing, Fazio (1986) states, "People do not at every moment in their daily lives engage in deliberate reasoning processes by which they decide how they intend to behave." We agree with this statement, although we believe it is likely that uncertainty-oriented persons spend more time and have greater reliance on controlled processing than do certainty-oriented persons. Where things become interesting, however, is what happens when the attitude becomes important (e.g., deciding whether to go to college). Here is where people assume the role of rational decision makers (Fazio, 1986). Similar to our above conjectures, however, we entertain the idea that for certainty-oriented persons, the greater the importance of the attitude, the greater the reliance on automatic as opposed to controlled processing. It is not unreasonable to think of many college students (perhaps too many) who are in college solely because their parents or a high school counselor told them that is what they should do. If such students are probed, it soon becomes apparent that they had never really considered the issue. Such people are likely to be certainty-oriented and are even less likely to become rational decision makers given important as opposed to trivial behavioral decisions.

Other Processes.   There are many other areas of social influence that can be seen to be affected systematically by individual differences of an informational sort. As exemplified by the chapters by Wolf and Nemeth in this volume, for example, a controversy has emerged regarding whether minority and majority influence are two separate and distinct processes or whether they follow the same general laws. Without engaging in this controversy (once was enough—see Sorrentino, King, and Leo, 1980), there does appear to be an important individual difference consideration related to uncertainty orientation. Given the above arguments regarding peripheral, heuristic, and automatic forms of processing of information on the one hand, and central, systematic, and controlled forms on the other, it seems to follow that majority influence may be considered a consensus heuristic (the message must be right because everybody says it is), activating the former types of processing; whereas minority influence, because of its inconsistent nature, would activate the latter forms of processing (i.e., it forces the person to think about alternatives). From the above arguments, it follows that uncertainty-oriented persons should be most susceptible to minority influence whereas certainty-oriented persons should be most susceptible to majority influence. We have argued elsewhere (Sorrentino & Short, 1986) that only uncertainty-oriented persons would attend to inconsistencies with regard to the self or the environment. Uncertainty-oriented persons, then, would attempt to discover why the minority is so insistent on being correct in the face of a majority. In contrast, certainty-oriented persons would probably ignore this inconsistency and "go along with the crowd." It may be then that minority and majority influence are two qualitatively distinct processes as Moscovici & Personnaz (1980) and Nemeth (this volume) have argued.[4]

While we are on inconsistency, we must point out that dissonance theory is also a likely candidate for individual differences related to information value. In paying lip service to this area, Festinger (1957) points out that there may exist an individual difference in one's tolerance for dissonance. Olson and Zanna (1979, 1982) and Zanna and Olson (1982) have tied this difference into repression-sensitization.[5] However, to the extent that dissonance requires an inconsistency between two cognitions, and that a person changes his or her attitudes in order to reduce dissonance produced by this inconsistency (see Festinger, 1957), then the theory of cognitive dissonance applies mainly to uncertainty-oriented persons and not certainty-oriented persons.

Some support for this contention comes from a study by Shaffer and Hendricks (1974) in their study of dissonance and dogmatism. Using an effortful task technique, these authors found that dissonance reduction occurred only for the open-minded subjects. The closed-minded subjects not only did not reduce dissonance, but also derogated the experiment and the experimenter! Presumably, the closed-minded subjects (who are conceptually similar to our certainty-oriented subjects) thought it was pretty stupid to ask someone to expend a great deal of

---

[4]Thanks to Shelly Chaikin for helping us work this one through.
[5]Jim Olson urged me to mention this.

effort on a boring task. The open minded subjects (who are conceptually similar to our uncertainty-oriented persons), of course, needed to resolve the dissonance aroused by this situation, and grew to like the boring task.

Last, but not least, we turn to the still unresolved issue of the risky shift. Actually, since Fraser, Gouge and Billig (1971) discovered a group shift also works for cautious items, it is now called the polarization shift (Myers & Lamm, 1976). The polarization shift is the phenomenon that a group tends to polarize the judgment of its members in the direction towards which they were previously disposed. Hence the group makes "riskier" decisions than "risky" individuals on so-called risky items and more cautious decisions than cautious individuals on cautious items. As it stands, there are those who are convinced that the phenomenon can be explained on the basis of persuasive arguments (e.g., Burnstein & Vinokur, 1977); the group points out relevant arguments that the members individually had not included or considered, thus leading to group polarization. Others, however, argue for a value explanation (see Myers & Lamm, 1976); the group makes the value of risk or caution salient to the members, leading to group polarization. Now, we would argue that both processes are operating and that they affect individuals in accordance with one's uncertainty orientation. The uncertainty-oriented member would be most affected by persuasive arguments, the certainty-oriented person would be reminded of the risk (or caution) as value heuristic. Hence, there may be more than one cause of the polarization shift; each cause dependent upon individual differences.

Finally, between the time we presented the substance of this chapter at the Ontario Symposium and rewrote the chapter for publication, a study quite supportive of our position has been completed. In this study (Sorrentino, Gitta, Olson, & Hewitt, in preparation) first year college students were presented with a one-sided or two-sided argument in favor of requiring comprehensive exams for students prior to graduation. Half the subjects were told the exams could take place within 1 to 2 years (high involvement condition) and half were told 5 to 6 years (low involvement condition). We reasoned that since uncertainty-oriented persons engage in systematic (controlled, central) processing, as the importance of the issue increased (i.e., high involvement), they would be more influenced by a two-sided argument. A two-sided argument ostensibly presents all the issues and permits the person to process the pros and cons of the argument, deciding for him or her self what the appropriate opinion should be. One-sided arguments, however, are less likely to allow systematic processing of information, and therefore are more amenable to peripheral (heuristic, automatic) forms of processing. Here, as the importance of the issue increases, certainty-oriented persons should be even more likely to be persuaded by a one-sided and less likely to be persuaded by a two-sided message. Results confirmed predictions. Uncertainty-oriented persons were more likely to be persuaded by a two-sided argument and less likely to be persuaded by a one-sided argument under high than low involvement. The reverse occurred for certainty-oriented persons. As the importance of the issue increased, they were even more likely to be persuaded by a one-sided message and less likely to be persuaded by a two-sided message.

We also included the need for cognition measure in the above study (Cacippo et al., 1983). There was a small but significant correlation, r (214) = .20, p < .002, between this measure and our measure of resultant uncertainty orientation. Curiously, this correlation seems to be due to its negative relation to the certainty component of the resultant measure, i.e., authoritarianism, r (214) = $-.236$, p < .001, rather than the uncertainty component, i.e., n Uncertainty, r (214) = .05, p > .20.

Another interesting result from the above study has to do with when we called subjects back 2 weeks later, under the guise of a student survey. The three factor interaction we cited above, i.e., between resultant uncertainty-orientation, one vs. two-sided arguments, and high vs. low involvement on attitudes toward comprehensive exams, was even stronger here than immediately after the persuasive message.

It would seem then that our information processing variable of uncertainty orientation may have a great deal to contribute to the more cognitive aspects of social influence. Let us turn now to our affective side, the affiliation motive.

THE AFFILIATION MOTIVE AS AFFECTIVE VALUE

An obvious candidate as an important individual difference variable for the effective or "social" side of social influence is the affiliation motive. Since its beginning, however, the theoretical conceptualization of affiliation motivation and the research examining affiliation motivation has been less than clear. In fact, the various conceptions of affiliation have resulted in a plethora of conflicting evidence and confusion in the area. Traditionally, affiliation had been treated as a unidimensional motive. Heyns, Veroff, and Atkinson (1958) conceived of affiliation as an approach motive that can be viewed as a source of positive motivation. Their n Affiliation measure was meant to infer the strength of the tendency to establish, restore, and maintain social relationships.

Curiously, the same authors (Atkinson, Heyns, & Veroff, 1954) suggested two types of affiliative concerns, one positive and one negative; the positive tendency being conceived as a desire to affiliate, the negative tendency, the desire to avoid social rejection. Unlike the achievement motive, however, where both an approach motive (the motive to succeed) and an avoidance motive (the motive to avoid failure) were combined to form resultant achievement motivation (see Atkinson, 1964; Atkinson & Raynor, 1974). Atkinson and his colleagues did not pursue the avoidance or social rejection aspects of the affiliation motive.

Research pursuing the affiliation motive as a single positive dimension continued for some time. However, as Marlowe and Gergen (1968) point out in their review of personality and social interaction, no systematic relationship between affiliation motivation and group processes could be found. Indeed, they cite

Hardy's (1957) study of need affiliation and conformity as the epitome of this failure (they called it anticlimatic). Hardy (1957) found that those who score moderate in *n* affiliation were the only ones to respond to group pressure in a conformity situation (Not to steal their thunder, but we have subsequently interpreted this as a measurement problem we have called a "moderates" effect, having even less to do with the affiliation motive—see Sorrentino & Short, 1977). In another review, Boyatzis (1973) concludes that it is difficult to draw any conclusions from the data, "except that something is not right" (p. 261).

Perhaps because of the failure of research into the affiliation motive to produce clear results, research and theory on affective sources of social influence declined. To us, however, examining social situations without a viable measure of the affiliation motive as a tool for research and theory would be much like studying performance in an achievement-oriented situation without examining differences due to achievement-related motives (clearly a Cardinal Sin). Fortunately, in recent years, there have been alternative conceptualizations of affiliation motivation which may serve to reestablish its utility and stimulate further research. Both Mehrabian & Ksionsky (1974) and Sorrentino and Short (Short, 1980; Sorrentino & Sheppard, 1978), have independently derived two dimensional conceptualizations and measures of the affiliation motive. In their model, Mehrabian and Ksionzky (1974) suggest that the tendency to affiliate and the tendency to avoid social rejection combine additively to form a measure of affiliation. For example, according to their model the tendency to conform would be an additive function of the two sources of motivation. Our model of affiliation, while similar in some respects, does not assume additivity. Indeed, it will be seen that very different behaviors are exhibited as a function of various combinations of the two sources of motivation.

In our model, affiliation-oriented persons (i.e., persons high in need for affiliation and low in fear of social rejection) are generally attracted to activities that allow them to restore, establish, or maintain positive relationships with others. All other things equal, they are not particularly interested in situations that do not permit them the opportunity of satisfying their affiliation need. They will, however, be positively motivated to perform any activity that they perceive will fulfill this goal (e.g., in one situation they may perceive that leadership activities are required, in another, conformity). In contrast, rejection-threatened persons (i.e., persons low in need for affiliation and high in fear of social rejection) will avoid or resist situations in which they may be required to interact interpersonally with others. Given their choice, they would much rather be in situations where there are no rejection incentives. These people are not concerned with friendship, they are mainly concerned with avoiding social rejection. All other things equal, they would rather be alone. When placed in a social situation, fear of social rejection will often lead to negative forms of behavior due to the inhibitory nature of the fear.

In the research to follow, we present some examples to show how a two dimensional conceptualization of the affiliation motive can, like uncertainty-

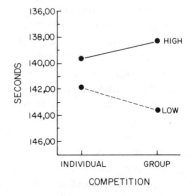

FIG. 11.2. Mean swimming performance in seconds for affiliation-oriented (High) and rejection-threatened (Low) swimmers in individual and group competition. From Sorrentino & Sheppard (1978). Effects of affiliation-related motives on swimmers in individual versus group competition: A field experiment. *Journal of Personality, 36*, 704–714. Copyright 1978 by the American Psychological Association. Adapted by permission.

orientation, lead to results not generally expected by others. These include interactions with situational determinants and/or somewhat surprising findings for some theorists in the areas of group performance, conformity, and leadership emergence.

Group Performance

Our first venture with a resultant measure of affiliation motivation was an unqualified success.[6] This was a field experiment by Sorrentino and Sheppard (1978), where we pretested experienced swimmers on the swimming teams of the universities of Toronto, McMaster, and Western Ontario. Later in the year, these swimmers were led to believe that they were to participate in the "First Annual Inter-Varsity Swimoff." They would be swimming in both an individual competition and a group competition composed of members of both their university and the other universities. In a 200 yd (186 m) free style swim, we predicted that in order to gain approval from the other group members, affiliation-oriented swimmers would swim faster in the Group as opposed to the Individual competition. Also, because of the rejection incentives in the group as opposed to individual competition, we predicted that rejection-threatened swimmers would be inhibited and swim slower in group than individual competition. Figure 11.2

---

[6]The resultant measure consists of z-scores on the TAT measure of n Affiliation (Heyns, Veroff, & Atkinson, 1958) which has to do with one's concern over establishing, maintaining, or restoring an affiliative relationship, minus z-scores on the Mehrabian fear of social rejection scale (Mehrabian & Ksionsky, 1974). Persons who score in the upper tertile are assumed to be affiliation-oriented. Those in the lower tertile are assumed to be rejection-threatened.

presents the results of that experiment. As predicted, affiliation-oriented swim-mers swam 1.48 seconds faster and rejection-threatened persons, 1.45 seconds slower, in the Group than in the Individual competition. Given that such meets are often won within 1/100ths of a second (the second author having missed being on the Olympic team by 3/100ths of a second in this event—ostensibly due to a sore thumb), we were most impressed. It should also be noted that Mehra-bian and Ksionzky's (1974) model would have predicted that both the affiliation-oriented and rejection-threatened person would have increased their speed from the Individual to the Group competition. The swimmer should swim faster in order to gain approval and/or avoid social rejection. This was not the case for the rejection-threatened swimmer as fear of social rejection is an inhibitor, as we predicted.

In another area of group performance, an experiment testing the implications of resultant affiliation motivation for Steiner's (1966) model of group productivi-ty, was run by Hancock (1983). The idea was that in a disjunctive task, where the group can go as fast as the fastest person, approval incentives would be stronger than rejection incentives as group size increased (more people to give approval to the fastest person). In a conjunctive task, where the group can go only as fast as the slowest person, social rejection incentives would be stronger than approval incentives as group size increases (more people to reject the slowest person). Hence, as group size increased, we expected affiliation-oriented persons to per-form best in disjunctive tasks and rejection-threatened persons to perform least well in conjunctive tasks. The latter prediction was supported, with rejection-threatened persons showing significantly lower performance in conjunctive tasks as group size increased. However, in the disjunctive task, both affiliation-ori-ented and rejection-threatened persons performed better as group size increased. It is clear that we need to know more about the incentive properties of various task demands before we can apply our knowledge of the affiliation motive, but we think this example provides an idea of what the researcher could look for.

Conformity

In the field of conformity research, consideration of resultant affiliation moti-vation has proved helpful in understanding the conformity process. Lewis, Lan-gan, and Hollander (1972), for example, predicted and found that where persons anticipate future interaction with the group, conformity will be greater than where they do not anticipate group interaction. Sorrentino and Hancock (in preparation) found, however, that only affiliation-oriented individuals con-formed more in a situation where they anticipated future interaction than when no such interaction was anticipated. Rejection-threatened persons actually con-formed less when they anticipated future interaction than when they did not. This was as expected as anticipation of group interaction should increase the approval and rejection-threatened incentives in the situation. The affiliation-oriented person would conform in order to build up "idiosyncracy credits" in the situation. The rejection-threatened person would deviate either because he or she did not know how to respond appropriately in the situation or he or she chose to be rejected now in order to avoid future rejection. This study serves as a good indication that affiliation-oriented persons will conform when there is a reason for doing so, and rejection-threatened persons behave quite differently. Let's see now what happens when leadership might be a good way to win friends.

The Affiliation Motive and Leadership Emergence

Table 11.1 presents some of the results of a recent study on leadership emergence (Sorrentino & Field, 1986). This was the culmination of over a decade of research investigating the impact of affiliation motivation on achievement-related motives and leadership (see Sorrentino, 1973, 1974). We argued that the reason no study was able to demonstrate a clear relationship between achievement-related motives and leadership emergence was because affiliation motivation was an important motive that also had to be considered. Task-oriented group activity not only has strong achievement incentives, but strong affiliation incentives as well.

In this study, twelve four-member male groups were run in group performance tasks over a period of five weeks, meeting once a week for 1–½ hours of group discussion. Subjects were paid a weekly wage and a bonus for their participation. Critical to the study was the fact that each member of the group differed from the other three members in his combination of achievement-related and affiliation-related motives. In Table 11.1, the ratings of each member of the group by the other members on leadership and related measures are presented. The ratings occurred at the end of the last session, and members were told to rate each other across the 5 weeks (weekly ratings were also taken; they are highly similar to the overall ratings). Note that on every measure shown in the Table, the person who is both success-oriented and affiliation-oriented (High Ach, High Aff) received the highest ratings by his group. The failure-threatened and rejection-threatened person (Low Ach, Low Aff) received the lowest ratings.

What is also interesting about the results shown in this Table is the somewhat weaker performance of achievement-related motives compared to those for affiliation-related motives. That is, the single motive that best predicts significantly high ratings on task and socioemotional leadership ability is the affiliation motive. This may of course be specific to the present study, and situations with stronger achievement incentives or weaker affiliation incentives could alter this differential. Both sources of motivation, however, would obviously have to be considered in future research. In addition to these measures, we also found very similar results for verbal participation rate, the single best predictor of leadership emergence (see Sorrentino & Boutilier, 1974). The two sources of positive motivation produced the highest participation rate and the two sources of nega-

TABLE 11.1

Overall Mean Ratings of Each Group Member by the Other Members as a Function of the Member's Achievement (Ach) and Affiliation (Aff) Related Motives

Measure	High Ach		Low Ach		p		
	High Aff	Low Aff	High Aff	Low Aff	Ach	Aff	Ach x Aff
Competence	3.89	3.58	3.75	3.20	.006	.017	n.s.
Confidence	3.92	3.56	3.78	3.16	n.s.	.01	n.s.
Interest	4.01	3.86	3.83	3.42	.001	.079	n.s.
Influence	3.98	3.33	3.64	2.96	.022	.002	n.s.
Contribution	4.09	3.56	3.74	3.26	.032	.009	n.s.
Motivation	3.98	3.72	3.78	3.20	.012	.05	n.s.
Task Leadership	3.89	3.50	3.78	3.11	.096	.015	n.s.
Socioemotional Leadership	3.69	3.47	3.61	3.03	.092	.042	n.s.
Leadership Elections 1st Choice	1.75	.67	1.00	.50	n.s.	.04	n.s.
1st and 2nd Choice	2.83	1.67	2.17	1.08	.068	.0005	n.s.

n = 12/cell. From Sorrentino & Field (1986). Emergent leadership over time: The functional value of positive motivation. *Journal of Personality and Social Psychology.* Copyright (1986) by the American Psychological Association. Adapted by permission.

tive motivation the lowest. Effects again were stronger for affiliation-related motives than for achievement-related motives.

In sum, the affiliation motive is an important area for the study of social influence. It is not a trait, but a disposition interacting with relevant situational determinants. It is a mistake to think of affiliation-oriented persons as conformers. This depends on the situation. Indeed, sometimes they will deviate, work very hard, swim very fast, or talk their heads off to make friendships or gain approval. It is also a mistake to think that the rejection-threatened person will necessarily take appropriate action to avoid social rejection when forced into a social situation. Fear of social rejection can be a powerful inhibitor.

Social Influence as a Function of Information and Affective Value

Let us briefly return to the distinction between normative and informational conformity. Although it is clearly recognized that both processes exist, it is virtually impossible to separate the two. In the Sherif (1935) study, one can argue that the group was being used as a source of social reality, but one can argue that normative demands were also being evoked. In the Asch (1951) line judgment study, the correct response was clear initially, but it is quite possible that the group made the subject question his or her own judgment, leading ironically to informational conformity (Asch, 1951, did point out that a number of subjects appeared to actually experience perceptual and judgment distortion).

Given that normative and informational influences appear to be inextricably embedded in the conformity process, it seems reasonable to argue that in most social influence situations both affective value and information value will be operating. We wonder, for example, to what extent both information value and affective value play a role in dissonance in group situations (see Zanna & Sander, this volume). This could occur because the group serves both as a source of social reality and approval or rejection. Hence, the magnitude of dissonance and the mode of reduction could be influenced by both factors. We also wonder if it wouldn't be useful to classify several of Cialdini's (this volume) major principles of social influence along informational and affective lines. For example, consistency, social validation, and authority, might best be thought as having information value, whereas reciprocation, liking, dependency, and perhaps scarcity would more appropriately influence affective value.

Finally, we must reiterate that we expect eventually to show that information value and affective value are not merely additive concepts for the study of social influence. In the area of achievement behavior, we have shown that one cannot precisely predict behavior without studying the two in combination, as they have systematic influences on each other. The same should hold in the area of social influence.

CONCLUSION

What we have attempted to show in this chapter, is that the study of social influence cannot go for long, and perhaps has already gone too long without examining the interactive nature of individual difference variables. We are not speaking merely of variables which quantitatively vary the *strength* of an effect, but which in fact qualitatively vary the *direction* of an effect. On the affective side, the study by Sorrentino and Shepard (1978) is a case in point. Here we demonstrated that not everybody swims faster when group incentives are available. However, the important point is we did not simply show that some people swim faster than others, but that group incentives systematically affect differences due to affiliation-related motives. Hence, while affiliation-oriented swimmers swim faster under group than individual incentives, rejection-threatened swimmers swim more poorly under group than individual incentives. This study is a direct analog to a similar illustration by Raynor (1968). Raynor challenged the assumption that everybody performs better in a course related to their major and/or future goals and he too did not merely find that this difference is more likely to hold for some people than for others. Rather, although success-oriented students performed better in a course they perceived as relevant for future goals than one that was not, the reverse occurred for failure-threatened students. These people actually performed worse in the relevant as opposed to the irrelevant course.[7]

The two studies cited above are related to the affective side of things with group incentives (such as approval, friendship, rejection) or achievement incentives (such as pride in accomplishment, shame over failure) determining the direction of the behavior as a function of the individual's personality. What we are speculating on in this chapter, and indeed this is high speculation, is that similar directional predictions may be made when it comes to social cognition. Hence while the importance, relevance, or involvement may increase cognitive activity on the part of some people (i.e., uncertainty oriented persons), it may actually serve to decrease such activity for others (i.e., certainty oriented persons). In other words, variables assumed to enhance systematic forms of information processing may work for some, but may actually dampen such tendencies in others. The thrust of information processing approaches to the study of social influence, then, may not be to investigate what types of variables increase controlled processing of information, but for whom?

Affective and informational approaches to the study of social influence may need to examine individual differences in order to understand underlying pro-

---

[7]This interaction, however, is also subsumed by a higher order interaction—with uncertainty-orientation (see Sorrentino, Short, & Raynor, 1984).

cesses. As Alice Eagly pointed out in her comments at the Ontario Symposium, perhaps now we have a clearer understanding of what processes may go with what people.

ACKNOWLEDGMENT

Our thanks to James Olson, Shelly Chaiken, Mark Snyder, Mark Zanna, Brendan Rule, and Gay Bisanz for their helpful comments regarding earlier drafts of this ms. Research reported here has been funded by the Social Sciences and Humanities Research Council (Canada) to the first author. Portions of this ms. were presented at the *Ontario Symposium*, Waterloo, Canada, 1984.

REFERENCES

Asch, S. (1951). Effects of group pressure upon the modification and distortion of judgement. In H. Guetzhaw (Ed.), *Groups leadership and men*. Pittsburgh, PA: Carnegie Press.

Atkinson, J. W. (1964). *An introduction to motivation*. New York: Van Nostrand.

Atkinson, J., Heyns, R., & Veroff, J. (1954). The effect of experimental arousal of the affiliation motive on thematic apperception. *Journal of Abnormal and Social Psychology, 49*, 405–410.

Atkinson, J. W., & Raynor, J. O. (1974). *Motivation and achievement*. Washington, D.C.: V. H. Winston.

Boyatzis, R. E. (1973). Affiliation motivation. In D. C. McClelland & R. S. Steel (Eds.), *Human motivation: A book of readings*. Morristown, NJ: General Learning Press.

Burnstein, E., & Vinokur, A. (1977). Persuasive arguments and social comparisons as determinants of attitude polarization. *Journal of Experimental Social Psychology, 13*, 315–330.

Byrne, D., & Lamberth, J. (1971). The effect of erotic stimuli on sex arousal, evaluative responses, and subsequent behavior. *Technical Reports of the Commission on Obscenity and Pornography* (Vol. 8, pp. 41–67). Washington, D.C.: U.S. Government Printing Office.

Cacioppo, J. T., Petty, R. E., & Morris, K. (1983). Effects of need for cognition on message evaluation, recall, and persuasion. *Journal of Personality and Social Psychology, 45*, 805–818.

Chaiken, S. (1980). Heuristic versus systematic information processing and the use of source versus message cues in persuasion. *Journal of Personality and Social Psychology, 39*, 752–766.

Deutsch, M., & Gerard, H. B. (1955). A study of normative and informational social influences upon individual judgement. *Journal of Abnormal and Social Psychology, 51*, 629–636.

Eagly, A. H., Chaiken, S. (in press). Cognitive theories of persuasion. *Advances in Experimental Social Psychology*.

Fazio, R. H. (1986). How do attitudes guide behavior? In R. M. Sorrentino & E. T. Higgins (Eds.), *Handbook of motivation and cognition: Foundations of social behavior* (pp. 204–243). New York: Guilford Press.

Festinger, L. (1957). *A Theory of Cognitive Dissonance*. Stanford, CA: Stanford University Press.

Fraser, S., Gouge, C., & Billig, M. (1971). Risky shifts, cautious shifts, and group polarization. *European Journal of Social Psychology, 1*, 7–29.

Fredrick, J. E., Sorrentino, R. M., & Hewitt, E. C. (1985). Need for uncertainty scoring manual. *Research Bulletin #618, The University of Western Ontario*, London, Ontario.

Hancock, R. D. (1983). *Models of group productivity and affiliation-related motives*. Unpublished doctoral thesis. University of Western Ontario, London, Ontario.

Hardy, K. R. (1957). Determinants of conformity and attitude change. *Journal of Abnormal and Social Psychology, 54*, 289–294.

Heckhausen, H. (1968). Achievement motive research: Current problems and some contributions toward a general theory of motivation. *Nebraska Symposium on Motivation* (Vol. 16, pp. 103–174). Lincoln: University of Nebraska Press.

Hewitt, E., & Sorrentino, R. M. (in preparation). The role of uncertainty orientation and gender in games of chance and skill.

Heyns, R. W., Veroff, J., & Atkinson, J. W. (1958). A scoring manual for the affiliation motive. In J. W. Atkinson (Ed.), *Motives in fantasy, action, and society.* New York: Van Nostrand.

Higgins, E. T., & King, G. (1981). Accessibility of social constructs: Information processing consequences of individual and contextual variability. In N. Cantor & J. F. Kihlstrom (Eds.), *Personality, cognition, and social interaction* (pp. 69–121). Hillsdale, NJ: Lawrence Erlbaum Associates.

King, G. (1980). *Individual differences in construct accessibility: A cognitive structural approach to uncertainty orientation.* Unpublished doctoral dissertation, University of Western Ontario, London, Ontario.

King, G., & Sorrentino (1983). The psychological dimension of goal-oriented interpersonal situations. *Journal of Personality and Social Psychology, 44*(1), 140–162.

Kirscht, J., & Dillehay, R. (1967). *Dimensions of authoritarianism.* Lexington: University of Kentucky Press.

Kohlberg, L. (1976). Moral state and moralization. In T. Lickman (Ed.), *Moral development and behavior* (pp. 31–53). New York: Holt, Rinehart, & Winston.

Lewis, S. A., Langan, C. J., & Hollander, E. P. (1972). Expectation of future interaction and the choice of less desirable alternatives in conformity. *Sociometry, 35,* 440–447.

Markus, H. (1977). Self-schemata and processing information about the self. *Journal of Personality and Social Psychology, 35,* 63–78.

Marlowe, D., & Gergen, J. J. (1968). Personality and social interaction. In G. Lindsey & E. Aronson (Eds.), *The handbook of social psychology* (pp. 590–665). Reading, MA: Addison-Wesley.

Mehrabian, A., & Ksionsky, S. (1974). *A theory of affiliation.* Lexington, MA: D. C. Heath.

Moscovici, S., & Personnaz, B. (1980). Studies in social influence. V. minority influence and compulsive behavior in a perceptual task. *Journal of Experimental Social Psychology, 16,* 270–282.

Myers, D. G., & Lamm, H. (1976). The group polarization phenomenon. *Psychological Bulletin, 83,* 602–627.

Olson, J. M., & Zanna, M. P. (1979). A new look at selective exposure. *Journal of Experimental Social Psychology, 15,* 1–15.

Olson, J. M., & Zanna, M. P. (1982). Repression-sensitization differences in responses to a decision. *Journal of Personality, 50,* 46–57.

Petty, R. E., & Cacioppo, J. P. (1984). The effect of involvement on responses to argument quantity and quality: Central and peripheral routes to persuasion. *Journal of Personality and Social Psychology, 46,* 69–81.

Raynor, J. O. (1968). Achievement motivation, grades and instrumentality. In D. S. Bushnell (Chairman), *Background factors, achievement, and mental health in adolescent boys.* Symposium presented at the meeting of the American Psychological Association, San Francisco.

Raynor, J. O., & McFarlin, D. B. (1986). Motivation and the self-system. In R. M. Sorrentino & E. T. Higgins (Ed.), *Handbook of motivation and cognition: Foundations of social behavior* (pp. 315–349). New York: Guilford Press.

Raynor, J. O., McFarlin, D. B., Zubek, J. M., & Sorrentino, R. M. (in preparation). Information value and cognitive functioning: Reinterpretation of cognitive-developmental and ego-identity theory in terms of uncertainty and certainty orientation.

Rokeach, M. (1960). *The open and closed: Investigations into the nature of belief systems and personality systems.* New York: Basic Books.

Shaffer, D. R., & Hendricks, C. (1974). Dogmatism and tolerance for ambiguity as determinants of differential reactions to cognitive inconsistency. *Journal of Personality and Social Psychology, 29*, 601–608.

Sherif, M. A. (1935). A study of some social factors in perception. *Archives of Psychology*, No. 187.

Short, J. C. (1980). *Effects of affiliation on achievement related performance.* Unpublished doctoral dissertation, University of Western Ontario, London, Canada.

Snyder, M. L. (1974). Self-monitoring of expressing behaviour. *Journal of Personality and Social Psychology, 30*, 531.

Sorrentino, R. M. (1973). An extension of theory of achievement motivation to the study of emergent leadership. *Journal of Personality and Social Psychology, 26*, 356–368.

Sorrentino, R. M. (1974). Extending initial and elaborated theory of achievement motivation to the study of group processes. In J. W. Atkinson & J. O. Raynor (Eds.), *Motivation and achievement.* Washington, D.C.: Winston.

Sorrentino, R. M., & Boutilier, R. G. (1974). Evaluation of a victim as a function of fate similarity/dissimilarity. *Journal of Experimental Social Psychology, 10*, 84–93.

Sorrentino, R. M., & Field, N. (1986). Emergent leadership over time: The functional value of positive motivation. *Journal of Personality and Social Psychology.*

Sorrentino, R. M., Gitta, M. Z., Olson, J., & Hewitt, E. (in preparation). Uncertainty orientation and persuasion: One-sided vs. two-sided communication.

Sorrentino, R. M., & Hancock, R. D. (in preparation). The effects of anticipated future interaction on conformity as a function of affiliated-related motives.

Sorrentino, R. M., & Hewitt, E. C. (1984). The uncertainty reducing properties of achievement tasks revisited. *Journal of Personality and Social Psychology, 47*, 884–889.

Sorrentino, R. M., King, G., & Leo, G. (1980). The influence of the minority on perception—a note on a possible alternative explanation. *Journal of Experimental Social Psychology, 16*, 293–301.

Sorrentino, R. M., & Roney, C. (in press). Task diagnosticity as a determinant of action.

Sorrentino, R. M., & Sheppard, B. H. (1978). Effects of affiliation-related motives on swimmers in individual versus group competition: A field experiment. *Journal of Personality, 36*, 704–714.

Sorrentino, R. M., & Short, J. C. (1977). The case of the mysterious moderates: Why motives sometimes fail to predict behavior. *Journal of Personality and Social Psychology, 35*, 478–484.

Sorrentino, R. M., & Short, J. C. (1986). Uncertainty orientation, motivation, and cognition. In R. M. Sorrentino & E. T. Higgins, (Eds.), *Handbook of motivation and cognition: Foundations of social behaviour* (pp. 379–403). New York: Guilford Press.

Sorrentino, R. M., Short, J. C., & Raynor, J. O. (1984). Uncertainty orientation: Implications for affective and cognitive views of achievement behaviour. *Journal of Personality and Social Psychology, 46*, 189–206.

Steiner, I. A. (1966). Models for inferring relationships between group size and potential group productivity. *Behavioral Science, 11*, 273–246.

Trope, Y. (1975). Seeking information about one's own ability as a determinant of choice among tasks. *Journal of Personality and Social Psychology, 32*, 1004–1013.

Trope, Y. (1979). Uncertainty-reducing properties of achievement tasks. *Journal of Personality and Social Psychology, 37*, 1505–1518.

Trope, Y. (1982). Self-assessment and task performance. *Journal of Experimental Psychology, 18*, 201–215.

Tversky, A. & Kahneman, D. (1973). Availability: A heuristic for judging frequency and probability. *Cognitive Psychology, 5*, 207–232.

Weiner, B. (1972). *Theories of motivation: From mechanism to cognition.* Chicago: Markham.

Zanna, M. P., & Olson, J. M. (1982). Individual differences in attitudinal relations. In M. P. Zanna, E. T. Higgins, & C. P. Herman (Eds.), *Consistency in social behavior: The Ontario Symposium* (Vol. 2). Hillsdale, NJ: Lawrence Erlbaum Associates.

COMMENTARY

12 Social Influence Research: New Approaches to Enduring Issues

Alice H. Eagly
Purdue University

This Ontario Symposium has provided us with a selection of the newest and most important theory and research on social influence. This quite diverse group of presentations spans a variety of theoretical perspectives and methodologies. Reflecting current trends within social psychology, most authors emphasized cognitive processes, yet some dealt in addition with motivational themes. Most authors considered the situational determinants of attitudes and beliefs, yet some focused on the role of enduring personality dispositions. Most authors discussed relatively new concepts or theories, yet others made good use of more traditional perspectives.

At first glance, the diversity of the chapters might suggest some disarray—or, at the very least, a lack of agreement on common themes and theories. Yet multiple approaches are needed to account for the complexity of the processes that social influence investigators seek to understand. Furthermore, within this diversity there is both continuity with long-standing themes of social influence research and significant growth as accounts of how influence occurs have broadened.

Both the choice of social influence as a theme for the Ontario Symposium and the content of the symposium papers themselves suggest that investigators have recovered from the disappointments of the 1960s and 70s. That period was characterized by widespread discouragement with the limitations the classic theories of attitude change and social influence (see Eagly & Himmelfarb, 1974) and with the apparently conflicting and nongeneralizable quality of many research findings in this area. There was also outright boredom with the repetitious quality of research within some paradigms—for example, persuasion experiments varying factors such as communicator credibility and level of fear, and conformity experiments utilizing the Crutchfield apparatus or similar methods for simulating group process.

The Cumulation of Knowledge.   In contrast to the pessimism that investigators often expressed in the 1960s and 70s about the growth of systematic knowledge concerning attitude change and social influence, the symposium authors appear relatively optimistic. Each author seems to believe that substantial progress has been made on certain research problems. Although the collective progress of social psychologists in understanding social influence cannot be described as rapid, the research and theory presented in this symposium show that the history of these research problems is not fairly described as the "slow progress of soft psychology" that Meehl (1978) and others have claimed is typical of social psychology.

Progress might have been more continuous had investigators been more skilled at integrating research findings. The need for insightful integration and accurate aggregation of findings has been particularly great for social-influence research because of its early popularity. The existence of large and complex empirical literatures at a relatively early point left this research area unusually vulnerable to various critiques of the 1960s and 70s, especially to the claim that research findings in social psychology are unstable or "fragile" (e.g., Cronbach, 1975; Gergen, 1973). Perhaps the belief in instability grew primarily because this area was the most popular research area in social psychology in the period immediately prior to these critiques. Indeed, this instability theme has not disappeared from descriptions of social-influence research (see Snyder & DeBono, Chapter 4). Yet I suspect that a comparative assessment of research findings would *not* support the claim of any greater inconsistency in these findings, compared with those in other areas of social psychology.

Some of the reviewers and commentators who fostered belief in the presumed instability of social-influence findings offered as evidence for their contention only their personal opinion. Others offered convenience samples of research findings, which they compared and evaluated by their statistical significance, generally without regard even to sample size and other determinants of statistical power. These relatively primitive methods of judging findings did very little to establish the validity of the claim that findings are unstable.

Fortunately meta-analytic methods (e.g., Cooper, 1984; Glass, McGaw, & Smith, 1981; Hedges & Olkin, 1985; Rosenthal, 1984) now provide statistically justified decision rules for integrating findings and for determining whether they are consistent or inconsistent across studies. Although these methods have been applied to a few social-influence problems (e.g., Beaman, Cole, Preston, Klentz, & Steblay, 1983; Eagly & Carli, 1981; Tanford & Penrod, 1984), uses in this area have been limited so far. The potential of these new methods for assessing the empirical status of basic social-influence research questions is exciting and should at long last allow the development of a tradition of cumulative findings. Impact of this sort has already been seen in other research areas, such as sex differences in abilities and social behaviors (Hall, 1984; Hyde & Linn, 1986).

Although the symposium contributors have not contended in a formal way with these issues of research integration, many of their efforts are nevertheless encouraging to those of us who believe that social-science knowledge can be cumulative. In particular, some of the contributors to this volume have incorporated into their current perspectives certain of the very imperfect understandings generated by older theories. For example, Snyder and DeBono (Chapter 4) utilized functional theories of attitudes, Wolf (Chapter 9) and Sorrentino and Hancock (Chapter 11) considered the classical distinction between normative and informational influence, Fazio (Chapter 5) chronicled the continuing history of self-perception theory, and Zanna and Sande (Chapter 6) evaluated the relevance of dissonance and attributional processes to group processes. I illustrate these and other trends by commenting on several specific themes that have been addressed by contributors to the symposium.

MODES OF INFORMATION PROCESSING

It is not surprising that a major focus of several symposium papers is the cognitive processes that underlie social influence. Emphasis on the cognitive mediation of influence is a long-standing tradition, stemming from the work of investigators such as Asch (1956) and various cognitive consistency theorists (e.g., Heider, 1958; Osgood & Tannenbaum, 1955). Early cognitive themes evolved into a concern with information processing (e.g., McGuire, 1972) and narrowed to a focus on message- and issue-relevant thinking as well as the more specific inferences that were thought to be carried out by the recipients of messages. Recipients of persuasive information were thought to engage in various cognitive processes—namely, (a) to logically draw conclusions from the premises contained in messages (e.g., McGuire, 1960; Wyer, 1974), (b) to reason about the consequences of recommended actions (e.g., Fishbein & Ajzen, 1975), (c) to causally explain communicators' positions on issues (e.g., Eagly, Chaiken, & Wood, 1981), and (d) to silently argue in favor of or counter to messages (e.g., Petty, Ostrom, & Brock, 1981). Although approaches based on these aspects of information-processing have been and remain important, they produced a somewhat one-sided view of the cognitions that underlie social influence. They depicted a rather rational, thoughtful, and careful information-processor who is quite receptive to new and challenging information. This view of the information-processor has been contested by some of the new work reported in the symposium. There is growing appreciation of the short-cuts that people sometimes take in reacting to information.

The idea that people may often exert little cognitive effort in judging the validity of messages and may base their agreement or disagreement on a superficial assessment of a variety of cues has been considered in a number of presentations in the symposium—particularly in Chaiken's (Chapter 1) discussion of heuristic processing of persuasive messages, Cacioppo and Petty's (Chapter 2) discussion of peripheral modes of processing, and Cialdini's (Chapter 7) consideration of compliance heuristics. Sherman (Chapter 3) also made use of this idea as an effective organizing principle in his discussion of attitude formation and change.

In contrast to the earlier approaches that emphasized relatively detailed processing of message content and the role of message- and topic-relevant cognitions in determining attitudes and beliefs, these new approaches deemphasize detailed processing and propose alternative routes to persuasion and compliance. Chaiken (1980, Chapter 1) proposed that simple decision rules often mediate the persuasive impact of a variety of persuasion variables. For example, with respect to communicator expertise, people may have learned that statements by experts are more veridical than statements by persons who lack expertise and may then apply the expert credo, "Statements by experts can be trusted," in response to a cue conveying high expertise. Belief in the communicator's recommended position would follow, without any more elaborate information processing than the use of this simple decision rule.

Under other circumstances, message recipients would turn to the more thorough information processing that Chaiken (e.g., 1980) has labeled "systematic" and Petty and Cacioppo (e.g., 1981) have labeled "central." When examined in more detail, this more thorough processing might encompass the logical, attributional, configural, or other types of inferences explored in detail by other investigators working in the information processing tradition.

Similar issues of mode of cognitive processing are beginning to be raised concerning the influence that occurs in group contexts. This emphasis is a new departure in this literature because, aside from some forays into attributional inferences (e.g., Moscovici & Nemeth, 1974; Ross, Bierbrauer, & Hoffman, 1976) and cognitive restructuring (Allen & Wilder, 1980), the information processing underlying conformity and minority influence has not been thoroughly examined. According to Moscovici (1980), a minority's opinion, if consistently stated, elicits careful scrutiny by group members. This detailed processing of the minority's position, which seems to resemble systematic or central processing, is held to bring about *latent, indirect,* or *covert* influence, an internalized change of opinion that is not necessarily manifested publically. Apparently this form of influence can best be detected on dependent variables not directly related to the influence induction. Wolf (Chapter 9) provided a helpful discussion of latent influence and noted the somewhat ambiguous status that this concept has, on both conceptual and empirical grounds.

In contrast, influence by the majority is held to bring about *manifest, direct,* or *overt* influence, a type of public compliance. Perhaps this influence by the majority is genuine opinion change, mediated by some sort of compliance heuristic or simple decision rule (see Sorrentino & Hancock, Chapter 11). Such compliance would be accompanied by change in private opinions. Alternatively, manifest influence may represent mere public compliance, unaccompanied by any shift of underlying opinions, however temporary.

To understand the extent to which agreement responses reflect internalized opinion change, researchers should continue to assess opinions under various conditions (e.g., with and without surveillance by the other group members). In addition, because temporal stability of opinion change suggests internalization, the persistence of influence over time should be examined within minority influence studies. Also important in building an understanding of majority and minority influence is the assessment of the intervening cognitive processes that have been proposed as mediators of these forms of influence. Demonstrating the usefulness of process-oriented measures, Nemeth (Chapter 10) reported minority influence research that assessed the number and uniqueness of subjects' associations to stimuli and the quality and variety of subjects' problem solutions. She argued that these measures provide evidence that influence by a minority, compared with influence by a majority, fosters attention to more aspects of the situation and encourages more divergent thought processes.

Wolf (Chapter 9) also addressed the issue of the processes that account for minority and majority influence. Wolf presented Latané and Wolf's (1983) argument that both minority and majority influence can be explained as a single process within the framework of social impact theory. As suggested by Maass and Clark's (1984) recent review of minority influence research, the Latané and Wolf position remains controversial, and investigators are directing considerable attention to understanding whether one or two processes account for minority and majority influence. Issues of cognitive mediation are increasingly important in this debate, and cognitive measures provide important indices of the extent to which a two-process theory is viable.

Zanna and Sande's (Chapter 6) paper on the effects of counterattitudinal essay writing in group contexts also addresses the cognitive processes underlying attitude change among group members. Their account, which emphasizes freedom of choice and the diffusion of personal responsibility for taking an attitudinal position, raises important attributional issues concerning how people explain their own counterattitudinal behavior. These issues are somewhat different from the attributional issues considered in the minority influence (e.g., Moscovici & Nemeth, 1974) and persuasion literatures (e.g., Eagly, Chaiken, & Wood, 1981), where the focus has been on explanations of influencing agents' behavior. Zanna and Sande's research suggests that group processes raise a complex set of attributional issues involving both explanations of one's own behavior and explanations of the behavior of other group members. Although consideration of attributional issues in the social influence literature has been sporadic and somewhat scattered (see Eagly & Chaiken, 1984), a general theory of how people explain their own and others' opinions might have considerable potential to account for attitude formation and change in group settings.

Determinants of Processing Mode.   To return to the general issue of modes of information processing, I note that this symposium displays the considerable progress that has been made in identifying the determinants of processing information in one mode or another (e.g., heuristically, systematically, attributionally). In the persuasion literature, variables that have been shown to affect the extent to which people use heuristic versus systematic processing include motivational variables such as personal involvement (e.g., Chaiken, 1980; Petty, Cacioppo, & Goldman, 1981) and need for cognition (Cacioppo, Petty, & Morris, 1983), ability variables such as distraction (e.g., Petty, Wells, & Brock, 1976) and issue-relevant knowledge (Wood, Kallgren, & Priesler, 1985), and other variables such as the salience of persuasion cues typically processed heuristically (e.g., Chaiken & Eagly, 1983; Pallak, 1983). Perhaps group-level variables such as the source's minority or majority status also affect processing mode, as Nemeth's (Chapter 10) analysis implies. Sherman (Chapter 3) delineated a range of conditions that may initiate central or heuristic processing. Also, in a recent analysis, Eagly and Chaiken (1984) suggested that broader principles, such as the sufficiency of a processing mode for determining the message's overall validity, may explain the effects of the particular variables that appear to affect processing mode.

One reason that demonstrations of the impact that a number of variables have on processing mode have been reasonably convincing is that investigators often included process-oriented measures along with measures of persuasion. Persuasion researchers have shown commendable creativity in obtaining indices of covert psychological processes. Not only has thought-listing (see Petty, Ostrom, & Brock, 1981) proven to be a flexible and informative method, but also psychophysiological measures are beginning to provide valuable evidence concerning the nature and intensity of psychological processes that underlie influence. Cacioppo and Petty (Chapter 2) have provided promising evidence that psychological processes relevant to social influence can be tracked through assessments of physiological reactions. Especially promising is the ability of muscle action potentials across the face to serve as indicators of positive or negative affective reactions.

Finally, in conceptualizing how people decide whether to use one or another processing mode, we would do well to note Sherman's (Chapter 3) suggestion that Shiffrin and Schneider's (1977; Schneider & Shiffrin, 1977) distinction between automatic and controlled processing is relevant. This decision may proceed automatically—that is, without much active control or attention by message recipients. Alternatively, an individual may choose a processing mode in a more controlled manner by actively thinking about the extent to which more or less effortful modes of processing are warranted or by using some other controlled or attentional method of evaluation. Although Sherman suggested that the decision about processing mode is typically a controlled, attentional process, this interesting issue clearly deserves empirical exploration.

MOTIVATION FOR INFORMATION PROCESSING

The new understanding that is emerging concerning variability in modes of cognitive processing raises motivational issues that have been neglected for a number of years. The open-minded information processor described in the recent past by many cognitively oriented investigators was not well endowed from a motivational standpoint. Any motives seemed to consist mainly of a desire to attain valid opinions that are in line with the relevant facts. Motivational issues were considerably more important in the prior generation of social influence theories. For example, in theories such as dissonance, reactance, and social judgment, people were thought to be motivated to defend their attitudes and beliefs from the implications of information that might disturb existing cognitions to which they were importantly committed. In addition, theories such as Katz's (1960) functional theory of attitudes featured attempts to delineate the range of motivations that may guide people's reactions to persuasive messages.

Motivational issues of this general type will have to be reintroduced to enable investigators to predict the conditions under which one rather than another processing mode will be used. In recognition of this need, Cacioppo and Petty (Chapter 2) used the concept of motivation in their elaboration likelihood model, and Chaiken (Chapter 1) incorporated the concept in a similar way. Within these frameworks, people must be motivated to expend the effort needed to process information centrally or systematically. Yet these investigators' ideas about what motivates message recipients to process message content thoroughly have remained largely intuitive or have been borrowed from other theoretical perspectives (see Eagly & Chaiken, 1984).

To achieve more progress on motivational issues, investigators should consider adopting a perspective that can be termed functional, following from the use of this term by an earlier generation of attitude theorists (e.g., Katz, 1960; Kelman, 1961). Functional perspectives take into account people's goals in social influence settings and posit that these goals are influenced by features of the setting as well as by ingrained dispositions of the recipients. Along these lines, Wolf (Chapter 9) explored the motivational implications of the distinction between normative and informational influence (Deutsch & Gerard, 1955). She argued that whether influence is informational or normative is determined by the needs or motives of the recipient of influence. These needs or motives are in turn a function of situational attributes such as characteristics of the influencing agent and the influence induction itself. The situational determinants of the goals that people hold in attitude-relevant situations have also come to the fore in Fazio's (Chapter 5) consideration of the conditions under which people form attitudes from observations of their recent behavior. His research suggested that they form attitudes from their behavior when they have a reason to do so—for example, when they receive a direct inquiry about an attitude, or when they perceive a cue implying that it may be useful or desirable to have an attitude. In contrast, Snyder and DeBono (Chapter 4) emphasized the dispositional determinants of the functions that attitudes serve for the recipient of persuasive information. They assumed that the attitudes of persons high in the personality trait of self-monitoring tend to serve a social adjustive function, whereas the attitudes of people low in self-monitoring tend to serve a value-expressive function. To the extent that this proposition is valid, persons differing in self-monitoring would tend to be influenced by different kinds of information—namely, by information that has implications for the functional base of their attitudes.

Also relevant to motivational issues is the taxonomy that Rule and Bisanz (Chapter 8) provided of the goals that people report that they hold in influence settings. The kind of self-report data on which this taxonomy is based allowed these investigators to display the implicit theories that people hold about social influence. It is not clear whether these implicit theories resemble social psychological theories that would account for the actual influence that occurs in natural settings. This challenging issue of the relation between knowledge structures of this type and interpersonal behavior deserves exploration. Nevertheless, as Rule and Bisanz argued, such knowledge structures no doubt affect the processing of information about interpersonal relations. Furthermore, investigators' thinking about how motivational issues can be incorporated into theories of persuasion and influence should be sharpened by these findings, especially by the evidence they provide of the range of goals that people believe they hold and methods they believe they use in influence situations.

INDIVIDUAL DIFFERENCES

People differ in the goals they hold in a given social influence setting mainly because they differ in their prior experience. Although it is difficult to assess the relevant aspects of prior experience directly, people's goals can be assessed, at least indirectly, by personality measures. Therefore, it is appropriate that individual differences are being considered once again in the social influence literature. Of course, individual differences is an old theme in this research area. Not only was the existence of a general trait of persuasibility considered by early researchers (Hovland & Janis, 1959), but also numerous personality variables such as self-esteem, anxiety, and internal-external control were considered as determinants of response to influence inductions. As several scholars have noted (e.g., Eagly, 1981; McGuire, 1968), the ability to predict responses to influence attempts from knowledge of message recipients' personal characteristics has remained poorly developed. This limited success was perhaps not surprising to social psychologists in view of Mischel's (1968) critique of personality research, which suggested that poor prediction of behavior was typical of personality research in general.

Some of the past difficulties in this area of social influence research stem from the manner in which influenceability hypotheses were most commonly derived: The derivations were by-products of personality theory and had little to do with the detailed knowledge that had developed concerning how attitudes and beliefs change. The result was primarily simplistic main-effect predictions—for example, predictions that individuals with high self-esteem are less influenceable than those with low self-esteem, and that individuals with an external locus of control are more influenceable than those with an internal locus of control (see Eagly, 1981). More substantial progress has resulted in those few instances in which personality variables were explicitly linked to theories of attitude change and social influence. For example, McGuire (1968, 1969) developed a theory of attitude change based on intervening processes of reception and yielding and hypothesized that personality variables such as self-esteem relate to the capacity to receive information as well as to the likelihood that recipients yield to what they receive.

It is encouraging that the work on individual differences included in this symposium has explicit links to theory about the psychological processes that underlie social influence. In particular, Sorrentino and Hancock's (Chapter 11) personality variables—uncertainty orientation and affiliation motivation—link explicitly to the processes of informational and normative influence (Deutsch & Gerard, 1955) that have remained important in theories of social influence. In addition, their ideas about orientations to certainty and uncertainty link nicely to newly developed distinctions between processing modes. If certainty-oriented people tend to process heuristically and uncertainty-oriented people tend to process systematically, we have a new base for predictions about modes of processing messages. Similarly, considerable interest in individual differences has been generated by a personality variable named *need for cognition*, originally proposed by Cohen (1957). Petty and Cacioppo (e.g., Cacioppo, Petty, & Morris, 1983) have shown that people high in need for cognition tend to engage in systematic or central processing of message content, and Chaiken (Chapter 1) has noted that people low in need for cognition may prefer to process messages heuristically. Also, Wood (1982; Wood, Kallgren, & Priesler, 1985) demonstrated the existence of topic-bound individual differences in processing. Her research suggested that people who are able to retrieve a relatively large amount of information relevant to a persuasion topic counterargue counterattitudinal messages more energetically and process their content more systematically. Yet another tie between attitude theories and dispositional variables has been provided by Snyder and DeBono (Chapter 4). As I already noted, these investigators related self-monitoring to functional theories of attitude change.

It is wise to adopt a cautious view toward the future of individual differences approaches to the study of social influence. Because the lowering of interest in such approaches during the 1970s reflected the Mischel (1968) critique of personality research as well as generally increased stringency in evaluating the outcomes of research, it may be helpful to consider the means by which personality research has managed to recover from the Mischel critique. This recovery has stemmed in part from the Epstein (e.g., 1979, 1980) response to the critique—that is, from the realization that personality dispositions, being very general predictors, are more successful in accounting for general behavioral tendencies averaged over time and/or situations than for specific behaviors. Yet the tradition in social-influence research has not been one of breadth in measurement of responses, either over time or across situations. Perhaps personality-oriented investigators will give some greater consideration to broadening dependent measures, as suggested by Snyder and DeBono's examination of their subjects' responses to several instances of image-oriented and product-oriented advertisements. Unless research strategy changes in this direction, weak predictions of influenceability from personality variables may again ensue, and investigators may become discouraged with the new generation of individual-difference approaches.

Another way to account for more substantial variability in influenceability is to take the situational determinants of behavior into account along with personality variables. Rather than average responses over situations, investigators can use situational variables as predictors of responses. This interactionist strategy (see Endler, 1982) is also reflected in the work reported at this symposium. As Snyder and DeBono (Chapter 4) explained, neither high nor low self-monitors should be generally persuasible; instead, there are circumstances in which persons of each type become persuasible because of special vulnerability to a particular type of advertising appeal. Numerous interaction predictions were also noted in the research reported by Sorrentino and Hancock (Chapter 11).

INFLUENCE IN NATURAL SETTINGS

Another trend evident in the work reported in the symposium is a greater use of natural settings for studying social influence. Of course, the great majority of the systematic research in this area has been conducted in the laboratory—from Asch's (1956) conformity experiments and Hovland, Janis, and Kelley's (1953) persuasion experiments to the more modern work on minority influence and processing of messages reported in this symposium. On the one hand, this focus on laboratory experiments is a strength because such research usually enables investigators to have enough control to test detailed and specific hypotheses. On the other hand, the laboratory experiment and the associated use of college-student subjects can lower the external validity of conclusions drawn from research. For example, reliance on laboratory experimentation has led researchers to underestimate the importance of message-reception processes in persuasion (see Eagly & Chaiken, 1984). In this and other instances, constraints of the laboratory have caused investigators to draw conclusions that probably lack external validity in relation to the natural settings to which they desire to generalize.

Because over-reliance on laboratory experiments often yields a biased view of social influence, it is reassuring to find that some of the new research in the area has been conducted in natural settings. In particular, Cialdini's (Chapter 7) work on compliance strategies provides insights into the social-psychological processes by which influence occurs in daily life. The feats of influence carried out by salespeople, politicians, and religious proselytizers deserve our attention, and classification of their compliance strategies is an important first step in developing a systematic psychology of naturally occurring persuasion.

Cialdini's emphasis on *how* people induce compliance in natural settings rather than on *whether* influence occurs will no doubt be shared by other investigators who study natural settings, which generally allow a much wider range of behavior than do laboratory settings. Rule and Bisanz's (Chapter 8) research also deals with influence techniques, although their emphasis is not on compliance specialists but on people in general, who must influence others to carry out the tasks of everyday living. Over the years, research on strategies of influence has been sparse, and I hope that the new research on this problem reported at the symposium is a sign of growing interest. For much too long social scientists have ceded description of styles and strategies of influence mainly to popular writers such as Vance Packard, Dale Carnegie, and Wilson Brian Key.

In order to study strategies of influence in natural settings, social psychologists will have to invoke a wider set of methods than is traditional in research on social influence. Cialdini's (Chapter 7) use of participant observation methods is refreshing and worth emulation. Rule and Bisanz's (Chapter 8) method of asking people to report on the persuasion that occurs in their daily lives also has considerable merit: People can be very intelligent informants about social interaction in natural settings.

SOCIAL ROLES AND SOCIAL INFLUENCE

As investigators continue to study influence in daily life, they will have some difficulty in achieving systematic accounts if the only type of theory linked to everyday persuasion remains the sort of individual psychological-process theory currently popular in social psychology. Cognitive processes and structures provide a molecular description of the psychology of compliance strategies, but they do not provide a perspective that allows prediction of the conditions under which various persuasion techniques will be used and with what degree of success. Rule and Bisanz (Chapter 8) may be correct in their claim that people possess knowledge structures of a schematic sort that allow them to process and store information pertaining to social influence. Yet these schemas no doubt are complex, largely because the culture provides elaborated sets of rules about the behavior that is appropriate in various roles, given various situations. To account for this complexity, we must have broader, sociologically grounded theoretical perspectives—what I will call macrotheories of persuasion. Such macrotheories should emphasize the normative constraints that regulate social influence and cause influence strategies to be recognized by people as legitimate or illegitimate.

As part of a consideration of normative constraints, it will prove helpful to introduce social role concepts into our accounts. People may come to use various compliance strategies largely because they are expected in terms of the social roles that they occupy in daily life. Each of the role relationships of everyday life, such as husband and wife, professor and student, and salesperson and customer, defines a set of expectations that people hold about each other's behavior, and these expectations constrain the ways in which people exert influence and react to others' attempts to exert influence. Although Rule and Bisanz did not obtain much evidence that persuasion strategies or methods are thought to vary depending on role relationships, their study constrained the range of roles on which their subjects reported.

In research that Valerie Steffen and I (Steffen & Eagly, 1985) carried out on styles of influence, we found that subjects reported substantial variation in the likelihood of various styles of making requests, depending on the relative status of the influencing agent and the target. In particular, subjects predicted more use of direct (versus indirect) and impolite (versus polite) styles of making requests when high-status persons induced low-status persons to carry out a task than when low-status persons induced high-status persons. In general, this research suggested that variation of roles on sociologically meaningful dimensions such as status and authority is associated with substantial differences in the way influence is carried out. In general, people come to rely on specific techniques of influence when they are legitimized by the roles and norms that regulate social interaction.

CONCLUSION

There are several reasons to be encouraged about the current status of social-influence research. Judging from this Ontario Symposium, I would even hazard the prediction that social influence research is entering a very fruitful period. A number of trends are very positive, especially the broader and more sophisticated attention to the cognitive processes that underlie social influence. Furthermore, there is a tentative realization that motivational issues must be introduced to account for the conditions under which people take cognitive short-cuts or bother to process information in more effortful and thorough ways. Finally, there is enough increased attention to natural settings that our new accounts of social influence may have increased power to explain behavior in daily life as well as in more structured laboratory settings.

REFERENCES

Allen, V., & Wilder, D. (1980). Impact of group consensus and social support on stimulus meaning: Mediation of conformity by cognitive restructuring. *Journal of Personality and Social Psychology, 30,* 1116–1124.

Asch, S. E. (1956). Studies of independence and conformity: I. A minority of one against a unanimous majority. *Psychological Monographs, 70* (9, Whole No. 416), 1–70.

Beaman, A. L., Cole, C. M., Preston, M., Klentz, B., & Steblay, N. M. (1983). Fifteen years of foot-in-the-door research: A meta-analysis. *Personality and Social Psychology Bulletin, 9,* 181–196.

Cacioppo, J. T., Petty, R. E., & Morris, K. J. (1983). Effects of need for cognition on message evaluation, recall, and persuasion. *Journal of Personality and Social Psychology, 45,* 805–818.

Chaiken, S. (1980). Heuristic versus systematic information processing and the use of source versus message cues in persuasion. *Journal of Personality and Social Psychology, 39,* 752–766.

Chaiken, S., & Eagly, A. H. (1983). Communication modality as a determinant of persuasion: The role of communicator salience. *Journal of Personality and Social Psychology, 45,* 241–256.

Cohen, A. R. (1957). Need for cognition and order of communication as determinants of opinion change. In C. I. Hovland (Ed.), *The order of presentation in persuasion* (pp. 79–97). New Haven, CT: Yale University Press.

Cooper, H. M. (1984). *The integrative research review: A systematic approach.* Beverly Hills, CA: Sage.

Cronbach, L. J. (1975). Beyond the two disciplines of scientific psychology. *American Psychologist, 30,* 116–127.

Deutsch, M., & Gerard, H. B. (1955). A study of normative and informational social influence upon individual judgment. *Journal of Abnormal and Social Psychology, 51,* 629–636.

Eagly, A. H. (1981). Recipient characteristics as determinants of responses to persuasion. In R. E. Petty, T. M. Ostrom, & T. C. Brock (Eds.), *Cognitive responses in persuasion* (pp. 173–195). Hillsdale, NJ: Lawrence Erlbaum Associates.

Eagly, A. H., & Carli, L. L. (1981). Sex of researchers and sex-typed communications as determinants of sex differences in influenceability. *Psychological Bulletin, 90,* 1–20.

Eagly, A. H., & Chaiken, S. (1984). Cognitive theories of persuasion. In L. Berkowitz (Ed.), *Advances in experimental social psychology* (Vol. 17, pp. 267–359). New York: Academic Press.

Eagly, A. H., Chaiken, S., & Wood, W. (1981). An attribution analysis of persuasion. In J. H. Harvey, W. J. Ickes, & R. F. Kidd (Eds.), *New directions in attribution research* (Vol. 3, pp. 37–62). Hillsdale, NJ: Lawrence Erlbaum Associates.

Eagly, A. H., & Himmelfarb, S. (1974). Current trends in attitude theory and research. In S. Himmelfarb & A. Eagly (Eds.), *Readings in attitude change* (pp. 594–610). New York: Wiley.

Endler, S. (1982). Interactionism comes of age. In M. P. Zanna, E. T. Higgins, & C. P. Herman (Eds.), *Consistency in social behavior: The Ontario Symposium* (Vol. 2, pp. 209–249). Hillsdale, NJ: Lawrence Erlbaum Associates.

Epstein, S. (1979). The stability of behavior: I. On predicting most of the people much of the time. *Journal of Personality and Social Psychology, 37,* 1097–1126.

Epstein, S. (1980). The stability of behavior: II. Implications for psychological research. *American Psychologist, 35,* 790–806.

Fishbein, M., & Ajzen, I. (1975). *Belief, attitude, intention, and behavior: An introduction to theory and research.* Reading, MA: Addison-Wesley.

Gergen, K. J. (1973). Social psychology as history. *Journal of Personality and Social Psychology, 26,* 309–320.

Glass, G. V., McGaw, B., & Smith, M. L. (1981). *Meta-analysis in social research.* Beverly Hills, CA: Sage .

Hall, J. A. (1984). *Nonverbal sex differences: Communication accuracy and expressive style.* Baltimore: Johns Hopkins University Press.

Hedges, L. V., & Olkin, I. (1985). *Statistical methods for meta-analysis.* New York: Academic Press.

Heider, F. (1958). *The psychology of interpersonal relations.* New York: Wiley.

Hovland, C. I., & Janis, I. L. (Eds.). (1959). *Personality and persuasibility.* New Haven, CT: Yale University Press.

Hovland, C. I., Janis, I. L., & Kelley, H. H. (1953). *Communication and persuasion: Psychological studies of opinion change.* New Haven, CT: Yale University Press.

Hyde, J., & Linn, M. (Eds.). (1986). *The psychology of gender: Advances through meta-analysis.* Baltimore: Johns Hopkins University Press.

Katz, D. (1960). The functional approach to the study of attitudes. *Public Opinion Quarterly, 24,* 163–204.

Kelman, H. D. (1961). Processes of opinion change. *Public Opinion Quarterly, 25,* 57–78.

Latané, B., & Wolf, S. (1983). The social impact of majorities and minorities. *Psychological Review, 88,* 438–453.

Maass, A., & Clark, R. D. (1984). Hidden impact of minorities: Fifteen years of minority impact research. *Psychological Bulletin, 95,* 428–450.

McGuire, W. J. (1960). A syllogistic analysis of cognitive relationships. In C. I. Hovland & M. J. Rosenberg (Eds.), *Attitude organization and change* (pp. 65–111). New Haven, CT: Yale University Press.

McGuire, W. J. (1968). Personality and susceptibility to social influence. In E. F. Borgatta & W. W. Lambert (Eds.), *Handbook of personality theory and research* (pp. 1130–1187). Chicago: Rand McNally.

McGuire, W. J. (1969). The nature of attitudes and attitude change. In G. Lindzey & E. Aronson (Eds.), *The handbook of social psychology* (2nd ed., Vol. 3, pp. 136–314). Reading, MA: Addison-Wesley.

McGuire, W. J. (1972). Attitude change: The information-processing paradigm. In C. G. McClintock (Ed.), *Experimental social psychology* (pp. 108–141). New York: Holt, Rinehart, & Winston.

Meehl, P. E. (1978). Theoretical risks and tabular asterisks: Sir Karl, Sir Ronald, and the slow progress of soft psychology. *Journal of Consulting and Clinical Psychology, 46,* 806–834.

Mischel, W. (1968). *Personality and assessment.* New York: Wiley.

Moscovici, S. (1980). Toward a theory of conversion behavior. In L. Berkowitz (Ed.), *Advances in experimental social psychology* (Vol. 13, pp. 209–239). New York: Academic Press.

Moscovici, S., & Nemeth, C. (1974). Social influence II: Minority influence. In C. Nemeth (Ed.), *Social psychology: Classic and contemporary integrations* (pp. 217–249). Chicago: Rand McNally.

Osgood, C. E., & Tannenbaum, P. H. (1955). The principle of congruity in the prediction of attitude change. *Psychological Review, 62,* 42–55.

Pallak, S. R. (1983). Salience of a communicator's physical attractiveness and persuasion: A heuristic versus systematic processing interpretation. *Social Cognition, 2,* 156–168.

Petty, R. E., & Cacioppo, J. T. (1981). *Attitudes and persuasion: Classic and contemporary approaches*. Dubuque, IA: Wm. C. Brown.

Petty, R. E., Cacioppo, J. T., & Goldman, R. (1981). Personal involvement as a determinant of argument-based persuasion. *Journal of Personality and Social Psychology, 41*, 847–855.

Petty, R. E., Ostrom, T. M., & Brock, T. C. (1981). Historical foundations of the cognitive response approach to attitudes and persuasion. In R. E. Petty, T. M. Ostrom, & T. C. Brock (Eds.), *Cognitive responses in persuasion* (pp. 5–29). Hillsdale, NJ: Lawrence Erlbaum Associates.

Petty, R. E., Wells, G. L., & Brock, T. C. (1976). Distraction can enhance or reduce yielding to propaganda: Thought disruption versus effort justification. *Journal of Personality and Social Psychology, 34*, 874–884.

Rosenthal, R. (1984). *Meta-analytic procedures for social research*. Beverly Hills, CA: Sage.

Ross, L., Bierbrauer, G., & Hoffman, S. (1976). The role of attribution processes in conformity and dissent: Revisiting the Asch situation. *American Psychologist, 31*, 148–157.

Schneider, W., & Shiffrin, R. M. (1977). Controlled and automatic human information processing: I. Detection, search, and attention. *Psychological Review, 84*, 1–66.

Shiffrin, R. M., & Schneider, W. (1977). Controlled and automatic human information processing: II. Perceptual learning, automatic attending, and a general theory. *Psychological Review, 84*, 127–190.

Steffan, V., & Eagly, A. H. (1985). Implicit theories about influence style: The effects of status and gender. *Personality and Social Psychology Bulletin, 11*, 191–205.

Tanford, S., & Penrod, S. (1984). Social influence model: A formal integration of research on majority and minority influence processes. *Psychological Bulletin, 95*, 189–225.

Wood, W. (1982). The retrieval of attitude-relevant information from memory: Effects on susceptibility to persuasion and on intrinsic motivation. *Journal of Personality and Social Psychology, 42*, 798–810.

Wood, W., Kallgren, C. A., & Priesler, R. M. (1985). Access to attitude-relevant information in memory as a determinant of persuasion. *Journal of Experimental Social Psychology, 21*, 73–85.

Wyer, R. S. (1974). *Cognitive organization and change: An information-processing approach*. Hillsdale, NJ: Lawrence Erlbaum Associates.

Author Index

Page numbers in *italics* refer to reference pages.

Subject Index

A

Ability
  individual differences in, 15–21
  levels, learning of, 251–252
  role, related to persuasion, 7–15
Achievement
  behavior, determinants of, 247
  dimensions for, 248
  incentives, 265
  -related motives, performance of, 262
Actions, human, understanding of, 189
Activation, automatic, 87
Advertising
  as applied persuasion, 120–122
  psychology of, applicational to functional
    approach, 113–119
Affect(s), 46–47
  expression of, 62
  patterns of, 56–60
  primary, 46–47
Affective approaches to social influence study,
    265–266
Affective experience, link to spontaneous fa-
    cial efference, 66–67
Affective reactions, valence and intensity of,
    56–57
Affective states, positive and negative, 48
Affective value, 247, 265
  affiliation motive as, See Affiliation motive

differences in, 248
distinguished from information value, 250
Affiliation motive, as affective value, 258–260
  conformity, 261–262
  group performance, 260–261
  leadership emergence, 262–264
  social influence as a function of information
    and affective value, 264
Agreement
  heuristics, 27
  responses, 275
Altruism, 196
Antecedent conditions, variations in, 208
Antithesis, principle of, 47–48
Argument(s)
  -acceptance processes, 6
  issue-relevant, 45
  quality, 16
    effectiveness of, 16
  -reception processes, 6
Attention, *See also* Self-attention model
  direct, primary effects on, 86
  selective allocation of, 81
Attentive processes, 87
Attitude
  -behavior relation, 146, 152, 255
    related to communication processes, 94–
    99
  change, 151–152
  of group members, 275–276

297